Reading Biblical Greek

Reading Biblical Greek is aimed at students who are studying New Testament Greek for the first time, or refreshing what they once learned. Designed to supplement and reinforce *The Elements of New Testament Greek*, by Jeremy Duff, each chapter of this textbook provides lengthy, plot-driven texts that will be accessible as students study each chapter of *The Elements*. Each text is accompanied by detailed questions, which test comprehension of content from recent lessons and review challenging topics from previous chapters. The graded nature of the texts, together with the copious notes and comprehension questions, makes this an ideal resource for learning, reviewing or re-entering Greek. The focus of this resource is on reading with understanding, and the exercises highlight how Greek texts convey meaning. Finally, this book moves on from first-year Greek, with sections that cover the most important advanced topics thoroughly.

Steffen G. Jenkins is Senior Lecturer in Greek and Biblical Studies at Union School of Theology in the United Kingdom. He has served as Lecturer in Old Testament at various seminaries in Cuba and was previously a tutor in Biblical Languages at Tyndale House, in Cambridge, England. He is the author of *Imprecations in the Psalms: Love for Enemies in Hard Places*; *Scripture Is Inspired*; and the forthcoming *Hearing God's Voice in Leviticus* and *Enjoy the Psalms*

'This is a wonderful book! It is designed to be used alongside Jeremy Duff's *Elements of New Testament Greek*. As a student, it guides you through the subjects as though taught by a friendly, encouraging and highly knowledgeable Greek professor. Complicated aspects of Greek grammar, such as aspect and voice, are explained with crystal clarity, using the latest linguistic scholarship. It is highly recommended for students who want to master the beautiful, yet sometimes challenging, language of Greek.'

Rutger Allan, Professor of Ancient Greek Linguistics and Literature, Free University of Amsterdam

'Jenkins' *Reader* skilfully shows that competent use of NT Greek for interpretation is grounded in reading actual ancient texts. His engaging style along with his pedagogical good sense and unsurpassed linguistic expertise is just what beginners need – as well as those desiring to recover their rusty Greek. Highly recommended!'

Buist Fanning, Senior Professor Emeritus of NT Studies, Dallas Theological Seminary USA

'I have seen firsthand the excellence Steffen Jenkins invests in teaching and the care he invests in students. Those same qualities can be observed throughout these pages. Whether you are learning Greek from scratch, deepening your knowledge of it or building your reading fluency, this book will serve you well.'

Christopher Fresch, Lecturer in Biblical Languages and Linguistics at the Bible College of South Australia

'Steffen Jenkins' *Reader* offers a wonderfully helpful, supplemental tool, especially for first-year students using Duff's *The Elements of New Testament Greek*. With keen pedagogical instincts and no small measure of wit, Jenkins reinforces, clarifies and elaborates Duff's grammar, even while offering elementary students a more immersive experience of the language. Highly recommended!'

George H. Guthrie, Professor of New Testament, Regent College, Vancouver, Canada

'Steffen Jenkins' fine *Reader* builds on the tradition of several generations of Greek textbooks (Nunn, Wenham, Duff), with a treasure trove of additional explanations, insights into the structure and internal logic of the language, and numerous exercises designed to enhance students' understanding and sharpen their skills. Highly recommended.'

Steve Jeffery, Pastor, All Saints Presbyterian Church, Fort Worth

'Pastors like me, who once knew Greek but have forgotten much, need the encouragement and support of a book like this. Luther said that reading the Bible in translation was like kissing your bride through her wedding veil. This book helps to take the veil away (again).'

Andy Mason, Minister, St John's Church, Chelsea, & Mission Director for the Co-mission Network

'I'm delighted to commend Steffen Jenkins' *Reader* as a well-designed textbook which will help students learn Greek well or revise their flagging Greek knowledge.'

>**Robert L. Plummer,** PhD, Collin and Evelyn Aikman Professor of Biblical Studies, The Southern Baptist Theological Seminary

Steffen Jenkins draws on a wealth of knowledge in this comprehensive textbook. Familiar not only with the classical and biblical languages, but also with the most up-to-date findings of modern – not least contrastive – linguistics, he endeavours to guide more or less experienced students of Ancient Greek, especially of the New Testament variety, to real linguistic competence. The starting point is Jeremy Duff's proven textbook *The Elements of New Testament Greek*. On the one hand, Dr Jenkins guides the learner through the twenty chapters of Duff's textbook. On the other hand, he provides valuable additional information (this on the use of the accents and all areas of morphology and syntax). A particular focus of Dr Jenkins' textbook is on the readings, which include some from the New Testament as well as numerous classical and post-classical texts based on the originals. Those who take the time to work through this impressive material step by step will, I believe, be richly rewarded!'

>**Heinrich von Siebenthal,** Professor Emeritus, Freie Theologische Hochschule Giessen and Staatsunabhängige Theologische Hochschule Basel

'Steffen Jenkins is one of the most incredible language teachers I know. He encourages students to reach higher than they think they can go. Who else could motivate a group of Cuban pastors to give a public recitation of the Greek optative verb in front of an English audience? This *Reader* will be an inspiration to many.'

>**Peter J. Williams,** Principal, Tyndale House, Cambridge

Reading Biblical Greek
A Graded Reader for Beginners

STEFFEN G. JENKINS
Union School of Theology

CAMBRIDGE
UNIVERSITY PRESS

Shaftesbury Road, Cambridge CB2 8EA, United Kingdom

One Liberty Plaza, 20th Floor, New York, NY 10006, USA

477 Williamstown Road, Port Melbourne, VIC 3207, Australia

314–321, 3rd Floor, Plot 3, Splendor Forum, Jasola District Centre, New Delhi – 110025, India

103 Penang Road, #05–06/07, Visioncrest Commercial, Singapore 238467

Cambridge University Press is part of Cambridge University Press & Assessment, a department of the University of Cambridge.

We share the University's mission to contribute to society through the pursuit of education, learning and research at the highest international levels of excellence.

www.cambridge.org
Information on this title: www.cambridge.org/9781108844413
DOI: 10.1017/9781108951111

© Steffen G. Jenkins 2026

This publication is in copyright. Subject to statutory exception and to the provisions of relevant collective licensing agreements, no reproduction of any part may take place without the written permission of Cambridge University Press & Assessment.

When citing this work, please include a reference to the DOI 10.1017/9781108951111

First published 2026

A catalogue record for this publication is available from the British Library

A Cataloging-in-Publication data record for this book is available from the Library of Congress

ISBN 978-1-108-84441-3 Hardback
ISBN 978-1-108-94815-9 Paperback

Additional resources for this publication at www.cambridge.org/jenkins-greek

Cambridge University Press & Assessment has no responsibility for the persistence or accuracy of URLs for external or third-party internet websites referred to in this publication and does not guarantee that any content on such websites is, or will remain, accurate or appropriate.

For EU product safety concerns, contact us at Calle de José Abascal, 56, 1°, 28003 Madrid, Spain, or email eugpsr@cambridge.org

To Sally

Contents

Foreword by Jeremy Duff — xi
Preface — xiii
Copyright Notices — xviii
List of Abbreviations — xix
Sources of Ancient Texts — xxv

How to Use This Book — 1

1 The Alphabet – Accents — 7
2 Basic Sentences – Present Indicative — 16
3 Cases and Gender – Genitive Case — 37
4 Prepositions – Dative Case — 55
5 Adjectives – Consolidation Greek Readings — 71
6 The Tenses – Imperfect Indicative — 85
7 Moods – Aorist Indicative — 112
8 Other Patterns of Nouns and Verbs – Aspect in the Infinitive — 136
9 Pronouns and Conjunctions – Accusative Case; Conjunctions — 155
10 Complex Sentences – Indirect Discourse; 'Little Words' — 171
11 Special Verbs – Consolidation Greek Readings – Aspect in Imperatives — 186
12 The Third Declension, Part 1 — 212
13 The Third Declension, Part 2 – Nominative Case — 219
14 Participles – Participles — 228
15 The Passive and Voices – The Middle Voice — 251
16 The Perfect – Consolidation Greek Reading – The Perfect System — 263
17 The Subjunctive – Aspect in the Subjunctive — 297
18 Using Verbs — 306
19 Extra Verbs – Future Indicative — 315
20 Final Pieces – Consolidation Greek Reading — 326
21 Next Steps – Atticising Greek (Optative; Future in Other Moods; Perfect in Other Moods; Hyperbaton) — 334

Indexes — 340
  Topics — 340
  Ancient Texts — 355

Foreword
by Jeremy Duff

I am delighted to see this *Reader*, based on my *The Elements of New Testament Greek*, published to help the next generation of Greek students. It is particularly timely as the new, fourth, edition of *The Elements* is going to press.

Dr Steffen Jenkins shares my passion for helping students. He has an encyclopaedic knowledge of Greek, and a mind tuned to seek clarity, but this is coupled with humility. Humility about himself, so he shows his workings and explains the limitations, rather than projecting a false authority. Humility, perhaps more importantly, about all our analysis and categorisation of the language and grammar of the New Testament. This book encourages and helps the student to read and understand Greek, guiding the student to focus on what the Greek means, not how it might or might not correspond to English, or what grammatical label might be put on it. This makes him a reliable guide for the student – immensely helpful, but honest about the challenges and uncertainties. It has been a pleasure to get to know Dr Jenkins over the last three years, as he shared the *Reader* with me, and responded kindly to my comments.

This *Reader* is a great addition to *The Elements*. It will be a notable help for those who study *The Elements* on their own, or without a teacher, since it is carefully indexed to *The Elements*, guiding you through it and giving further explanations and examples. It is ideal for those needing a refresher, who have learnt the basics of Greek using *The Elements* or another textbook, but want to consolidate their knowledge. It is particularly pleasing to see the '**Extra Material**' section. This revisits the material from each chapter of *The Elements* from the perspective of having studied the entire book. Because *The Elements* proceeds 'step by step', inevitably there is more to be said about, for example, the present tense than it is helpful to put in Chapter 2. This *Reader* gives that extra detail – what it would have been good to say about the present tense, but which would have overwhelmed the student in their second week. Plunge too deep into the 'Extra Material' too quickly and you will soon rejoice that *The Elements* didn't give you all the detail first time around! It is also good that the *Reader* provides a guide to accents, for those who wish to learn them after having studied with *The Elements*, and more generally gives a wise 'second opinion' at a number of points. Not setting up an argument, as if the student is equipped to decide between different approaches to certain grammatical issues, but giving the committed learner a broader perspective, and alternative ways of thinking, which undoubtedly will 'click' for some.

Aside from all of this, the *Reader* gets the student reading Greek. I rejoice that Dr Jenkins, for all of the careful grammatical analysis and the tons of examples, keeps the focus on reading Greek. The story of Phoebe, and Joseph and Aseneth, will appeal to many. Reading the whole of Philemon after Chapter 11 is a great encouragement. I applaud his attempt to set New Testament Greek in the wider world of Greek. May it help prevent future generations of biblical commentators trying to wring precision out of vocabulary or grammatical forms which might be rare in the New Testament, but are not uncommon more broadly in Greek. The New Testament is, in the end, such a small corpus.

I want to thank Dr Jenkins for producing this *Reader*, which forms a valuable companion to *The Elements*. Teaching Greek, just like learning Greek, is best done in company. The 'second-year' textbook, the text to help you revise or refresh your Greek, the guide for those studying on their own – it cleverly hits all three targets. I commend it to teachers and students alike, believing it will help many to achieve *The Elements*' aim, 'to help you learn enough Greek to read the New Testament'.

Preface

For those who like reading prefaces, I'll begin by explaining the approach to teaching Greek that makes use of this *Reader*. I'll narrate the almost comical sequence of accidents that led to me writing it: no one is more surprised than I am, and I hope that it might encourage others who are surely more able than me to knock on the doors of publishers. Finally, I will enjoy the opportunity to thank wonderful women, men and children who have helped to make this *Reader* possible.

Like so many, I was given excellent teaching at theological college in the Biblical languages, and I loved them and worked hard at them. Within a few years, I was aware that my Greek was disappearing. I had joined the great international body of graduates who *used to know Greek*. When I resolved to refresh the language, I found it tedious and demoralising to start again with a grammar. When I tried switching to reading New Testament texts instead, I found that too much was too far gone: I couldn't easily look up what I needed and refresh some basics.

A few years on, and I realised that learning Classical Greek would be a good idea anyway, and I thought that might provide an interesting way back in. I heard about the JACT *Reading Greek* course (CUP),[1] which combines an introductory grammar (complete with the usual exercises) with reading Greek texts from the very start. These texts were made up for beginners and only contained the most basic grammatical forms, but they meant that one was enjoying reading extended texts immediately. The texts became fuller and more complex as one learnt more grammar; eventually, made-up texts gave way to real texts, suitably edited, and I enjoyed the exhilaration of reading Plato, Demosthenes and the like, even if simplified and with plenty of helpful annotations. I had started this process determined that this would be the *last* time that I would learn Greek from scratch. (To compound my shame, I had started learning Greek using the edition of *Elements of New Testament Greek* (*ENTG*) by John Wenham. That was by the kindness of the Divinity Faculty in Cambridge, but I was really meant to be studying Physics, and soon the complexities of fluid dynamics required my full attention. Nonetheless, this was now my *third* time staring at the very basics.)

Meanwhile, I had the privilege of teaching Biblical Hebrew at Tyndale House in Cambridge, to a wonderful cohort of future seminary lecturers from the seminaries I had previously served in Cuba. I reflected on the fact that one reason

---

[1] Many thanks to Steve Walton and Chris Fresch for that conversation!

why my Hebrew was still strong was that I had taken a fourth-year course that required a huge volume of weekly reading of Hebrew Bible. I made that the cornerstone of this Cuban 'boot camp': we were reading four chapters per day of Hebrew Bible by the time we were done.

When the time came to teach Biblical Greek in a similar Cuban 'boot camp', I wanted to make sure that reading lots of Greek text was central. However, there wasn't a beginner's grammar that took this approach, so we worked through Classical Greek (using the JACT course, as above), and then switched to reading New Testament and surrounding texts.

When I was given the privilege of teaching New Testament Greek at Union School of Theology, it was easy enough to make sure that students in the second, third and fourth years were immersed in Greek texts, but what to do about first years? I wanted them to have even longer (and even easier) texts each week than the exercise C at the end of every chapter in *ENTG*, helpful and excellent though those exercises were. I thought that adapting the JACT made-up texts and turning them into texts that followed the order of topics in *ENTG* might work. I set about that editing, hoping to use it with students one day, but conscious that I would first need permission from CUP. I didn't dare to ask.

What follows is not only to express my thanks to the wonderful staff at CUP and the CUP bookshop, but to encourage any readers who are nervous about approaching publishers.

My colleagues at Union very kindly allowed me to adapt our curriculum and include a large volume of reading into my classes, and also to allow fourth-year students the option to learn Classical Greek composition. As a result, I was eagerly awaiting the new *Cambridge Grammar of Classical Greek* (I am grateful to Rutger Allan for alerting me to it, as well as other resources). For several years, the publication date on the CUP website was always listed as the following month, and I eventually stopped checking.

Then one day I was leaving Cambridge market, walking past the CUP bookshop, and there it was in the window! I bought a copy straight away, shared my excitement with the lovely staff and thanked them for bringing it out in paperback at an affordable price. The wonderful Alastair Lynn overheard this, and generously offered me a discount for my students.

Not long after, Stuart Hughes, from CUP, got in touch to ask why a theological college was using a Classical grammar. In my reply, I took the opportunity to explain my desire to adapt the JACT texts for my students in-house, and asking how I could seek permission and make any necessary payments. Mr Hughes very kindly arranged a phone call, in which he uttered a line that I won't soon forget: 'Wouldn't you want to publish that with us?'

From there, the amazing Dr Beatrice Rehl got in touch and shepherded my initial vague idea into a serious proposal, obtaining peer review, securing the approval of the Press Syndicate, and keeping me on track until today.

If you're anxiously teetering on the edge of pitching a book to a daunting publisher, let me assure you that I have only known kindness, helpfulness and even gentleness from all at CUP. It's as if publishers are on the same side as authors; who knew?

So many have been involved that I wonder whether my name deserves to be on the cover!

I would like to thank Beatrice Rehl for her indefatigable kindness and patience throughout, and especially for granting an extension to the original deadline at a very trying time.

My agent, Pieter Kwant, for steadfast cheerfulness and reassuring responses to my boundless store of anxiety throughout this project. It took *years* before I would overcome my need to ask Pieter to check every email to my editor.

Thanks to Alastair Lynn, Stuart Hughes (as above), Eilidh Burrett, Nicola Chapman and Chris Jackson at CUP. To those at CUP working on this MS after this preface is immutable: thank you!

ENTG would not exist without the work of H. P. V. Nunn and J. W. Wenham, who wrote the first and second editions.

I would like to thank Tyndale House, in Cambridge, for the honour of teaching Hebrew and Greek to Cuban lecturers there, for constantly encouraging us to set our aspirations higher in the languages, for countless encouraging conversations, and for being the kind of welcoming environment where a project like this book can be dreamt of and given shape, not least through fellowship with scholars who are far more senior but treat students as friends and fellow Christians. I'd especially like to thank Dirk Jongkind for providing an endorsement to my initial proposal to CUP; and Peter Williams and Simon Sykes for setting such a congenial tone at the House, as well as for their personal encouragement.

At Union, without simply listing every colleague (since they are all and always supportive), some were enthusiastic at key moments of decision: Mike Reeves, Joel Morris, Cor Bennema, Stephen Moore and Paul Spear.

Perhaps the most frightening moment in writing was the day that I realised that, while the print edition of *Joseph & Aseneth* is well outside copyright, I had been using an electronic edition which was in copyright. I sought permission to use it from Dr Craig Evans, who must be one of the busiest men alive, and received his generous response by return of post. Thank you!

The skill, artistry, imagination and finesse that went into producing *Phoebe's Banquet* was outsourced entirely to my better half. Sally wrote this novella to the exacting specification of only using certain vocab and tenses in English, and my task was happily limited to turning that into Greek. The original is, of course, far superior.

Students of Greek Grammar at Union School of Theology suffered through drafts of chapters of the *Reader* in various stages of completion and polish: I thank you all for your patient forbearance. As promised, those of you who offered corrections are hereby acknowledged, with thanks: Mia Anderson, Jane

Beeching, George Brand, David van den Broek, Bosco Bukeera, Oliver Butler, Lewis Cameron, Jarod Kary, Steven King, Jacob Lees, Pei Zhi Cheung, Remon Rizk, Nicolas Schoofs, Henrik Steinbrecher and Kenny Wiles. Thanks to Manus Wong for the mnemonic σα σimple αspect and John McCabe for 'α males'. Whenever you ask a question in class, ten others are grateful; just think how many more future students will avoid confusion and puzzlement because you helped to correct a textbook!

In the summer of 2022, a group from Reformation Fellowship test-drove an early draft of the *Reader* to learn or re-learn Greek. The idea came from Justin Schell, and it was kindly organised by Harley Wideman. Members of that cohort who provided feedback were: Marty Lenski, Simon Field, Jukka Heimonen, Agnes Balmer, Marco Uliana, Paul Cheung, Adrian Yeboah, Ashley Cruz, Chris Murphy, Daniel Bennett, Dustin Scott, Joel Kendall, John Duffy and Harley Wideman. The *Reader* is in better shape because of you all. The narrative of how the *Reader* came to be is included above at the behest of one of you: thanks for that suggestion!

During the autumn term of 2022, Zoe O'Neill of Union Theological College, Belfast (no relation!) most kindly shared drafts of the *Reader* with first-year students of Greek and passed on kind words of encouragement: I thank her, her colleagues who taught the class, and their students for their patience.

My predecessor at Union, John Kendall, expected (and obtained) the highest standards from his Greek students. His generosity in letting me build on the culture that he passed on to me is pure grace. I'm grateful for the excellent feedback he offered on early chapters of this *Reader*. He didn't want credit for the accented paradigms in the Online Material, but he does deserve it.

I'm grateful to my colleagues at Union for a sabbatical in the second semester of 2022–3, and especially to Peter Newton for picking up a great deal of Greek teaching, as well as for his helpful comments on drafts of this *Reader*; I'm grateful to my Pentateuch students for suffering through a year's worth of material in one semester too! As difficult family events unfolded, I'm grateful to our Provost, Clive Bowsher, for allowing me to work mostly from home for an extended period.

I have enjoyed the immense privilege of seeing some of our graduate students work through portions of the *Reader*. Marie-Josée Fortin and Kevin Hale offered excellent feedback, for which I thank them. My pastor, and unaccountably also my student, Andrew Graham has kindly and steadfastly worked through the book, refreshing his Greek with humility, and been a much-needed voice of reassurance. Soon-to-be-Dr Raj Sangha is not a man to miss a single detail, and he has painstakingly combed through the MS, spotting all manner of things, bringing consistency where there was carelessness, and producing the indexes.

Peter Harris and Chris Fresch have offered superb comments on several sections quite recently, for which I thank them, even if space, time and skill have limited the results that their comments deserve.

One of my recurring flash-forwards as I have been writing is the certainty that better men and women than me will roll their eyes at the crass errors that I have failed to spot as I revise the work, even with all the eagle-eyed help listed above; responsibility for the remaining errors is entirely mine; responsibility for gleeful eye-rolling is yours.

Since September of 2022, Canon Prof Jeremy Duff has blessed me with his time, hospitality, encouragement, and patience. He has very kindly shared the changes in his forthcoming fourth edition of *ENTG*, so that this *Reader* didn't become obsolete while in press, commented on draft chapters and been a gracious conversation partner as I've pondered how best to present some material.

Penultimately, I'm always in the debt of my wonderful Sally and our awesome Ben and Daniel. As I type this, we are hoping for the first annual 'all clear' after a year of treatment for Sally, and yet she has never wavered in her support and enthusiasm for this writing project. She is worth more than rubies. The boys have been the wise sons to make their father glad, and we thank their saviour for blessing us with them.

Finally, while I trust that this *Reader* will help any who want to read Greek in and around the New Testament for any reason, I didn't write it for the sake of antiquarian curiosity. As the final example in the *Reader* reminds us, the New Testament was written

>ἵνα εἰδῆτε ὅτι ζωὴν ἔχετε αἰώνιον 1 John 5:13
>'that you may know that you have eternal life'.

This book would be largely pointless apart from the life, death, resurrection and ascension of our saviour, Jesus Christ. In thankful worship and adoration, I express my indebtedness, devotion and love to the one who gave and sustains our life daily.

Copyright Notices

Unless otherwise stated, translations of all texts are my own.

'The Rich Man and the Precious Stone' (in Chapter 5), *Joseph & Aseneth* (in Chapters 6–20) and short example fragments (in **Extra Material** of various chapters) were adapted from the *Old Testament Greek Pseudepigrapha* using the electronic edition © Dr Craig A. Evans, with his kind permission.

The quotations from Smyth are from the earlier version, now in the public domain:

> Herbert Weir Smyth, *A Greek Grammar for Colleges*. New York: American Book Company, 1920.

The English original of 'Phoebe's Banquet' is © Sally-Ann Jenkins. A Greek translation is used with her kind permission.

Abbreviations

1 GENERAL

EH 7 2.4.1	**Extra Help** of Chapter 7, Section 2.4.1.
EM 7 5.4.1	**Extra Material** of Chapter 7, Section 5.4.1.
Reader	This book that you are now holding.
ENTG	Jeremy Duff, *Elements of New Testament Greek*: the textbook of which this *Reader* is a companion. I will point you at section numbers, which are the same in both editions.
GNT	Greek New Testament. (You do not need a copy to use *ENTG* or this *Reader*.)

2 REFERENCE GRAMMARS AND OTHER SOURCES

These are used mostly under the headings of **Extra Material**; they are mentioned so that you know where to look if you want to take matters further. References are to paragraph or section numbers, where available. I'm not expecting you to invest in buying any of these at this stage; see the **Next Steps** in Chapter 21, instead.

B-D-R	Blass, Friedrich, Albert Debrunner and Friedrich Rehkopf. *Grammatik des neutestamentlichen Griechisch*. 16th ed. Göttingen: Vandenhoeck & Ruprecht, 1984. English Translation with the same section numbers, but missing the most recent updates: Blass, Friedrich, Albert Debrunner and Robert W. Funk. *A Greek Grammar of the New Testament and Other Early Christian Literature*. Chicago: University of Chicago Press, 1961.
CGCG	Boas, Evert van Emde, Albert Rijksbaron, Luuk Huitink and Mathieu de Bakker. *The Cambridge Grammar of Classical Greek*. Cambridge: Cambridge University Press, 2019.
EAGLL	Giannakis, Georgios K., ed. *Encyclopedia of Ancient Greek Language and Linguistics*. Leiden; Boston: Brill, 2014.

Fanning	Fanning, Buist M. *Verbal Aspect in New Testament Greek*. Oxford Theological Monographs. Oxford: Oxford University Press, 1990.
Gildersleeve	Gildersleeve, Basil L. *Syntax of Classical Greek from Homer to Demosthenes*. Medford, MA: American Book Company, 1900.
Goodwin	Goodwin, William W. *A Greek Grammar*. Revised and enlarged. Boston: Ginn, 1892.
GVR	*The Greek Verb Revisited: A Fresh Approach for Biblical Exegesis*. Edited by Steven E. Runge and Christopher J. Fresch. Bellingham, WA: Lexham, 2016.
Harris, *Prepositions*	Harris, Murray J. *Prepositions and Theology in the Greek New Testament: An Essential Reference Resource for Exegesis*. Grand Rapids: Zondervan, 2012.
Horrocks	Horrocks, Geoffrey. *Greek: A History of the Language and its Speakers*. 2nd ed. Chichester: Wiley Blackwell, 2014.
JACT	Joint Association of Classical Teachers
Jobes & Silva	Jobes, Karen H. and Moisés Silva. *Invitation to the Septuagint*. 2nd ed. Grand Rapids: Baker Academic, 2015.
Köstenberger	Köstenberger, Andreas J., Benjamin L. Merkle and Robert L. Plummer. *Going Deeper with New Testament Greek: An Intermediate Study of the Grammar and Syntax of the New Testament*. Revised ed. Nashville: B&H Academic, 2020.
Kühner-Gerth	Kühner, Raphael and Bernhard Gerth. *Ausführliche Grammatik der griechischen Sprache*. Hanover: Hahn, 1890–1904.
LNTG	*Linguistics and New Testament Greek: Key Issues in the Current Debate*. Edited by David Alan Black and Benjamin L. Merkle. Grand Rapids: Baker Academic, 2020.
MH	Moulton, J. H., W. F. Howard and Nigel Turner. *A Grammar of New Testament Greek*. 4 vols. 3rd ed. Edinburgh: T&T Clark, 1908–76.
Mounce, *Morphology*	Mounce, William D. *The Morphology of Biblical Greek*. Grand Rapids: Zondervan, 1994.
Muraoka	Muraoka, Takamitsu. *A Syntax of Septuagint Greek*. Leuven: Peeters, 2016.
Probert	Probert, Philomen. *A New Short Guide to the Accentuation of Ancient Greek*. Bristol: BCP, 2003.

Rijksbaron	Rijksbaron, Albert. *The Syntax and Semantics of the Verb in Classical Greek: An Introduction*. 3rd ed. Amsterdam: Gieben, 2002.
Robertson	A. T. Robertson, *A Grammar of the Greek New Testament in the Light of Historical Research*. 4th ed. Nashville: Broadman, 1934.
Runge, DGGNT	Steven E. Runge. *Discourse Grammar of the Greek New Testament: A Practical Introduction for Teaching and Exegesis*. Peabody: Hendrickson, 2010.
Schwyzer-Debrunner	Schwyzer, Eduard. *Allgemeiner Teil; Lautlehre; Wortbildung; Flexion*. Vol. I of *Griechische Grammatik: Auf der Grundlage von Karl Brugmanns Griechischer Grammatik*. Reprinted in Handbuch der Altertumswissenschaft 2.1.1. Munich: Beck, 1939. Schwyzer, Eduard, and Albert Debrunner. *Syntax und syntaktische Stilistik*. Vol. II of *Griechische Grammatik: Auf der Grundlage von Karl Brugmanns griechischer Grammatik*. Reprinted in Handbuch der Altertumswissenschaft 2.1.2. Munich: Beck, 1950.
Sihler	Sihler, Andrew L. *New Comparative Grammar of Greek and Latin*. Oxford: Oxford University Press, 1995.
Smyth	Smyth, Herbert Weir. *Greek Grammar*. Revised by Gordon M. Messing. Cambridge, MA: Harvard University Press, 1956.
vS	Siebenthal, Heinrich von. *Ancient Greek Grammar for the Study of the New Testament*. Oxford: Peter Lang, 2019.
Wallace	Wallace, Daniel B. *Greek Grammar beyond the Basics: An Exegetical Syntax of the New Testament*. Grand Rapids: Zondervan, 1996.

3 ANCIENT TEXTS

1–2 Cor	1–2 Corinthians
1 En.	1 Enoch
1–2 Esd	1 Esdras (apocryphal, contains passages similar to portions of Ezra, Nehemiah and Chronicles); 2 Esdras (= Ezra, Nehemiah)
1–3 John	1–3 John
1–2 Kgdms	1–2 Kingdoms (= 1–2 Samuel)
1–4 Macc	1–4 Maccabees
1–2 Pet	1–2 Peter

1–2 Thess	1–2 Thessalonians
1–2 Tim	1–2 Timothy
1–2 Chr	1–2 Chronicles
1–2 Clem.	1–2 Clement
3–4 Kgdms	3–4 Kingdoms (= 1–2 Kings)
Acts	Acts
Acts Pil.	Acts of Pilate
Aesop, *Fab.*	Aesop, *Fables*
Appian	Appian
Bell. civ.	*Civil Wars*
Pun.	*Punic Wars*
Aristophanes, *Vesp.*	Aristophanes, *Wasps*
Aristotle, *Rhet.*	Aristotle, *Rhetoric*
Barn.	Barnabas
Col	Colossians
Demosthenes	Demosthenes
1 Olynth.	*1 Olynthiac*
Andr.	*Against Androtion*
Cor.	*On the Crown*
Lept.	*Against Leptines*
Deut	Deuteronomy
Did.	Didache
Dio Chrysostom, *Ven.*	Dio Chrysostom, *The Hunter (Eubeoan Discourse)*
Diogn.	Diognetus
Eccl	Ecclesiastes
Eph	Ephesians
Euclid, *Elements*, CN	Euclid, *Elements*, Common Notions
Euripides, *Iph. taur.*	Euripides, *Iphigeneia at Tauris*
Exod	Exodus
Ezek	Ezekiel
Gal	Galatians
Gen	Genesis
Gos. Pet.	Gospel of Peter
Heb	Hebrews
Herm.	Shepherd of Hermas
Sim.	Similitude(s)
Vis.	Vision(s)
Herodotus, *Hist.*	Herodotus, *Histories*
Ign.	Ignatius
Pol.	*To Polycarp*
Rom.	*To the Romans*
Smyrn.	*To the Smyrnaeans*
Trall.	*To the Trallians*

Inf. Gos. Thom.	Infancy Gospel of Thomas
Isa	Isaiah
Jas	James
Jdt	Judith
Jer	Jeremiah
Job	Job
John	John
Josh	Joshua
Jub.	Jubilees
Jude	Jude
Judg	Judges
Lam	Lamentations
Let. Aris.	Letter of Aristeas
Lev	Leviticus
Luke	Luke
Mark	Mark
Mart. Pol.	Martyrdom of Polycarp
Matt	Matthew
Num	Numbers
Pausanias, *Descr.*	Pausanias, *Description of Greece*
Phil	Philippians
Philo	Philo
Confusion	*On the Confusion of Tongues*
Heir	*Who Is the Heir?*
Sacrifices	*On the Sacrifices of Cain and Abel*
Unchangeable	*That God Is Unchangeable*
Phlm	Philemon
Pindar	Pindar
Ol.	*Olympian Odes*
Plato	Plato
Apol.	*Apology of Socrates*
Gorg.	*Gorgias*
Leg.	*Laws*
Menex.	*Menexenus*
Pol.	*Politicus*
Tim.	*Timaeus*
Plutarch, *Cic.*	Plutarch, *Cicero*
Pol. *Phil.*	Polycarp, *To the Philippians*
Prot. Jas.	Protoevangelium of James
Prov	Proverbs
Ps	Psalm
Rev	Revelation
Rom	Romans

Ruth	Ruth
Sib. Or.	Sibylline Oracles
Sir	Sirach/Ecclesiasticus
Sophocles	Sophocles
Aj.	*Ajax*
Oed. tyr.	*Oedipus tyrannus*
Strabo, *Geogr.*	Strabo, *Geography*
T. Benj.	Testament of Benjamin
T. Dan.	Testament of Dan
T. Iss.	Testament of Issachar
T. Jos.	Testament of Joseph
T. Naph.	Testament of Naphtali
T. Sim.	Testament of Simeon
Thucydides, *P.W.*	Thucydides, *History of the Peloponnesian War*
Tob	Tobit
Wis	Wisdom of Solomon
Xenophon	Xenophon
Anab.	*Anabasis*
Cyr.	*Cyropaedia*
Mem.	*Memorabilia*
Zech	Zechariah

Sources of Ancient Texts

You can find almost all the ancient texts quoted in the public domain, as follows. These are all available on the internet, as are translations of most of them. I have sometimes simplified the Greek texts, used alternative readings from the critical apparatus of these editions or edited slightly by comparison with other editions.

Greek New Testament:
Scrivener, F. H. A. *The New Testament in Greek*. Cambridge: Cambridge University Press, 1881.

Greek Old Testament:
Swete, Henry Barclay. *The Old Testament in Greek: According to the Septuagint*. Cambridge: Cambridge University Press, 1909.

Apostolic Fathers:
Lightfoot, Joseph Barber and J. R. Harmer. *The Apostolic Fathers*. London: Macmillan, 1891.

Texts in Chapter 5 of this *Reader* were adapted from:
'An Interview with Pericles' and '300!' – Moss, Charles M. *A First Greek Reader*. Revised ed. Boston: John Allyn, 1887.
'Aesop's Fables: The Goose That Laid the Golden Eggs' – Abbott, Evelyn. *Easy Greek Reader*. Oxford: Clarendon, 1886.
'Aesop's Fables: The Wolf and the Lamb' – Smith, William. *A First Greek Reading Book*. London: John Murray, 1868.

Short examples used throughout the Extra Material of each chapter:
'Acts of Pilate' from *Evangelia Apocrypha, Adhibitis Plurimis Codicibus Graecis et Latinis, Maximam Partem Nunc Primum Consultis atque Ineditorum Copia Insignibus*. Edited by Konstantin von Tischendorf. Leipzig: Avenarius and Mendelssohn, 1853.
Appian, *The Foreign Wars*. Edited by L. Mendelssohn. Medford, MA: Teubner, 1879.
Aristophanes, *Aristophanes Comoediae*. Edited by F. W. Hall and W. M. Geldart. Vol. I. Medford, MA: Clarendon, Oxford, 1907.
Aristotle. *Ars Rhetorica*. Edited by W. D. Ross. Medford, MA: Clarendon, 1959.
Chrysostom. *Patrologia Graeca*. Edited by J.-P. Migne. Vol. LXII. 1862.

Demosthenes, *Demosthenis Orationes*. Edited by S. H. Butcher. Medford, MA, 1903.
Dio Chrysostom. *Dionis Prusaensis Quem Vocant Chrysostomum Quae Exstant Omnia*. Edited by J. de Arnim. Vol. I (*Orationes*). Medford, MA: Weidmann, 1893.
Euclid, *Euclidis Elementa*. Edited by J. L. Heiberg. Medford, MA: Teubner, 1883–8.
Euripides, *Euripidis Fabulae*. Edited by Gilbert Murray. Vol. II. Oxford: Clarendon, 1913.
'Gospel of Peter' from *The Akhmîm Fragment of the Apocryphal Gospel of Peter*. Edited by H. B. Swete. London: Macmillan, 1893.
Herodotus, *The Histories*. Trans. A. D. Godley. Medford, MA: Harvard University Press, 1920.
'Infancy Gospel of Thomas' from *Evangelia Apocrypha, Adhibitis Plurimis Codicibus Graecis et Latinis, Maximam Partem Nunc Primum Consultis atque Ineditorum Copia Insignibus*. Edited by Konstantin von Tischendorf. Leipzig: Avenarius and Mendelssohn, 1853.
Pausanias, *Pausaniae Graeciae Descriptio*. 3 vols. Leipzig: Teubner, 1903.
Philo, *Philonis Alexandrini opera quae supersunt*. Edited by Paul Wendland. Berlin: Reimer, 1896–.
Pindar, *The Odes of Pindar*. Edited by John Sandys. Cambridge, MA: Harvard University Press, 1937.
Plato, *Platonis Opera*. Edited by John Burnet. Oxford: Oxford University Press, 1903.
Plutarch, *Plutarch's Lives*. Edited by Bernadotte Perrin. Medford, MA: Harvard University Press, 1919.
'Protoevangelium of James' from *Evangelia Apocrypha, Adhibitis Plurimis Codicibus Graecis et Latinis, Maximam Partem Nunc Primum Consultis atque Ineditorum Copia Insignibus*. Edited by Konstantin von Tischendorf. Leipzig: Avenarius and Mendelssohn, 1853.
Sophocles, *Oedipus Tyrannus*. Edited by Sir Richard Jebb. Medford, MA: Cambridge University Press, 1887.
Ajax. Edited by Sir Richard Jebb. Medford, MA: Cambridge University Press, 1887.
Strabo. *Geographica*. Edited by A. Meineke. Leipzig: Teubner, 1877.
Thucydides, *Thucydides*. Edited by John William Donaldson. New York: Harper, 1885.
Xenophon, *Xenophontis Opera Omnia*. Vols. I–IV. Oxford: Clarendon, 1900–10.

How to Use This Book

1 IS THIS BOOK FOR ME?

This book is for you if:

- you are learning Greek from scratch, or
- you *used to know* Greek and want to refresh what you've forgotten in a fun way, or
- you have covered a first-year course in Greek and want an introduction to the kinds of topics that are usually taught in second and third-year courses.

The book is designed to be used week by week. However, it can be particularly helpful for revision before exams, or to keep Greek alive during term breaks or while you wait for your second year of Greek to start.

This book works with *Elements of New Testament Greek* by Jeremy Duff (Cambridge University Press). It works *both* for the 2005 third edition and the revised fourth edition. I'll refer to this book as the *Reader* and to *Elements of New Testament Greek* as *ENTG*, throughout.

2 HOW DO I USE THIS BOOK?

2.1 I'm (Re-)Learning Greek from Scratch

Each of Chapters 1–20 in the *Reader* accompanies the corresponding chapter of *ENTG*.

When you begin a chapter, first, make sure you've found the **Online Material** for that chapter (see Section 3 in this chapter). Check for any *errata* there either to *ENTG* or to this *Reader* and correct your copy as necessary.

What will you find in each chapter of the *Reader*?

Each chapter begins with a brief **How to Use This Chapter** box. Follow the instructions on how to use the *Reader* and *ENTG* for that chapter. Start there, not in *ENTG*. Often I will simply tell you to work through the whole chapter of *ENTG* and to refer to **Extra Help** (EH) after each section of *ENTG*. Sometimes there are more detailed instructions, explaining how each section of **Extra Help** relates to *ENTG*. Working through a section of *ENTG* includes doing the exercises and checking your answers.

This is how each chapter works:

- The first major part of each chapter is **Extra Help**. This guides you through that chapter of *ENTG* and provides supplementary explanations and advice,

as a teacher in a classroom might. At the end of each chapter, make sure you've learned the vocabulary, any grammar tables and grammar rules. I would suggest turning straight to the **Greek Readings** before you attempt the end-of-chapter exercises.
- Second, there are one or more **Greek Readings** which you can read confidently once you have completed *ENTG* up to the current chapter. Translate each **Reading** using the notes provided, answering the comprehension questions as you go. To save you from flicking around this book, the notes and study questions are in the **Online Material**. When you are not sure about something, keep reviewing the relevant section of *ENTG*; the notes and answers to questions will point you to the right place. You will find a translation and answers to the questions in the **Online Material**; check your work against them.
- Thirdly and finally, there is the **Extra Material** (**EM**) which goes beyond *ENTG* and explains more advanced matters. If you are learning Greek from scratch, you should not attempt this until you have worked through *ENTG*, *except* the introduction to Greek accents, which you can follow from the start. There are further notes, questions and answers on each **Greek Reading** based on the **Extra Material** (again, in the **Online Material**).

2.2 I've Let My Greek Rust: How Do I Use This *Reader*?

I especially hope that this *Reader* will help you if you used to know Greek but have let it go: in which case you have my fullest sympathy! I remember the horrible dilemma while trying to get back into Greek. Do I work through a textbook from scratch, tediously and painfully reviewing material that I sort of know? Or do I dive into the Greek New Testament (GNT), not knowing where to turn when I'm stuck?

This book is for you: start with the **Greek Reading** in Chapter 1. If there is anything there that you struggle with, it is explained in chapter 1 of *ENTG* or the *Reader*. The comprehension questions and notes after the reading will point you to the exact point in *ENTG* or the *Reader* which explains what you're struggling with.

Next, tackle the **Greek Reading** in Chapter 2. If there is anything there that you struggle with, the comprehension questions and notes after the reading will point you to the exact points in Chapters 1 or 2. Keep going through the chapters, enjoying the **Greek Readings**, reviewing the grammar only when you need to. I really hope you find that satisfying and enjoy yourself!

If you have previously covered more advanced material and your Greek isn't too rusty, feel free to dive into the **Extra Material** before moving on to the next chapter, since the notes and study questions will walk you through the *same* **Greek Readings** in more detail. These topics are never met earlier than the more basic introduction to that topic in *ENTG*. Alternatively, come back to them once you've been through the whole book.

2.3 What Is the Extra Material?

If you complete *ENTG* and haven't got a second-year course available to you, the **Extra Material** gives you a window into the kind of further study that you need. It helps you with the most important matters of syntax that are the bread and butter of reading with understanding. I have chosen to give a fairly full introduction to two topics: how authors use *cases* in a variety of contexts, and likewise for *verbs*.

Since it concerns matters beyond *ENTG*, it will include pointers to specific sections of helpful reference grammars, so that you can take the topic further. For more controversial matters, I refer to books or articles that I've relied on. The **Extra Material** is hardly ever original to me; it is my attempt to teach you the excellent work of others.

2.4 What If I Own the Third Edition of *ENTG* (2005)?

That's no problem: this *Reader* was written to work with that edition too. Before you start each chapter, turn to the **Online Material**, and particularly pay attention to two things:

- There is a list of *errata* in *ENTG* going back to quite early printings. You should annotate your copy with these corrections.
- For a couple of chapters, there will be slightly different instructions for how to combine this *Reader* with *ENTG*: this is where the fourth edition of *ENTG* made a significant change. Follow those instructions rather than the instructions in this *Reader*.

2.5 Accents

ENTG doesn't teach you much about accents, on principle. If you need, or want, to understand accents, I include the basics in the **Extra Material**, and supply accented forms of all the grammar and vocabulary in the **Online Material**. Accents are the only part of **Extra Material** that is designed for beginners; therefore, they will always be the first topic in the **Extra Material** of a chapter where they appear. If you want to learn Greek with accents, add them to *ENTG* from the accented versions of vocab and paradigms found in the **Online Material**, chapter by chapter.

3 ONLINE MATERIAL

Our companion website (www.cambridge.org/jenkins-greek) provides **Online Material** to supplement each chapter, including:

1 Translations of the **Greek Readings**.
2 The questions and notes for each **Reading**.

3 Answers to the comprehension questions.
4 *Errata* in *ENTG* and in this *Reader*.
5 *Errata* in the third edition of *ENTG*.
6 Separate instructions for some chapters, if you're using the third edition of *ENTG*.
7 Accented versions of the grammar and vocabulary in *ENTG*.
8 Tables helping you to understand how the various patterns of nouns and verbs relate to each other.

4 ENCOURAGEMENTS ALONG THE WAY

Be encouraged: once you've covered Chapters 1–11, you will read the Epistle to Philemon (an entire NT book!) with plenty of notes to help you. Each chapter from 16 onwards has an extra **Greek Reading**: an unedited extract from the GNT, with very little help needed.

Chapters 5, 11, 16 and 20 contain some consolidation material, to help you with any mid-year or mid-term breaks at those points. This involves longer Greek passages, with a much greater number of cross-references to earlier chapters of *ENTG*, so you can revise all the content you've learned up to that point. In Chapter 20, the passage is from the Early Church Fathers.

After Chapter 20, you can read anything that John wrote while only looking up (on average) one word of vocab every other verse.

Finally, Chapter 21 introduces you to a couple of features of Greek which are not covered in *ENTG*.

5 WHY GREEK TEXTS FROM OUTSIDE THE NT?

It may well be that your only interest in Greek is to read the NT. You'll notice that the majority of **Readings** are from outside. I'm convinced that this will help you to be a better reader *of the NT*, even if that's all you care about.

Let's think about what happens when you try to improve your Greek by reading Greek from the NT.

First, you already know what the text says, from your familiarity with translations. You can't help but take short-cuts. For myself, it was only when I opened the Gospel of Thomas that I realised that I hadn't really understood how the relative pronoun works: I had always worked it out from the sense in the NT. But here were sentences that I couldn't guess! Let me quote from the first edition of *ENTG*:

> The following selection of passages from Christian authors of the first two centuries has been added to this book in the hope that it may be useful to those who wish for some further knowledge of Greek *than*

that which can be obtained from the study of a book whose contents are so familiar to them in an English version as are the contents of the Greek Testament.[1]

Secondly, not only do you know what it means, you also care a great deal about the meaning. It's difficult to relax and consider various options when you feel the danger of overturning important truths which you've learned from translations. If you're always going to correct yourself from translations, why bother reading Greek at all?[2]

Thirdly, if you're reading God's word devotionally, you might feel uncomfortable breaking off to look up a point of grammar or the like, as though you were rudely terminating a conversation mid-sentence. You have other business in mind than improving your Greek.

Fourthly, because of that pressure to 'get something out of' your reading of the NT, we have a wealth of resources designed to 'help you gain insights' from the Greek text. These will stunt your growth in Greek. They can fool you into thinking that you can make minutely detailed decisions about the meaning of a text when you aren't competent to read the language at that level at all.[3] This would be incomprehensible with any other body of literature. Germans who study Shakespeare don't spend their time clicking on electronic German translations.

It is when we read texts that we're not already familiar with, and where we're not under pressure over how to interpret them, that we can become better readers of Greek. We then enjoy that improvement when we turn to the NT in Greek. Learn to read what translations have to leave out, and see for yourself the decisions that they have to make. Engage with commentaries, knowing when they've exhausted what the Greek can tell them and have moved on to other (important) factors for exegesis. My aim for you is a habit of *reading* Greek with understanding.

Finally, here is how C. S. Lewis viewed experts in the Gospels who talked as if they understood literature (his own field); the same applies to us when we become 'experts' in the Greek of the NT but are frightened by any Greek that isn't in the NT:

> A man who has spent his youth and manhood in the minute study of NT texts and of other people's studies of them, whose literary experience of those texts lacks any standard of comparison such as can only grow from a wide and deep and genial experience of literature in general, is, I should think, very likely to miss the obvious thing about

---

[1] H. P. V. Nunn, *A Short Syntax of New Testament Greek* (Cambridge: Cambridge University Press, 1920), 134 (italics added).

[2] Bradley H. McLean, *Hellenistic and Biblical Greek: A Graduated Reader* (Cambridge: Cambridge University Press, 2014), 3.

[3] Ibid., 4.

them. If he tells me that something in a Gospel is legend or romance, I want to know how many legends and romances he has read, how well his palate is trained in detecting them by the flavour; not how many years he has spent on that Gospel.[4]

Similarly, if all your experience of understanding Greek comes from reading NT texts whose meaning you already know, helped by commentaries and other resources, you don't have much expertise *of understanding Greek texts* to bring to the NT. There really is nothing harder about extra-Biblical Greek: it just exposes the short-cuts you've been taking in the NT. Getting confident outside the NT will increase your reading competence within the NT.[5]

If you use the **Extra Material**, every new idea is illustrated with Greek examples. I usually include at least one from the NT, to help you *recognise* the idea: for example, you have always known what 'the temple *of* his body' meant, and now you will learn why the genitive means that. I often include some examples from outside the NT: practising your understanding works better when you don't already know what you think the sentence means!

As for the made-up and adapted texts which make the first **Greek Reading** in each chapter, let me quote the four classicists who have just written a landmark Greek grammar:

> We also decided to dispense almost entirely with fabricated sentences ... from what we consider a healthy mistrust of our ability to produce Greek that would have sounded true to an ancient hearer.[6]

I have dared to do what they dare not; that's not because I'm more confident, but because there is no choice: I want you to practise the Greek that you have learned, chapter by chapter, when you only have a limited range of grammar and vocab, but giving you an extended prose text. For the many mistakes and infelicities in my attempt at writing simplified Greek, I plead guilty in advance. My aim is to serve the student, not save face nor parade my (laughably limited) knowledge.[7]

---

[4] C. S. Lewis, 'Fern-Seed and Elephants' in *Fern-Seed and Elephants: And Other Essays on Christianity* (Glasgow: Fount, 1977), 107.

[5] A quite separate reason is this: if you're engaging in any kind of scholarship (even just using commentaries), you will keep seeing these texts from outside the GNT cited, and you might develop a sense of awe at the specially trained mystics who are able to read them. This can be cured in half an hour by picking up any such text and reading it: it's just plain Greek from the NT age.

[6] *CGCG* xxxiv.

[7] A similar sentiment is in *ENTG* (3rd ed.) xi and 1. I'm immensely grateful to Professor Duff for reinforcing this principle of self-abnegation over the last year.

CHAPTER 1

The Alphabet
—
Accents

> **How to Use This Chapter**
>
> Please follow the general instructions in the **How to Use This Book** chapter above, which tells you what to do for each chapter, including this one.
> In this box at the start of each chapter, I give you instructions specific to this chapter. These will only ever involve how the sections of **Extra Help** relate to *ENTG*. **Extra Help** is always the beginning of the chapter, before the **Greek Readings**; in this chapter that's Sections 1 to 1.3.1.
>
> Work through chapter 1 of *ENTG*, section by section. As you complete each section, read the **Extra Help** below for that section.
>
> **Extra Material** introduces us to the basics of accents. **Extra Material** is always the end of the chapter, after the **Greek Readings**; in this chapter that's Sections 3 to 3.7.

1 ALPHABET

1.1 After *ENTG* 1.1.2: Pronunciation

You may well hear others pronouncing Greek quite differently when they read the GNT out loud, and there are some strongly held views out there on the subject. Follow your teacher, if you have one.

As far as this *Reader* goes, I am aiming to accompany *ENTG*, not change it. I will help you to follow what *ENTG* teaches, on this and on every other topic. Where there are different views on a topic among Greek scholars, any discussion will be reserved for the **Extra Material**, which goes beyond the topics in *ENTG*.

1.2 After *ENTG* 1.4: Diphthongs

Rule of thumb: diphthongs end in ι or υ. You needn't worry about exceptions to this rule.

1.3 After *ENTG* 1.5: Accents

ENTG makes a good case for not bothering with accents. If you want to learn about accents, the **Extra Material** throughout this *Reader* includes what you need to know.

Either way, I would advise you to learn your vocabulary and your grammatical patterns ('paradigms') by stressing the same syllable consistently, since this will make memorisation easier. You might as well, therefore, stress the syllable that the accent indicates. You'll find accented versions of all the vocabulary and paradigms in the **Online Material** that accompanies this *Reader*.

1.3.1 If You're Not Sure What a Syllable Is

You may not realise this, but whenever you pronounce English (whether out loud or while reading silently), you naturally break longer words up into pieces that normally have one vowel sound or one diphthong (two combined vowel sounds). These pieces are called **syllables**. Don't worry too much at all about which syllable the consonants belong to: it's really the vowel sounds you care about. *In Greek, each syllable has exactly one vowel or one diphthong*. Whenever a word has more than one syllable, you will put the stress on one of them, always the same one for each word. That's a frequent problem whenever we learn a language: we often stress the wrong syllable and become much harder to understand. On the other hand, putting the stress in the right place will reduce wasted effort when learning vocab.

Here are a few words from the last couple of sentences, with bold where the stress lies (at least the way I pronounce them):

> re**a**lise when**ev**er pron**ounce** **Eng**lish **wheth**er com**bined** **fre**quent

2 THE GREEK READING: PHOEBE'S BANQUET

> **Before You Start: How to Use the Vocabulary Lists**
> Vocab learnt up to the current chapter in *ENTG* is assumed (here, in Chapter 1, we don't give you καί in the list below). Any other words in the passage are given in the vocab list, in alphabetical order.

The only purpose of the text below is to help you practise the Greek alphabet. The text introduces the main characters of the story that you'll read in the next few chapters.

You don't need to understand the grammar in these little sentence fragments: looking up each word and replacing it with the English equivalent will give you the sense. I realise that looking every word up will feel tedious, but that will help you to practise the alphabet!

Keep pronouncing each word in your head. Be consistent in how you pronounce each letter, looking them up when in doubt. Stress the accented syllable.

The numbers in the text below are for ease of reference in the notes and study questions.

Ἡ ὈΝΟΜΑΤΟΓΡΑΦΙΑ ΤΩΝ ἈΝΘΡΩΠΩΝ ΤΗΣ ἹΣΤΟΡΙΑΣ

[1] Φοίβη – Ἀδελφὴ τοῦ Πέτρου. ποιεῖ δείπνους. μεριμνᾷ.

[2] Οὐρβανός – Δοῦλος τῆς Φοίβης. ἄγγελος ἀνεξίκακος.

[3] Πέτρος – Ἀδελφὸς τῆς Φοίβης. κατοικεῖ ἑτέρῳ οἴκῳ.

[4] Ἐπαίνετος – Δοῦλος καὶ οἰκονόμος τοῦ Πέτρου.

[5] Ἀμπλιᾶτος – Δοῦλος τοῦ Πέτρου καὶ διδάσκαλος τοῦ Παύλου. [6] ἀγαπᾷ τὴν Φοίβην κρυφῇ. [7] φιλεῖ τὸ ἔργον αὐτοῦ, ἀλλ' οὐ φιλεῖ διδάσκειν τὸν Παῦλον.

[8] Παῦλος – Ὁ υἱὸς τοῦ Πέτρου. διδάσκεται ὑπὸ τοῦ Ἀμπλιάτου. [9] ὁ Ἀμπλιᾶτος νομίζει δαιμόνιον εἶναι τὸν Παῦλον.

[10] Μαρία – Ἀδελφὴ τοῦ Παύλου. ἀγαθή.

[11] Περσίς καὶ Ἰουλία – Ἕτεραι ἀδελφαὶ τοῦ Παύλου. ἱλαραί.

[12] Τρύφαινα καὶ Τρυφῶσα – Δουλαὶ ἐν τῷ οἴκῳ τοῦ Πέτρου. κόσμιαι.

[13] Ῥοῦφος – Ταλαίπωρος κηπουρός. [14] δεῖ αὐτὸν τηρεῖν τὸν Παῦλον, τὸ δαιμόνιον. [15] εὔχεται πρὸς τὸν θεὸν καὶ πρὸς τὸν Χριστὸν καὶ πρὸς τοὺς ἀγγέλους ἐν τῷ οὐρανῷ.

2.1 Vocabulary

You don't need to memorise these words, and there are some here you won't learn in this course at all. In this chapter, I'll encourage you with pointers to how they've landed in English.

People's names should be guessable; have a look through Rom 16 if you need a bit of help.

Sometimes I have given you some short phrases instead of every word: check for it below whenever you encounter a very short word (three letters or fewer).

ἀγαθή – noble[1]
ἀγαπᾷ – he loves
ἄγγελος – a messenger, or an **angel** (heavenly beings often used as divine *messengers*); in this story, 'messenger'
ἀγγέλους – messengers (see above)
ἀδελφαί – sisters; see next entry
ἀδελφή – sister; see next entry
ἀδελφός – brother (Phil**adelphia** is the city of *brotherly* love; see below on φιλεῖ)
ἀλλά – but
ἀνεξίκακος – unflappable
δαιμόνιον – a demon
δεῖ αὐτόν – he is compelled
δείπνους – dinner parties
διδάσκαλος – teacher (*didactic*)
διδάσκειν – to teach (see previous entry)
διδάσκεται – he is taught (see previous entry)
δοῦλος – slave; not surprisingly, there is controversy over how to understand this noun. It is a good example of how learning a language, especially vocabulary, requires understanding the culture that uses that language. Translations seldom translate it consistently, often using 'servant', which makes the places where they choose 'slave' look unnecessarily pointed. I will stick with this single gloss throughout, in line with *ENTG*. If you find the term problematic, bear in mind that Paul called the government God's δοῦλος, himself *our* δοῦλος, Moses is honoured as God's δοῦλος, and this is the word Jesus promises to use when he congratulates his disciples as 'good and faithful …'
δουλαί – female slaves (see previous entry)
εἶναι – to be [the word before εἶναι comes after 'to be' in English]
ἐν – **in**
ἑτέρῳ – another (**hetero**doxy – *another* teaching)
ἕτεραι – [more than one] other (see previous entry)
εὔχεται – he prays
ἡ ὀνοματογραφία – the list of names, that is, the cast of characters (**onomato**poeic is something *named* after what it sounds like; **graph**ic design is all about *writing*)
θεόν – God (**theo**logy)
ἱλαραί – cheerful (from which we get **hilar**ious)
κατοικεῖ – he inhabits (see below on words related to οἶκος)
κηπουρός – gardener
κόσμιαι – diligent
κρυφῇ – secretly (**crypt**ic)
μεριμνᾷ – she frets
νομίζει – he considers; he reckons
ὁ υἱός – the son
οἰκονόμος – steward, household manager (οἶκος *house*, νόμος *rule, law* – the rules for governing a household)

---

[1] Fans of P. G. Wodehouse: Bertie Wooster's aunt Agatha is ironically named.

οἴκῳ – house (see above on οἰκονόμος)
οὐ – 'not' (οὐ denies what comes after it in Greek, so you'll have to move some words around in your English translation)
οὐρανῷ – Heaven
ποιεῖ – she makes (in this context, you'll want an English idiom) (we get English words like **poet** from this – one who 'makes it up')
πρός – to
ταλαίπωρος – hapless
τηρεῖν – to guard
τῆς ἱστορίας – of the story (**history**)
τῆς Φοίβης – of Phoebe
τὸ ἔργον αὐτοῦ – his job (**ergo**nomics – <u>rules</u> for **working** well; cf. οἰκονόμος above)
τοῦ Παύλου – of Paul
τοῦ Πέτρου – of Peter
τῶν ἀνθρωπῶν – of the people (**anthropo**logy is the study of people; λόγος is 'word' in a very broad sense, including the subject of study)
ὑπὸ τοῦ Ἀμπλιάτου – by Ampliatus
φιλεῖ – he loves, likes, enjoys (**Phil**adelphia is the city of brotherly *love*; see above on ἀδελφός)
Χριστόν – **Christ**

3 ACCENTS

FURTHER READING: vS 5

Remember that accents are not required for you to navigate *ENTG* successfully, which is why they are in **Extra Material**, rather than **Extra Help**. However, they are the one element of **Extra Material** which you can learn even if you're learning Greek from scratch, which is why accents are the first section of **Extra Material**, where it appears.

There are various honourable reasons for learning about accents, including:

1 You have no choice: your human right to self-determination is being erased by a teacher or by the expectations of the academy.
2 You don't want to be embarrassed when you quote Greek words out of context. I'll especially point out the rules that will help you with this.
3 You find this kind of thing fascinating; your spouse confiscates your wallet before you're allowed near the British Museum, in case you come out of the bookshop with *Peter Rabbit* re-written in Middle Egyptian hieroglyphs. True story.
4 You're not willing to trust that something doesn't make a difference until you've tried it for yourself and seen that it makes no difference. I feel for you.

Books have been written on accents;[2] what I'm going to do is focus on the rules that allow you to do two things:

1. Know when accents make a difference in meaning. (Whether you trust the provenance of the accents or not is up to you.)
2. Know how to quote Greek words out of context without looking like you don't understand accents.

As *ENTG* says, accents in the age of the NT simply indicate the stressed syllable. However, accents move around in the same word depending on context and on any endings added to the word. The rules which explain how accents move around date back to an older period of Greek, when the accent wasn't about stress, but about pitch.

Greek used to be pronounced by raising and lowering the tone, as if it were musical. The accents were used to show you when the pitch rises and falls within each word.

> To *understand* why an accent is where it is, you need to understand the rules of pitch. This will help you understand those places where accents distinguish different meanings, and to quote Greek out of context.
>
> To *pronounce* Greek when reading out loud or in your head, you don't need to worry about pitch: the accents tell you where to put the stress.

Remember:

1. Each syllable contains only one vowel or diphthong.
2. Two vowels together only form a diphthong if the second one is υ or ι; otherwise they are two separate syllables.

There are three accents:

Acute indicates where the pitch rises: ά.
Grave indicates where the pitch falls: ὰ.
Circumflex indicates that the pitch rises and falls in the same syllable: ᾶ.

In this chapter, we will explain how accents work generally. It will begin to fall into place in the next chapter, when we see how they work on verbs specifically.

3.1 Vowel Length

As far as accents are concerned, short vowels have one unit of length (λόγος), long vowels have two (ἀμήν) (*ENTG* 1.1.3 note 1). Diphthongs have the length

---

[2] See D. A. Carson, *Greek Accents: A Student's Manual* (Grand Rapids: Baker, 1985) and Philomen Probert, *A New Short Guide to the Accentuation of Ancient Greek* (Bristol: BCP, 2003).

of their combined vowels (φα**ί**νει, προσ**η**ύχετο) (*ENTG* 1.4). When discussing accents, a unit of vowel length is called a *mora*, plural *morae*.

3.2 The Rise and Fall of the Greek Pitch

Every word has a single rise in pitch, which falls immediately. The rise is marked by the acute accent, ά.

Accents combine with breathings: ἄ Ἄ αὔ, etc.

To illustrate, I'll use grave accents to show you where the pitch falls after it has risen. Note that these grave accents are never written, except at the end of words (**EM 1** 3.3). **Bold** shows which vowels are involved:

- λόγος = λόγὸς
- ἐγένετο = ἐγένὲτο
- ἄνθρωπος = ἄνθρὼπὸς (the fall in pitch takes up the whole of the syllable after the rise)
- πιστεύσωσιν = πιστεύσὼσὶν
- φῶς (**circumflex is shorthand for rise and fall**)
- ἀνθρώπων = ἀνθρώπὼν
- τοῦ = τόὺ (as with breathings, the circumflex is put on the second vowel of diphthongs, but it means a rise on the first vowel and a fall on the second)
- φαίνὲὶ: the diphthong in the first syllable has two *morae*. The pitch is constant on the first vowel (α), rising on the second (ι). It then falls over the second syllable, using up both *morae* in that diphthong too.

3.3 The Grave Accent

If the last syllable of a word has an acute accent, and that word is followed by another word rather than punctuation, then it is turned into a grave accent (ὰ). No one is quite sure why, but it probably means that there is no rise in pitch. This might be to make sure the next word starts at the same pitch as all the others.

In the first two sentences in the final exercise in chapter 1 of *ENTG*, the accents are as follows. **Bold shows where acute becomes grave**, and underlining shows where there is no change:

Ἐν ἀρχῇ[1] ἦν ὁ λόγος,[2] καὶ[3] ὁ λόγος ἦν πρὸς τὸν θεόν,[4] καὶ θεὸς ἦν ὁ λόγος.[5]

[1] No change; accent on final syllable isn't acute.
[2] No change; accent not on final syllable.
[3] Acute accent on final syllable, followed by another word without punctuation intervening, so turned into grave.
[4] Acute accent on final syllable, but followed by punctuation.
[5] Punctuation, and accent not on final syllable, so no change.

When you're quoting a few words of Greek out of their context, you might need to turn a grave accent on the last word into an acute.

If you find yourself wanting to know how to pronounce the pitch in a word that ends in a grave accent, or indeed in a word that ends in an acute accent, let me remind you that:

- you should merely pronounce accents by stress, not pitch
- the rules of pitch which we're dealing with here explain where the accents are and how they change, but are not there to guide your pronunciation
- nobody likes a show-off.

3.4 The Rule of Limitation

After the fall in pitch, we are allowed **at most a single *mora* (i.e. one short vowel)**. This produces the following derived rules:

If the final syllable has only one short vowel:

- An acute accent (ά) can go on any of the last three syllables (θεόν, λόγος, γέγονεν), but no earlier.
- A circumflex accent (ᾶ) can *only* go on the second-to-last syllable (οὗτος).

If the final syllable is longer than one short vowel (one *mora*):

- An acute accent can go on either of the last two syllables (ζωή, ἀνθρώπων), but no earlier.
- A circumflex accent can only go on the last (ἀρχῆ).

Can you work out how the rule of limitation leads to the rules above? Keep checking until you can.[3]

3.5 Exceptions

Further Reading: vS 74c

The diphthongs οι and αι, if they are the very last two letters of a word, count as having a length of one (except in some -όω contractions, **EM 19** 4.1, and optative endings, **EM 21** 1.1).

To illustrate, I'm using grave accents to show you where the pitch falls after it has risen:

> ἄνθρὼπὸς: acute on antepenultimate, pitch falls on the long vowel in the second syllable, leaving one *mora* (the short omicron) after the fall.

---

[3] Almost every description of accents gives you these derived rules, rather than the basic rule of limitation, which is set out beautifully in Donald J. Mastronarde, *Introduction to Attic Greek*, 2nd ed. (Berkeley: University of California Press, 2013), Unit 2.

ἀνθρώπων: final syllable has two *morae*, so the pitch can't fall *before* that. It rises right before that and falls on the final syllable.

ἀνθρώποις: exactly as above, because the οι in the final syllable aren't the very last letters of the word, they still count as two *morae*.

ἄνθρωποι: the οι in the final syllable are the very last letters of the word, so they have a combined length of one *mora*. That means the pitch can fall just before that, and therefore rise even earlier, just as in ἄνθρωπος.

Some little words have no accent and can interfere with the accent of the word before it (so that it can have two accents, or the wrong accent on the wrong syllable); don't worry for now.

3.6 Accents in Summary

1 Pitch only involves vowels.
2 Every word will have a single rise in pitch, and it then falls immediately.
3 After that fall, there can be *at most* a short vowel.

3.7 Quoting Greek out of Context

There are only two things you need to watch when you're quoting some Greek text out of context.

1 A grave accent might be on the final syllable, and should become acute instead. You already know all you need about this.
2 Some words break the rules and affect the words around them. You'll learn about these 'enclitics' in later chapters.

CHAPTER 2

Basic Sentences
—
Present Indicative

> **How to Use This Chapter**
>
> Work through chapter 2 of *ENTG*, section by section, completing exercises as you go. As you complete each section, read **Extra Help** below for that section.
>
> **Extra Help** advises you on how to learn grammatical endings. You will learn the logic behind the verb endings, which will save you time with new endings later. Chiefly, you'll learn how to tackle any Greek sentence.
>
> **Extra Material** focusses on the different contexts in which Greek uses the present tense. We also go a little further with accents, explaining how they work on verbs.

1 BASIC SENTENCES

1.1 After *ENTG* 2.1 (before 2.1.1)

An older rule for the 'optional ν' might help you understand what it's doing. For pronunciation reasons, it appears when the next word begins with a vowel and before punctuation. (Compare the English word 'an' before 'apple' but 'a' before 'bushel'.) This convention is very often not followed in the NT, however.

1.2 After *ENTG* 2.1.2

As *ENTG* points out, the Greek present tense can be found in a range of contexts, whereas English uses a different tense for each one. 'I untie' and 'I am untying' (and other English forms) are all expressed by the one Greek present tense λύω.

Similarly, every element of grammar that you will learn this year can appear in its own range of contexts. That's one reason you need further study after *ENTG*. In the **Extra Material** throughout this book, we introduce the different contexts in which authors can use each element of Greek. We begin to practise deciding what an author is likely and unlikely to mean by them. Once you've worked through *ENTG* once, you can proceed to the **Extra Material**.

1.3 After *ENTG* 2.3.3: Tackling Any Greek Sentence: A Tree with Trunk and Branches

Any Greek sentence is like a tree, with a trunk and some branches. The key to reading it is to identify the trunk.

First find your verb: you might add this as 'step zero' in the Hint box on *ENTG* 2.3.3. That's always in the trunk. See whether there is a subject other than the verb ending (*nominative*). See whether there is an object (*accusative*). That's your trunk. Anything else in the sentence will be telling you more about one of these three things on the trunk, hanging off one of them like a branch.

> **Word order is *not* what tells you what each word does in the sentence; *cases* do that.**

1.4 After *ENTG* 2.3

1.4.1 All That Tedious Memorising …

There will be many paradigms[1] and a lot of vocabulary to learn as you work through this course. Be encouraged by the endgame: you'll be able to pick up John's Gospel and just *read* without looking up more than a word every other verse or so! It is crucial to your success in Greek that you memorise the paradigms with a high degree of accuracy as soon as possible. Here are some tips to help you:

- At the beginning, there is relatively little to learn. It can be tempting to take short-cuts of various forms; resist! Don't rely on a process of elimination ('it isn't nominative so it must be accusative'). It will fail once more options appear later.
- When learning vocab, picture in your mind what the word means: a loaf of bread for ἄρτος, someone listening for ἀκούω.
- The **Online Material** has two resources that will especially help you as you work through *ENTG*:
  ○ The *Accented Vocabulary* file marks the accent on each word to help with consistent pronunciation.
  ○ Consider using software to help you test yourself more efficiently. Some programs will keep track of your progress and work out when you need re-testing on each word. You'll find all the vocab there in a form that will work with one such program.
- Copying out a paradigm repeatedly, and reading it out loud, will help you remember it.
- Keep reviewing older paradigms as we meet new ones.

---

[1] Verbs follow *conjugations* (*ENTG* 2.1.1), nouns follow *declensions* (*ENTG* 2.3.1). The catch-all word for all grammatical patterns is *paradigms*.

- **Little and often**. Carry your notebook or flashcards (or app on your phone) around in your pocket and refer to them throughout the day at odd spare moments. Pretend that it's as important as checking your 'social media' (or whatever kids are calling it these days).
- Use a study-buddy for a weekly meeting, even if it means video-conferencing someone in another town. You can swap tips and mnemonics. The deadline of meeting together will spur you on.
- Testing yourself from English to Greek for vocabulary is hard work but can help, if you have time. Be fussy about spelling.
- Notice synonyms and near-synonyms (λέγω 'I say' is in this chapter, but you will meet other verbs to do with speaking soon).

1.4.2 Learning Paradigms: A Method

There are considerably fewer different endings in Greek than you might think. Whenever new paradigms appear in *ENTG*, I'll give you some extra help to spot patterns and understand the hidden rules which produce the apparent variety of paradigms. You're more than free to ignore this advice: many students prefer just to learn endings by rote; many like understanding the underlying logic. Between *ENTG* and this *Reader*, both are catered for, but understand that there is no difference in the end result. The paradigms are the same either way, and the aim is the same either way.

Your aim is to **know the paradigms well enough to recognise any form on sight**. Whenever you encounter a new paradigm that's related to an earlier one:

1 Apply the rules and try to write out the new paradigm from them.
2 Check the result against *ENTG*. That will correct mistakes, misunderstanding of rules, and alert you to exceptions.
   For example, memorise the endings in *ENTG* 2.1. Then apply the rules for contract verbs to those same endings to try to reproduce the endings in *ENTG* 2.2.
3 Keep writing out the paradigms from memory, checking until perfect; 100 times is <u>not</u> too many; you'll use them every day for the rest of your life!
4 Use your study-partner and/or software to test yourself, making sure you can parse any form as you meet it. Initially you'll have to go down your paradigm in your head, counting as you go, until you find the one you're looking at. You see λύομεν and you go (1) λύω (2) λύεις (3) λύει (4) λύομεν. Got it! Number 4. So that's 1st person plural. Eventually, you'll recognise them on sight, but that takes practice. So practise!

1.4.3 Building Your Verb

We'll gradually meet the components that can be added to a verb. So far we have met three, which combine to produce the form that you meet in a Greek text.

Understanding how the contract vowel interacts with the *same* endings saves us from learning two sets of endings, as you can see in Table 2.1.

Table 2.1 Building Your Verb

Stem	Contract vowel	Ending	Result
λυ	–	ομεν	λύομεν
		ετε	λύετε
φιλ	ε	ομεν	φιλοῦμεν
		ετε	φιλεῖτε

2 THE GREEK READING

As you work through this **Reading**, remember:

1 Keep pronouncing each word in your head. Be consistent in how you pronounce each letter, looking them up when in doubt. Stress the accented syllable.[2]
2 If you get stuck with a sentence, move on to the next one.
3 Once you've worked out what a sentence means, try reading it out loud with feeling, emphasising the right words. (If you're in a library or a café, read it in your head, actively enough to feel your mouth muscles working.)

The saga begins!
Phoebe decides to host a dinner party for a large crowd, including her brother Peter and all his household. She sends a messenger to convey the invitation. The messenger teams up with one of Peter's slaves, and a hunt for Peter begins. Ampliatus, private tutor to Peter's son, seizes the opportunity to be near to his (secretly) beloved Phoebe. Some catering arrangements are made.

¹ Φοίβη καλεῖ δοῦλον· Φοίβη καλεῖ τὸν Οὐρβανόν. λέγει·

² Ἔχω λόγον.

³ Ποιῶ δεῖπνον καὶ καλῶ ὄχλον.

⁴ Καὶ καλῶ τὸν Πέτρον· καλῶ τὸν ἀδελφόν μου.

⁵ Ὁ Οὐρβανὸς λέγει·

---

[2] If you have worked through **EM 1 3** (to remind you, this means **Extra Material** in chapter 1, section 3), remember that the rules of pitch are only there to help you understand which syllable is stressed. By the NT era, variations in pitch were no longer part of speaking Greek. As you read, just stress the accented syllable.

⁶ Ἄγω ἄγγελον.

⁷ Ὁ Οὐρβανὸς ἄγει τὸν ἄγγελον πρὸς τὸν Πέτρον.

⁸ Βλέπει ὁ Οὐρβανὸς δοῦλον τοῦ Πέτρου.

⁹ Βλέπει ὁ Οὐρβανὸς Ἐπαίνετον, καὶ λέγει·

¹⁰ Ἔχομεν λόγον.

¹¹ Ὁ Ἐπαίνετος ἀκούει τοὺς λόγους, καὶ λέγει·

¹² Τί λαλεῖς; Λόγον ἔχετε;

¹³ Λέγει Οὐρβανός·

¹⁴ Φοίβη καὶ πολλοὶ ἄνθρωποι ποιοῦσι δεῖπνον.

¹⁵ Καλοῦμεν τὸν Πέτρον καὶ τὸν οἶκον.

¹⁶ Ἄνθρωπον βλέπουσι ὁ Οὐρβανὸς καὶ ὁ Ἐπαίνετος.

¹⁷ Τίνα βλέπει ὁ Οὐρβανός; ¹⁸ τίνα βλέπει ὁ Ἐπαίνετος; ¹⁹ τίνα βλέπουσιν οἱ ἄνθρωποι;

²⁰ Ἀμπλιᾶτον βλέπουσιν. (²¹ Ὁ Ἀμπλιᾶτος διδάσκει τὸν Παῦλον. ²² ὁ Ἀμπλιᾶτος διδάσκει τὸν υἱὸν τοῦ Πέτρου.)

²³ Λέγει ὁ Ἐπαίνετος·

²⁴ Ὁ ἄγγελος ζητεῖ τὸν κύριον, καὶ ζητῶ τὸν κύριον. ²⁵ ζητοῦμεν τὸν Πέτρον. ²⁶ Φοίβη ποιεῖ δεῖπνον καὶ καλεῖ τὸν ἀδελφὸν καὶ τὸν οἶκον.

²⁷ (Φιλεῖ ὁ Ἀμπλιᾶτος Φοίβην.)

²⁸ Ὁ Ἀμπλιᾶτος λέγει·

²⁹ Τί λέγετε;

Τὸν Πέτρον ζητεῖτε;

³⁰ Λαμβάνω τὸν λόγον.

³¹ Διδάσκω τὸν Παυλόν· τὸν υἱὸν τοῦ Πέτρου τηρῶ.

³² Φοίβη καλεῖ τὸν οἶκον· Φοίβη καλεῖ με.

³³ Ὑπάγουσιν ὁ Οὐρβανὸς καὶ ὁ Ἐπαίνετος. ³⁴ ζητεῖ τὸν Πέτρον ὁ Ἐπαίνετος.

³⁵ ζητεῖ Φοίβην ὁ Οὐρβανός.

³⁶ Λέγει ὁ Οὐρβανός, καὶ ἀκούει Φοίβη·

³⁷ Λαμβάνουσιν ὁ Πέτρος καὶ ὁ οἶκος τὸν λόγον.

³⁸ Ὑπάγει ὁ Ἐπαίνετος καὶ ζητεῖ Φοίβην. ³⁹ βλέπει Φοίβην ὁ Ἐπαίνετος καὶ

λέγει·

⁴⁰ Ποιοῦμεν ἄρτους, ὡς λέγει ὁ νόμος.

2.1 Vocabulary

A Reminder
You don't need to memorise these words, and there are some here you won't learn in this course at all.

Inflected forms are explained unless you've learnt their meaning in this chapter.

Words which you are supposed to have memorised in Chapters 1 and 2 are not given, unless they are in a form which you do not recognise.

Bold font means that you will learn that word in a later chapter; that's purely for your encouragement. I will keep giving these to you as vocab until the chapter when you're supposed to learn them.

Ἀμπλιᾶτος – Ampliatus
δεῖπνος – dinner party
Ἐπαίνετος – Epaenetus
με – me (acc)
μου – my (follows whatever is mine)
Οὐρβανός – Urbanus
Παῦλος – Paul
Πέτρος – Peter
πολλοί – many

πρός – to (followed by the target, in the acc case)
τί; – what? (acc)
τίνα; – whom? (acc)
τοῦ Πέτρου – of Peter
ὑπάγω – I depart
Φοίβη – Phoebe (nom sing)
Φοίβην – Phoebe (acc sing)
ὡς – as

3 ACCENTS

Remember that accents do not form part of *ENTG*, which is why they're in **Extra Material** rather than **Extra Help**. They are the one part of **Extra Material** that you can follow if this is your first time learning Greek, which is why they're always before any other **Extra Material** in any chapter.

3.1 Accents on Finite Verb Forms Are Regressive

FURTHER READING: vS 74A

We have described where accents *can* go: the 'rule of limitation' (**EM 1** 3.4). Now we'll explain where they *do* go in verbs. This is really easy: the accent goes as close to the start of the verb as it can, without breaking the rule of limitation. Take a moment to write out the paradigm in *ENTG* 2.1 and work out where the accent goes; then compare that with the accented paradigm in the **Online Material**.

For contract verbs, look at the table in *ENTG* 2.2. In the right-hand column, the uncontracted verb φιλέω is given:

1 Copy it out, and add the accents to *the uncontracted verb* according to the same principle: put it as far to the left as the rule of limitation allows.
2 Now look at the underlined pairs of vowels/diphthongs in that column, which will contract. If the accent is on the first one of them, then the pitch would have dropped on the second one; **when you contract them, you indicate this with a circumflex.**

For example, φιλε + ω: pitch rise must be on the ε; if it were to rise on the ι, it would fall on the ε, but then there are *two* vowel lengths in the ω after that, which isn't allowed. If the pitch were to rise on the ω, then it wouldn't be as far to the left as allowed by the rules. It must be φιλέ + ὼ. This then contracts to φιλῶ.

NB: you add the accent before the contraction of contract vowels with endings. For example, φιλ-ε-ομεν. Put the accent as far to the left as possible. φιλ-έ-ομεν. Then the contract vowel combines with the ending, φιλ-έ + ὸ-μεν → οῦ. Result: φιλοῦμεν.

As before, check your work against the online paradigm.

You will always need to know whether the final syllable is long or short. For verbs, this happens in the aorist and perfect active, and the α is always short.

3.1.1 Finite vs Non-Finite Verb Forms

Verb forms that have person and number are called 'finite' (indicative, imperative, subjunctive, optative). The participles and infinitives do not decline for person and number, and are often called 'verbal nouns' or 'non-finite'.

Finite verb forms obey the rules explained above (I'll point out the tiny number of exceptions as we meet them). Non-finite verbs are more complicated; I believe they give you too little payoff for the effort it takes to learn them.

3.2 Proclitics

Further Reading: vS 6

Some short words break the rules of accents. One set of these is called **proclitics**. These words lack their own accent, and rely on the accent of the following word. They were originally not separate words, but attached as a prefix to the following word. One example is the article in the nominative (ὁ οἱ), but not in the accusative (τόν, τούς). There aren't many others, and I'll point them out as they arise in the vocab of *ENTG*.

4 THE PRESENT TENSE

If you're learning Greek for the first time, the **Extra Material** covering accents will have been accessible to you. However, these other topics should wait until you have mastered the first-year material, not least because the examples illustrating them require the whole of first-year grammar.

4.1 Present Tense = Ongoing + Now

As discussed in chapter 6 of *ENTG* and in the **Extra Help** for that chapter, indicative tenses combine aspect with time.[3] The present system, which includes the present and imperfect tenses, has 'ongoing' aspect. It presents the action as in progress: it doesn't include both the beginning and the end, but refers to a point in time when the action was still ongoing, as shown in Figure 2.1. By contrast, the aorist system presents the action as a simple whole, including the beginning and the end.

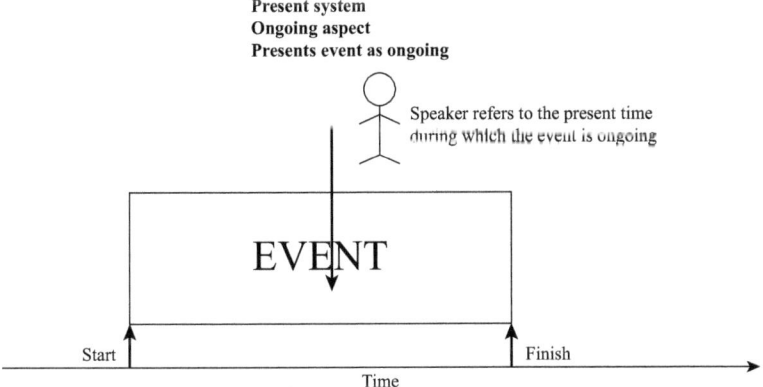

Figure 2.1 Aspect of Present Indicative

---

[3] For a summary of aspect in all the systems, see **EH 18** 4.2.

Much of what we will cover below for the present tense will be almost identical when we cover the imperfect tense in Chapter 6, because they share the 'ongoing' aspect of the present system. The imperfect tense is even more straightforward, so be encouraged.

When a Greek author is referring to an action that is going on at the time of speaking/writing, the **present tense is the default tense** to use. In later chapters, we will see why they might choose a different tense, and below we will see how a present tense might refer to something that isn't present. Nonetheless, the present tense is the default for present time and generally refers to the present time.

4.2 English vs Greek: The Label Maker

As *ENTG* 2.1 explains, English distinguishes between:

- I am eating a carrot. (Once, right now.)
- I eat carrots. (As a general rule, or by force of habit.)
- I keep eating carrots. (It happens repeatedly.)

The Greek tense doesn't mean those three things: it means one thing which includes any of those three situations. The Greek author is describing one event, regardless of whether that one event is a single action, a series of actions, a habitual action, etc. The problem is that you start your Greek journey by translating, and English forces you to decide what the Greek text does not tell you.

Even worse, in order for English-speaking scholars to communicate with each other, the different situations that *English* distinguishes between are each given neat labels. This might help us to talk about whether λύω in a particular sentence refers to one act of untying ('descriptive present') or a habit of untying people ('habitual present'). This can make us forget that there is **one** *Greek present tense* and that it doesn't make these distinctions.

Context and other factors might make us say that ποιεῖ in a particular sentence means 'she keeps on making'. We have handy labels to express such decisions compactly, described below. But ποιεῖ is just a Greek present tense, not an 'iterative present'. English has forced your hand, because 'he is making' and 'he makes' mean different things, and you have to choose one.

5 CONTEXTS FOR THE PRESENT TENSE

FURTHER READING: FANNING 4.1; vS 197; WALLACE 513–39

The present tense refers to an action ongoing now. Sometimes, the author might stress the fact that the action is not yet completed. By extension, it can refer to actions that haven't even started yet. The list of headings below might look daunting, but if you keep that basic meaning in view, it will all make sense.

> **This Is Easy**
> Don't let the list of contexts below put you off. Almost all of them work the same way in English.
>   Only two will be new to you, and both are very rare: perfective and conative. If you're daunted by this, take a quick look at the English examples in **EM 2** 5.5 and see how familiar they are.

5.1 Focus on Present Time

The present tense is the default tense for actions that are happening 'now'. While the aspect of the present system presents the action at a point when it is 'ongoing', the first few contexts we will consider are more to do with the *present time* of the action. Later, we will consider contexts where the 'ongoing' aspect comes to the fore (**EM 2** 5.2).

5.1.1 Descriptive

This is the first of the two most obvious uses: the focus is on a particular action, and its 'nowness' is highlighted.

>   Ἀκούεις τί οὗτοι λέγουσιν; Matt 21:16
>   Do you hear what these are saying?

>   ἢ ἡμῖν τί ἀτενίζετε; Acts 3:12
>   Why are you staring at us?

>   καλῶς ποιεῖτε Jas 2:8
>   you are doing well

>   ἰδοὺ ἀπόλλυμαι λύπῃ μεγάλῃ ἐν γῇ ἀλλοτρίᾳ. 1 Macc 6:13
>   Look, I'm dying of great grief in a foreign country.

Some verbs don't refer to actions, but to states of being.[4] If you think the author meant a particularly short-lived or temporary state, then this is labelled 'descriptive'.

>   Κύριε, ἴδε ὃν φιλεῖς ἀσθενεῖ. John 11:3
>   Master, look, the one you love is ill.
>   In context, he is currently suffering from a particular illness, rather than being generally sickly.

>   ἐγὼ ὀργίζομαι ἐπὶ τὰ ἔθνη Zech 1:15
>   I am angry against the nations

---

[4] Different verb types are explained in more detail when we cover the aspect in other moods: see **EM 8** 5.1.1.

In English, such a short-lived state is sometimes written in the same way as ongoing states, even when we are referring to a very focussed 'now'.

> γινώσκεις ἃ ἀναγινώσκεις; Acts 8:30
> Do you understand what you are reading?
> Not, 'Are you understanding …?'

5.1.2 English Idiom: Durative

In English, 'they are with me for three days' implies that their total stay will be three days long, and that some of that is future. If you mean that the stay so far has been going on for three days, and continues, then you must say 'they have been with me for three days'. This is an English issue, not a Greek one.[5] Greek will just use a present tense in that situation, but English requires a perfect tense.

> ἤδη ἡμέρας τρεῖς προσμένουσί μοι Mark 8:2
> they have been with me **for three days already**
>
> ἀπὸ τῶν ἡμερῶν Ἰωάννου τοῦ βαπτιστοῦ **ἕως ἄρτι** ἡ βασιλεία τῶν οὐρανῶν βιάζεται Matt 11:12
>
> **From the days** of John the Baptist **until now**, the kingdom of heaven has endured violence
>
> εἴκοσι ἔτη ἐγώ εἰμι μετὰ σοῦ Gen 31:38
> I have been with you **for twenty years** [accusative of time, *ENTG* 10.4]

5.1.3 Iterative / Customary / Habitual

This is the second of the two most obvious uses: actions over a longer period, when that period includes the present time. The focus is on the present, even though the action itself might not be happening at this very instant.

The most general sense is given by the **iterative present**: the action keeps happening, but not necessarily with any regularity, such as checking the time often throughout an exam.

> ὑμεῖς ποιεῖτε τὰ ἔργα τοῦ πατρὸς ὑμῶν John 8:41
> you are doing the works of your father
>
> σεληνιάζεται καὶ κακῶς πάσχει· **πολλάκις** γὰρ πίπτει εἰς τὸ πῦρ. Matt 17:15
>
> He has seizures, and suffers awfully, because he falls into the fire **often** …

---

[5] Languages that use the present tense in such a context don't have a 'durative' present in their Greek grammars.

ὃ ἔστι δ' ὅτε κατορθοῦν ἐν οἷς πταίουσι μεγάλα νομίζουσιν Philo, *Unchangeable*, 134
and yet there are times ['there is a when'] when they reckon to be upright, concerning matters in which they are erring greatly.
The context contrasts this with what they do habitually or customarily.

[On trial, Socrates has to explain why he has acquired such a terrible reputation. In part, he says, some young men are trying to act like him, but, lacking his wisdom, are winding people up.]

χαίρουσιν ἀκούοντες ἐξεταζομένων τῶν ἀνθρώπων, καὶ αὐτοὶ **πολλάκις** ἐμὲ μιμοῦνται. Plato, *Apol.* 23c
They keep delighting in hearing men being interrogated: they even mimic me **often**.

Knowing whether an author intends you to understand a present tense as descriptive rather than, say, iterative is a matter of interpretation. However, authors want to be understood and will often make it perfectly plain. Notice the use of πολλάκις in the last two examples above. They tell us that the acts of imitating (μιμοῦνται) and falling (πίπτει) are iterative.

Similar to iterative is the present referring to customs: **customary present** (which is also a repetition of the action over a period of time, including now):

ἐὰν μὴ πυγμῇ νίψωνται τὰς χεῖρας, οὐκ ἐσθίουσι Mark 7:3
unless they wash their hands, they don't eat.

τὰ ἴδια πρόβατα καλεῖ κατ' ὄνομα, καὶ ἐξάγει αὐτά. John 10:3
He calls his own sheep by their name, and leads them out.
Jesus is describing the *expected* behaviour of good shepherds.

πᾶν οὖν δένδρον μὴ ποιοῦν καρπὸν καλὸν ἐκκόπτεται καὶ εἰς πῦρ βάλλεται Luke 3:9
so every tree which doesn't bear good fruit is cut down and is thrown into a fire

However, it can also refer to the **habitual** behaviour of a particular person or group:

λέγουσι καὶ οὐ ποιοῦσι Matt 23:3
They speak, but they do not do.
The context tells us that the Pharisees habitually speak, teaching others, v2, and habitually fail to do that which they teach, v4.

οὕτω γράφω. 2 Thess 3:17
[I'm writing this greeting myself] ... this is how I write.

γαμοῦσιν ὡς πάντες, τεκνογονοῦσιν· ἀλλ' οὐ ῥίπτουσι τὰ γεννώμενα Diogn. 5.6

> like everyone else, they marry and have children; however, <u>they</u> don't
> <u>cast away</u> their offspring
>
> In the wider argument, the point is that this refusal to abandon sick or unwanted children is a distinctively **characteristic** behaviour of Christians.

Verbs that describe states of being don't usually refer to multiple events, but to a single period of existence in that state. We call this 'customary' unless it is particularly short-lived ('descriptive').

> ἡμεῖς ἀσθενοῦμεν ἐν αὐτῷ 2 Cor 13:4
> We <u>are weak</u> in him.
>
> ὁ πένης ἐργάζεται τὴν ἔντευξιν ἐν ᾗ <u>πλουτεῖ</u> Herm. Sim. 2.7
> The poor man works at intercession, concerning which <u>he is rich</u>.

5.1.4 Remember the Focus on 'Now'

Remember that all the situations above are just a single Greek tense. However much we need to distinguish them in English, that is not the focus of the Greek verb. The Greek present tense above focusses on the 'now' of the event. Regardless of whether the event is a single act or a long sequence or a lifelong habit, the author chose a present tense to say that the event is happening *now*.

This doesn't mean that one action within the event is happening now: someone is in the habit of washing *now* even if they aren't *currently* in the bathroom. It's the *current* habit that is in view.

In deciding whether you're dealing with descriptive, iterative or a state, etc., don't lose sight of what the Greek is telling you: *now*.

5.1.5 Gnomic

We have seen the present focussed on narrow points of time (descriptive) and for broader periods, including life-long habits (iterative, etc.). We can take that to the extreme and consider actions which are *always* true: proverbial statements and truisms. 'There are eight pints to a gallon.' 'A stitch in time saves nine.'

> πᾶς ὁ αἰτῶν <u>λαμβάνει</u> Matt 7:8
> Everyone who asks <u>receives</u>.
>
> Πᾶσα βασιλεία ἐφ' ἑαυτὴν διαμερισθεῖσα ἐρημοῦται. Luke 11:17
> Every kingdom that is divided against itself <u>is made desolate</u>.
>
> Τὰ τῷ αὐτῷ ἴσα καὶ ἀλλήλοις ἐστὶν ἴσα. Euclid, *Elements*, CN 1
> Things which are equal to another thing <u>are</u> also equal to each other.
>
> Σοφία ἐν ἐξόδοις ὑμνεῖται Prov 1:20
> Wisdom <u>sings</u> aloud in the streets.

> ὃν γὰρ ἀγαπᾷ Κύριος ἐλέγχει, μαστιγοῖ δὲ πάντα υἱὸν ὃν παραδέχεται.
> Prov 3:12
> for, whom the Lord loves, he rebukes, and scourges every son whom he receives.

> ὡς καὶ ὁ χοῖρος ... ὅταν δὲ πεινᾷ κραυγάζει, καὶ λαβὼν πάλιν σιωπᾷ.
> Barn. 10.3
> Just as a pig ... cries out whenever it's hungry, but once it has received [food] is quiet again.

> Φθείρουσιν ἤθη χρηστὰ ὁμιλίαι κακαί. 1 Cor 15:33
> Evil associations ruin honourable habits.

5.1.6 Performative (a.k.a. Aoristic, a.k.a. Instantaneous)

At the other end of the scale, we can shrink the period in view to be only as long as the act of speaking. The action is *ongoing* during the exact moment of speaking: not before, and not after. The 'now' really comes to the fore.

> Παραγγέλλω σοι ἐν τῷ ὀνόματι Ἰησοῦ Χριστοῦ, ἐξελθεῖν ἀπ' αὐτῆς.
> Acts 16:18
> I command you, in Jesus Christ's name, to come out of her.

This is where saying something *is* the action: to say that you are doing it, is to do it. 'I pray', 'I warn', 'I beg', 'With this ring, I marry you', anything beginning 'I hereby...'

This includes times when, for rhetorical effect, you say or write, 'I tell you ...' before you say what you want to say. The period of time of the present includes the time it takes to say your message. (Beware of thinking that the present *must* mean 'I tell you repeatedly'.)

> ὡς προειρήκαμεν, καὶ ἄρτι πάλιν λέγω, εἴ τις ὑμᾶς εὐαγγελίζεται παρ' ὃ παρελάβετε, ἀνάθεμα ἔστω. Gal 1:9
> As we have said, so I tell you again: 'If someone proclaims a gospel to you, contrary to the one that you received, let him be anathema.' Notice how the use of πάλιν and the contrast with the perfect tense would make no sense of 'I keep on telling you'.

> Λέγω σοι ὅτι οὐκ ἔστιν αὕτη νηστεία Herm. Sim. 5.1.3
> I'm telling you that this is not a fast at all.
>> He is explaining what he has just said; he isn't repeatedly telling you that it is not a fast.

5.2 Focus on Ongoing Aspect

We turn now to situations where the author focusses on the action as 'not yet finished'.

This particularly applies to actions that have a natural completion point: eating a meal, reading a whole book, teaching a lesson, running a marathon. If the action breaks off before that point, then it is unsuccessful: you haven't filled in the form, you haven't written the assignment, you haven't run a marathon.[6]

The 'ongoing' aspect of the present tells us that the endpoint *hasn't* yet been reached, in a variety of situations.

5.2.1 Conative

Conative applies to actions that have a natural completion point.

The present tense describes an action in progress. Therefore, the action is *not yet successfully complete*. If you think the context (or the nature of the action) implies some difficulty or opposition in reaching the intended outcome, you call this **conative**. English will require a bolder translation, because we don't use the present tense like this:

> ἄρτι γὰρ ἀνθρώπους πείθω ἢ τὸν Θεόν; Gal 1:10
> for am I now **seeking to** win over people or God?
>> The difficulty in completing the action is explicitly stated in the next few words, using ζητῶ: ἢ **ζητῶ** ἀνθρώποις ἀρέσκειν; 'Or **am I seeking** to please people?'

> ἐν νόμῳ δικαιοῦσθε Gal 5:4
> you are **trying** to be justified by the law.
>> Paul is clear that not only have they not yet succeeded, but also that they never will be justified by the law. 'You are being justified' would miss the point. Unfortunately, you can't sit on the fence; to translate a present tense in a 'default' way is to exclude the conative meaning in English. Remember that the Greek is just a present tense, δικαιοῦσθε: **EM 2** 5.1.4.

5.2.2 Voluntative (Beware: a.k.a. Conative)

The 'not yet successful' sense, which comes to the fore in the conative, can be applied to actions that haven't even started yet. Someone wants to, or is about to, do something. However, unlike the conative, this need not cast doubt on whether it will succeed or not. It isn't always easy to decide which of the two is in view.[7]

Both conative and voluntative apply to actions that have a natural endpoint which hasn't yet been reached. The difference is that *conative* has begun the

---

[6] Different verb types are explained in more detail when we cover the aspect in other moods: see **EM 8** 5.1.1.

[7] Be aware that many authors call both these uses 'conative'. Both the conative and voluntative uses of the present are quite rare, whereas they are common enough for the imperfect. We introduce them here because they are features of the 'ongoing' aspect which both tenses share.

action, it is meeting resistance, and its completion is in doubt. *Voluntative* hasn't begun at all yet, whether or not it will face resistance or be likely to complete.

Here are some possible examples, but these are matters of the reader's interpretation, not the grammar of the verbs. Each could be conative, rather than voluntative, or even something else:

> Εἰδότες οὖν τὸν φόβον τοῦ Κυρίου ἀνθρώπους πείθομεν 2 Cor 5:11
> Therefore, because we know the fear of the Lord, we **aim to** persuade people.

> ἐλεύσομαι δὲ πρὸς ὑμᾶς, ὅταν Μακεδονίαν διέλθω· Μακεδονίαν γὰρ διέρχομαι 1 Cor 16:5
> I will come to you after I have been through Macedonia – for I plan to pass through Macedonia

> οἱ Ἐγεσταῖοι ... ἡμᾶς ἐκφοβοῦσι. Thucydides, *P.W.* 6.11.2
> the Segestians **want to** frighten us.
>
> The speaker is explaining that the course of action which the Segestians are warning *against* is actually the best one. The Segestians are *trying to frighten* – but the speaker is making sure that we aren't frightened.
>
> NB: φοβέομαι 'I fear' has no endpoint, but the active form φοβέω means to frighten. That has a natural endpoint: when they're afraid.

> τὰ δ' εἰς ἅπαντα τὸν λοιπὸν χρόνον ἐγκώμι' ὑμῶν ἀφαιρεῖται Demosthenes, *Cor.* 18.207
> [Demosthenes explains that his opponent wants to deprive him of glory, and now shows the implications for his hearers] he would deprive you of praise for all the rest of time.

5.2.3 Futuristic

As with conative, if an action has a natural endpoint, the present tense implies that the endpoint has not been reached yet. The author can stress the certainty that the endpoint will be reached (as in English).

> ἔρχεται εἰς συνάντησίν σοι Gen 32:6
> he is coming to meet you.
>
> The context is that they have already seen Esau on his way. The action has a clear endpoint that is in focus here: Esau's arrival.

By extension, an author can talk about an action that hasn't even started yet (with or without an endpoint), to make it imminent or otherwise vivid. There is a fine line between this and **voluntative**.

> Ἡ γῆ εἰς ἣν εἰσέρχεσθε κληρονομῆσαι 1 Esd 8:80
> The land into which you are **about to** enter to possess it ...
>   Imminent.

ὁ υἱός σου ζῇ John 4:50
your son <u>will live</u>
   Vivid.

See also Gen 19:14; 4 Kgdms 2:5.

In a clearly predictive *context*, a future event can be described with the present tense to highlight its certainty.

βασιλείαν **οὔπω** ἔλαβον, ἀλλ' ἐξουσίαν … λαμβάνουσι. Rev 17:12
they have **not yet** received a kingdom, but they <u>will receive</u> authority.

See also John 16:22; 20:17; Sib. Or. 3.45; T. Jos. 7.3.

As ever, remember that the present tenses in these three 'futuristic' contexts are simply *present tenses* in Greek; it is up to the reader to decide whether they are futuristic and why. For example:

καὶ ὑμεῖς οὖν γίνεσθε ἕτοιμοι· ὅτι ᾗ ὥρᾳ οὐ δοκεῖτε ὁ υἱὸς τοῦ ἀνθρώπου ἔρχεται. Luke 12:40
So, as for you, be ready: for you do not know the time at which the son of man <u>comes/is coming/is trying to come/is already on his way and will most certainly arrive/wants to come/is about to come/will come</u>, etc.

Whether you understand ἔρχεται as descriptive, habitual, prophetic, futuristic (and in what sense) will make a huge difference to what Jesus told his disciples to do. Despite the great significance of that decision, the Greek present tense doesn't help you out at all: Jesus expected his hearers to know what he meant from what he had already taught them. His choice of a present tense wasn't designed to inform them on that point. English translations might not be able to duck out of making a decision, and commentaries will use labels to discuss the options, but the Greek verb doesn't give anything away.

Figure 2.2 shows how the focus on ongoing aspect combines with time in the examples above.

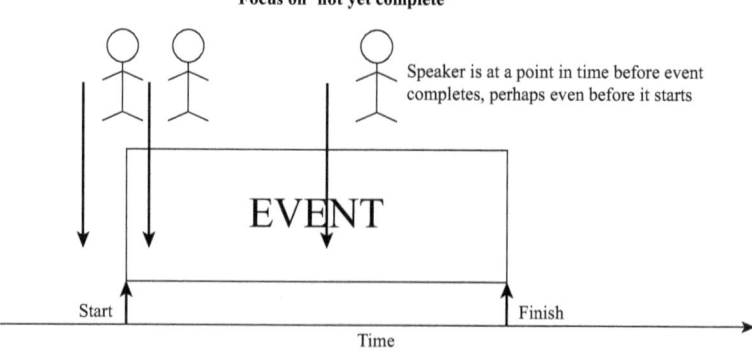

Figure 2.2 Focus on Ongoing Aspect

5.3 Other Contexts

The present tense can be used in two other contexts that don't really fit our expectations.

5.3.1 Historical

As also in English, an obviously past narrative will sometimes use a present tense to refer to a past action. That past context is what tells us that the present tense is doing the job of an aorist.

τότε παραλαμβάνει αὐτὸν ὁ διάβολος … καὶ λέγει αὐτῷ … Matt 4:4
then the devil took him … and said to him …

καὶ ἀκολουθοῦσιν αὐτῷ οἱ μαθηταὶ αὐτοῦ. Mark 6:1
And his disciples followed him.

καὶ ἐξάγουσιν αὐτὸν ἵνα σταυρώσωσιν αὐτόν. Mark 15:20
They led him out, to crucify him.

Quoting an autobiographical inscription, clearly referring to past events:
νικῶ πὺξ δύ' Ὀλυμπιάδας. Pausanias, *Descr.* 6.9.9
I won at the Olympics twice at boxing.

The significance is not easy to pin down. Understanding why a text chooses to use a historical present instead of an aorist appears to be a matter of getting to know *that* author.[8]

5.3.2 Perfective

This only applies to a very small number of verbs. Their present indicative has an obviously perfect meaning. The verb ἥκω almost always means 'I have come' (not 'I am coming'). A few other verbs can sometimes have a perfective meaning: ἀπέχω, ἀκούω, πάρειμι.

εἶπεν Βαλαὰμ πρὸς Βαλάκ Ἰδοὺ ἥκω πρός σε νῦν. Num 22:38
Balaam said to Balak: 'Look, I have come to you now.'

ἀπέχεις ὁλοτελῆ τὴν ἀποκάλυψιν. Herm. Vis. 3.13.4
You have received the revelation fully.

---

[8] Fanning 4.1.8; more specific proposals (such as Runge, *DGGNT* chapter 6) seem limited to particular authors. See further: Stephen H. Levinsohn, 'Verb Forms and Grounding in Narrative', *GVR*, 163–83 and Patrick James, 'Imperfects, Aorists, Historic Presents, and Perfects in John 11: A Narrative Test Case', *GVR*, 184–220.

5.4 What the Present Tense Doesn't Tell You

You will sometimes read that the present tense can only refer to actions that are repeated or even constant. The claim is that the aspect of the present tense requires this sense of repetition (labelled 'linear aspect', for example).

We have seen plenty of examples where the present tense refers to actions that are repeated, and plenty of examples where it refers to actions that aren't repeated.

Authors have ways of making it clear that an action is repeated (e.g. πολλάκις), or constant (e.g. πάντοτε). Context might show that too. But that is not a feature of the present tense: an author can use a present tense to refer to all manner of actions. We misread the author if we insist that the present must be constant/repeated/etc.

For example, Paul may or may not have been *constantly* thanking God when he wrote 1 Tim 1:12, but that is not why he chose a present tense, nor does the present tense tell you that it's true:

> Καὶ χάριν ἔχω [idiom, similar to 'I give thanks'] τῷ ἐνδυναμώσαντί με
> 1 Tim 1:12
> I thank the one who has strengthened me.

Elsewhere, Paul uses expressions such as πάντοτε when that is his point:

> **ἀδιαλείπτως** μνείαν ὑμῶν ποιοῦμαι, **πάντοτε** ἐπὶ τῶν προσευχῶν
> Rom 1:9–10
> I mention you **ceaselessly, always** in my prayers.

> Εὐχαριστῶ τῷ Θεῷ μου **πάντοτε** περὶ ὑμῶν 1 Cor 1:4
> I thank my God for you **always**.

Moreover, there are plenty of texts using the exact same expression where a permanent state of thankfulness would not fit:

> Μυκήνα φίλα, χάριν ἔχω ζόας, χάριν ἔχω τροφᾶς Euripides, *Iph. taur.* 847
> Beloved Mycene, I thank you for life, I thank you for food
> Nothing in the context suggests anything ongoing.

> ὦ Σώκρατες, ἐγὼ χάριν ἔχω τούτου τοῦ λόγου Plato, *Menex.* 249d
> Socrates, I'm grateful for this speech.

> ἥδομαι ... καὶ χάριν ἔχω καὶ εὔχομαι Xenophon, *Anab.* 6.1.26
> [in a one-off context] I am pleased ... and I thank you, and I pray ...

5.5 Quick Summary of Contexts for the Present Tense

In summary, a simple Greek present tense can appear in the following contexts. Note that, in some of them, English expresses the idea more explicitly, but be encouraged by how many of them are uses that you already understand from the English present tense.

Focus on 'now':

> Do you hear what these are saying? **Descriptive**
> I have been with you **for twenty years**. **Durative (English idiom)**
> He keeps on falling into the fire. **Iterative**
> Unless they wash their hands, they don't eat. **Customary**
> They speak, but they do not do. **Habitual**
> Everyone who asks receives. **Gnomic**
> I command you, in Jesus Christ's name, to come out of her. **Performative**

Focus on 'not yet':

> You are **trying** to be justified by the law. **Conative**
> We **aim to** persuade people. **Voluntative**
> He is coming to meet you. **Futuristic (Future endpoint)**
> I am **about to** go to Jerusalem. **Futuristic (Entirely future)**
> They will receive authority. **Futuristic (Prophetic)**

Other uses:

> Then the devil took him ... and said to him ... **Historical**
> I have come to you now. **Perfective (Certain verbs only)**

5.5.1 Beware of the Labels

> Let me stress that these labels are **not** telling you about different present tenses. They describe an interpretive decision. There is no such thing as a 'habitual present' in Greek; there is only a present tense.
>
> 'And here it must be confessed that categories have done harm. We are all too apt to take our pigeon-holes for pilgrim shrines.'[9]

When you read commentaries or articles, please bear in mind the translation in Table 2.2.

Table 2.2 What Labels Mean

What they write:	This is an 'iterative present'.
What that doesn't mean:	I, the holder of the secret Greek knowledge, have decoded the language scientifically, and found that this is an 'iterative present'.
What they mean:	I, a humble interpreter, have concluded that the Greek author intended me to understand this as referring to a regularly repeating action in the present, rather than a habit or a single ongoing action.

---

[9] Basil Gildersleeve, 'Temporal Sentences of Limit in Greek', *The American Journal of Philology* 24 (1903): 388–407 (392); I'm grateful to David Reimer for this source.

5.6 Some Good News

This first exposure to a variety of contexts for a single tense is a baptism of fire. Rest assured that all the other tenses exist in fewer contexts. The most important of the ones above will also be reviewed when we meet the same ideas for the imperfect (**EM 6**).

Until then, every verb in the **Greek Readings** will be present, and many of them will seem forced (for example, you would never write a past story using only 'historic presents'). After Chapter 6, you will only meet the present tense in more natural contexts. Until then, the questions and notes on each passage, based on the **Extra Material**, will point out the few present tenses that are worth thinking about.

> **Keep Going!**
> Don't try to digest all these now, much less learn them. Re-read the **Greek Reading** above, using the notes and questions in the **Online Material**. Eventually, as you read plenty of Greek, they will be second nature to you.

CHAPTER 3

Cases and Gender
—
Genitive Case

> **How to Use This Chapter**
>
> Work through this chapter of *ENTG*, section by section, completing exercises as you go. As you complete each section, read **Extra Help** below for that section.
>
> **Extra Help**, in this chapter, gives you the logic behind the noun endings, vastly reducing the number of endings you need to learn. We then continue to learn how to tackle any Greek sentence as a 'trunk with branches'.
>
> **Extra Material** introduces some of the different jobs that the Greek genitive case can do. It also takes us a little further with accents.

1 AFTER *ENTG* 3.2: TRUNK AND BRANCHES CONTINUED

In **EH 2** 1.3, I advised you to tackle all Greek sentences as a tree, with a trunk and some branches. Start by finding the trunk, and only then work out what the branches are doing.

We saw that the first step is to find the verb, then any subject (nominative) and direct object (accusative). In this chapter of *ENTG*, we meet the final member of the trunk and the first of many branches.

1.1 Trunk: Indirect Object (Dative)

ENTG 3.1 explains one of the things that the dative case does: the indirect object. It answers the question, 'to or for whom was the action done?' If the trunk so far tells you 'He threw a rock', then we want to know 'At whom?' The answer goes in the **dative** case.

Before going further in your typical Greek sentence, look for the verb, then the other trunk members: subject (nominative), direct object (accusative), indirect object (dative). Word order does not identify these: cases do.

1.2 Branch: Genitive

These 'branches' are properly called **modifiers**. They modify a member of the trunk and tell you more about it. For clarity, the noun being modified is called the **head** noun.

3 Cases and Gender

The genitive case is one of the most common modifiers. It often tells you that the head noun and the modifier are connected *somehow*, which English can express by 'of' (*ENTG* 3.1). The idea of ownership is just one of many connections expressed by the Greek genitive and English 'of', such as:

- 'Superman: man *of* iron.' Iron is not the owner of superman.
- 'The goblet *of* fire.' Fire does not own the goblet.
- Neither does glass own the jug in: 'a jug *of* glass'.
- Nor does water in 'a jug *of* water'.

This is the kind of thing that makes further study of Greek necessary and is the main topic in the **Extra Material** throughout this book.

The *modifier* can branch off the **subject**: *Bob's* **dog** bit me.

It can branch off the **direct object**: he bit the *postman's* **trousers**.

It can modify the **indirect object**: he brought the newspaper **for the wife** *of the butcher*.

> It isn't *word order* that tells you what each word does in the trunk of the sentence: *cases* do.

However, when it comes to modifiers, it is generally sound to assume that they modify whichever element in the trunk is nearest to them; we will meet further rules in Chapter 4.

You can now tackle the **Half-Way Practice** in *ENTG*.

Now to learn the endings!

2 BEFORE *ENTG* 3.3: THE GREAT MEMORY SAVING

In this chapter of *ENTG* we will meet the endings on the article (twenty-four endings), masculine nouns (eight), neuter nouns (eight), feminine nouns (twenty-four) and αὐτός (twenty-four), for a possible **total of eighty-eight**.

By learning some simple rules about endings, we can reduce this to **a mere 10**. Even better, those same rules will keep reappearing later, in different families of words.

If you are learning Greek with accents, you will find accented versions of all the paradigms in the **Online Material** for this chapter.

2.1 Before *ENTG* 3.3.2: Neuter Endings

Anything **neuter** always has the following pattern:

1. The gen and dat are the same as the masc.
2. The neut acc is always the same as the neut nom, both in the sing and pl.
3. The neut nom pl is always -α. (So is the acc pl, because of rule 2.)

Write out λόγος in full, then apply these rules to write out ἐργόν. Check your answer against the table in *ENTG* 3.3.2. This will save you a lot of work in the rest of *ENTG*!

2.2 Before *ENTG* 3.3.2: Feminine Endings Are (Mostly) Masculine Endings

If you simply learnt the feminine endings in *ENTG* 3.3.2, and kept the masculine endings in mind as you did so, you would notice a pattern. Two sets of rules make that pattern clear, and will keep reappearing in other contexts: **thematic vowels** and **vowel lengthening**.

2.2.1 Thematic Vowels

Instead of thinking of λόγος as λογ- plus endings, break the ending down into a **thematic vowel** -o- and then the ending proper. The nominative singular is λογ-ο-**ς**, the accusative singular λογ-ο-**ν**. As well as adding endings to the thematic vowel, the vowel itself sometimes lengthens.[1]

2.2.2 λόγος Revisited

In *ENTG* 1 we learnt that there are short and long vowels, and diphthongs. The long form of ο is ω, but sometimes omicron will lengthen to the diphthong ου. With that in mind, try to work out what the actual endings of λόγος are. Check your result against Table 3.1.

2.2.3 Feminine Endings: ἀρχή

For now, the thematic vowel in ἀρχή is η in the singular, and α in the plural. We can't lengthen η any further. Now apply the pattern of λόγος to ἀρχή, write out the result, and compare it with the table in *ENTG* 3.3.2.

It isn't quite right. However, all you have to do is move the -ς ending from nominative singular to genitive singular, and the endings are identical, as you can see in Table 3.2. Hardly anything to learn at all!

---

[1] Grammars don't usually use the term 'thematic vowel' for nouns, but only in verbs. The principles are identical to those which we find in verbs, so it will keep things simple for you if you approach nouns this way.

3 Cases and Gender

Table 3.1 Endings and Thematic Vowels

		Ending proper	Ending added to o thematic vowel	Result	Notes
Sing	Nom	-ς	λόγ-ο-ς	λόγος	
	Acc	-ν	λόγ-ο-ν	λόγον	
	Gen	lengthen	λόγ-ου	λόγου	
	Dat	lengthen + ι	λόγ-ω-ι	λόγῳ	1
Pl	Nom	-ι	λόγ-ο-ι	λόγοι	
	Acc	lengthen then ς	λόγ-ου-ς	λόγους	
	Gen	-ων	λόγ-ο-ων	λόγων	2
	Dat	-ις	λόγ-ο-ις	λόγοις	

[1] Whenever ι is in a diphthong with a long vowel, it becomes subscript.
[2] Why has the thematic vowel disappeared in the genitive plural? Thematic vowels are subject to the same rules of **contract** as the contract vowels on verbs. See *ENTG* 2.2; notice that learning rules in one context will help you again in different contexts.

Table 3.2 Feminine Endings and Thematic Vowels

		Ending proper	Ending added to η / α thematic vowel	Result	Real pattern
Sing	Nom	-ς	ἀρχ-η-ς	ἀρχής	ἀρχή
	Acc	-ν	ἀρχ-η-ν	ἀρχήν	ἀρχήν
	Gen	lengthen	ἀρχ-η	ἀρχῆ	ἀρχῆς
	Dat	lengthen + ι	ἀρχ-η	ἀρχῇ	ἀρχῇ
Pl	Nom	-ι	ἀρχ-α-ι	ἀρχαί	ἀρχαί
	Acc	lengthen then ς	ἀρχ-α-ς	ἀρχάς	ἀρχάς
	Gen	-ων	ἀρχ-α-ων	ἀρχῶν	ἀρχῶν
	Dat	-ις	ἀρχ-α-ις	ἀρχαῖς	ἀρχαῖς

2.2.4 Embedding the Endings

Now apply the method described in **EH 2** 1.4.2.

1. You have already memorised the paradigm of λόγος. Write it out again to learn the rules above as you go.
2. Write out ἀρχή, without looking anything up, by applying the rules.
3. Check what you've written against the pattern, and use that to reinforce the rules.
4. Keep doing that until you never get it wrong.

We have reduced the eight feminine endings to two (the nominative and genitive singular).

2.3 After *ENTG* 3.3.3: The Article

Look closely at *ENTG* 3.3.4, where the article is put side by side with three noun patterns: λόγος, ἀρχή and ἔργον. Spend a moment noticing where the endings for the article and the corresponding noun are different and where they are the same.

They are the same everywhere, except:

1 The nom (both sing and pl), where:
   ○ The masc and fem replace the opening τ with a rough breathing on the article.
   ○ The masc sing drops the ς on the article (notice how this is also a difference in the masc and fem noun endings).
   ○ The neut sing drops the ν on the article.
2 The neut acc sing (which copies the nom: **EH 3** 2.1).

2.4 Before *ENTG* 3.3.5: Feminine Endings Simplified Further

2.4.1 Optional Background

The masculine and neuter noun patterns of λόγος and ἔργον are referred to as the '**o-declension**', and the feminine pattern of ἀρχή the '**α-declension**', after their thematic vowels. Wait – why is ἀρχ-ή not called the **η**-declension?

A quirk of Greek is that long α (ᾱ) often became η. So ἀρχή was really ἀρχᾱ, with the long alpha thematic vowel becoming an eta in the singular.

Δόξα, on the other hand, has a short thematic alpha. Start with the rules for feminine nouns (which are identical to masculine, except for the ς moving from nominative singular to genitive singular), and apply them to δόξα. Compare with *ENTG* 3.3.5: it works, right?

Long alphas refused to change to eta after an ι, ρ or an ε. With that in mind, try applying the endings to ἡμέρα (its thematic vowel is a short alpha). Compare with *ENTG* 3.3.5: it works, right?

2.4.2 The Anger Rule: ιρε

With or without that bit of archaeology (which I know some of you can't live without, and others can't live with): the *only* difference between the three feminine nouns is in the singular endings, which either have α or η: everything else is identical. You can tell what will happen from the nominative singular, which is what you learn as vocab:

- If the noun has η in the nom sing, it has η throughout the sing (ἀρχή).
- If the noun has α in the nom sing, it switches to η for the gen and dat sing (δόξα) ...
- ... unless the stem of the noun (the bit before the thematic vowel) ends in ρ or a vowel,[2] in which case it remains α throughout (ἡμέρα).

The table in 'Nouns So Far' for Chapter 3, in the **Online Material**, has all the noun endings side by side. I will keep adding to this as we meet more nouns.

2.4.3 Very Few Endings

Notice that we barely have anything new to learn in this chapter.

1. The masc endings give you nearly every other noun ending.
2. Learn two rules, which give you the neut endings.
3. Move a ς to get the fem ones, and learn a rule to tell you whether the sing endings have α or η.

2.4.4 Embedding the Endings

Now apply the method described in **EH 2** 1.4.2.

> 1. Learn the rules of how to turn the patterns you already know into δόξα, ἀρχή and ἡμέρα.
> 2. Write out δόξα, ἀρχή and ἡμέρα, without looking anything up, by applying the rules.
> 3. Check what you've written against the right pattern, and use that to reinforce the rules.
> 4. Keep doing that until you never get it wrong.

2.5 After *ENTG* 3.5: Ἰησοῦς

This will look irregular for now, but the pattern will be obvious after *ENTG* 8.3.1.

2.6 After *ENTG* 3.6: You Already Know αὐτός

As you can see, this pronoun largely follows λόγος, ἀρχή and ἔργον. The exception is that the neuter nominative singular (and therefore the accusative singular) pronoun αὐτό follows the article τό, not ἔργον.

---

[2] In practice, the vowel will be ι or ε. A mnemonic is ι-ρ-ε: think 'ire', 'anger'. These words say 'Aaaa!!!' (αααα) all through the singular.

As before, make sure you can write out αὐτός from what you already know. Don't stop until you never get it wrong.

> **That Neuter ν**
>
> The neuter nominative and accusative singular ending is only **-ο** on the article and on pronouns. Otherwise, it is always **-ον**, even on word types you are yet to meet.

2.7 After *ENTG* 3.6: Agreement in Grammar, Not Appearance

Sometimes, two words are parsed the same way, while looking different:

ὁ	λόγος	masc nom sing
ἔργον	αὐτο	neut nom sing
ἡμέρας	δόξης	fem gen sing

The reason for understanding endings (morphology) is to decode the grammatical information they give (gender, case, number). In *ENTG* chapter 2 we learnt that the article has to agree with its noun: ὁ and λόγος do agree – that's the important thing, even though they look different.

It needs to become second nature to see no longer αν but rather α-declension **feminine accusative singular.** The rules above are designed to get you to the important information faster, not just to save you memory work.

Conversely, and we will keep meeting this, endings may look the same but not agree:

τά (neut nom/acc pl) is nothing to do with ἡμέρα (fem nom sing)

δόξας (fem acc pl) could agree with ἡμέρας (fem acc pl) but not with the identical ἡμέρας (fem gen sing)

3 THE GREEK READING

The epic of the party continues ...
The appointed day of Phoebe's feast arrives, and we find Ampliatus desperately trying to teach Paul (Peter's son) who turns up without his textbook. Paul's sister is passing through and kindly brings him his book, but he then uses her for target practice and pays no attention to his tutor.
Female slaves arrive with news that the dinner party is ready, which is music to love-struck Ampliatus' ears.

¹ Ἐγένετο ἡ ἡμέρα τοῦ δείπνου τῆς Φοίβης.

² Ἐγένετο ἡ ἀρχὴ τῆς ὥρας ὅτε ὁ Ἀμπλιᾶτος διδάσκει τὸν Παῦλον.

³ Ὁ ἄνθρωπος ἔχει βιβλίον τῆς δόξης.

⁴ Ὁ Παῦλος οὐκ ἔχει τὸ βιβλίον αὐτοῦ.

⁵ Ὁ Παῦλος, ὁ υἱὸς τοῦ Πέτρου, καλεῖ τὴν ἀδελφὴν αὐτοῦ·

⁶ Μαρία, οὐκ ἔχω τὸ βιβλίον.

⁷ Ἡ ἀδελφὴ αὐτοῦ λέγει αὐτῷ·

⁸ Ἀδελφέ, αὐτὸ φέρω.

⁹ Τὴν δόξαν ἔχω.

¹⁰ Ἡ ἀδελφὴ φέρει τὸ βιβλίον τοῦ ἀδελφοῦ αὐτῆς.

¹¹ Φέρει τῷ ἀδελφῷ τὸ βιβλίον.

¹² Ὁ Παῦλος λαμβάνει τὸ βιβλίον.

¹³ Ὁ Ἀμπλιᾶτος καὶ ὁ Παῦλος ἀνοίγουσι τὰ βιβλία αὐτῶν.

(¹⁴ Φιλεῖ ὁ Ἀμπλιᾶτος τὸ ἔργον αὐτοῦ. ¹⁵ τὸ τέκνον οὐ φιλεῖ ὁ Ἀμπλιᾶτος. ¹⁶ ἔχει ὁ Παῦλος πρόσωπον ἀγγέλου, καὶ ἔχει καρδίαν δαιμονίου. ¹⁷ ἁμαρτίας ποιεῖ τὸ τέκνον, καὶ ἡ ψυχὴ τῆς ἀδελφῆς οὐχ ἁμαρτίας ποιεῖ.)

¹⁸ Ὁ Ἀμπλιᾶτος διδάσκει τὸν Παῦλον.

¹⁹ Τὸ τέκνον λάλει τῇ ἀδελφῇ αὐτοῦ.

²⁰ Ὁ Ἀμπλιᾶτος λέγει τῷ τέκνῳ·

²¹ Παῦλε, ἀκούεις τοὺς λόγους;

²² Ἀκούεις τὴν ἀρχὴν τῶν λόγων;

²³ Τὸ τέκνον βάλλει γῆν τῇ ἀδελφῇ.

²⁴ Ἀκούουσι φωνήν. ²⁵ ἀκούει ὁ ἄνθρωπος. ²⁶ ἀκούει τὰ τέκνα.

²⁷ Δοῦλαι φέρουσι λόγον, καὶ λέγουσιν ὁ Ἀμπλιᾶτος καὶ τὰ τέκνα·

²⁸ Τί ποιεῖτε, Τρύφαινα καὶ Τρυφῶσα;

²⁹ Λέγουσι τῷ Ἀμπλιᾶτῳ αἱ δοῦλαι·

³⁰ Ἀκούομεν λόγον τῆς Φοίβης.

³¹ Φέρομεν τὸν λόγον τῷ Πέτρῳ.

³² Ἡ Φοίβη ζητεῖ τὸν Πέτρον.

³³ Ζητεῖ τὸν ἀδελφὸν αὐτῆς.

³⁴ Ἀκούουσι τῶν δούλων, καὶ λαλεῖ ὁ Ἀμπλιᾶτος ταῖς δούλαις. ³⁵ λέγει τῇ Τρυφαίνᾳ καὶ τῇ Τρυφώσῃ·

³⁶ Εὐαγγέλιον ἔχετε.

(³⁷ Ὁ ἄνθρωπος φιλεῖ τὴν Φοίβην.)

3.1 Vocabulary

You don't need to memorise these words, and there are some here you won't learn in this course at all.

Inflected forms are explained unless you've learnt their meaning in *ENTG* by now.

Words which you are supposed to have memorised in previous chapters are not given, unless they are in a form which you do not recognise.

Bold words indicate that you will learn these in a later chapter; that's purely for your encouragement. I will keep giving these to you as vocab until you're supposed to learn them.

ἀνοίγω – I open
δεῖπνος – dinner party
δούλη – female slave
ἐγένετο – it arrived
ὅτε – when

οὐ, οὐκ, οὐχ – indicates that what follows isn't true
τί; – what?
φέρω – I carry

4 ACCENTS

4.1 Some More Proclitics

We met a couple of proclitics in **EM 2** 3.2: words which lack their own accent and rely on the accent of the following word. You have met four more in this chapter: the article in the nominative, masculine and feminine, singular and plural: ὁ ἡ οἱ αἱ. See the accented article paradigm in the **Online Material**.

4.2 Accents on Nouns

FURTHER READING: VS 23E

In Chapter 1 we learnt where accents can and cannot go in general. In Chapter 2 we learnt where they *do* go on finite verbs: they are nice and predictable. They go as far to the left as possible: they are 'regressive'.

When it comes to nouns, the rules of Chapter 1 still tell us where they *can* go. The accent that you learn as vocab will generally stay there, if it is allowed: it is 'persistent'.

However, if it cannot stay there, because the ending on the noun becomes longer, you can't always predict where it will move to. Unlike verbs, noun accents hardly ever give you useful information. It isn't worth the trouble to learn the extremely complicated rules that govern them.[3]

5 GENITIVE CONTEXTS

FURTHER READING: VS 158–72; WALLACE 72–136

The major topic of the **Extra Material** throughout this *Reader* is the variety of contexts in which you can find the elements of grammar that *ENTG* introduces, as we have begun to see with the present tense.

We turn now to the genitive case, and we will consider different contexts under several groupings. The main point of these groupings is to help your understanding and your memory, by seeing how they fit together.

5.1 Reminder: Beware of the Labels

I have given some caveats concerning the different contexts in which the present tense can appear (**EM 2** 5.5.1). So it is with cases: each case has one, two or (at most) three distinct meanings, which can apply to many different contexts. Two warnings, especially about the first meaning of the genitive below ('pertaining to'):

---

[3] You will find them throughout the morphology section of vS, generally following each paradigm.

Firstly, this list of contexts is *not* exhaustive. These are the most common applications of the basic meanings. There are plenty of niche uses of genitives in Greek literature, and you needn't force them into one of these neat boxes.

Secondly, we must resist the urge to multiply categories. Focus on the overall meaning, using these examples as just that: illustrations of what an author might mean. A longer list still won't be complete, but you'll be more tempted to think it is.

> While such labels are helpful, they often do not distinguish between intrinsically different uses, but between different nuances of a general syntactic function. For example, the genitive is often used to express a close relationship between two nouns … without expressing the precise nature of that relationship. [That] depends on the meaning of the nouns involved and on the context …[4]

5.2 Pertaining to …

The genitive noun is *somehow* closely connected with the noun that it modifies.[5]

ENTG asked you to translate the genitive as 'of'. You may well have thought of that as meaning 'ownership', but English uses 'of' in all sorts of other ways. The father 'of' Peter isn't Peter's property. The fellow servants 'of' a butler do not belong to him. The way 'of' life isn't owned by life. Likewise: 'God of love', 'person of interest', 'day of rest'.

However, many uses of the genitive don't work with 'of' in English, and it's best to banish 'of' from your thinking for now. The contexts we will meet first are genitives *pertaining to* something. Replace 'of' with 'to do with', and then think about what you really mean by that.

In what follows, the **head noun** is the noun being modified by the genitive noun.

The genitive will tell you that the head noun is somehow to do with the genitive noun, or pertains to the genitive noun.

5.2.1 Obvious Examples

Let's begin with some contexts where it is obvious how the genitive *pertains to* the head noun, and English happily accepts 'of'. One example of each will do, and the typical label is given in brackets with each example.

Please do not treat this list as exhaustive: it's just a set of relatively frequent examples, illustrating the loose connection between the genitive and its head noun as 'pertaining to'. Don't waste your time trying to 'classify' 'the fame *of David*'; it's perfectly obvious what it means.

---

[4] *CGCG* 30.1 n1.
[5] **Gen**itive here refers to '**gen**us': the kind or type of something, but that's just one way that the genitive noun and the other noun can be connected.

ἡ δὲ πενθερὰ Σίμωνος κατέκειτο πυρέσσουσα Mark 1:30
Simon's mother-in-law was laid up with a fever.
Relationship

ὁ δοῦλος ἐκεῖνος εὗρεν ἕνα τῶν συνδούλων αὐτοῦ Matt 18:28
that servant found one of his fellow-servants.
Association

ἑτοιμασίᾳ τοῦ εὐαγγελίου Eph 6:15
the readiness (which arises from) the gospel.
Origin / Source

Ὁδοὶ δύο εἰσί, μία τῆς ζωῆς καὶ μία τοῦ θανάτου Did. 1.1
There are two roads, one leads to life, the other leads to death.
Destination

Δός μοι τὸν ἀμπελῶνά σου 3 Kgdms 20:2
Give me your vineyard
Possession

λέγει αὐτῷ **εἷς** τῶν μαθητῶν Mark 13:1
one of the disciples says to him ...
Partitive: the genitive is the whole of which the head noun is **a part**.

As ever, it is not the grammar of the genitive which tells you how to take it, but your understanding of the words, the context, the way the world works, etc. For example:

πολλοὶ ἀδελφοί που γένοιντ' ἂν ἑνὸς ἀνδρός τε καὶ μιᾶς ὑεῖς, Plato, Leg. 627c
suppose that there were somewhere **many brothers** of one man and indeed of the same woman
The point here isn't their **relationship** to the parents, but that the same parents are the **source** of all the children who will go on to display different qualities nonetheless. It's the nature of the argument that tells you this.

The looseness of the connection doesn't mean that any two uses of the genitive are interchangeable. The author of two genitives might have two very different relationships in mind. C. S. Lewis helpfully warns against conflating the meaning of 'my' in 'my teddy bear', 'my father' and 'my God'.[6] The point is that these different meanings are not different 'genitives': they are the same genitive ('pertaining to ...') describing different relationships between different nouns.

---

[6] C. S. Lewis, *The Screwtape Letters* (London: Geoffrey Bles, 1942), Letter 21.

5.2.2 Descriptive (Pertaining to Quality)

The genitive works like an adjective, modifying the head noun.

> τέχνη ἀνθρώπου Acts 17:29
> human skill
>
> ἦλθεν τῇ ἡμέρᾳ τῶν σαββάτων 1 Macc 9:43
> he went on the Sabbath day
>
> Γινώσκετε δὲ ὅτι ἔρχεται ἤδη ἡ ἡμέρα τῆς κρίσεως 2 Clem. 16.3
> You know that judgment day is already coming
>
> ὁ θεὸς τοῦ αἰῶνος ἐπὶ γῆν πατήσει 1 En. 1:4
> the eternal God will walk on earth

English 'of' is used archaically in this sense: 'a thing *of* beauty' for 'a beautiful thing'.

5.2.3 Described (Pertaining to *Emphasised* Quality)

Much more rarely than the 'descriptive' genitive, the head noun and the genitive are reversed. The head noun indicates the quality which the genitive noun possesses. This strongly emphasises the quality.

> **τὴν περισσείαν** τῆς χάριτος Rom 5:17
> **the abundance** of grace
>
> ἵνα **ἡ ὑπερβολὴ** τῆς δυνάμεως ᾖ τοῦ Θεοῦ 2 Cor 4:7
> to demonstrate that **the extraordinary quality** of power is God's
> > Logically, it is the power which is to be demonstrated: if you remove τῆς δυνάμεως, the sentence makes no sense – 'to show that extraordinariness is God's'. Nonetheless, that's merely the modifier, not the head noun. The focus is on the *extraordinary quality*.
>
> παρώξυνεν ἐνβριμήματι ὀργῆς αὐτοῦ βασιλέα Lam 2.6
> he provoked a king by the furious quality of his anger
> > A translation such as 'his furious anger' misses the focus and treats this as though ἐμβρίμημα were the genitive and ὀργή the head noun – a 'descriptive genitive'.

An archaic 'of' in English captures the emphasis better than turning the head noun into an adjective: 'the abundance of grace'; 'the extraordinariness of his power'; 'the fury of his anger'.

5.2.4 Explanatory (Pertaining to What I Really Mean)

When the meaning of a noun is a bit mysterious or metaphorical, an author can use a genitive to clarify what it really means.[7]

> ἐκ τοῦ οἴνου <u>τοῦ θυμοῦ</u> τῆς πορνείας αὐτῆς πεπότικε πάντα ἔθνη.
> ... πίεται ἐκ τοῦ οἴνου <u>τοῦ θυμοῦ</u> τοῦ Θεοῦ, τοῦ κεκερασμένου ἀκράτου ἐν τῷ ποτηρίῳ <u>τῆς ὀργῆς</u> αὐτοῦ Rev 14:8–10
> all nations have drunk from the wine <u>which is the passion</u> of her sexual immorality ... he will drink of the wine <u>which is the passion</u> of God, mixed neat in the cup <u>which is his</u> <u>anger</u>

> κλυδωνιζόμενοι καὶ περιφερόμενοι παντὶ ἀνέμῳ <u>τῆς διδασκαλίας</u> Eph 4:14
> tossed and carried about by every wind, <u>which is to say, by teaching</u>

See also Eph 6:14–17.

5.2.5 Contents / Material (Pertaining to What It's Made For / Of)

The genitive can describe what the head noun is made for, 'a wine jug' (**contents**), or made of, 'a glass jug' (**material**).

> ποτήριον <u>ὕδατος</u> Mark 9:41
> a cup <u>of water</u>

> τὸ δίκτυον <u>τῶν ἰχθύων</u> John 21:8
> the net <u>for fish</u>

> ἀγέλη <u>χοίρων</u> Mark 5:11
> a herd <u>consisting of pigs</u>

> λίτραν μύρου <u>**νάρδου πιστικῆς**</u> πολυτίμου John 12:3
> a pound <u>consisting of costly perfume</u> **consisting of unadulterated nard**

> ἀργυρίου <u>ἐπισήμου</u> ἑξακισχιλίων ταλάντων Thucydides, *P.W.* 2.13.3
> 6,000 talents <u>consisting of coined silver</u>

5.2.6 Partitive of Time and Space

We saw that the partitive sense of the genitive is generally obvious in English, meaning that the genitive is the whole of which the head noun is a part.
  Greek, unlike English, applies this to time and space too.

> εἰς δὲ τὴν δευτέραν ἅπαξ <u>τοῦ ἐνιαυτοῦ</u> μόνος ὁ ἀρχιερεύς, Heb 9:7
> but into the second [chamber of the sanctuary], only the high Priest [goes], and only once <u>during the year</u>

---

[7] This is sometimes labelled a 'Genitive of Apposition', which is not to be confused with a genitive that is simply in apposition.

> ἐκλεκτοῖς παρεπιδήμοις <u>διασπορᾶς</u> <u>Πόντου, Γαλατίας, Καππαδοκίας,</u>
> <u>Ἀσίας, καὶ Βιθυνίας</u>, 1 Pet 1:1
> to the chosen exiles <u>within the diaspora</u> <u>within Pontus, within Galatia,</u>
> <u>within Cappadocia, within Asia and within Bithynia</u>

The genitive of time can sometimes be descriptive, calling to mind the properties of that time or region:

> ὁ δὲ ἐγερθεὶς παρέλαβε τὸ παιδίον καὶ τὴν μητέρα αὐτοῦ <u>νυκτός</u>, καὶ ἀνεχώρησεν εἰς Αἴγυπτον Matt 2:14
> He got up, took the child and his mother <u>during the night</u> [i.e. under cover of darkness, 'by night'], and set off for Egypt.
>
> Νικόδημος ... ἦλθε πρὸς τὸν Ἰησοῦν <u>νυκτός</u> John 3:1–2
> Nicodemus ... approached Jesus <u>by night</u>
>
> See also: 1 Thess 5:7.

It's easiest to understand this sense by seeing how different cases apply to time and space: **EM 9** 4.4.

5.2.7 Price (Pertaining to Value)

The genitive can indicate the price to be paid for the head noun.

> ὁ δὲ ἀποκριθεὶς εἶπεν ἑνὶ αὐτῶν, Ἑταῖρε, οὐκ ἀδικῶ σε· οὐχὶ <u>δηναρίου</u> συνεφώνησάς μοι; Matt 20:13
> But he replied to one of them: 'My dear chap, I'm not wronging you: didn't you agree with me on <u>a denarius [as the price]</u>?'
>
> ἀπεκρίθη δὲ αὐτῇ ὁ Πέτρος, Εἰπέ μοι, εἰ <u>τοσούτου</u> τὸ χωρίον ἀπέδοσθε. ἡ δὲ εἶπε, Ναί, <u>τοσούτου</u>. Acts 5:8
> Peter replied to her: 'Tell me whether you sold the field <u>for this much</u>.' She said, 'Yes, <u>for this much</u>.'
>
> ἐγένετο λιμὸς μέγας ... ἐγενήθη κεφαλὴ ὄνου <u>πεντήκοντα ἀργυρίου</u> 4 Kgdms 6:25
> there came a harsh famine ... a donkey's head became <u>[priced at] 50 silver pieces</u>
>
> νέας <u>τούτων τῶν χρημάτων</u> ποιήσασθαι Herodotus, *Hist.* 7.144.3
> to make ships <u>[paid for by] this much money</u>

5.2.8 Subjective / Objective (Pertaining to Action)

Sometimes a head noun is related to an *action*: faith ↔ believe; punishment ↔ punish; meal ↔ eat; desolation ↔ destroy.

What does 'The Desolation *of Smaug*' mean? I once was invited to see the film, by someone who thought that the title meant that Smaug is destroyed, or left desolate. As every well-read person knows, the title refers to what Smaug has destroyed: the desolation he has caused.

Smaug is the *subject* of the implied action: 'of Smaug' is a **subjective genitive**. Smaug destroyed Dale etc. It was left desolate. It became 'The Desolation of Smaug'. Were it the other way around, 'of Smaug' would be an **objective genitive**: somebody destroyed Smaug; Smaug was left desolate.

A subjective genitive tells you that the genitive noun *did* the action that the head noun relates to; an objective genitive tells you that the genitive noun is the object of the action.

> ὑμεῖς ἐστε τὸ **φῶς** τοῦ κόσμου Matt 5:14
> you are the **light** of the world
> > Objective: you illuminate the world.

> μνήσθητι τὰ **ἐλέη** Δαυείδ 2 Chr 6:42
> remember the **mercies** of David
> > Objective: David received mercy.

> Μίνως ἔπεμψε μηνίων δακρύματα ὑμῖν ἐκ τῶν Μενελάου **τιμωρημάτων**
> Herodotus, *Hist.* 7.169 [word order simplified]
> Minos sent grief angrily against you because of your **assistance** of Menelaus
> > Objective: they assisted Menelaus, they didn't receive assistance from him.

> ἰδὼν τὴν **πίστιν** αὐτῶν, εἶπεν αὐτῷ, Ἄνθρωπε, ἀφέωνταί σοι αἱ **ἁμαρτίαι** σου Luke 5:20
> when he saw their **faith**, he said to him, 'Sir, your **sins** are forgiven for you.'
> > Subjective: they believe [they exercise faith]; he has committed the sins.

> ἀξιοπιστότερά ἐστιν **τραύματα** φίλου ἢ ἑκούσια **φιλήματα** ἐχθροῦ
> Prov 27:6
> worthier of trust are the **hurts** of a friend than the gratuitous **kisses** of an enemy
> > Subjective: the friend hurts you; the enemy kisses you.

The subjective genitive has the same idea as the genitive with ὑπό, denoting the agent.

As usual, there is nothing in the grammar to tell you whether a genitive is subjective or objective; the meaning of the head noun, the genitive noun, the context and common sense should make it obvious; at least, the author thought it was obvious. For example:

> ἐν τῷ ἀπολείπειν ἕκαστον τὸν **φόβον** τοῦ Θεοῦ 1 Clem. 3.4
> while each one abandoned the **fear** of God
> > Objective: people fear God, God doesn't fear people.

ἡγιασμένοις ἐν **θελήματι** Θεοῦ 1 Clem. Salutation
sanctified by the **will** of God
    Subjective: sanctified according to God's will, not by our desiring God.

'Of' in English will often cover both options, but translations can't always avoid making the choice for you. Sometimes the head noun could be understood in different ways depending on whether the genitive is understood as subjective or objective:

    ἐγενόμην ἐν τῇ νήσῳ τῇ καλουμένῃ Πάτμῳ, διὰ τὸν λόγον τοῦ Θεοῦ καὶ διὰ τὴν **μαρτυρίαν** Ἰησοῦ Χριστοῦ Rev 1:9
    I was on the island called Patmos, on account of God's word and on account of ...
        [my] **witness** about Christ (objective: John bore witness to Christ)
        the **testimony** by Christ (subjective: Christ testified)

    [πεφανέρωται] δικαιοσύνη δὲ Θεοῦ διὰ **πίστεως** Ἰησοῦ Χριστοῦ Rom 3:22
    A righteousness from God [has been revealed] through ...
        faith in Jesus Christ (objective: people exercising faith in Jesus)
        the faithfulness of Jesus Christ (subjective: Jesus exercising faithfulness)

5.3 'From'

The genitive can be found with a sense of *separation from* something. (This is called *ablative*.)

5.3.1 Separation

The head noun has been *separated from the genitive noun*.

    Λῦσον τὸ ὑπόδημα τῶν ποδῶν σου Acts 7:33
    Untie your sandals off your feet

    τοῦ ἀπέχεσθαι τῶν ἀλισγημάτων τῶν εἰδώλων καὶ τῆς πορνείας Acts 15:20
    to keep away from things polluted by idols and from sexual immorality

5.3.2 Comparison

In English we say, '*greater* than B' or '*less busy* than B'. A comparative of some kind, followed by 'than' indicates what is being compared and on what terms. Greek uses the same formula, but instead of 'than B' puts B in the genitive.

    ἔστιν ἀπίστου **χείρων** 1 Tim 5:8
    he is **worse** than an unbeliever

περισσότερον αὐτῶν πάντων ἐκοπίασα 1 Cor 15:10
I worked **harder** than all of them

5.4 General Uses of All Cases

There are some uses which all cases have; I list them here to avoid confusing the distinctive uses.

5.4.1 Apposition

If you repeat a concept immediately with another word or phrase, then the repeated one has to have the same case as the one before it. They refer to the same thing, so they have the same case.

Nom: ἀκούσας δὲ Ἡρώδης ὁ βασιλεὺς ἐταράχθη Matt 2:3
When Herod the King heard, he became troubled

Acc: παράκλητον ἔχομεν πρὸς τὸν πατέρα, Ἰησοῦν Χριστὸν δίκαιον 1 John 2:1
We have an advocate with the Father, Jesus Christ, the righteous one

Gen: ὑμεῖς ἐκ πατρὸς τοῦ διαβόλου ἐστέ John 8:44
You are of your father, the devil

Dat: οὐαὶ ὑμῖν τοῖς Φαρισαίοις Luke 11:43
Woe to you, Pharisees!

5.4.2 Governed by Prepositions

FURTHER READING: HARRIS, PREPOSITIONS 28–44; WALLACE 355–63; vS 183

You know this from *ENTG* 4.1; all prepositions govern cases. On the exact relationship between prepositions and case, see the discussions in the FURTHER READING for this section (below the section heading above).

5.4.3 Governed by Certain Verbs

As you know from *ENTG* 3.2, some verbs govern certain cases. This is a matter of getting to know the verbs as vocab.

Even then, you can often see that these are just following an expected use of the relevant case. We have learnt that ἀκούω 'takes the genitive' to tell you who is speaking, and the accusative of the sound that you hear. But the genitive is just a straightforward genitive of **source** (EM 3 5.2.1), telling you who is making the sound that you hear.

CHAPTER 4

Prepositions
—
Dative Case

> **How to Use This Chapter**
> Work through this chapter of *ENTG*, section by section, completing exercises as you go. As you complete each section, read **Extra Help** below for that section.
>   In the **Extra Help**, you will continue to learn how to tackle any Greek sentence as a 'trunk with branches'. You will then begin to meet some of the logic behind spelling changes in Greek.
>   **Extra Material** introduces some of the different jobs that the Greek dative case can do. It also takes you a little further with accents.

1 *ENTG 4*

1.1 After *ENTG* 4.1: Trunk and Branches

As you know, you tackle a sentence by finding the few words in the *trunk* (EH 2 1.3). That gives you the basic meaning. After that, work out how the other words hang off something in the trunk, like *branches*.

The trunk consists of a **verb**, a **subject** (which is either just the verb ending or a *nominative* word), perhaps **direct objects** (in the *accusative*), and **indirect objects** (in the *dative*).

Branches will *modify* something in the trunk. You have previously met the first type of branch, or *modifier*:

- The *genitive*, which narrows down a noun in the trunk (ὁ ἄγγελος τοῦ θεοῦ God's messenger).

You have now met one more branch:

- The **preposition** with the words that it governs.
  I will refer to the combination of 'preposition + words governed' as a **prepositional branch**.

1.2 After *ENTG* 4.2: Vocab

Note the warning on memorisation in *ENTG* 4.2.1. You might find it helpful to memorise short phrases, such as those in tables 4.2.2–4. Don't settle for memorising glosses without the case they take. When you read κατὰ τὸν νόμον, it's not much use remembering 'according to, or against' if you can't remember which one takes the accusative.

1.3 After *ENTG* 4.2: Shorthand Consonants

In this chapter you will begin to meet ways that words change their spellings in context. Two principles will help you here:

1. Some consonants are shorthand for a combination of sounds.
2. Greek spelling is honest.

In English, letters such as *t*, *k*, *p* are sometimes pronounced by exhaling air afterwards ('aspirated') and sometimes not.

Hold your hand in front of your mouth and feel the air when you say *p*ot and compare that with *sp*it. The former is aspirated, and the latter not, but they are written the same way.[1]

Greek writes these two sounds differently.[2] Θ wasn't pronounced *th*, but an aspirated *t* (*tip tunnel*). The unaspirated *t* (*stiff, part*) is written τ. This is the same aspiration that is marked by a rough breathing on vowels and on ρ at the start of words, so I will write it ʽ. Thus θ is shorthand for τʽ. Likewise χ = κʽ. φ = πʽ. See Table 4.1.

Table 4.1 Aspirated Consonants

	unaspirated	aspirate
p	π	φ
k	κ	χ
t	τ	θ

You will meet more such combinations when they become helpful. Now to the second principle: honesty.

Try saying this, in the middle of a sentence at reasonable speed: μετ' ὥραν. You can't do it: the rough breathing (or aspiration) before the vowel ω comes right after the consonant τ. You say *met + aspiration + ōran*. The combination *t + aspiration* is spelt θ. Greeks write what they really say, which is μεθ' ὥραν not μετ' ὥραν.

---

[1] Variations in aspiration are one feature of regional and national accents in English, so my apologies if that didn't work for you!
[2] I am not making any claim about how Greek should be pronounced or how it was spoken in the days of the NT. However, there is a logic behind Greek spellings which is best explained by a certain pronunciation, even if that pronunciation is merely historical.

This explains footnote 6 in *ENTG* 4.2.5 and the various spellings in 4.6. (In 4.6, the addition of κ before a vowel is much like the addition of a ν after some verb endings: compare **EH 2** 1.1.)

1.4 After *ENTG* 4.3: The Dative Review

When you see a dative, you need to decide whether it's:

- the indirect object (*ENTG* 3.1)
- governed by a verb (*ENTG* 3.2 and **EH 3** 1.1)
- governed by a preposition (*ENTG* 4.1)
- the instrument of the action (*ENTG* 4.3)

The rest is easy: find the trunk, work out the meaning of the trunk, then add the branches and see how they add to the meaning.

2 THE GREEK READING

The epic of the party continues ...
  Phoebe is looking for her brother to tell him about the feast. Love-struck Ampliatus spots her and takes the opportunity to escort her on her quest.
  (A slave, in the wrong place and wrong time, is ordered to substitute for Ampliatus and look after the demon-child, Paul. His prayer for deliverance goes unanswered, and he faces his doom stoically.)
  Phoebe and Ampliatus spot Peter, her brother, fishing with some of his daughters. Phoebe tells him about the feast, and they conclude their fishing expedition.

¹ Ἡ Φοίβη περιπατεῖ ἔξω τῆς οἰκίας οὗ κατοικεῖ ὁ Πέτρος.

² Ὁ Ἀμπλιᾶτος ζητεῖ τὴν Φοίβην ἔξω. ³ αὐτὴ βλέπει αὐτόν.

ΦΟΙΒΗ·

    ⁴ Ζητῶ τὸν Πέτρον.

    ⁵ Ἐπικαλῶ τὸν Οὐρανόν· Πέτρε, ποῦ περιπατεῖς;

⁶ ΑΜΠΛΙΑΤΟΣ·

    ⁷ Ὑπάγει ἀπὸ τῆς οἰκίας ὁ Πέτρος σὺν τῷ Οὐρβανῷ πρὸς τὴν

    θάλασσαν.

⁸ Παρακαλεῖ ἡ Φοίβη τὸν Ἀμπλιᾶτον. ⁹ ὁ Ἀμπλιᾶτος, διὰ τὴν ἀγάπην αὐτοῦ

πρὸς αὐτήν, λέγει·

¹⁰ Ζητοῦμεν τὸν Πέτρον.

¹¹ Πέμπει ἡ Φοίβη δοῦλον πρὸς τὸν Παῦλον. ¹² λέγει τῷ δουλῷ·

¹³ Κηπουρέ· Τηρεῖς τὸ τέκνον ὑπὲρ τοῦ Ἀμπλιατοῦ.

¹⁴ Ὁ δοῦλος λέγει ἐν αὐτῷ·

¹⁵ Οὐ πιστεύω τῷ τεκνῷ.

¹⁶ Πῶς τηρῶ αὐτό;

¹⁷ Ἐνώπιον τῆς Φοίβης, ἐπικάλει τὸν Θεὸν καὶ τὸν Χριστὸν τῆς βασιλείας καὶ τοὺς ἀγγέλους ἐν τῷ οὐρανῷ. ¹⁸ ἀναβλέπει καὶ οὐ παραλαμβάνει σημεῖον. οὐ πέμπει ὁ Θεὸς σημεῖον αὐτῷ. ¹⁹ οὐκ ἀπολύουσιν αὐτὸν οἱ ἄγγελοι. ²⁰ οὐ προσκύνει τῷ Θεῷ, καὶ ὑπάγει καὶ διδάσκει τὸ τέκνον.

²¹ Ὑπάγει ὁ Ἀμπλιᾶτος μετὰ τῆς Φοίβης παρὰ τῆς οἰκίας, καὶ περιπατοῦσι παρὰ τὴν θάλασσαν.

²² Ζητοῦσι τὸν Πέτρον περὶ τὴν θάλασσαν, καὶ μεθ' ὥραν ἀκούουσι τοῦ Πέτρου ἐν πλοιῷ σὺν ταῖς ἀδελφαῖς τοῦ Παύλου.

²³ Ἁλιεύουσιν ἐνάλια αἱ ἀδελφαὶ δικτύοις. ²⁴ τὰ δίκτυα αὐτῶν ἀμφιβάλλουσιν.

²⁵ τὰς φωνὰς τῶν ἀδελφῶν ἀκούει ἡ Φοίβη. ²⁶ καλεῖ τὸν Πέτρον. ²⁷ ὁ Πέτρος καὶ αἱ ἀδελφαὶ ἀναβλέπουσι καὶ ἀκούουσιν·

²⁸ Συνάγω ὄχλον καὶ ποιῶ δεῖπνον τῇ οἰκίᾳ.

²⁹ Κατὰ τὴν ἀγάπην, καλῶ τὴν οἰκίαν εἰς τὸ δεῖπνον.

³⁰ Οὐκ ἀπολύουσι τὰ ἐνάλια αὐτῶν αἱ ἀδελφαί· ἐκβάλλουσιν αὐτὰ ἐκ τοῦ πλοιοῦ ἐπὶ τὴν γήν.

2.1 Vocabulary

ἁλιεύω – I fish
ἀμφιβάλλω – I cast (in the context of fishing)
δεῖπνος – dinner party
δίκτυον – a net

ἐνάλιον – a fish
κηπουρός – gardener
οὗ – where
πέμπω – I send

3 ACCENTS

3.1 Proclitics

In this chapter you meet nearly all the remaining proclitics, adding to ὁ ἡ οἱ αἱ (**EM 2** 3.2).

- Οὐ οὐκ οὐχ, except right before punctuation.
- The prepositions ἐκ/ἐξ, εἰς, ἐν.

3.2 Compound Verbs

FURTHER READING: PROBERT 90-2

With compound verbs (*ENTG* 4.4), the accent doesn't always go as far to the left as possible.

The general rule is that it cannot go further to the left than the last syllable of the preposition: ἐπίθες, not ἔπιθες (Matt 9:18).

When the preposition is followed by the **augment** (*ENTG* 6.5.2) or by **reduplication** (*ENTG* 16.2.1), the accent cannot go further to the left than the augment or reduplication: ἀπῆλθον not ἄπηλθον (Gen 14:11), ἐπισυνῆκται not ἐπισύνηκται (1 Macc 15:12).

Certain verbs break the rules when they become compounds, in some of their forms, leaving the accent further to the right than it needs to be. For example, the 3s future of compounds of εἰμί: παρέσται, not πάρεσται (Rev 17:8).

4 CONTEXTS FOR THE DATIVE

FURTHER READING: VS 173-81; WALLACE 137-75

There are three basic ideas behind the dative, and we met all of them in *ENTG*. First, the **indirect** object. By extension, it can indicate various ways that someone or something is involved in the action. Secondly, the **instrument** with which the action is performed; this too is extended to include a couple of related ideas. Finally, we have met the dative indicating *location* in space or time; this is the *locative* dative and is very straightforward.

All the caveats we gave for the different contexts of the genitive apply here too: this is not an exhaustive list, but a set of illustrations of common uses, to give you the general sense. However, unlike the genitive, it is much easier to see almost any use of the dative as a simple extension of the three main uses above.

4.1 Indirect Object

4.1.1 With Verbs and Related Words

The difference between direct and indirect objects isn't always as clear cut as the examples we use in textbooks. Loosely speaking, the direct object is most closely involved in the action, and the indirect object less so. Nonetheless, many verbs in English have to be learnt as idioms, to know what the direct or indirect object refers to. The recipient of a piece of writing is the direct object in US English but the indirect object in British English: 'I wrote *to* my MP' vs 'I wrote my Congressman'.

Sometimes Greek will view something/someone as the indirect object where an English equivalent views it as the direct object, and vice versa. We just need to learn that as vocab, as we did in *ENTG* 3.2 for some verbs of speaking or hearing. Part of looking up an unknown verb is discovering whether it has certain uses for one or more cases.

If a verb can take a dative, the participle can too; by extension, an adjective with similar meaning can as well, as can an adverb. See the family of 'follow' (ἀκολουθ-) words:

> **ἠκολούθησαν** τῷ Ἰησοῦ John 1:37
> they **followed** Jesus

> οἱ **ἀκολουθοῦντες** τῷ ἀρνίῳ Rev 14:4
> the **followers** of the lamb

> ἔστησαν οἱ ἱερεῖς ... **ἀκολούθως** τῇ Μωυσέως βίβλῳ 1 Esd 7:9
> the priests stood ... **following** the book of Moses
> ['following' in the sense of 'obeying']

> ἵνα τούτοις **ἀκόλουθα** καὶ λέγῃς καὶ διανοῇ Let. Aris. 218
> so that those things which **follow** from these things you should both
>   speak and think
> [in the sense of 'follow logically and ethically']

The point of telling you this is that we can save ourselves from creating new categories of dative when these *only* exist if they're governed by such words. One such example is the 'dative of measure', where the whole idea of 'measure' comes from a comparative word governing the dative, and isn't something the dative could mean by itself.

> πόσῳ ... **χείρονος** ἀξιωθήσεται τιμωρίας Heb 10:29
> how much **worse** punishment will be deserved
>   The sense of measure comes from the explicit word of comparison **χείρονος**.

As in English, some verbs do not always take a dative, but do so sometimes as part of an idiom. For example, κατακρίνω ('condemn') does not usually take the dative, except in the idiom 'condemn to death':

> κατακρινοῦσιν αὐτὸν θανάτῳ Mark 10:33
> they will condemn him to death

Very often, when a verb 'governs' a dative, this really means that the verb routinely expresses one of the meanings of the dative below, and usually the obvious one for that verb.

4.1.2 Indirect Object

The dative can identify the indirect object. It answers the question: *to* or *for* whom (or what) do you do the verb? (*ENTG* 3.1.) The following other uses of the dative are extensions of this idea.

> δοθήσεται αὐτῷ Jas 1:5
> it will be given to him

4.1.3 Advantage

The 'dative of **advantage**' benefits the indirect object.

> ἣν ἐνεκαίνισεν ἡμῖν ὁδὸν πρόσφατον, καὶ ζῶσαν Heb 10:20
> the new and living way, which he opened for our benefit

> καὶ ἐπλάτυνεν δόξαν τῷ λαῷ αὐτοῦ 1 Macc 3:3
> So he increased the glory for his people

4.1.4 Disadvantage

The 'dative of **disadvantage**' hurts the indirect object.

> Κύριε, μὴ στήσῃς αὐτοῖς τὴν ἁμαρτίαν ταύτην. Acts 7:60
> 'Master: do not hold this sin against them.'

Sometimes you might think a dative is either advantage or disadvantage, but you're not sure which; the umbrella label is 'dative of **interest**'. An example might be:

> καθὼς γὰρ ἐγένετο Ἰωνᾶς σημεῖον τοῖς Νινευίταις, οὕτως ἔσται καὶ ὁ
> υἱὸς τοῦ ἀνθρώπου τῇ γενεᾷ ταύτῃ. Luke 11:30
> for just as Jonah became a sign to the Ninevites, in the same way the Son
> of Man will be to this generation.

4.1.5 Possession

Verbs of existence (εἰμί, γίνομαι or ὑπάρχω) with the dative tell you that someone owns something. It's an extension of advantage: 'there exists, <u>for your sake</u> ...'

> ἡ σκηνὴ τοῦ μαρτυρίου **ἦν** <u>τοῖς πατράσιν</u> Acts 7:44
> the fathers **had** the tent of witness
>
> λύπη <u>μοι</u> **ἐστί** μεγάλη Rom 9:2
> <u>I</u> **have** deep anguish.

4.1.6 Ethical

> FURTHER READING: *CGCG* 30.52–3; vS 176c; MURAOKA 22WH

This expresses a sense of interest or involvement in the action, but not always one that is tangible. It often can't be brought out in English at all.

> ἑορτὴν ἑβδομάδων ποιήσεις <u>μοι</u> Exod 34:22
> The feast of weeks you will observe
>> There is no clear sense that this is for the advantage of God, or that he is in any way the indirect object; the dative pronoun just means that he's the one commanding it; this is quite intuitive in other European languages, but the closest I can come to it in English is the over-translation '<u>because I say so</u>'.
>
> <u>ἐμοὶ</u> δὲ μὴ γένοιτο καυχᾶσθαι Gal 6:14
> may it never happen that I boast
>> As above, the dative pronoun underlines that this is the wish of the speaker, but the optative already means that.
>
> προστατεύειν <u>ἡμῖν</u> διανενόησαι τῆς πόλεως; Xenophon, *Mem.* 3.6.2
> have you decided whether to be the leader of the city <u>for us</u>
>
> Θεοῦ γὰρ διάκονός ἐστί <u>σοι</u> Rom 13:4
> He (the government) is God's servant <u>for you</u>

For English-speakers, the ethical dative is often quite confusing.

4.1.7 (Agent)

> FURTHER READING: vS 176c (c); WALLACE 163–6; MURAOKA 22WO; *CGCG* 30.50

Very rarely, the dative marks an agent rather than an instrument. I only mention this use at all to warn you, because it is appealed to far more often than it deserves. If you think you have found a dative indicating an agent, you probably haven't. See the thorough discussion in Muraoka 22wo.

It generally requires a *passive verb in the perfect system*.

> ἰδού, οὐδὲν, ἄξιον θανάτου **ἐστὶ πεπραγμένον** [perfect passive] αὐτῷ
> Luke 23:15
> Look: nothing deserving death **has been done** by him

We can feel pressure to see such a category when the Holy Spirit appears as an instrumental dative, and we want to avoid the conclusion that the Spirit is impersonal. Wallace 431–5 (esp. 434), suggests that some NT authors use ὑπό + genitive of the Father as the ultimate agent and διά + genitive of the Son as the intermediate agent: this is a normal grammatical distinction. They then want a distinct way of expressing the agency of the Spirit, and bend the rules by using an 'instrumental' dative. In other words, this specifically *trinitarian* bending of the rules shouldn't lead us to invent a 'dative of agent'.

4.2 Instrumental Dative

As it happens, the English word 'with' will help us to see how these various ideas are related.

4.2.1 Instrument (Means, Manner)

The dative identifies the **instrument** through which an action is performed (*ENTG* 4.3).

> τῷ δὲ δακτύλῳ αὐτῶν οὐ θέλουσι κινῆσαι αὐτά. Matt 23:4
> but they aren't willing to move [the heavy burdens] with their finger

The dative might focus less on 'with *what*?' than on 'by what means?'. For example, when Herod condemned James to death, it's not as if he needed to use a sword to execute him. Rather, he had a choice of means of execution. This is called a dative of **means**.

> ἀνεῖλε δὲ Ἰάκωβον τὸν ἀδελφὸν Ἰωάννου μαχαίρᾳ. Acts 12:2
> [Herod] executed James, John's brother, with the sword [by means of the sword].

> τίς στρατεύεται ἰδίοις ὀψωνίοις ποτέ; 1 Cor 9:7
> Whoever engages in soldiery by means of his own finances?
> That is, 'at his own expense'.

Remember that ἐν + dative is a common way of indicating *instrument*, and that includes these extended senses (*ENTG* 4.3):

> σκεπάζων παρεμβολὴν ἐν ῥομφαίᾳ. 1 Macc 3:3
> protecting his camp with the sword [by means of the sword].

Pushing that idea a little further, the dative can describe the **manner** of an action. Compare 'He hit the nail *with a hammer*' and 'He hit the nail *with a blow*'.[3] 'A blow' isn't some external instrument that he picked up to do the action (like a hammer) but is similar, in that it answers the question: 'How did he do it?' He did it like this, in this manner.

> ἔκραξε φωνῇ μεγάλῃ Acts 7:60
> he cried out with a loud voice
>> It's not as if he wanted to cry out and found a loud voice somewhere to do it with; the loud voice is *how* he cried out; it is the *manner* by which he chose to cry out. He cried out *loudly*.
>
> ἀκατασχέτῳ θυμῷ καὶ μεγάλῃ φωνῇ ἐπεβόα Mart. Pol. 12:2
> [the crowd] shouted with out-of-control anger and with a loud voice
>
> συμμαχήσει τὸ ἔθνος ... καρδίᾳ πλήρει. 1 Macc 8:25
> the people will fight ... with full heart [wholeheartedly]
>
> προσεφώνησε τῇ Ἑβραΐδι διαλέκτῳ Acts 21:40
> he called out in the Hebrew language

4.2.2 Cognate

FURTHER READING: MURAOKA 22WR; 56B; vS 180C, 240; B-D-R 198.6

There is a Hebrew idiom which was translated woodenly into Greek by the translators of the OT, giving us a verb and another word which is cognate to the verb. Cognate means that two words of different types come from the same root: sing ↔ song; dying ↔ death. It is often extended to words with a similar idea rather than strictly the same root: eating ↔ food.

One option is to put a cognate noun in the dative, as a dative of manner; however, the result doesn't always make a lot of sense in Greek:

> Ἀπὸ παντὸς ξύλου τοῦ ἐν τῷ παραδείσῳ βρώσει **φάγῃ**· [17] ἀπὸ δὲ τοῦ ξύλου τοῦ γινώσκειν καλὸν καὶ πονηρόν, οὐ φάγεσθε ἀπ' αὐτοῦ· ᾗ δ' ἂν ἡμέρᾳ φάγησθε ἀπ' αὐτοῦ, **θανάτῳ** ἀποθανεῖσθε. Gen 2:16-17
> From every tree in the paradise you may eat **as (?) food**, but from the tree of knowing good and evil do not eat: on the day that you eat from it you will die **to (?) death**.

The underlying Hebrew is an emphatic statement of the verb: 'you may **most certainly** eat'; 'you will **most assuredly** die'.

You will especially find this in quotations from the Old Greek translation of the OT:

---

[3] Cf. the 'internal object' accusative (**EM 9** 4.3.1).

καὶ ἀναπληροῦται ἐπ' αὐτοῖς ἡ προφητεία Ἠσαΐου, ἡ λέγουσα,
Ἀκοῇ ἀκούσετε, καὶ οὐ μὴ συνῆτε· καὶ **βλέποντες βλέψετε**, καὶ οὐ μὴ ἴδητε. Matt 13:14
so Isaiah's prophecy will be fulfilled with respect to them, which says:
You will certainly hear but won't understand; and **you will assuredly look** but won't see.

The use of a cognate participle, **βλέποντες βλέψετε**, is the other way of capturing this Hebrew idiom: **EM 14** 4.2.2.

ὁ γὰρ Θεὸς ἐνετείλατο, λέγων,

...

Ὁ κακολογῶν πατέρα ἢ μητέρα θανάτῳ τελευτάτω Matt 15:4
For God commanded:

...

'The one dishonouring father or mother must assuredly die.'

Like a number of other features of Hebrew, this caught on as a way of marking emphasis in the Old Greek translation of the OT more generally, and that idiom spilled over into Jewish and Christian Greek:[4]

χαρᾷ **χαίρει** διὰ τὴν φωνὴν τοῦ νυμφίου John 3:29
he rejoices greatly owing to the groom's voice

Ἀναθέματι **ἀνεθεματίσαμεν** ἑαυτούς, μηδενὸς γεύσασθαι ἕως οὗ ἀποκτείνωμεν τὸν Παῦλον. Acts 23:14
We have bound [on pain of cursing] ourselves most strictly, not to taste anything until the time when we have killed Paul.

Translations will often, correctly, render the verb as 'put ourselves under an oath' or something like that; that the idea of 'oath' or 'curse' is *already* there in the verb ἀναθεματίζω. The cognate noun ἀνάθεμα in the dative adds the idea of *emphasis*, not the idea of 'curse' or 'oath'.

However, we need to be careful not to jump to the conclusion that a dative of a cognate noun is this kind of emphatic cognate dative, rather than a more regular dative:

καλέσαντος κλήσει ἁγίᾳ, 2 Tim 1:9
called us with a holy calling

This might mean that he called us *emphatically*, but it might also simply indicate that the *means* of calling us was a calling which is holy (see **EM 4** 4.2.1).

---

[4] Something similar appears *very rarely* in earlier Greek, with datives of a cognate noun being used, but there is very little evidence that this was an expression of emphasis rather than occasional word play (see Schwyzer-Debrunner II:166). It is so rare that this use isn't even mentioned by *CGCG*, Smyth or Kühner-Gerth. For a discussion from an NT perspective, see Robertson 531.

καί τινες αὐτὸν ἐμάστιζον λέγοντες <u>Ταύτῃ τῇ τιμῇ</u> **τιμήσωμεν** τὸν υἱὸν τοῦ θεοῦ Gos. Pet. 3.9

Some whipped him saying: 'Let's **honour** God's son <u>with this kind of honour</u>.'

Again, this could mean 'emphatically honour him' but more likely is an ironic dative of manner: 'let's honour him *like this*' '*with this kind of honour*'.

4.2.3 Instruments vs Agents

FURTHER READING: vS 187M, 187O, 191A, 259G, 259L

ENTG 4.3 presents two ways of identifying both instruments and agents; there are others, which you can see in a reference grammar at your leisure.

4.2.4 Association

The idea of doing something in someone's company (*with* them) isn't a million miles away from doing it *with* their help.

σύμφημι <u>τῷ νόμῳ</u> ὅτι καλός Rom 7:16
I am in agreement <u>with the law</u>, that it is good.
Paul and the law are *together*, agreeing.

ὃς καὶ **συν**επολιτεύσατο <u>τῷ Εἰρηναίῳ</u> Mart. Pol. 22:2
who also was a compatriot <u>with Irenaeus</u>
The man referred to was *associated* with Irenaeus by a shared citizenship.

συναντήσαντός ποτε <u>τῷ ἁγίῳ Πολυκάρπῳ</u> Μαρκίωνος Mart. Pol. 23:2
when Marcion once met <u>with holy Polycarp</u> …
Marcion and Polycarp met *together*.

Note how in these examples the verbs have the idea of association by being compounds with **σύν**.

> **Dative vs Genitive: 'Association' as an Example**
> You will remember that there is also a genitive to do with 'association' (**EM 3** 5.2.1). This illustrates a helpful difference between the genitive and the dative. The dative tends to be about *actions*: it relates to verbs either as the *indirect object* that is somehow affected by the action or the *instrument* that somehow brings the action about or the *location* where the action takes place. The genitive tends not to modify the verb, but one of the other elements in the 'trunk': it tends to qualify nouns and the like. I don't simply mean that it is nouns which are put in the genitive, since that's true of the dative and of all

cases. I mean that the genitive noun tells you something about another noun, whereas the dative is telling you about the action.

The dative of association tells you *how* you perform the action of walking: you do it in the company of a friend. Peter walks *with a friend*.

The genitive of association tells you nothing about the action, but about the friend. One of *Peter's* friends means that Peter and the friend are associated by the friendship.

4.2.5 Cause

If the dative can say what helped you (instrument), it can also say what *moved* you to do something.

The dative indicates the **cause**.

> καὶ τῇ ὑπερβολῇ τῶν ἀποκαλύψεων ἵνα μὴ ὑπεραίρωμαι, ἐδόθη μοι σκόλοψ 2 Cor 12:7
> a thorn was given to me, so that I should not puff myself up <u>because of the greatness</u> of the revelations

> χάριτί ἐστε σεσῳσμένοι Eph 2:5
> <u>because of grace</u> you are saved.
>> This could, of course, be a dative of **means** instead, or indeed both; all examples in the *Reader* are illustrations, not explanations of particular texts.

4.2.6 Reference (a.k.a. 'Respect') 'as far as *dative* is concerned'

The 'dative of **reference**' tells us in what sense the statement is true. It answers the question, 'By reference <u>to what</u> is this so?' The statement is not generally true, but is true within the limits set by the dative.

> νωθροὶ γεγόνατε Heb 5:11
> You have become sluggish.

Sluggish in general? Not going to work? Not making the beds? No:

> νωθροὶ γεγόνατε <u>ταῖς ἀκοαῖς</u>. Heb 5:11
> You have become sluggish <u>as far as your ears are concerned</u>.
>> 'You're not listening.'

> ἀπερίτμητοι <u>τῇ καρδίᾳ καὶ τοῖς ὠσίν</u> Acts 7:51
> uncircumcised <u>as far as your hearts and ears are concerned</u>
>> They were, of course, the very opposite of uncircumcised in the normal sense.

> Τὸν δὲ ἀσθενοῦντα <u>τῇ πίστει</u> προσλαμβάνεσθε Rom 14:1

Welcome the one who is weak <u>as far as his faith is concerned</u>
He might be very strong physically.

ἔπεχε σεαυτῷ καὶ τῇ διδασκαλίᾳ. ἐπίμενε <u>αὐτοῖς</u> 1 Tim 4:16
be mindful of yourself and the teaching. Be persistent <u>in these</u>
He may or may not need to be persistent in other things, but the command is limited to <u>these things</u> just mentioned.

πιστὸν ὄντα <u>τῷ ποιήσαντι αὐτόν</u> Heb 3:2
being faithful <u>as far as the one who created him is concerned</u>

You might wonder how this has anything to do with the other instrumental uses.

Καὶ εἶπε Λευὶς πρὸς τὸν υἱὸν Φαραὼ **ἱλαρῷ** <u>τῷ προσώπῳ</u> *Jos. Asen.* 22:10a, Chapter 16 of this *Reader*
Levi said to Pharaoh's son **with cheerfulness** <u>as far as his face is concerned</u>
ἱλαρῷ is a dative of manner, which means that he spoke <u>cheerfully</u>. But he was specifically cheerful <u>in his face</u>. His face was the *means* by which he was cheerful. He spoke cheerfully 'with his face'.

This limiting sense of the dative of reference (or respect) can be found with all the cases, but is most often (by a long way) found with the dative.[5]

Don't confuse it with the locative dative (below), which tells you something that doesn't limit the truth of the statement, whereas the dative of reference does.

4.3 Locative

You may have noticed that prepositions take the dative to indicate a static position: *in* ἐν + dative, *beside* παρά + dative, *on* ἐπί + dative.

This is the final and simplest thing which the dative can communicate: **location**. The dative tells you where the action takes place.

4.3.1 Location in Space or Time

The locative looks at a choice of regions (Spain, Portugal) or periods (Monday, Tuesday) and tells you *in which* of them the action takes place.

Relating to time, it can have this meaning with or without ἐν:

<u>τῇ</u> μὲν γὰρ <u>πρώτῃ ἡμέρᾳ</u> ἐποίησε τοὺς ἀνωτέρους οὐρανούς, τὴν γῆν, τὰ ὕδατα, Jub 2:2
For <u>on the first day</u> he created the upper heaven, the earth, the water,

---

[5] Wallace 145.

Νόμον ἔχομεν ἐν σαββάτῳ μὴ θεραπεῦσαί τινα. Acts Pil. 1.1
We have a law not to heal anyone on the Sabbath.

Relating to space, it has hardly ever existed without ἐν:

οὐ δύνασαι μεθ' ἡμῶν οἰκεῖν ἐν τῇ κώμῃ. Inf. Gos. Thom. 4.2
You can't live with us in the village.

except in ancient poetry:

ἀλλ' ἔα με ναίειν ὄρεσιν Sophocles, Oed. tyr. 1451
but let me dwell in the hill country

It can be used metaphorically to refer to entities that are neither regions of space nor periods of time. This is sometimes called a 'dative of **sphere**', but there is no need for a separate category.

For a comparison of the locative dative with the other cases in time and space, see **EM 9** 4.4.

4.3.2 'Locative' and 'Reference' Compared

Especially with metaphorical or abstract nouns, the difference between a dative in the sense of 'locative' is worth comparing with the sense of 'reference'. Here are some examples:

ἔγνω τῷ σώματι ὅτι ἴαται ἀπὸ τῆς μάστιγος Mark 5:29
she knew in her body that she had been healed from her illness.
> If you remove the dative, the sentence is still true: 'She knew that she had been healed.' The statement is generally true, and the dative gives more information, rather than restricting the truth of the statement. If you think it means, 'She didn't know that she had been healed, *except* with respect to her body' you would understand this as a dative of 'reference'. Compare: 'Uncircumcised *in your hearts*', 4.2.6.

ἐν σαρκὶ τυγχάνουσιν, ἀλλ' οὐ κατὰ σάρκα ζῶσιν. Diogn. 5.8
they happen to be in the flesh, but they do not live according to the flesh
> A more metaphorical locative; compare the next one.

ἐπειδὴ γὰρ ἀσθενέστερος τῇ σαρκὶ ἦς Herm. Sim. 9.1.2
for when you were weaker in the flesh
> This doesn't mean, 'when you were weaker, and you happened to be "in the flesh" …', which would be locative; it is a dative of reference. You may have been strong in all sorts of ways, but at that time you were weak as far as the flesh was concerned. If you remove the dative, the sentence is no longer true.

> ἐν σαρκὶ ἔδει αὐτὸν φανερωθῆναι Barn. 5.6
> it was necessary for him to be revealed <u>in the flesh</u>
>> Once you say 'it was necessary' there is no way for 'in the flesh' not to be compulsory; if you try to read it as 'locative' it will mean the same as 'reference'.

4.3.3 Authors Have Ways of Being Explicit

Throughout the **Extra Material** in this *Reader*, you're discovering that an element of grammar by itself (such as the dative case) can refer to different things (such as disadvantage or association), depending on the context. This doesn't mean that authors are forced into losing their meaning in ambiguity. *Anything that can be implied by the use of a dative can be made explicit.* Sometimes it means adding a whole explanatory sentence, but many of these nuances can be clarified quite simply and elegantly. For example:

> ἥν τινες ἀπωσάμενοι <u>περὶ τὴν πίστιν</u> ἐναυάγησαν 1 Tim 1:19
> by rejecting which, some have made shipwreck <u>as far as their faith is concerned</u>
>> The use of περί + acc clarifies what would be merely implied by a dative alone: 'reference'.

The same is true for all the other elements.

4.4 Reminder

> As before, with genitives and present tenses, please remember what these labels are: a compact way of communicating to others *how you believe the dative is being used*. You have **not** decoded an inherently different type of dative. It's just a dative, but you're telling me why you think the author put it there.

CHAPTER 5

Adjectives
—
Consolidation Greek Readings

How to Use This Chapter

This chapter includes some extra work for consolidation, for those who have a mid-term break.

Work through this chapter of *ENTG*, section by section, completing exercises as you go. As you complete each section, read **Extra Help** below for that section.

In the **Extra Help**, you'll keep learning how to tackle any Greek sentence, including the next 'branch': the adjective. We will see how the article is used with any branch, and how to turn branches into nouns.

There is twice as much **Greek Reading** in this chapter, to help you consolidate Chapters 1–5. We conclude *Phoebe's Banquet* and read several shorter texts: adapted classics, including a couple of Aesop's fables.

Extra Material takes you a little further with accents. Otherwise, you have a break from new ideas to help you practise the material so far.

1 *ENTG* 5

Let me stress that this **Extra Help** is entirely optional. All that you need is in *ENTG*. In this chapter, I'm giving you some broader rules and patterns, which explain the patterns in *ENTG*. Some students enjoy learning that way. If that's not you, skip straight to the **Greek Readings**.

1.1 Before You Start: Memorisation

If you have mastered the paradigms for nouns we have met so far, there are virtually no new endings in this chapter. Before you go any further, please make sure that you're absolutely confident in your parsing and declining of the nouns from previous chapters.

In the next chapter, you will meet some new verb forms and the same applies: rejoice if you have learnt the present endings thoroughly, or weep at unnecessary extra work if you have not.

1.2 After *ENTG* 5.2: Trunk and Branches: A New Branch, Same Rules

Further Reading: vS 136

The adjective is another 'modifier' (or 'branch') that can qualify a part of the main sentence (or 'trunk'), just as the genitive (*ENTG* 3.1; **EH 3** 1.2) and prepositional branches (*ENTG* 4.1; **EH 4** 1.1) do. These uses of modifiers are called 'attributive'. We need to know this label, because the adjective also has other uses, and we need to be able to talk about them easily. It's also helpful to know the label 'head noun'; this is the noun that is being modified by a branch.

ENTG describes all this perfectly, and here I want to help you see how all these attributive modifiers obey the same basic rules of word order. This is especially important with the article.

ENTG 5.2 shows you two different ways to modify a noun that has the article with an adjective.

The sandwich, which is how we do it in English:

 ἡ **καλὴ** γῆ the **good** land

Or the repeated article:

 ἡ γῆ ἡ **καλή** the **good** land

In the **sandwich construction**, the **attributive modifier** goes in between the article and the noun, making it obvious what is being modified. In the **repeated article construction**, the attributive modifier is preceded by the same article as the noun. The repeated article says, 'I relate to my twin back there, and I'm telling you something about the noun that followed my twin.' (To help you remember: the word order is similar to the English expression 'the land *which is* good'.)

Both of these also work with the genitive and with prepositional branches.

ἡ **τοῦ Πέτρου** γῆ	
ἡ γῆ ἡ **τοῦ Πέτρου**	**Peter's** land
ἡ **περὶ θάλασσαν** γῆ	
ἡ γῆ ἡ **περὶ θάλασσαν**	The land **around a sea**

1.2.1 Watch Out: Which Article?

Notice how the genitive modifier can have its own article, or not. ἡ **τοῦ ἱεροῦ** γῆ 'the land **of the temple**' vs ἡ **ἱεροῦ** γῆ 'the land **of a temple**'. Do not confuse this with the article that agrees with the head noun.

1.2.2 Watch Out: Dropping the Repeated Article

It is more common for the genitive modifiers and for prepositional modifiers to take the repeated article construction (they follow the noun, rather than being sandwiched before it) *but to drop the repeated article*. In fact, this is the only version that we have seen so far of genitives and prepositions.

ἡ γῆ ἡ **τοῦ Πέτρου**	Peter's land
ἡ γῆ ἡ **περὶ θάλασσαν**	The land **around a sea**

This *cannot* happen when the modifier is an adjective, because it would change the meaning (*ENTG* 5.4). This means that the options are as shown in Table 5.1.

Table 5.1 Modifier Options

Modifier	Sandwich	Repeated article
Adjective	ἡ **καλή** γῆ	ἡ γῆ ἡ **καλή**
Genitive	ἡ **τοῦ Πέτρου** γῆ	ἡ γῆ [ἡ] **τοῦ Πέτρου**
Prepositional branch	ἡ **περὶ θάλασσαν** γῆ	ἡ γῆ [ἡ] **περὶ θάλασσαν**

For example, in Eph 1:15 we read, 'For this reason, because I have heard …'

τὴν καθ' ὑμᾶς πίστιν ἐν τῷ Κυρίῳ Ἰησοῦ καὶ τὴν ἀγάπην τὴν εἰς πάντας τοὺς ἁγίους …

τὴν πίστιν is modified twice:

1 a prepositional branch in sandwich construction, between the article and the noun:
   τὴν καθ' ὑμᾶς πίστιν – your faith
2 another prepositional branch in repeated article construction, dropping the article:
   τὴν καθ' ὑμᾶς πίστιν [τὴν] ἐν τῷ Κυρίῳ Ἰησοῦ – your faith in the Lord Jesus.

τὴν ἀγάπην is then modified by

a prepositional branch in repeated article construction
τὴν ἀγάπην τὴν εἰς πάντας τοὺς ἁγίους – and love for all the saints.

1.3 After *ENTG* 5.4: Trunk and Branches: A New Type of Tree

So far we have talked about tackling Greek sentences by identifying the 'trunk of the tree': first the verb, then the subject, direct object, and indirect object (if present). Only after you have identified the elements of the trunk should you deal with any branches (modifiers).

ENTG 5.4 introduces a different type of sentence, a new type of 'tree trunk'. Don't worry: there aren't any others! Instead of a 'doing' tree, this is a 'being' tree, more or less equating A with B. You therefore have two nominatives, not a nominative and an accusative. We need to pay close attention to the rules of word order and of the article to work out which nominative is the **subject** and which is the **complement**.

Once you have mastered how adjectives can be the complement, you'll see why the adjective cannot drop the article in the 'repeated article' construction (discussed in 1.2.2). The adjective has the article before it when attributive, and not when predicative (assuming the noun has an article).

1.3.1 Attributive vs Predicative Made Simple

> If the noun has the article, then:
> the adjective comes straight after an article if it is **attributive**
> the adjective does not follow straight after an article if it is **predicative**.

1.3.2 Watch Out: αὐτός

We have met αὐτός in *ENTG* 3.6, which tells us that it is a pronoun. We discovered that it can be a modifier in the genitive, meaning 'his', 'hers', 'its'.

It does *not* take the article. This is because the article tells you that something is identifiable: 'you know which one I mean'. Since a pro*noun* stands in the place of a noun, that only works if it is obvious which noun you're referring to. The pronoun already implies what the article would have told you – 'you know which one I mean' – so there is no need for the article as well.

That lack of article makes it look, accidentally, as though this is predicative word order: ὁ λόγος αὐτοῦ. Sometimes it gets described that way, which is misleading. This is the attributive word order for pronouns, because they don't need the article.

1.4 After *ENTG* 5.5: Modifiers ('Branches') as Nouns

ENTG 5.5 explains that the adjective can also be used instead of a noun. This is called a **nominal** or **substantival** use.

1.4.1 No Article Needed

Sometimes *ENTG* 5.5 is misread as though nominal adjectives need the article. In fact, you can make indefinite adjectives into nouns too. Οἱ νεκροί is 'the dead people' (*ENTG* 5.5) but νεκροί is just 'dead people' generally. See exercise B3 in *ENTG* chapter 6. We hardly ever do this in English, but it can happen: 'a blonde' means 'a blonde lady'.

1.4.2 It's Just an Attributive Use

'Nominal' isn't really a separate use of the adjective: it's an attributive use where the noun is implicit. The noun will be ἄνθρωπος (if the adjective is masculine), γυνή (woman, if feminine) or πρᾶγμα ('thing', plural πράγματα, if neuter).

οἱ νεκροί	is shorthand for	οἱ νεκροί **ἄνθρωποι**
ἡ καλή	is shorthand for	ἡ καλή **γυνή**
τὰ ἅγια	is shorthand for	τὰ ἅγια **πράγματα**

1.4.3 It Works for All Attributive Modifiers

As we have seen, adjectives aren't the only attributive modifiers: genitives and prepositional branches are as well. These all follow the same rules of word order. As you might expect, you can use these other attributive modifiers with an implicit noun as well.

> λέγων τὰ περὶ τῆς βασιλείας 'speaking **the things** concerning the kingdom', Acts 1:3
> as if he had written
> τὰ περὶ τῆς βασιλείας **πράγματα** or τὰ **πράγματα** τὰ περὶ τῆς βασιλείας.

Jesus' famous 'get behind me Satan' (Matt 16:23) is followed by

> οὐ φρονεῖς τὰ τοῦ Θεοῦ, ἀλλὰ τὰ τῶν ἀνθρώπων,
> 'you are not considering **the things** of God, but **the things** of men'.

It is as if he had said:

> οὐ φρονεῖς τὰ τοῦ Θεοῦ **πράγματα**,
>   ἀλλὰ τὰ τῶν ἀνθρώπων **πράγματα**, or
> οὐ φρονεῖς τὰ **πράγματα** [τὰ] τοῦ Θεοῦ,
>   ἀλλὰ τὰ **πράγματα** [τὰ] τῶν ἀνθρώπων.

Sometimes you'll want 'which' in English:

> τὰ ἄνω Col 3:1
> the things which are above
> τὰ ἐπὶ τῆς γῆς Col 3:2
> the things which are on the earth

2 THE GREEK READINGS

If this is a normal week for you, then **Reading A** will probably keep you busy enough. If you have a mid-term break, the extra readings will help you not to lose your Greek.

2.1 Reading A: Phoebe's Banquet Concludes

The epic of the banquet concludes!

The day of the feast has arrived; Ampliatus is free from having to teach the unruly child, who is watched by his own father for the day, but gets to hang around his beloved Phoebe. Phoebe is initially concerned that they lack all that is needed for the party, so Peter sends his children to gather whatever is serviceable from the catch of fish in the boat. While he sends a slave to supervise, Mary decides that all is prepared and sends a slave to summon the guests. Ampliatus overhears Phoebe telling Mary that she has all the food they need.

Everyone is happy, each for their own reasons, and after the hosts say grace, all end by worshipping God.

¹ Ἔστι καινὴ ἡμέρα. ² ἡ ἡμέρα ἐστὶν ἡ ἡμέρα τοῦ δείπνου. ³ μακάριος ὁ Ἀμπλιᾶτος. ⁴ ἔχει ὁ μακάριος Ἀμπλιᾶτος τὴν εἰρήνην. ⁵ οὐ διδάσκει σήμερον τὸν Παῦλον τὸν τοῦ Πέτρου υἱόν. ⁶ ὁ Πέτρος τήρει τὸ τέκνον τὸ πονηρόν.

⁷ Λέγει ἡ Φοίβη·

⁸ Οὐκ ἔχομεν τὰ περὶ τοῦ δείπνου.

⁹ Λέγει ὁ Πέτρος τῷ τέκνῳ τῷ πονηρῷ καὶ ταῖς ἀδελφαῖς τοῦ τέκνου·

¹⁰ Ἀγαπητοί· ἐκβάλλω ὑμᾶς ἐκ τοῦ οἴκου καὶ πρὸς τὴν θάλασσαν.

¹¹ συνάγετε ἐνάλια πολλὰ ἐκ τοῦ πλοίου. ¹² συνάγετε τὰ καλὰ ἐνάλια, ἀλλὰ τὰ κακὰ οὐ παραλαμβάνετε.

¹³ Λέγει ὁ Πέτρος δούλῳ·

¹⁴ Δοῦλε ἀγαθὲ καὶ πιστέ· τηρεῖς τὰ τέκνα.

¹⁵ Πιστεύει ὁ Πέτρος τῷ δούλῳ. ¹⁶ ἀγαθὸς καὶ πιστὸς ὁ δοῦλος. ¹⁷ ἔστιν ἕτερος δοῦλος ἐν τῇ οἰκίᾳ. ¹⁸ ὁ δοῦλος καλός. ¹⁹ λέγει ἡ Μαρία τῷ δούλῳ·

²⁰ Ἔχω λόγον τῷ ὄχλῳ περὶ τοῦ δείπνου. ²¹ ὁ καιρὸς τοῦ δείπνου ἔστιν. ²² συνάγεις τὸν ὄχλον εἰς τὸν δεῖπνον.

²³ Ἀκούει ὁ Ἀμπλιᾶτος τῆς ἀγαπητῆς αὐτοῦ·

²⁴ Μαρία, τὸν ἄρτον τοῦ δείπνου ἔχω.

²⁵ Μακάριος ὁ Παῦλος· οὐ διδάσκει αὐτὸν ὁ Ἀμπλιᾶτος. ²⁶ μακάριος ὁ Ἀμπλιᾶτος· παρὰ τῇ Φοίβῃ ἐστίν. ²⁷ μακάριοι ἡ Φοίβη καὶ ὁ Πέτρος· μέγας

ὁ ὄχλος καὶ ἀγαθὸς ὁ δεῖπνος. ²⁸ ἀναβλέπουσι καὶ εὐχαριστοῦσι τῷ θεῷ.

²⁹ μακάριος ὁ ὄχλος· τὸν ἴδιον ἄρτον ἔχει ἕκαστος ἄνθρωπος. ³⁰ οἱ πιστοὶ

μακάριοι προσκυνοῦσι τῷ αἰωνίῳ θεῷ τῶν Ἰουδαίων.

2.1.1 Vocabulary

δεῖπνος, ου, ὁ – dinner party
ἐνάλιον, ου, τό – a fish
εὐχαριστέω – I give thanks

σήμερον – today
ὑμᾶς – you (acc pl)

2.2 Extra Reading B: 'The Rich Man and the Precious Stone'

This is an edited, not to say butchered, version of an ancient tale.

¹ Ἔστιν πλούσιος ἐν τῷ Ἰσραὴλ ἀλλὰ οὐ δίκαιος ὁ ἄνθρωπος. ² εὑρίσκει ἐν τῇ

σοφιᾷ τοῦ Σολομῶντος·

³ Εἰ σκορπίζεις τοῖς πτωχοῖς, τοῦ Θεοῦ λαμβάνεις.

⁴ Πιστεύει τῷ λογῷ, καὶ πωλεῖ ἕκαστα καλὰ τῆς οἰκίας αὐτοῦ, καὶ σκορπίζει

τοῖς πτωχοῖς, ἀλλὰ ἔχει ἀργύρια δύο. ⁵ ἀλλὰ πτωχός ἐστιν ὁ ἄνθρωπος, καὶ ὁ

λαὸς οὐ δίκαιοί εἰσιν αὐτῷ. ⁶ ἡ ψυχὴ αὐτοῦ ἐστιν μικρά, καὶ λέγει·

⁷ Ὑπάγω εἰς Ἰερουσαλὴμ καὶ ζητῶ τὸν Θεόν μου καὶ λαλῶ αὐτῷ.

⁸ ψευδολόγος ὁ Θεός. ⁹ λέγει ὁ ψευδολόγος Θεός·

¹⁰ Εἰ σκορπίζεις τοῖς πτωχοῖς, τοῦ Θεοῦ λαμβάνεις.

¹¹ Ὑπάγει καὶ βλέπει ἀνθρώπους δύο. ¹² πολεμοῦσιν ἀλλήλους περὶ λίθου

τιμίου. ¹³ συνάγει τοὺς ἀνθρώπους καὶ λέγει πρὸς αὐτούς·

¹⁴ Ἵνα τί, ἀδελφοί, πολεμεῖτε; ¹⁵ λαμβάνετε ἀργύρια δύο, καὶ λαμβάνω

τὸν λίθον τὸν τίμιον.

¹⁶ Ἔχει τὸν λίθον ἐν Ἰερουσαλὴμ καὶ ἐξετάζει χρυσοχόον περὶ τοῦ τιμίου λίθου.

¹⁷ ὁ χρυσοχόος ἀκούει τοὺς τοῦ ἀνθρώπου λόγους, καὶ βλέπει τὸν λίθον, καὶ προσκυνεῖ, καὶ ἐξετάζει·

¹⁸ Ποῦ τὸν τίμον καὶ θεῖον λίθον εὑρίσκεις; ¹⁹ Ἰερουσαλὴμ καὶ ὁ λαὸς ζητοῦσι τὸν λίθον. ²⁰ ὁ λίθος ἐστὶν ὁ λίθος ἐκ τῆς διπλοΐδος Ἀαρών.

²¹ Παρακαλεῖ ὁ χρυσοχόος τὸν ἄνθρωπον·

²² Εἰ τὸν λίθον βλέπουσιν οἱ ἀδελφοὶ τοῦ ἱεροῦ, τοῦ Θεοῦ λαμβάνεις.

²³ Ἀκούει καὶ πρὸς τὸ ἱερὸν ὑπάρχει. ²⁴ ἄγγελος κυρίου λέγει πρὸς τοὺς ἀδελφοὺς τοὺς τοῦ ἱεροῦ·

²⁵ Νῦν περιπατεῖ ἄνθρωπος ἐν τῷ ἱερῷ. ²⁶ τὸν ἐκ τῆς διπλοΐδος Ἀαρών λίθον ἔχει.

²⁷ Καὶ λέγει ὁ ἄγγελος λόγους περὶ τοῦ ἀνθρώπου τοῖς ἀδελφοῖς.

²⁸ σκορπίζουσιν οἱ ἀδελφοὶ τῷ ἀνθρώπῳ χρυσίον πολὺ καὶ ἀργύριον πολύ, καὶ παρακαλοῦσιν αὐτόν·

²⁹ Οὐ πιστεύεις τῷ θεῷ ἐν τῇ καρδίᾳ διὰ τὸν λογον·

³⁰ Εἰ σκορπίζεις τοῖς πτωχοῖς, τοῦ Θεοῦ λαμβάνεις;

³¹ Ὁ πλούσιος ἀκούει ἐν τῷ ἱερῷ, καὶ εὐχαριστεῖ, καὶ πιστεύει τῷ κυρίῳ, καὶ εὐχαριστοῦσιν οἱ ἀδελφοί.

2.2.1 Vocabulary

Ἀαρών – (indeclinable) Aaron
ἀλλήλους – one another, each other
ἀργύριον, ου, τό – silver (pl: silver coins)
διπλοΐδος – (fem gen sing) a double-cloak
δύο – two

ἐξετάζω – I enquire
εὑρίσκω – I find
θεῖος, θεία, θεῖον – divine
λίθος, ου, ὁ – stone
Ἵνα τί – why?
μικρός, ά, όν – small
νῦν – now

πλούσιος – rich
πολεμέω – I fight ('polemics')
πτωχός, ή, όν – poor
πωλέω – I sell
Σολομῶντος – Solomon; the preceding article will tell you the gender, case and number. Remember, the article *never* lies.

σοφία, ας, ἡ – wisdom
σκορπίζω – I scatter (metaphorically, to give liberally)
τίμιος, α, ον – precious
χρυσίον – gold
χρυσοχόος, ου, ὁ – goldsmith
ψευδολόγος, ον – lying, false (dealing in false *pseudo* words)

2.3 Extra Reading C: An Interview with Pericles, General and Leader of Athens

¹ Ἄνθρωπος τῷ Περικλεῖ λέγει·

² Περίκλεις, τὶ ἐν νῷ ἔχει ὁ ἀγαθὸς κύριος τῆς βασιλείας;

³ τί ἐστι τὸ πρῶτον;

⁴ Λέγει ὁ Περικλῆς·

⁵ Ὅτι ἄνθρωπός ἐστιν.

⁶ Καὶ τὸ δεύτερον;

⁷ Ὅτι κατὰ τὸν νόμον πάντοτε ἄρχει.

⁸ Καὶ τὸ τρίτον;

⁹ Ὅτι οὐ πάντοτε ἄρχει.

¹⁰ Ὁ ἄνθρωπος λέγει τῷ Περικλεῖ·

¹¹ Μακάριοι οἱ Ἀθηναῖοι.

¹² Οὐ μόνον ἐν νῷ ἔχεις, ἀλλὰ ποιεῖς.

2.3.1 Vocabulary

Ἀθηναῖος, α, ον – Athenian
ἄρχω – I rule
δεύτερος, α, ον – second
μόνον – only
νῷ – mind (masc dat sing)
ὅτι – that

πάντοτε – always
Περικλῆς – Pericles (voc: Περίκλεις; dat: Περικλεῖ)
πρῶτος, η, ον – first
τί – what?
τρίτος, η, ον – third

2.4 Extra Reading D: Aesop's Fables: The Goose That Laid the Golden Eggs

¹Ὄρνεον ἄνθρωπος ἔχει. ²τὸ ὄρνεον ᾠὰ χρυσοῦ τίκτει. ³λέγει ἐν αὐτῷ ὁ ἄνθρωπος·

⁴ἔστιν ἐν αὐτῷ ὄγκον χρυσοῦ.

⁵Ἀποκτείνει αὐτό, ἀλλὰ εὑρίσκει ὅμοιον τῶν λοιπῶν ὀρνέων. ⁶ἡ ἐλπὶς αὐτοῦ χρυσὸς πολύς. ⁷ἀλλὰ τὸ μικρὸν αὐτοῦ ὑπάγει.

⁸Ὁ μῦθος ἀποκαλύπτει·

⁹Εἰ μικρὸν πάρειμι, ἱκανὸν τὸ μικρόν. ¹⁰φεύγομεν τὴν ἐπιθυμίαν.

2.4.1 Vocabulary

ἀποκαλύπτω – I reveal
ἀποκτείνω – I kill
ἐλπίς – hope (fem)
ἐπιθυμία, ας, ἡ – greed
ἱκανός, ή, όν – sufficient
λοιπός, ή, όν – the rest
μικρός, ά, όν – little, small
μῦθος, ου, ὁ – story, myth, fable
ὄγκον – system, device, organ

ὅμοιος, οία, οιον – similar + gen of whatever is similar
ὄρνεον, ου, τό – bird (*orn*ithology)
πάρειμι – I am at hand
τίκτω – I give birth (think a bit about how to put this in English in this context)
φεύγω – I flee
χρυσός, οῦ, ὁ – gold
ᾠόν, οῦ, τό – egg

2.5 Extra Reading E: Aesop's Fables: The Wolf and the Lamb

¹ Λύκος ἀρνίον διώκει, ἀλλὰ τὸ ἀρνίον εἰς τὸ ἱερὸν ὑπάγει.

² Αὐτῷ λέγει ὁ λύκος·

³ Εἰ περιπατοῦμεν ἐν τῷ ἱερῷ, θύει ὁ ἱερεύς τῷ θεῷ.

⁴ Λέγει τὸ ἀρνίον·

⁵ Τί ἐστι τὸ ἀγαθόν; ⁶ θύει ὁ ἱερεύς τῷ θεῷ ἢ λύκος ἀποκτείνει;

⁷ Ὁ λόγος ἀποκαλύπτει·

⁸ Ἐν τῇ ὥρᾳ τῶν νεκρῶν ὑπάγομεν. ⁹ κακόν ἐστιν ὑπὸ τῶν πονηρῶν,

ἀλλὰ ἀγαθόν ἐστι μετὰ εἰρήνης καὶ μετὰ δόξης.

2.5.1 Vocabulary

ἀποκαλύπτω – I reveal	θύω – I sacrifice
ἀποκτείνω – I kill	ἱερεύς – priest (masc nom sing)
ἀρνίον, ου, τό – lamb	λύκος, ου, ὁ – wolf
διώκω – I chase	τί – which?

2.6 Extra Reading F: 300!

¹ Λεωνίδας ἐστὶν ὁ στρατηγὸς ἐν Θερμοπύλαις. ² οὐκ ἐστι φόβος ἐν τῷ ἀγαθῷ

Λεωνίδᾳ. ³ ἀλλὰ στρατιώτης ἔκφοβος λέγει αὐτῷ·

⁴ Στρατηγέ, ὁ ἀριθμὸς τῶν βαρβάρων μετὰ Ξέρξου ἐστὶ μέγας. ⁵ ὅτε

τὰ τοξεύματα αὐτῶν ἐν τῷ ἀέρι ἐστίν, ὁ ἥλιος οὐ φανερός ἐστιν.

⁶ Ἀναβλέπει ὁ Λεωνίδας καὶ λέγει·

⁷·Ἀλλά, ἔκφοβε, τὰ τοξεύματα ποιεῖ τὴν ζωήν. ⁸·οἱ βάρβαροί εἰσιν ἐν τῇ σκοτιᾷ.

⁹·Ἀκούει ὁ στρατιώτης, καὶ οὐκ ἔστιν ἔκφοβος ἀλλὰ εἰς τὴν μάχην ὑπάγει.

2.6.1 Vocabulary

ἀέρι – air (masc dat sing)
ἀριθμός, οῦ, ὁ – number (arithmetic)
βάρβαρος – foreign, barbarian
ἔκφοβος – terrified
ἥλιος, ου, ὁ – sun ('helium')
Θερμοπύλαις – Thermopylae (site of a famous-last-stand battle of Spartans holding off Xerxes and the Persian expeditionary force)
Λεωνίδας – Leonidas (dat Λεωνίδᾳ)
μάχη, ης, ἡ – battle, fighting

Ξέρξης, ου, ὁ – Xerxes
ὅτε – when
σκοτία, ας, ἡ – darkness
στρατηγός, οῦ, ὁ – general, military commander ('strategy')
στρατιώτης, οῦ, ὁ – soldier
τόξεύματα – arrow (neut pl nom/acc – you will meet this class of nouns in the next chapter.)
φανερός, ά, όν – visible
φόβος, ου, ὁ – fear

3 ACCENTS

We have seen that *proclitics* (such as ὁ, ἡ, οἱ or αἱ) simply attach to the following word. These don't affect accents nearby, but simply lack their own. This chapter has two more proclitics in the vocab: ὡς and εἰ.

3.1 Enclitics (εἰμί)

FURTHER READING: vS 6

Now we also meet *enclitics* which throw their accents *backwards* onto the preceding word and play merry havoc with their accent.

The enclitic in this chapter is the present tense of εἰμί. All its forms are enclitic, except for the 2s which has an accent (εἶ, vs εἰ, a *proclitic* meaning 'if').

3.1.1 Enclitics Throw Their Accent Back

Enclitics of two syllables have the accent on their second syllable. Single-syllable enclitics obviously have it on their only syllable. Enclitics then lose their accent by *throwing it back* onto the previous word. The enclitic is usually left with no accent, as we will see in the rules below.

When enclitics are referred to out of context (such as in a lexicon or a paradigm) they are written with the acute accent on the second syllable (εἰμί) or *no* accent if they have one syllable (τε – vocab in *ENTG* 9). This is because many enclitics are variations of words that *do* have an accent, as we will see in later chapters, and this convention tells them apart conveniently.

If the previous word has a grave on the final syllable, it becomes acute:

πονηρούς τε (cf. πονηρούς καί)
ἰδού τινες

Remember that it may be that the reason for turning acutes on final syllables into graves is that there is no room for the pitch to drop again on that word. In these cases, the pitch does have room to fall: over the enclitic.

If the previous word has the drop in pitch on the syllable before last, then it receives an extra acute accent on its final syllable.

A drop – marked in the version [in brackets] below – on the syllable before last can either come from an acute on the syllable before that:

ἄνθρωπός εἰμι   [ἄνθρὼπός εἲμι]
παρεκάλεσέν τε   [παρεκάλὲσέν τὲ]
συμβούλιόν τε   [συμβούλιόν τὲ]
ἄγγελόν μου   [ἄγγὲλόν μὸὺ]

or from a circumflex, so that the pitch rises and falls on the same syllable:

πλεῖόν ἐστιν   [πλέιόν ἒστιν]
Ἰουδαῖοί τε   [Ἰουδάιοί τὲ]

If the previous word has an acute on the syllable before last, and the enclitic has two syllables, the enclitic keeps its accent:

πρέπον ἐστίν
ἰσχύειν τινά

In all other cases, the previous word remains unchanged when the enclitic throws its accent back:

αὐτῷ τινες
ἀκούει μου
πλήσας τε

3.1.2 Enclitics Starting a Sentence

When a sentence begins with an enclitic, it cannot throw the accent back, so it keeps it. Compare:

καὶ γὰρ ἐγὼ ἄνθρωπός εἰμι ὑπὸ ἐξουσίαν Matt 8:9
Εἰμὶ μὲν κἀγὼ θνητὸς ἴσος ἅπασιν Wis 7:1

3.1.3 Preparatory Use of ἐστι

FURTHER READING: vS 125B

ENTG 5.8 explains that ἐστί and εἰσί can have a 'preparatory use' ('there is' 'there are') at the start of a sentence. As with other enclitics, at the start of the sentence, εἰσί takes the accent:

Εἰσὶν δέ μοι δύο θυγατέρες Gen 19:8

However, the 3rd person singular has a different form when it is preparatory:

Ἔστι παιδάριον ἓν ὧδε John 6:9

Its accent is regressive, like that of normal verbs (**EM 2** 3.1). It takes this form for all senses of 'there exists' or 'it is possible' *anywhere in the sentence*, and whenever it follows ἀλλά, εἰ, καί, οὐκ, τοῦτο or ὡς.

3.1.4 Combining Enclitics and Proclitics

If the word before an enclitic is a proclitic (which doesn't have its own accent), it receives an acute accent:

Εἴ τις ἑτεροδιδασκαλεῖ … 1 Tim 6:3

If two or more enclitics follow each other, each throws the accent back. Thus, the last enclitic in the sequence has no accent, while the word before the first enclitic receives an accent (according to the rules above).

εἴ τί ἐστιν ἐν τῷ … Acts 25:5[1]
τι throws its accent back onto εἰ which becomes εἴ.
ἐστιν throws its accent back onto τι which becomes τί.
ἐν is proclitic, and so leans forward onto τῷ for its accent.

---

[1] With thanks to vS 128b.

CHAPTER 6

The Tenses
—
Imperfect Indicative

> **How to Use This Chapter**
>
> In this chapter, you will meet different Greek verb 'tenses'. I will show you some patterns that will save you time in the long run, and will help you relate every stage of parsing a verb to the information the verb communicates. That means that the **Extra Help** is a little longer than usual and will need a bit more of your time.
>
> Follow the instructions throughout the **Extra Help** below, which will tell you when to work through various sections of *ENTG*. The instructions below are for the fourth edition of *ENTG*. If you have the third edition, please check the **Online Material**, which has different instructions for you for this chapter.
>
> The **Greek Reading** is no longer 'Phoebe's Banquet' but is now the ancient novella *Joseph & Aseneth*.
>
> In the **Extra Material** you'll discover some major uses of the imperfect tense, as we did with the present tense previously.

1 BEFORE YOU START: THE GREEK VERB

Few things in Greek (at least in NT Greek circles) cause more controversy than how to understand this simplest and most foundational matter: what the verb means. This *Reader* will help you to learn the view that *ENTG* presents.

We're going to skip over a few sections in this chapter of *ENTG*, but let me stress that this is not to change what *ENTG* teaches, but to present the material in a way that will make some connections between how verbs look, how they are built up and what they communicate. Even more than with nouns, understanding these connections will keep saving you time throughout later chapters.

There's an old German saying, 'Please don't help me, it's hard enough as it is.' If you're already finding Greek hard going enough without my 'help', let me stress that this **Extra Help** is optional. The prospect of saving time later by investing more now might be the opposite of what you need. If so, just use *ENTG*, and perhaps come back to the **Extra Help** in this chapter when you're revising at the end of term, or trying to keep your Greek fresh in the summer holidays. The perspective in this chapter might help things to click then. Nonetheless, the **Greek**

Reading below will be helpful once you've worked through the chapter of *ENTG*, without the **Extra Help**, if you have time.

Your choice is either:

- Follow the material in Sections 2–4 below, which is an alternative to *ENTG* 6.1–4 or
- Skip Sections 2–4 below, and work through *ENTG* 6.1–4.[1]

Either way, return to the usual **Extra Help** to accompany *ENTG* 6.5–8 onwards (**EH 6** 5 below).

2 TENSES: ENGLISH AND GREEK

2.1 The Past Tenses: Author's Choice

ENTG introduces the idea of **aspect** in this chapter.[2]

> **Aspect** is an author's *choice* of how to *present* an action.

What's the difference between the following two descriptions?

1 This morning, *I went* to chapel. After that, I taught Greek.
2 This morning, *I was going* to chapel, when my phone rang. Later, I taught Greek.

They both describe exactly the same morning, but I've chosen to give you more details the second time. The italicised verb in (1) is a simple statement that the event happened in the past. It's the English 'past simple'. The verb in (2) draws you in to the action and presents it while it was in progress. It is the 'imperfect'. It is *during* that ongoing action that my phone rang. In both (1) and (2), after chapel, 'I taught Greek'. That's the past simple again.

The English past simple is the default past tense; it tells you that something happened – no more, no less. If you choose the imperfect, you have a reason for doing so: perhaps the next thing you say happened while that imperfect was happening.

---

[1] However, if you're using the third edition of *ENTG*, you *must* use Sections 2–4 below.
[2] The third edition of *ENTG* uses 'aspect' to cover three quite separate things, whereas the fourth edition and this *Reader* limit 'aspect' consistently to one thing.

To help you if you are already familiar with the complex terminology: I will use 'aspect' to mean 'grammatical aspect' of Greek verbs. I will not use it for 'lexical aspect' (sometimes termed *Aktionsart*) of Greek verbs, or to refer to any kind of aspect of English verbs in translation. *ENTG* (3rd ed.) refers to all three as 'aspect' somewhat interchangeably. My discussion of 'lexical aspect' is reserved for the **Extra Material** of various chapters and is mentioned (as *Aktionsart*) in chapter 18 of *ENTG* in the fourth edition.

This difference between the past simple and the imperfect is called 'aspect'. Notice that it is *not* a difference in the nature of two actions: it is a difference in *how the author chooses to present* the exact same action. Both *I went* (1) and *I was going* (2) refer to **the same action**, but presented differently.

2.2 How Greek Tenses Relate to Each Other

2.2.1 Comparison with English

In Table 6.1 there are some English **tenses** and how they relate to each other, combining time and aspect:[3]

Table 6.1 English Tenses

	Past **time**	Present **time**	Future **time**
Ongoing **aspect:**	*Imperfect* I was loving	*Present Continuous* I am loving	*Future Continuous* I will be loving
Simple **aspect:**	*Simple Past* I loved	*Simple Present* I love	*Simple Future* I will love

Tenses communicate two things in English: **aspect** and **time**. Table 6.2 shows how it works in Greek.

Table 6.2 Greek Tenses

	Past **time**	Present **time**	Future **time**
Ongoing **aspect:**	Imperfect tense	Present tense	Future tense
Simple **aspect:**	Aorist tense	–	

Notice a couple of differences:

- Unlike English, the future does not allow you a choice of aspect. You cannot distinguish 'I will be going' from 'I will go'.
- Unlike English, there isn't a separate present tense which means 'I go' as opposed to 'I am going'. More on this below: **EH 6 4.1**.
- Like English, there are two past tenses, with different aspects, as described above.

Greek offers the author the same choice as English in the past. You can present an action simply, referring to it as a complete whole. I will refer to this as having **simple aspect**. That is the Greek **aorist** tense; it is the default past tense. The author can choose instead to draw you into the action, when it was in progress,

---

[3] This is in *ENTG* **Comparative English Grammar**, section 7, but only in the third edition.

referring to it when it was yet incomplete. I will refer to this as having **ongoing aspect**. That is the Greek **imperfect** tense.

The table is laid out to help you compare it with the English table, but as soon as we see how the different tenses look, it will make more sense to lay them out by something called **system**, as follows.

2.2.2 Greek Verb: Systems

Table 6.3 Verb Systems

	Present system	Aorist system	Future system
Stem: (communicating aspect, except in the future)	λυ- (ongoing aspect)	λυσα- (simple aspect)	λυσ- (no aspect specified)
Principal tense: (communicating default time)	Present tense λύω	–	Future tense λύσω
Historical tense: (communicating past time)	Imperfect tense ἔλυον	Aorist tense ἔλυσα	–

Table 6.3 shows how each tense fits within a system. The columns in the table are fundamental to *every* form of every Greek verb, without exception. Every form you will ever meet of any verb exists in one such column. They are called systems: present system, aorist system, future system.

How do you know which system a verb is in? Easy: you look at the stem. We have met the stem of the present system – the present stem: it is simply the form of every verb we've met, but without the endings: λυ-ω, βλεπ-ω, διδασκ-ω, ἐχ-ω.

The future tense simply adds a σ to the end of the stem, and the aorist adds σα. To help you remember: σ = σooner or later; σα = σimple αspect.

2.2.3 Greek Verbs: Time

The two rows in Table 6.3 tell us the time of the verb. The 'historical' tenses are used in past narratives (imperfect and aorist).

How do you know which row you are in?

The **principal** tenses have the endings you have already met. The future endings are identical to the present tense endings, but they are added to the **future stem**: λύσω (I will untie/be untying) instead of λύω; πιστεύσεις (you will believe) instead of πιστεύεις. What could be easier?

The **historical** tenses give us two clues. First, they add an 'augment' to the front of the stem: the ἐ- in the table. Λυ- and πιστευ- become ἔλυ- and ἐπιστευ-. Second, they take **historical tense** endings, which we'll learn below.

2.2.4 Parse with Meaning

It would be tempting to take a shortcut at this point in parsing. You could say, 'if I see an ἐ and a σ I know it's aorist; if I only see an ἐ, it's imperfect; if neither, then present' (*ENTG* 6.2). That will work *only in this chapter*. Get into good habits now. Say instead:

- The ἐ tells me that this is a **historical tense**.
- The **stem** tells me the **aspect** of the verb.

> **Tense**
> is a shorthand for
> **system** (communicating **aspect**)
> +
> **time**.

Note well this confusing point: the '*present*' stem has nothing to do with *present* time; it is an unfortunate label; it communicates *ongoing aspect* both in the present (present tense) and in the past (imperfect tense).

You might find it helpful to compare Figure 2.1 (p 23) with Figure 6.1 (p 99).

3 PARSING MADE SIMPLE

3.1 Thematic Vowels

Just like nouns, verb endings are made up of an 'ending proper' combined with a 'thematic vowel'. The thematic vowel is ε, but it can change. It becomes ο before μ or ν. In the **aorist system**, the stem (λυσα) changes the thematic vowel to α before an 'ending proper'.

In Table 6.4 you can see how the two past tenses share the same endings, and are only different in their stem, which tells us the system of the verb. The system is the author's way of telling us his choice of aspect: how he has decided to portray the action.

Table 6.4 Historical Endings

	Present system	**Aorist system**
Stem: (communicating aspect)	λυ- (ongoing aspect)	λυσα- (simple aspect)
Historical tense: (past time)	Imperfect tense	Aorist tense
	ἔ-λυ-ο-ν	ἔ-λυσ-α-
	ἔ-λυ-ε-ς	ἔ-λυσ-α-ς
	ἔ-λυ-ε- – (ν)	ἔ-λυσ-ε- – (ν)
	ἐ-λύ-ο-μεν	ἐ-λύσ-α-μεν
	ἐ-λύ-ε-τε	ἐ-λύσ-α-τε
	ἔ-λυ-ο-ν	ἔ-λυσ-α-ν

Note:

- The 3s takes an 'optional *nu*', just like the present 3p ending. It is not a true ending, but an aid to pronunciation, so it does not change the thematic vowel to o or to α. Compare that with the true ν ending in the 1s and the 3p, which does change the thematic vowel.
- The 1s of the aorist used to have an ending. It has dropped out, but the thematic vowel changes as though it were still there.
- The difference between aorist and imperfect is that the aorist has a longer stem (marked in bold) with σ and then the thematic vowel changes. (Even though the thematic vowel is not part of the stem, I will usually show the aorist stem as λυσα- rather than λυσ-, to distinguish it from the future stem, λυσ-.)

You may feel that this is more effort than just learning two sets of endings, but we will meet more tenses later which use the same endings, and it will be helpful for you to remember that the endings are to do with time, not with stem (and therefore not with aspect).

3.2 The Greek Tenses Laid out by System and Time

Table 6.5 Greek Tenses

	Present system	**Aorist system**	**Future system**
Stem: (communicating aspect, except in the future)	**λυ-** (ongoing aspect)	**λυσα-** (simple aspect)	**λυσ-** (no aspect specified)
Principal tense: (communicating default time)	Present tense λύ-ω λύ-εις λύ-ει λύ-ομεν λύ-ετε λύ-ουσι(ν)	–	Future tense λύσ-ω λύσ-εις λύσ-ει λύσ-ομεν λύσ-ετε λύσ-ουσι(ν)
Historical tense: (communicating past time)	Imperfect tense ἔ-λυ-ο-ν ἔ-λυ-ε-ς ἔ-λυ-ε- – (ν) ἐ-λύ-ο-μεν ἐ-λύ-ε-τε ἔ-λυ-ο-ν	Aorist tense ἔ-λυσ-α- ἔ-λυσ-α-ς ἔ-λυσ-ε- – (ν) ἐ-λύσ-α-μεν ἐ-λύσ-α-τε ἔ-λυσ-α-ν	–

See Table 6.5. The columns in this table are the three **systems**, which are identified by their respective **stem**. They communicate aspect. Present tense and imperfect tense have the same stem (present stem, **λυ-**) because they have

ongoing aspect, so they are in the same column. Imperfect tense and aorist tense have different stems (present stem, **λυ-** vs aorist stem **λυσ-α-**) because they have different **aspects**, so they are in different columns.

The rows are about time. Both aorist tense and imperfect tense have the past time markers: the prefix and the past endings, so they are in the same row. The present tense and imperfect tense have different time markers, so they are in different rows.

Notice how the systems (and their stems) are named after the tense that is at the top of their column. It's confusing: the imperfect tense uses the 'present stem' but is in the past, not the present; anyway, the stems tell you about aspect, not about time.

You may feel that we have made four simple things into a complex 2x3 grid, but we will be adding rows and columns, and so keeping track of what the stems (columns) tell us, and what the endings (rows) tell us, will make your life ever so easy. Shortcuts with parsing will not work when you meet verbs in the aorist stem that don't have the augment.

3.3 Embedding the Paradigms

Now apply the method described in **EH 2** 1.4.2.

1. Learn the basic pattern for historical tenses (ἔλυον). Don't stop when you get it right. Stop when you can no longer imagine getting it wrong. (Test yourself on λύω while you're at it.)
2. Learn the rules for turning the imperfect into the aorist.
3. Write out the imperfect and the aorist, without looking anything up, by applying the rules.
4. Check what you've written against the table, and use that to reinforce the rules.
5. Keep doing that until you never get it wrong.
6. Now do the same for turning the present (you already know the endings) into the future.

3.4 Parsing Practice

ἐπίστευσαν

- Which aspect? Stem has sigma and thematic vowel shifts to α, so this is the aorist stem. Therefore <u>presented simply</u>.
- Which time? Has augment and historical endings ἐ - πιστευσ - α - ν, so <u>past</u> tense.
  ○ Past action, presented simply.
  ○ Shorthand: 'aorist tense' = 'past time of the aorist stem (simple aspect)'.

πιστεύετε

- Which aspect? The stem has no σ, so it is the present. Aspect is: <u>presented as ongoing</u>.
- Which time? Has no augment so <u>it's not a past tense</u>.
  - A current action presented as ongoing.
  - Shorthand: 'present tense' = 'present time of the present stem (ongoing aspect)'.

ἐπίστευσεν

- Which aspect? Stem has sigma, so this is either the aorist or future stem.
  - εν is not a future ending, whereas it is the one ending in the aorist where the thematic vowel doesn't change to α (see **EM 6** 3.1)
  - It is the aorist stem, therefore the action is <u>presented simply</u>.
- Which time? Has augment and historical endings **ἐ** - πίστευσ - ε - **ν**, so <u>past tense</u>.
  - Past action, presented simply.
  - Shorthand: 'aorist tense' = 'past time of the aorist stem (simple aspect)'.
- Note that the ending does not change the thematic vowel to α because it is blank, with the optional *nu* being there for pronunciation reasons.

πιστεύσετε

- Which aspect? The stem is the future **πιστεύσ**ετε, so aspect is <u>not described at all</u>.
- Which time? (We already know this from the previous question, but it's always good to double-check and confirm.) Has no augment so <u>it's not a past tense</u>.
  - A future action.
  - Shorthand: 'future tense' = future time.

ἐπίστευον

- Which aspect? Stem has no sigma, so this is the present stem. Aspect: <u>presented as ongoing</u>.
- Which time? Has augment and historical endings **ἐ** - πίστευ - ο - **ν**, so <u>past tense</u>.
  - Past action, presented as ongoing.
  - Shorthand: 'imperfect tense' = 'past time of the present stem (ongoing aspect)'.

Now apply this to *ENTG* **Practice** 6.2, 6.3 and 6.4. Make sure you interpret the two different elements of parsing as you go: stem (aspect) and augment/endings (time).

3.5 Building Your Verb

We will continue to meet the various components that can make up a verb and which each contribute something to its meaning. In **EH 2** 1.4.3 we met the stem, contract vowel and ending. Now we add the augment, the fact that the stem can add something at the end (and after the contract vowel), and we break up the ending into thematic vowel + ending proper. For example, see Table 6.6.

Table 6.6 Building Your Verb

Augment	Stem		Thematic vowel	Ending proper	Result
	verb root	suffix			
	λυ	σ-	ε→ο	μεν	λύσομεν
	λυ	-	ε	τε	λύετε
ἐ	λυ	σα-	ε→α	τε	ἐλύσατε
ἐ	λυ	-	ε→ο	ν	ἔλυον

4 GREEK VERB: DIFFERENT MEANINGS

4.1 English vs Greek Aspect

Every Greek tense has a variety of contexts in which it can occur. Learning to expect these contexts is often the subject of second- and third-year Greek courses; it is also the subject of much of the **Extra Material** in this reader.

For now, *ENTG* expects you to be aware of the following options:

- The Greek present tense (λύω) can mean
  - 'I am doing it right now' or
  - 'I do this habitually.'
- The Greek imperfect (ἔλυον) can mean
  - 'I was doing it then' or
  - 'I used to do it back then' or
  - 'I *began* to do it back then.'
- The Greek future (λύσω) can mean
  - 'I will do it' or
  - 'I will be doing it.'

English forces you to make a choice in translation. You cannot avoid being an interpreter, whether you like it or not. Eventually, you will be able to read without translating, as you do in English, and you'll keep the options open naturally in your head. All it takes is several years of practice reading plenty of Greek texts, which is what you're planning to do anyway, right?

4.2 Labels Summarised

Table 6.7 Stem and Aspect Labels

Stem	Aspect	Meaning	English examples
Present	Ongoing	Action **is presented as** ongoing, incomplete, referring to a point in time that doesn't include the beginning and end	**Present**: I am singing (right now); I sing (habitually) **Past**: I was singing (at that moment); I used to sing (habitually); I started to sing
Aorist	Simple	Action **is presented** simply, as a complete whole, referring to beginning, end and everything in between	**Past**: I sang
Future	–	No information about aspect	**Future**: I will sing (later); I will be singing (when we meet)

4.3 Understanding the Verb: Summary

1. Parse independently for aspect (stem) and for time (augment and endings).
2. In our verb tables, tenses in the same column agree about aspect (the same stem).
3. Tenses on the same row agree about time (augment and endings).
4. Aspect is a *choice* of the author in presenting the action, not the *nature* of the action.

Now tackle the **Half-Way Practice** in *ENTG* and then work through *ENTG* 6.5–6.8, with the optional help below.

5 *ENTG* 6.5–6.8

5.1 Before *ENTG* 6.5.1: The Augment

The augment lengthens the initial vowel of the verb stem; if there is no vowel, it adds ἐ instead (as we have seen with λύω).[4]

---

[4] *ENTG* explains this accurately in the footnote. The body of the section explains that you add the ἐ by contraction. You already know from the rules of contract that ε + ε → ει, not η and ε + ο → ου, not ω. You can simply use the **Key Grammar** at the bottom of the page, but delete 'ἐ plus'. (Likewise in the Grammar Reference Tables at the back of *ENTG*.)

The rule of diphthongs with ι (*ENTG* 6.5.1) is familiar from noun endings: **EH 3** 2.2.2.

In summary, the *augment* means:

- If the word begins with a vowel, lengthen the vowel (short vowel → long vowel; *ENTG* 1.1.3 Note 1).
- Otherwise, add an ἐ.

Work through *ENTG* 6.5 and **Practice** 6.5.

5.2 Optional: Before *ENTG* 6.6: The σ Suffix

The second **Key Grammar** in *ENTG* 6.6 might look a bit daunting, but, as often with Greek, the underlying ideas are simple enough, and we have already met most of them (**EH 4** 1.3).

Some Greek letters are shorthand for combinations:

$$\psi = \pi + \sigma$$
$$\xi = \kappa + \sigma.$$

Some come in aspirated forms (as with rough breathings) or unaspirated (as with smooth breathings):

$$\varphi = \pi + {}^{\backprime}$$
$$\theta = \tau + {}^{\backprime}$$
$$\chi = \kappa + {}^{\backprime}$$

Try adding an *s* sound to a *p* sound, and you find that you can't really aspirate it either way. That's why both end up as the same:

$$\pi + \sigma \qquad\qquad = \psi$$
$$\varphi + \sigma = \pi + {}^{\backprime} + \sigma \rightarrow \pi + \sigma = \psi$$

If you try this with β, you'll soon discover how similar β is to π.[5] Try saying *bs* fast in the middle of a word: you really can't tell the difference between βσ, πσ and φσ, they all sound like πσ, which is spelt ψ.

The same principle explains why κσ, γσ, χσ, σσσ all end up sounding like κσ, spelt ξ.

Likewise, try pronouncing any of τ δ θ ζ followed by σ at speed in the middle of a word, and they will all end up sounding like a plain σ.[6] Greek spelling is just being honest about that.

Work through *ENTG* 6.6–8, including **Practice** 6.6 and 6.7, but not yet 6.8.

---

[5] The difference is that you make a sound with your vocal cords with *b* but not with *p*; *b* is therefore called 'voiced'.

[6] At the request of one student with a tender conscience, let me reassure you that you will not thereby open the Chamber of Secrets.

5.2.1 Consonant Groups

The footnote in *ENTG* 6.6 explains the above groupings of consonants and might help you remember them, as does Table 6.8. However, don't let this overwhelm you if you're not ready for it.

What all of these have in common is that you stop the air flow, and they are called 'stops'. With the *aspirated* ones, you then exhale.

Table 6.8 Stops

	unaspirated voiced	unaspirated unvoiced	aspirated	+ σ	NB
Lips	β	π	φ	ψ	πτ + σ → ψ
Teeth	δ	τ	θ	σ	ζ[7] + σ → σ
Throat	γ	κ	χ	ξ	σσ + σ → ξ

5.3 After *ENTG* 6.8: Building Your Verb (with Contract Verbs)

Contract verbs mean that we expand the table we met before (**EH 6** 3.5). The contract vowel goes at the end of the most basic stem. The suffixes in the other stems come after the contract vowel and lengthen it. Remember also that compound verbs will take a preposition at the very front (*ENTG* 4.4; 6.5.2). For example, see Table 6.9.

Table 6.9 Building Your Verb

Preposition	Augment	Stem			Thematic vowel	Ending proper	Result
		verb root	contract vowel	suffix			
		λυ	-	σ-	ε→ο	μεν	λύσομεν
		λυ	-	-	ε	τε	λύετε
	ἐ	λυ	-	σα-	ε→α	τε	ἐλύσατε
	ἐ	λυ	-	-	ε→ο	ν	ἔλυον
ἀπο→ἀπ	ε	λυ	-	-	ε	-	ἀπέλυε(ν)
		φιλ	ε→η	σ-	ε→ο	μεν	φιλήσομεν
		φιλ	ε	-	ε	τε	φιλεῖτε
	ἐ	φιλ	ε→η	σα-	ε→α	τε	ἐφιλήσατε
	ἐ	φιλ	ε	-	ε→ο	ν	ἐφίλουν

On the table at the end of *ENTG* 6.8 notice that the optional ν, which is there for pronunciation reasons, only follows -σι and -ε endings. It therefore never

---

[7] In older Greek, this was shorthand for σδ.

appears on the imperfect 3s of contract verbs (unlike non-contract verbs), but does continue to appear on the present and future 3p and the aorist 3s.

5.4 Embedding the Paradigms

Now apply the method described in **EH 2** 1.4.2.

1 Review all the tenses, checking against the table in 3.2. Don't stop when you get it right. Stop when you can no longer imagine getting it wrong.
2 Learn the rules above for contract verbs.
3 Write out all the tenses for contract verbs, without looking anything up, by applying the rules.
4 Check what you've written against the right pattern (*ENTG* 6.8), and use that to reinforce the rules.
5 Keep doing that until you never get it wrong.

Now tackle practice 6.8.

6 THE GREEK READING

Joseph & Aseneth *is a popular novella written in Greek not long before the NT, and simplified for you in the rest of this* Reader.[8]

The eponymous Joseph is the well-known patriarch of Genesis. God gave him the interpretation of Pharaoh's dreams, warning that all Egypt would enjoy seven years of plenty, followed by seven years of famine. Pharaoh put Joseph in charge of setting aside enough wheat during the plentiful harvests to get Egypt through the lean years. We meet him in the first year of plenty.

1:1 Ἐν τῷ πρώτῳ ἔτει ἔπεμψεν ὁ Φαραὼ τὸν Ἰωσὴφ εἰς τὴν γῆν Αἰγύπτου.

² καὶ ἄγουσιν οἱ τοῦ Ἰωσὴφ δοῦλοι αὐτὸν εἰς τὴν γῆν Ἡλιουπόλεως. ³ τότε

συνῆγον τὸν σῖτον του τόπου ὡς τὴν ἄμμον τῆς θαλάσσης.

⁴ Κατῴκει δὲ ἄνθρωπος ἐν Ἡλιουπόλει, δοῦλος τοῦ Φαραώ· καὶ αὐτὸς μόνος

εἶχεν ἀρχὴν τῶν σατραπῶν τοῦ Φαραώ. ⁵ καὶ ὁ ἄνθρωπος πλούσιος, καὶ αὐτὸς

---

[8] If you eventually want to go back and read the unedited original, it is available as a critical edition in the public domain (including on Google books) in P. Battifol, *Studia Patristica: Etudes d'ancienne littérature chrétienne* (Paris: Leroux, 1889), 39–87, and in more recent electronic editions (such as the one listed in the copyright notices of this *Reader*).

ἀγαπητὸς τοῦ Φαραώ, καὶ τὸ ὄνομα αὐτοῦ Πεντεφρός. καὶ Πεντεφρὸς ὁ ἱερεὺς Ἡλιουπόλεως. ⁶ καὶ εἶχεν θυγατέρα μεγάλην καὶ ὡραίαν ὑπὲρ τὰς ἐν τῇ γῇ.

⁷ Καὶ αὐτὴ οὐχ ὡς αἱ θυγάτερες τῶν Αἰγυπτίων, ἀλλὰ ὡς αἱ τῶν Ἑβραίων· ⁸ μεγάλη ὡς Σάρρα καὶ ὡραία ὡς Ῥεβέκκα καὶ καλὴ ὡς Ῥαχήλ· καὶ τὸ ὄνομα αὐτῆς Ἀσενέθ. ⁹ καὶ ἤδη ἐδόξαζον τὴν ψύχην αὐτῆς ἐν τῇ γῇ Ἡλιουπόλεως καὶ ἕως τῶν ἄκρων τοῦ Αἰγύπτου, καὶ ἐμνήστευον αὐτὴν οἱ υἱοὶ τῶν σατραπῶν καὶ τῶν κυριῶν. ¹⁰ καὶ ἔχουσιν ἔρις πολλὴ δι᾽ αὐτὴν καὶ ἐποίουν μάχας δι᾽ Ἀσενέθ. ¹¹ καὶ ἤκουσε περὶ αὐτῆς ὁ υἱὸς τοῦ Φαραὼ ὁ πρωτότοκος. Ὅτε ὁ Φαραὼ ἐκάλεσε τοὺς υἱοὺς αὐτοῦ, ὁ πρωτότοκος ᾔτησεν αὐτήν. ¹² πάντοτε ᾐτεῖ τὸν Φαραώ· Κράζει ἡ καρδία μου τῇ Ἀσενὲθ τῇ θυγατρὶ τοῦ Πεντεφροῦ τοῦ ἱερέως Ἡλιουπόλεως. ¹³ ἀλλὰ λέγει αὐτῷ ὁ Φαραώ·

Διὰ τί ζητεῖς θυγατερά; ¹⁴ ἀλλ᾽ ἡ θυγάτηρ τοῦ Ἰωακὶμ τοῦ κυρίου ἤδη ἐμνήστευσέ σοι, καὶ καλὴ μεγάλη ἐστίν, καὶ Ἰωακὶμ ἤνοιξέ σοι τὸν οἶκον αὐτοῦ. οὐ γράψομεν τῷ Πεντεφρῷ περὶ τῆς Ἀσενέθ, καὶ οὐ διώξεις τὴν ἀγάπην αὐτῆς. οὐκ ἐπείσεις με. ἐκήρυξα.

6.1 Vocabulary

Αἴγυπτος – Egypt
Αἰγύπτιος, ία, ιον – Egyptian
ἄκρον, ου, ἡ – end, limit, outer borders
ἄμμος, ου, ἡ – sand
ἀρχή, ῆς, ἡ – beginning, ruler, authority (the common idea is 'being first', whether in rank or in time)
Ἑβραῖος, ου, ὁ – a Hebrew
ἔρις – conflict (nom fem sing)

ἔτει – year (neut dat sing)
Ἡλιουπόλεως – Heliopolis (fem gen sing; dat Ἡλιουπόλει)
θυγάτηρ – daughter (fem nom sing; **θυγατερά** acc sing – you can work out the other forms from the article)
ἱερεύς – priest (masc nom sing; gen ἱερέως)
Ἰωακίμ (indeclinable) – Joakim
μάχη, ης, ἡ – battle, fighting

μνηστεύω – I woo, become engaged to
με – me
μου – my
ὄνομα – name (neut nom sing)
Πεντεφρός, οῦ, ὁ – Pentephres
πλούσιος, ία, ιον – wealthy
πρῶτος, η, ον – first
πρωτότοκος, ον – firstborn
Ῥαχήλ (indeclinable) – Rachel; together with Rebecca and Sarah, they were the Mothers of the nation, married to Abraham, Isaac and Jacob
Ῥεβέκκα, ας, ἡ – Rebecca
Σάρρα, ας, ἡ – Sarah
σατράπος, ου, ὁ – *satrap* (a regional governor)
σῖτος, ου, ὁ – wheat
σε – you (acc)
σοι – to you
τί – what?
Φαραώ – Pharaoh (indeclinable, but in this passage it will always have the article to help you)
χώρα, ας, ἡ – region
ὡραῖος, α, ον – beautiful

7 CONTEXTS FOR THE IMPERFECT TENSE

FURTHER READING: vS 198; WALLACE 540–53

As we saw in **EM 2** 4.1, the present tense combines 'ongoing' aspect with the present time. As we have seen at length in the **Extra Help** of this chapter, each indicative tense is a combination of a system, which communicates aspect, and a time value.[9]

The imperfect tense refers to an action presented as ongoing *back then*. Sometimes, the author might stress the fact that the action was not yet completed *back then*. By extension, it can refer to actions that hadn't even started yet *back then*. (Replace *back then* with *now* and this is exactly how the present tense works: **EM 2** 5.) See Figure 6.1.

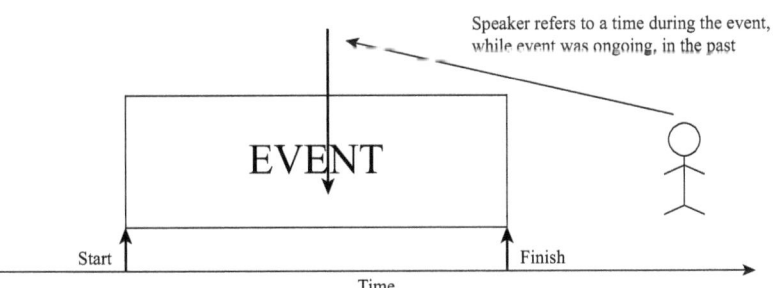

Figure 6.1 Imperfect Indicative

---

[9] For a summary and diagrams of aspect in all the systems and moods, see **EH 18** 4.2.

The good news is that about half of the contexts in which a present tense can occur do not apply to the imperfect. If you struggled to get your head around the present, you might find it easier to go back to it once you've understood the imperfect, which is much more straightforward. Nearly everything you learn below about the imperfect applies to the present.

7.1 Narrative Alternation with Aorist

FURTHER READING: *CGCG* 33.13, 48–53; RIJKSBARON 6.1

In a non-narrative context, such as a speech, a letter or a conversation, you can find the full range of Greek indicative tenses.

However, in narrative, the main verbs are aorists and imperfects, with the occasional historical present and pluperfect. *The aorist indicative is the default past tense*; usually, it simply tells us that something happened. It is when we see an imperfect that we need to ask why it isn't an aorist. Narrative is the easiest place to understand the significance of aspect; you can then apply it to non-narrative.

A story is usually told with a sequence of aorists telling you what happened in order. 'I got up, I had breakfast, I cycled to college.' Imperfects interspersed between them slow the story down and draw you in. An imperfect sets the scene for the next action. 'I cycled to college. *I was locking my bike.*' Clearly the story is incomplete: you're left waiting to find out what happened *while* I was locking my bike. 'I cycled to college. *I was locking my bike* when Bob warned me about the flood in the classrooms.' The imperfect 'I was locking' tells you that something interesting is about to happen (the warning about the flood), whereas the previous sequence of aorists was just moving the story along. The story can then continue with a sequence of aorists: 'I thanked him, I chose a different classroom', etc.

Multiple imperfects in sequence will usually refer to events that are all happening at the same time, combining to set the scene: 'I cycled to college. *I was locking my bike, the birds were chirping, Charlie was trying to clean his bike, passers-by used to greet us in those days, and we kept swatting at flies,* when Bob …' As you will see in the notes and questions on the **Greek Reading**, the first two chapters of *Joseph & Aseneth* consist almost entirely of imperfects, which work together to set the scene. They tell you what was going on at the point when the action begins in chapter 3.

All the following contexts for the imperfect are frequently used in past narrative; nearly all of them match contexts for the present tense, which you already know from **EM 2** 5: descriptive, iterative, habitual, customary, conative. However, as with the present, the Greek imperfect isn't telling you about the nature of the action (once, repeated, attempted, etc.); the point of the imperfect is to tell you that this was going on *then*.

7.2 Focus on Time

The imperfect tells you that something was going on at a point in the past; whether that something is a single event, or a habit, or a state, is not what the imperfect itself tells you, but is something that unfortunately has to be decided for English translation. Your aim is not to translate, but to understand what the Greek tells you. The Greek tells you that something *was happening back then*.

7.2.1 Descriptive

As with the descriptive present, the imperfect is used to describe a single past action, and to present it while it was going on.

> ὁ δὲ Πέτρος ἠκολούθει αὐτῷ ... **ἐκάθητο** Matt 26:58
> Peter <u>was following</u> him ... then **he sat down**.
> > The aorist ἐκάθητο completes Peter's following, and invites us to see what happened next.

> καὶ ἐτήρει καιρὸν τοῦ ἀπατῆσαι αὐτὴν ἀφ' ἧς ἡμέρας εἶδεν αὐτήν. Jdt 12:16
> He <u>was looking out</u> for an opportunity to deceive her from the day on which he had seen her.

> καὶ καθίσαντες ἐπὶ τὴν κεραίαν ἑκατέρωθεν οἱ μὲν ἐβόων, οἱ δ' ἔκοπτον τὰς τῶν μηρυμάτων ἀρχάς, Plutarch, *Cic.* 47.5
> [A flock of crows approaches Cicero's ship], and settled on both sides of the sail yard. Some of them <u>were shouting</u> (i.e. cawing), while others <u>were striking</u> (i.e. pecking) at the ends of the ropes.

> τὰ στέρνα ἔκοπτον ὡς ἐπὶ πένθει Appian, *Pun.* 77
> <u>they were beating</u> their chests because of their grief.

> αὐτὴ ἀπέθνησκεν Luke 8:42
> She was dying.

> Ἦν δὲ τὸ πάσχα καὶ τὰ ἄζυμα **μετὰ δύο ἡμέρας**· καὶ <u>ἐζήτουν</u> ... Mark 14:1
> The Passover and the Feast of Unleavened Bread were **two days later**, and <u>they were seeking</u> ...
> > Notice again the focus on telling you *when* this background activity was happening, so the imperfect sets the scene for the next action. Whether we think 'seeking' was a single act, or repeated, or something else, is a decision that comes from factors other than the imperfect.

As with the present tense, beware of translation and English idiom for states which you deem to be temporary ('descriptive') rather than settled ('customary'):

ἐπεθύμει γεμίσαι τὴν κοιλίαν αὐτοῦ … · καὶ οὐδεὶς ἐδίδου αὐτῷ. Luke 15:16
He longed to fill his stomach [with the pigs' swill], but no one gave him a thing.

The imperfects are setting the scene for what happened: he came to his senses *while* in such a desperate state of longing and while not being given anything.

But English insists on: 'He longed' not 'he was longing'; 'they gave' not 'they were giving'.

ἐνόμιζε δὲ συνιέναι τοὺς ἀδελφοὺς αὐτοῦ … · οἱ δὲ **οὐ συνῆκαν**. Acts 7:25
He supposed that his brothers would understand … but **they didn't understand**.

Again, the imperfect gives us a temporary state which sets the scene. The aorist resolves the situation and moves us on to the next thing.

'He supposed', not 'He was supposing'.

εἶχον δὲ **τότε** δέσμιον ἐπίσημον, λεγόμενον Βαραββᾶν Matt 27:16
they had **then** a well-known prisoner called Barabbas

They had him *then*; it sets the scene for the choice that's about to happen.

7.2.2 Iterative / Habitual / Customary

As with the present tense, the imperfect can refer to an action that was repeated (perhaps so often as to be a habit, or even a cultural norm). It does not necessarily describe the action at a time when it was taking place, but at a point in time during a period of time when it kept on happening.

καθ' ἡμέραν πρὸς ὑμᾶς ἐκαθεζόμην διδάσκων ἐν τῷ ἱερῷ Matt 26:55
Day after day, I would sit to teach in the temple
    habitual

ἐμνήσθημεν τοὺς ἰχθύας οὓς ἠσθίομεν ἐν Αἰγύπτῳ δωρεάν Num 11:5
we remember the fish which we used to eat for free in Egypt.
    habitual

ταῦτα ἔφερεν αὐτῷ βασιλεὺς Ἀμμὼν κατ' ἐνιαυτόν 2 Chr 27:5
the Ammonite king would bring these to him annually
    habitual

πολλοὶ πλούσιοι ἔβαλλον πολλά Mark 12:41
many rich people were putting in many [coins]

Iterative because a sequence of people were each doing it. The fact that the action is iterative comes from the plural subject, πολλοί. The point of the imperfect is that *while this was going on back then* ... a poor widow did something interesting, and Jesus responds to that.

καὶ ἐγενήθη ἀναγινώσκοντος Ἰουδεὶν τρεῖς σελίδας καὶ τέσσαρας, ἀπέτεμνεν αὐτὰς τῷ ξυρῷ τοῦ γραμματέως καὶ ἔριπτεν εἰς τὸ πῦρ Jer 43:23
whenever Jehudi would read three or four pages, he cut them off with a scribe's knife and threw them into the fire
Iterative, because Jehudi kept repeating the same action multiple times, which the context says explicitly.

ἀναβαίνοντας ... οἱ βάρβαροι ἐτόξευον καὶ ἔβαλλον. Xenophon, *Anab.* 4.2.12
while [the Greeks] were climbing up ... the barbarians would loose arrows and hurl [things].
Iterative: it wasn't a custom or a habit; on this one occasion, the barbarians kept on attacking to impede the Greeks, as long as the Greeks kept climbing.
The imperfect is setting the scene for what happened next: the barbarians failed to keep the Greeks at bay and fled.

οἱ δὲ Χαναναῖοι **τότε** κατῴκουν τὴν γῆν. Gen 12:6
the Canaanites were living in the land **then**.
This was their long-term abode, so this is a 'customary' imperfect, as far as English translation goes. But that's irrelevant to the Greek: the imperfect tells you that they were living there *then*, setting the scene for Abraham's visit to the land.

Authors usually want to be understood clearly, so you needn't fear that you're going to have to stare at every imperfect in Greek and wonder what it means from a menu of options. The likely meaning should be self-evident; where it isn't, the author has ways of being explicit. For example:

ἐλάλει Ἰωσὴφ **ἡμέραν ἐξ ἡμέρας** Gen 39:10
she kept speaking to Joseph, **day after day**.

7.3 Focus on Ongoing Aspect

As with the present tense, we turn now to situations where the author focusses on the action as 'not yet finished *back then*'. It helps to understand a distinction between two types of situation. Compare:

ἀνάγω – 'I lead up, I restore, I offer up' comes to end when the object has reached the 'up' destination, or been fully restored, or been offered. If you get halfway there, the action is obviously incomplete.

ἄγω – you can lead someone along indefinitely, and at some point you might stop. ἄγω by itself would never be seen as *incomplete*; it just happened for a while and then stopped.

When you stop doing ἀνάγω, you either say 'job done' or 'I didn't manage it'; neither applies to ἄγω. Some situations, such as ἀνάγω, **have an end in view**. Likewise, eating a meal, reading a whole book, teaching a lesson, running a marathon.

An author can use the imperfect to stress that 'not yet' (as with the present), but only if the action does have a natural endpoint that 'hasn't yet been reached'.[10] The action might *go on* to complete successfully, and we might already know this from our hindsight; but the focus of the imperfect is on the *then* when the action was not yet complete.

Figure 6.2 shows how the focus on ongoing aspect combines with time.

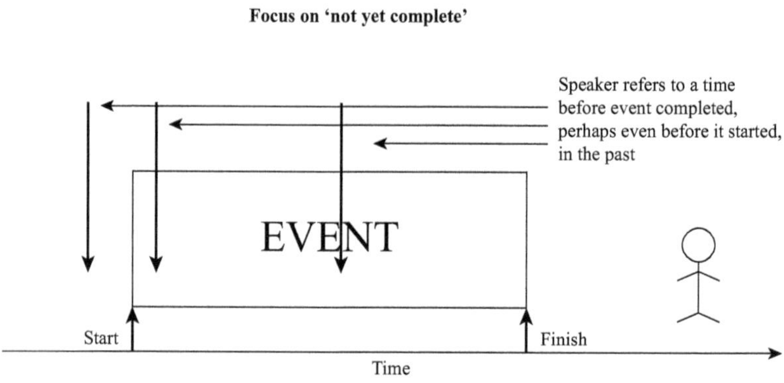

Focus on 'not yet complete'

Figure 6.2 Focus on Ongoing Aspect

7.3.1 Conative

As with the present tense, the imperfect can be used in a conative context. This works for verbs that have a natural endpoint, in a context where there is some impediment.

καταλοίποις τῶν ἱερέων οἳ ἦσαν φοβερίζοντές με 2 Esd 16:14
the rest of the priests who were trying to frighten me.

---

[10] Different verb types are explained in more detail when we cover the aspect in other moods: see **EM 8** 5.1.1.

ἔμβλεπον εἰς ἀντίλημψιν ἀνθρώπων καὶ οὐκ ἦν Sir 51:7
I tried to see [i.e. 'looked for', which has an endpoint, rather than 'saw', which doesn't] help from people, but there wasn't any.

ἔπειθον παρακαθεζόμενοι καὶ λέγοντες· ... Mart. Pol. 8:2
sitting next to him, they tried to persuade him, saying: ...
The ensuing dialogue shows that they didn't succeed.

ξύμβασίν ... ἔπρασσε Thucydides, P.W. 3.75.1
he tried to bring about a reconciliation
The ensuing narrative shows that he failed.

ὡς οἷόν τε ἦν ἐκώλυον 4 Macc 4:7
[complaining and opposing] to the extent that they were able, they tried to prevent it.
The idiom οἷός τέ εἰμι means 'to be able', and makes the conative sense explicit here.

ὁ δὲ Ἰωάννης διεκώλυεν αὐτὸν λέγων Matt 3:14
Now John tried to stop him, saying: ...
[The ensuing dialogue ends with John not succeeding in preventing Jesus from being baptised.]
Matthew uses λέγων to tell us that John 'was preventing him, by saying ...'. That means that he's describing the action of preventing as in progress, rather than entirely future. An unsuccessful action in progress, rather than a purely future action, is all that stands between conative and voluntative – a fine line that isn't always clear.

As ever, authors have ways of making a conative sense explicit:

ἐζήτει **ἀνελεῖν** Μωυσῆν Exod 2:15
he was trying **to kill** Moses

7.3.2. Voluntative

The 'not yet successful' sense, which comes to the fore in the conative, can be applied to actions that haven't even started yet. Someone wants to, or is about to, do something. However, unlike the conative, this need not cast doubt on whether it will succeed or not. It isn't always easy to decide which of the two is in view.[11]

Both conative and voluntative apply to actions that have a natural endpoint which hadn't yet been reached. The difference is that *conative* had begun the action, it was meeting resistance, and its completion was in doubt. *Voluntative*

---

[11] Be aware that many authors call both these uses 'conative'. Both the conative and voluntative uses of the present are quite rare, whereas they are common enough for the imperfect.

hadn't begun yet and needn't have been meeting resistance or be unlikely to complete.

> εἰ διαλέκτων γένεσιν αὐτὸ μόνον ἐδήλου Philo, *Confusion*, 191
> If <u>he had intended to reveal</u> only the creation of languages
>> Context: a discussion over what was intended.

> καὶ ἐκάλουν αὐτὸ ἐπὶ τῷ ὀνόματι τοῦ πατρὸς αὐτοῦ Ζαχαρίαν. Luke 1:59
> <u>they wanted to name</u> him after his father, Zechariah
>> The ensuing narrative shows that they have expressed the intention to name him, but haven't managed it yet.

A voluntative sense can be made explicit:

> Ῥαχὴλ κλαίουσα τὰ τέκνα αὐτῆς, καὶ <u>οὐκ ἤθελε</u> **παρακληθῆναι**, ὅτι οὐκ εἰσί. Matt 2:18
> Rachel weeping for her children, and she <u>didn't want</u> **to be comforted**, because they are no more.

7.3.3 Idiom: Desiderative

With verbs that in themselves mean 'I wish', an author might use the imperfect to refer to a present desire, to present it in a less blunt and direct way. English has similar idioms:

> ἐγὼ ἐβουλόμην πρὸς ἐμαυτὸν κατέχειν Phlm 13
> <u>I would like</u> to keep him for myself.

> ἤθελον δὲ παρεῖναι πρὸς ὑμᾶς ἄρτι Gal 4:20
> <u>I should wish</u> to be with you already.

The sense of desire is already explicit in the meaning of the verb itself.

7.3.4 Inceptive

The aspect of the present system can point to the beginning of an action, as we have seen with the conative present and imperfect, for example. The imperfect, in some contexts, seems to indicate that 'at that point, the action began'.

> ἡ δὲ πενθερὰ Σίμωνος κατέκειτο πυρέσσουσα, καὶ εὐθέως λέγουσιν αὐτῷ περὶ αὐτῆς· καὶ προσελθὼν ἤγειρεν αὐτήν, κρατήσας τῆς χειρὸς αὐτῆς· καὶ ἀφῆκεν αὐτὴν ὁ πυρετὸς εὐθέως, καὶ <u>διηκόνει αὐτοῖς</u>. Mark 1:30–1
> Simon's mother-in-law was laid up with a fever, and straight away they told him about her: so he approached her, raised her up taking her hand, and immediately the fever left her alone. <u>That's when she began to serve</u> them.

This use might be less common than is often claimed. Many imperfects will be used to describe actions that follow as a result of a previous action. That means that of course they *begin* at that point: regardless of whether they are presented as an imperfect or an aorist. Remember that we want to ask what the author means by choosing the imperfect. The question is whether the author intends to highlight the *beginning* of the action, or is using the imperfect for another reason: see the discussion in **EM 6** 7.5.3.

As with the conative use of the present, a use can be very rare but nonetheless real. Certainly in the other moods, we will see this inceptive sense attach to the present system.

7.4 Contexts for the Present System: Summary Table

Table 6.10 summarises the tenses that an author can use to express certain meanings in specific contexts.

You might want to go over the **Greek Reading** again now, using the questions on the **Extra Material** to help you, and leave the following section until you have more time.

7.5 What the Imperfect Does and Does Not Tell You

Feel free to skip this section for now, and return to it later.

Let me give you a couple of cautions about the imperfect, which all add up to the same idea that *ENTG* and this *Reader* want to keep reinforcing. Make it your aim to read Greek, understanding what it is (and isn't) telling you. Translating is not your aim. Keep asking *why* an author chose an imperfect.

7.5.1 Interpret the Greek, Not Your Translation

We have seen that English will force you to translate in certain ways. It is one reason for the adage 'something is lost in translation'. Make sure that you understand the Greek text that you're reading, rather than trying to understand your English translation instead.

> ἔλεγον οὖν οἱ Ἰουδαῖοι, Ἴδε πῶς ἐφίλει αὐτόν. John 11:36
> Some of the Jews were saying, 'Look at how he loved [Greek **imperfect** rendered by English **past simple**] him.'

They go on to wonder why he wasn't able to save someone whom he clearly loved. John has anticipated this with a scene-setting imperfect before the action began:

> ἠγάπα δὲ ὁ Ἰησοῦς τὴν Μάρθαν καὶ τὴν ἀδελφὴν αὐτῆς καὶ τὸν Λάζαρον v5
> Jesus loved [Greek **imperfect** rendered by English **past simple**] Martha, her sister and Lazarus.

Table 6.10 Present System Contexts

Context	Present tense	Imperfect tense	Notes
Focus on the time of the action			
Descriptive	Do you hear what these are saying?	Peter was following him	
Durative (English idiom)	I have been with you **for twenty years**	N/A	
Iterative / Habitual / Customary	He keeps on falling into the fire.	they were casting out many demons	
Gnomic	Everyone who asks receives	N/A	
Performative	I command you	N/A	What you say is the act itself.
Focus on the action as incomplete			
Conative	You are **trying** to be justified by the law.	they **tried** to persuade him	Must have a natural endpoint, and face some resistance.
Voluntative	We **aim to** persuade people.	they **wanted** to name him	Must have a natural endpoint.
Desiderative	N/A	I should wish to be with you	Only verbs of desire.
Inceptive	N/A	That's when she began to serve them.	Rare.
Futuristic	he is coming to meet you (future endpoint) I am **about to** go to Jerusalem (entirely future) the Son of Man is coming (prophetic)	N/A	Must have a natural endpoint. Only in context of prophecy.
Other contexts			
Historical	They led him out, to crucify him	N/A	Only in context of past narrative.
Perfective	I have come	N/A	Handful of verbs only.
Immediative	N/A	Then she was serving them.	Older Greek, possibly still in use.

(Uses which are very rare, or matters of English translation, are in italics.)

The imperfect tells us that the narrative that follows, and which Jesus explains in verse 4, happens at a time when Jesus loved not only Lazarus, but his sisters too. Perhaps the point is that his perplexing actions weren't done for lack of love; or perhaps it is more positive: his teaching and demonstration of the Resurrection are an act of love for them. The reason for this imperfect is for us to work out, whereas any reasonable English translation will hide it.

7.5.2 Not Necessarily Repeated

As we saw with the present tense, the imperfect can be used of an action that is repeated, and some will insist that this must be what it means. We have seen plenty of examples showing that this is not so. Every tense, and every aspectual stem, can be used for single or repeated actions, as we will see in the following chapters.

When you read Jesus' prayer for his enemies to be forgiven on the cross, Luke tells you what Jesus was doing with an imperfect: ἔλεγεν (Luke 23:34). Discard the idea that it *must* mean '*he kept* saying this *over and over*'. Such a notion would come from the context or be stated explicitly, not from the imperfect itself. Even if that is what was going on, that will not be what the *imperfect* is telling you. Ask yourself *why* Luke chose an imperfect when he could perfectly well have used an aorist. Look at the wider passage and see why Luke uses an imperfect. His prayer becomes poignant as the background to the callous behaviour of the soldiers gambling for his clothes while he hung there praying for them.

7.5.3 Not 'Inceptive' All That Often

Sometimes, the imperfect describes an action that begins as a consequence of the previous aorist. Some would say that the imperfect can communicate the idea of beginning an action (inceptive),[12] while more recently some have questioned this.[13] I don't want to rule an inceptive use of the imperfect out of court entirely; nevertheless, I would urge you to consider carefully what else an imperfect might be doing in that context.

In English, compare: 'I got the mower, I *was cutting* the grass' with 'I got the mower, I *cut* the grass.' *Either way*, cutting the grass must begin after I got the mower; the alternative is impossible. The point of the imperfect is therefore not 'beginning'. To make that point I would say 'I got the mower, I *began to cut* the grass.' The point of the imperfect, rather, is to set up what happened during the cutting. It makes you ask, 'What happened *while I was cutting the grass*?'

In the same way, when Greek wants to tell you that an action begins, it uses ἄρχομαι (**EM 7** 5.1.2). This doesn't mean that the imperfect isn't used in contexts where an action begins: it often will, but that's not necessarily the point of the

---

[12] A good description is in Wallace 544–5.
[13] Rijksbaron 6.2.3; vS 198e.

imperfect. The imperfect will usually be doing one of the jobs we have identified earlier in this chapter, most often setting up the following action. Let's see some examples.

Immediately after Jesus tells the disciples to watch out for the yeast of the Pharisees, we find:

> οἱ δὲ <u>διελογίζοντο</u> ἐν ἑαυτοῖς, λέγοντες "Ὅτι ἄρτους οὐκ ἐλάβομεν. Matt 16:7
> But <u>they were discussing</u> among themselves, saying: 'It's because we didn't have loaves.'

The point isn't that the disciples *began* a discussion (though that is what happened; every action has a beginning, and they can hardly have discussed the meaning of his question before they asked it), but that *they were discussing this* when Jesus sets them straight in the very next sentence:

> γνοὺς δὲ ὁ Ἰησοῦς εἶπεν αὐτοῖς ... (v8)
> But Jesus, knowing that, said to them ...

Even when the context highlights the beginning of the action, that's not the point of the imperfect. Consider:

> **ἀπὸ τότε** <u>ἐζήτει</u> εὐκαιρίαν ἵνα αὐτὸν παραδῷ Matt 26:16
> **from then on**, <u>he kept looking</u> for an opportunity to betray him

You might think that the imperfect must be inceptive because we're told expressly 'from then on', but notice two things. First, even with ἀπὸ τότε an author doesn't trust us to know that the meaning is inceptive, and must supply that expressly:

> **Ἀπὸ τότε** <u>ἤρξατο</u> ὁ Ἰησοῦς <u>δεικνύειν</u> Matt 16:21
> **From then on** Jesus <u>began teaching</u>
> See also Matt 4:17.

Second, you find ἀπὸ τότε in contexts where the meaning can't be inceptive:

> **ἀπὸ τότε** ἡ βασιλεία τοῦ θεοῦ εὐαγγελίζεται Luke 16:16
> **Since then** God's kingdom <u>has been preached</u> [the translation is 'durative', **EM 2** 5.1.2]

What then is the purpose of the imperfect in Matt 26:16? It puts everything in vv17–46 in suspense, until we get the resolution of Judas' attempt in v47: Judas came and betrayed him. The institution of the Lord's Supper, the prediction of Peter's denial, and Jesus' prayer prior to his passion are all set against the background of the time when Judas was seeking to betray him. It comes to an end with Jesus announcing that 'his betrayer had arrived' (v46). Judas may have wanted to betray Jesus, but it was Jesus who kept the initiative, and continued teaching until he was good and ready.

7.5.4 Immediative

FURTHER READING: RIJKSBARON 6.2.3; SMYTH 1899

In older Greek, the imperfect can be used to describe the scene that results from the action. The imperfect will immediately follow that action (hence the name),[14] but its purpose is to paint a picture of the resulting state of affairs.

> [After a description of competitions being set up and prizes promised:]
> ταῦτα μὲν δὴ προείρητό τε καὶ <u>ἠσκεῖτο</u> ἡ στρατιά. Xenophon, *Cyr.* 2.1.24
> These, then, had been promised, and the army <u>was training</u>.

This function of the imperfect doesn't seem to be discussed in grammars of NT Greek, but it does seem to occur in the Greek of the period:

> οἱ δὲ λαβόντες τὸν κύριον <u>ὤθουν</u> αὐτὸν τρέχοντες Gos. Pet. 3.6
> So, once they had taken the Lord, <u>they were pushing</u> him at a run.
> NB: Λαβόντες here isn't nominal, οἱ ... λαβόντες; rather οἱ δὲ indicates the change of subject [*ENTG* 9.4.3], and λαβόντες is adverbial, qualifying ὤθουν.

It might shed light on some places where an 'inceptive' sense is usually seen:

> ἡ δὲ πενθερὰ Σίμωνος κατέκειτο πυρέσσουσα, καὶ εὐθέως λέγουσιν αὐτῷ περὶ αὐτῆς· καὶ προσελθὼν ἤγειρεν αὐτήν, κρατήσας τῆς χειρὸς αὐτῆς· καὶ ἀφῆκεν αὐτὴν ὁ πυρετὸς εὐθέως, <u>καὶ διηκόνει</u> αὐτοῖς. Mark 1:30–1
> Simon's mother-in-law was laid up with a fever, and straight away they told him about her: so he approached her, raised her up taking her hand, and immediately the fever left her alone. <u>Then she was serving</u> them.

If this is 'immediative', then the imperfect isn't setting up the following action. Rather it's showing you the end result that followed immediately. It paints the resulting scene.

The point wouldn't be that she *began* to serve them, as though that's what they had been waiting for, and Jesus' healing fixed that problem. Rather, look at this lady before and after Jesus intervened: lying in bed helpless, then well enough to serve others.

---

[14] Do not confuse this with the 'immediative' sense of the present stem in the other moods, which we will meet later.

CHAPTER 7

Moods
—
Aorist Indicative

> **How to Use This Chapter**
>
> In this chapter, you will meet different Greek verb 'moods'. Simply work through the chapter of *ENTG*, consulting the **Extra Help** below as you complete each section. If you invested time in the **Extra Help** in Chapter 6, you will reap the benefits in this chapter.
>
> In the **Extra Material** we'll examine the contexts for the aorist tense.

1 MOODS, IMPERATIVE AND INFINITIVE

1.1 After *ENTG* 7.1: Idea of Moods

You might find these short summaries of the moods helpful:

> **Indicative** *describes* the world.
>
> > (It doesn't have to deal with the world accurately or truthfully. It includes questions.)
>
> **Imperative** *changes* the world.
>
> > '*Learn* your paradigms!'
>
> **Infinitive** is a *noun* which expresses the idea of a verb.
>
> > 'What's your favourite thing? Do you love apples?' 'No: I love *to read*.'
>
> **Participle** is an *adjective* which expresses the idea of a verb.
>
> > Was the man slow? No, he was a *running* man.

You will now see the pay-off of how the verb fits together in the last chapter (**EH 6 2**). Every new mood is simply a new row in our verb table. The table is updated as the verb grows, so do look at 'The Greek Verb So Far', in the **Online Material** for Chapter 7.

For example, in *ENTG* 7.1, you read that there is no *imperfect* in the **other moods**. That's because the moods apply to each **system** (present, aorist, future).[1] The imperfect is not a system, but is the combination of the present system with *past* time in the indicative. The online table shows you this at a glance: the imperfect is a cell, not a column.

Likewise, 'Parsing Made Simple' (**EH 6** 3) will now make parsing the verbs in this chapter a doddle. The augment marks *past time* for each system in the indicative (**EH 6** 2.2.3). The aorist *only* has the augment in the indicative. Remember that the labels we give to indicative tenses are a shorthand for the system plus time (**EH 6** 2.2.4).

1.1.1 Parsing and Meaning: Aspect in the Other Moods

Parsing like that points you towards meaning. What do the two tenses you have met in the 'present' system (present tense and imperfect tense) have in common? Regardless of time, they present the action as 'ongoing'. That's the meaning of everything in that system: the infinitive, imperative and participle all present the action as ongoing. By contrast with the imperfect, what does the aorist tense mean? It presents the action 'simply'. That's the contrast all the way through: the aorist infinitive, imperative and participle refer to an action 'simply'.

For a quick reminder of how aspect, time and tenses relate, see **EH 6** 4.2. Remember that 'ongoing' in Greek covers two situations that we distinguish in English: an action happening right now is ongoing; a habit is also ongoing now: you dance habitually, even if you're not dancing *right* now. When the present of the other moods is 'ongoing', it can be for either reason, because Greek doesn't distinguish between them.

1.2 After *ENTG* 7.2: The Imperative

1.2.1 After *ENTG* 7.2.1: Formation

The 2s aorist imperative is the one rule breaker: it does not change the thematic vowel to an α. No one knows why.

The 2s present imperative is blank, leaving just the thematic vowel ε, but without an optional ν (cf. the imperfect and aorist indicative 3s, **EH 6** 3.1).

1.2.2 After *ENTG* 7.2.2: Aorist vs Present

The choice between present and aorist is central to the Greek verb. In English, we have a similar choice in the indicative tenses (**EH 6** 2.1). What is much harder for us to grasp is that Greek also has this in the 'other moods': a choice of ways of saying: '*close* the door', 'I like *to eat*'.

---

[1] For now, 'system' and 'stem' are interchangeable.

Please resist the temptation to get so excited by this that you see significance in the choice of every imperative or infinitive, and start correcting the translations or informing your hearers of what is lost in translation. You need to have read a lot more Greek text and got a feel for how this choice works, with the help of some instruction, before rushing in where angels fear to tread. We cover this in the **Extra Material**, beyond *ENTG*.

As you saw in Chapter 6, *every* form of every Greek verb, without exception, is part of one of the systems, and therefore built on the stem of that system. Every Greek verb form has a surname, even the imperatives: they're either *present* imperative or *aorist* imperative.

1.3 After *ENTG* 7.3: The Infinitive

Once again, *every* form of every Greek verb, without exception, is part of one of the systems, and therefore built on the stem of that system. That's why every Greek verb form has a surname. What that means in the infinitive is a matter for further study (**EM 8** 5).

2 AFTER *ENTG* 7.4: THE PARTICIPLE

If you learn the verb as I'm advising you, the paradigms for participles become the easiest thing. You are simply combining the stems of verbs (which you already know how to do) with the endings of adjectives (which you also know how to do). You haven't yet met all the forms of adjectives, which is why you don't *yet* recognise the endings on participles.

2.1 After *ENTG* 7.4.1: Formation

You have begun to see that some endings are duplicates of each other, such as -ας in the 1st declension, which can be both genitive singular and accusative plural of some nouns. It reappeared in the aorist indicative, 2s, and here as the aorist masculine nominative singular participle. Likewise, -ων is the genitive plural ending on *all* nouns, but is also the present masculine nominative singular participle.

2.2 After *ENTG* 7.4.2: Meaning

2.2.1 Parsing and Meaning

Get into the habit of parsing the participle in two separate parts, each telling you something different.

1 The participle is an adjective like any other, so parse for: gender, case and number. (You will only meet masculine and nominative for now, but get into the habit of including gender and case in your parsing, to reinforce the fact that you're parsing an adjective.)

Once you parse an adjective, you know what it agrees with. You then look up the adjective to find out what it means: strong, blue, happy. These adjectives have the meaning of a verb, and like all verbs, they have a surname, so that needs to be part of the meaning. So:

2 Parse the verb stem: is it the aorist stem or the present stem? And of which verb?

That gives you the meaning of the verb, which might be 'running' or 'having painted' or 'dancing' or 'having eaten'. *ENTG* 7.4.2 explains further. Once again, *every* form of every Greek verb, without exception, is part of one of the systems, and therefore built on the stem of that system. That's why every Greek verb has a surname: even the participles.

2.2.2 These Are 'Adverbial' Participles

You may feel that the uses in *ENTG* 7.4.2 aren't like adjectives at all. We'll meet more obvious ways of using the participle like an adjective in later chapters, but even here you can see it. Look at the examples at the end of *ENTG* 7.4.2:

> Περιπατῶν Ἰησοῦς παρὰ τὴν θάλασσαν τῆς Γαλιλαίας εἶδεν δύο ἀδελφούς. Matt 4:18

Analyse the trunk of the tree:

> Subject: Ἰησοῦς (Jesus)
> Verb: εἶδεν (he saw)
> Direct Object: δύο ἀδελφούς (two brothers)

Ἰησοῦς εἶδεν δύο ἀδελφούς – Jesus saw two brothers.

Now tell me more about Ἰησοῦς, by adding a branch to it (a modifier). You could imagine a number of adjectives plausibly: 'Exhausted Jesus saw two brothers' or 'Delighted Jesus saw two brothers.'

Instead, we have 'Walking-by-the-lake-of-Galilee Jesus saw two brothers.'

Περιπατῶν παρὰ τὴν θάλασσαν τῆς Γαλιλαίας is a branch modifying Ἰησοῦς like any other adjective. However, because you are modifying the subject of the verb, it is easier to think of it as modifying the verb itself. 'Jesus *saw (while walking by the lake)* two brothers.'

Likewise with Mark 6:16 ἀκούσας ὁ Ἡρῴδης ἔλεγεν. The trunk of the tree is ὁ Ἡρῴδης (subject) ἔλεγεν (verb). The branch is ἀκούσας modifying the subject. 'The having-heard Herod said'. It makes more sense as modifying the verb, since ὁ Ἡρῴδης is the subject of the verb, so 'Herod *said (after he heard)*'.

Because these participles are modifying the *verb*, they are called ad*verbial*.

> When a participle functions like a normal adjective, it will follow the normal rules concerning the article: it will lack it when predicative; it will lack it when the noun lacks it; it will have it when it is attributive and the noun has it (**EH 5** 1.3.1).
> When it is *adverbial* it *never* has the article.

2.2.3 Verb Systems, Not Tenses

As we saw in **EH 6** 3.2, the labels 'present' and 'aorist' are unfortunate descriptions for the stems/systems. The labels are borrowed from one indicative tense in each system. However, in the other moods you can see that there is nothing 'present' about the present imperative or participle. Rather, the 'ongoing' aspect is what is relevant here: the 'present' participle describes an action that was ongoing at the time of the main verb. The 'aorist' participle describes an action simply at the time of the main verb: this 'simple' aspect presents the action as a competed whole, which means that the action is complete before the main verb. (See **Key Grammar** in *ENTG* 7.4.2.)

Do not think of the other moods as having 'tenses'; tenses only occur in the indicative as a combination of stem and time. The labels 'present' and 'aorist' in the other moods are not tenses, but indicate the system of the verb, which communicates its aspect.

2.3 After *ENTG* 7.4.3: Participles with Objects

As an adjective, the participle is a modifier (or branch). What makes it so flexible is that, as a verb, it can turn an entire 'tree' into a 'branch'. *ENTG* will introduce more of this later, but it might help you make sense of participles with objects for now.

If you have two sentences (trees) with the same *subject*, you can turn the verb in one of them into a participle. You then hang that branch off the other tree, and you have a 'complex sentence'.

When you turn that verb into a participle, you need to decide whether it will be present or aorist; at that point, the tense of the original verb is irrelevant. If the action of that verb is simultaneous with the verb in the main tree, you want a 'present' participle; if the action is complete before that of the other verb, then 'aorist'.

Taking the examples at the end of *ENTG* 7.4.2 again, here are the two original sentences:

>Ἰησοῦς περιπάτει παρὰ τὴν θάλασσαν.

>Ἰησοῦς βλέπει ἀδελφούς.

If he saw while walking (simultaneous action):

>Περιπατῶν παρὰ τὴν θάλασσαν, Ἰησοῦς βλέπει ἀδελφούς.

Otherwise:

>Περιπατήσας παρὰ τὴν θάλασσαν, Ἰησοῦς βλέπει ἀδελφούς.

And again:

>ὁ Ἡρώδης ἤκουσεν.

>ὁ Ἡρώδης ἔλεγεν.

ἀκούσας ὁ **Ἡρῴδης** ἔλεγεν.

or, if the actions were simultaneous:

ἀκουῶν ὁ **Ἡρῴδης** ἔλεγεν.

2.4 After *ENTG* 7.5: Participles as Nouns

Remember that 'adjectives as nouns' is really just an attributive adjective with an implicit noun (**EH 5** 1.4). Since participles are adjectives, they can also be used with an implicit noun (meaning man/person, woman or thing).

Περιπατῶν Ἰησοῦς	'Walking Jesus'
ὁ περιπατῶν	'the walking man'

Please heed the hint in *ENTG* 7.5 and the section on 'Good English' in *ENTG* 7.4.2. The NT has already been translated accurately plenty of times. You're not aiming to improve on that, but to learn to read what a translation cannot convey. Learn to understand the Greek text itself; then put that into good English as best you can.

3 THE GREEK READING

The story so far ...

Pharaoh has sent Joseph into the country, and he approaches the grand city of Heliopolis. The ranking governor, a favourite of Pharaoh's, who is also the local priest (Pentephres) has a daughter (Aseneth). We learn that she is much more Hebrew than Egyptian, but that her beauty is causing fighting to break out among her suitors, who are a Who's Who of Egyptian nobility. Finally, her fame reaches Pharaoh's firstborn, who pesters his father on every occasion to 'get her for me'. Pharaoh reminds his brat-in-chief of a little something called 'your engagement to the daughter of Lord Ioakeim' and considers the matter closed. But is it ...?

2:1 Οἱ σατράποι ἔπεμπον ἀποστόλους εἰς αὐτήν, μετὰ τῶν υἱῶν αὐτῶν, καὶ ἔλεγον αὐτοῖς·

² Μαρτυρήσατε περὶ τῆς δικαιοσύνης τοῦ υἱοῦ μου. μὴ μετανοεῖτε ἀλλὰ κηρύσσετε παρρησίᾳ.

³ Ἀλλὰ οὐκ ἤθελεν ἡ Ἀσενὲθ ἄνθρωπον. ⁴ ἀνάγοντες οἱ ἀπόστολοι τοὺς υἱοὺς εἰς αὐτήν, οὐκ ἔπειθον αὐτήν. ⁵ ἔβλεπε τοῖς ὀφθαλμοῖς τοὺς υἱοὺς ὀπίσω τῶν

ἀποστόλων, ἀλλὰ ἐδόκει πρόβατα βλέπειν. ⁶ οὐ παρελάμβανε τοὺς υἱοὺς. ⁷ ὁ Πεντεφρὸς οὐκ ἀπεκάλυψε τὴν Ἀσενέθ· οὐκ ἄνθρωπος ἐθεώρησεν αὐτήν.

3:1 Καὶ ἦγον τὸν Ἰωσὴφ πρὸς τὸν τόπον. ² καὶ ἐγγίζων Ἡλιουπόλει, Ἰωσὴφ ἔπεμψεν ἀποστόλους αὐτοῦ πρὸς τὸν Πεντεφρὸν καὶ ἐλάλησαν λέγοντες·

³ Ἐν τῷ οἴκῳ σου ἤθελον κατοικῆσαι σήμερον, καὶ δεῖ αἰτῆσαι ἄρτον.

⁴ Καὶ ἀκούσας ὁ Πεντεφρὸς χαίρων λέγει·

Εὐλογητὸς ὁ θεὸς τοῦ Ἰωσήφ.

⁵ Καὶ καλέσας ὁ Πεντεφρὸς δοῦλον ἐλάλησεν αὐτῷ ἐντολήν. ὁ δοῦλος ὁ ἔχων τὴν ἐξουσίαν ἐπὶ τῆς οἰκίας προσέχων τῷ κυρίῳ αὐτοῦ ἤκουσε τὸν λόγον·

⁶ Χαῖρε· δεῖπνον μέγαν ποίησον. σπεῦσον.

Μέλλουσιν ἀγεῖν ἄρτι τὸν Ἰωσὴφ τὸν τοῦ θεοῦ ἀγαπητὸν εἰς τὴν οἰκίαν· εὐλόγει τὸν θεόν.

⁷ Καὶ βλέψαντες οἱ δοῦλοι τῆς Ἀσενέθ τὸν Πεντεφρὸν ἀπεκάλυψαν εὐαγγέλιον τῇ Ἀσενέθ λέγοντες·

⁸ Ὁ Πεντεφρὸς καὶ ἡ γυνὴ αὐτοῦ εἰσιν ἐν τῇ οἰκίᾳ.

⁹ Καὶ ἡ Ἀσενὲθ ἤθελε βλέπειν αὐτοὺς. καὶ ἡ Ἀσενὲθ ἐλάλησε τοῖς δούλοις·

¹⁰ Λύσατε τὰ ἱμάτια καὶ δήσατε τὴν καλὴν στολὴν τῇ ἁγίᾳ ζώνῃ.

¹¹ Καὶ ἠκολούθει πάντοτε ἡ Ἀσενὲθ τοῖς τῶν Αἰγυπτίων θεοῖς καὶ ἐποίει τὰς ἐντολὰς αὐτῶν. ¹² (ἀλλὰ ποῦ εἰσιν οἱ τίμιοι λίθοι οἱ ἔχοντες τὰ τῶν εἰδώλων θηρία;) ¹³ ᾔτει τοὺς δούλους τοὺς λίθους, καὶ ὑπῆγον οἱ δοῦλοι ζήτουντες τοὺς λίθους, ἀλλὰ οὐκ ἔβλεψαν αὐτοὺς. ¹⁴ καὶ ἔδησεν ἡ Ἀσενὲθ θηρία ἐπὶ τῆς κεφαλῆς αὐτῆς.

3.1 Vocabulary

Αἰγύπτιος, ία, ιον – Egyptian
γυνή, ἡ – wife
δεῖπνος, ου, ὁ – dinner party
εἴδωλον, ου, τό – idol
εὐλογητός, ή, όν – blessed (in the sense of 'praised', rather than 'happy', cf. μακάριος)
ζώνη, ης, ἡ – belt
λίθος, ου, ὁ – stone

μου – my
Πεντεφρός, οῦ, ὁ – Pentephres
σατράπος, ου, ὁ – *satrap* (a regional governor)
σου – your
σπεύδω – I hurry
στολή, ῆς, ἡ – robe
τίμιος, α, ον – precious
χαίρω – I rejoice

4 ACCENTS

4.1 Contract Verbs

FURTHER READING: VS 83

In **EM 2** 3.1, we saw that verb accents are 'regressive' (rising in pitch as early as possible), but that the accents on contract verbs are resolved *before* the contraction. Below, we see that this helps us to distinguish two uses of the ει ending: present indicative 3s vs present imperative 2s.

Present imperative 2s: present stem + contract vowel + thematic vowel + ending proper

φιλ - ε - ε - –

If the pitch rises on φιλ, it falls on the contract ε, leaving a single short vowel after the fall, which meets the rule of limitation (**EM 1** 3.4).

φίλ - ὲ - ε - –

When we resolve the contraction, the rise in pitch is not in the contracted vowels:

φίλ - ὲ + ε - –

The accent therefore is unaffected:

φίλει

Present indicative 3s: present stem + contract vowel + ending.[2]

φιλ - ε - ει

If the pitch were to rise on φιλ, it would fall on the contract ε, leaving more than a single short vowel after the fall, which breaks the rule of limitation (**EM 1** 3.4).

---

[2] Remember that the singular principal indicative endings have the contract vowel and the ending baked together.

It must rise on the contract ε, and fall on the whole of the following syllable, the diphthong ει.

φιλ - έ - εὶ

When we resolve the contraction, the rise in pitch is within the contracted vowels, as is the fall:

φιλ - έ + εὶ

The result is a circumflex accent:[3]

φιλεῖ

Thus, the accent distinguishes φίλει from φιλεῖ.

5 CONTEXTS FOR THE AORIST INDICATIVE

FURTHER READING: vS 199; WALLACE 554–65

The aorist is very easy to understand, yet often made unnecessarily complicated. Apart from a couple of easy idioms and extremely rare uses, the aorist tells you that something happened, no more and no less. That 'something' can be one action or a series of actions, just as we saw with the present and imperfect.

The aorist is the tense you use to tell you that something happened without any further nuances. If you want to say that the event was attempted, or difficult, or enduringly relevant, you need a different tense.

We'll handle the few idioms and exceptions in **EM 7** 5.3. Apart from those, what you mostly need with the aorist is *not* a lot of different labels (on which **EM 7** 5.2).

5.1 Past Action, 'Simple' Aspect

As we saw in **EH 6** 2.2, the aorist indicative combines two pieces of information:

- an action is presented simply (aorist stem)
- the action is in the past (historical tense).

Its typical use is, therefore, to refer to a past action simply; it refers to the whole action, including the beginning and the end; there is no focus on any point of time within that. It is the default past tense. Whereas we generally need to ask why an author would use an imperfect or a perfect, we seldom need to ask why an aorist is used. You use an aorist to avoid making the point that is made by the imperfect or the perfect.

---

[3] Remember that this means that the pitch rises on the first vowel of the diphthong and falls on the second, even though it is written on the second vowel.

Unlike the present stem, it presents that action simply, without drawing you into the action.

See Figure 7.1.

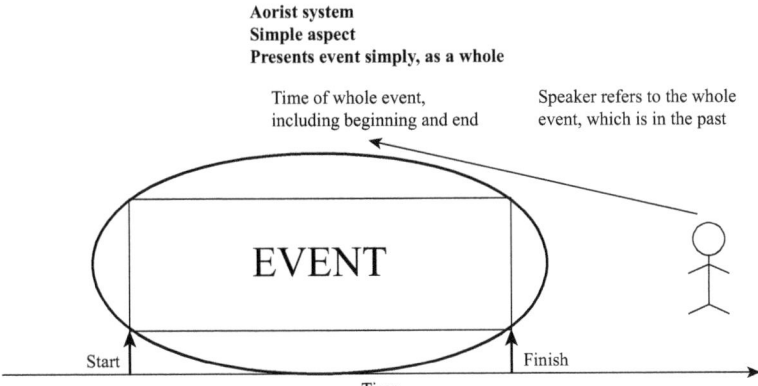

Figure 7.1 Aorist Indicative

The most common mistake with the aorist is to assume that it tells you that the *action* itself was simple: a single event, or a completed event, or some other property of the *action*, rather than an author's choice in how to *present* the action. We will see below that the aorist can refer to the full range of events that the present stem can (customs, habits, etc.). But it *presents* them simply: that is the aspect of the aorist.

5.1.1 Default Aorist (a.k.a. Global)

The most common use of the aorist, which I like to call '**default** aorist', does exactly what you would expect: it refers to a past event simply. It goes by various labels, including 'global'. It includes the whole event, including the beginning, the end and everything in between, but presents that whole *simply*.

> ἐλάλησεν Μωυσῆς πρὸς πάντας υἱοὺς Ἰσραήλ. Deut 1:3
> Moses spoke to all the sons of Israel.

For actions that have no natural endpoint,[4] the aorist indicates that the action happened for a while and then stopped. In such cases, the author would have been free to use an imperfect to present the same situation as ongoing, perhaps to set the scene (**EM 6** 7.1). Table 7.1 shows some examples.

---

[4] Different verb types are explained in more detail when we cover the aspect in other moods: see **EM 8** 5.1.1.

Table 7.1 Verbs without Endpoint

Aorist of verb without endpoint	**Imperfect** of verb without endpoint
ἐνέπαιξαν αὐτῷ, ἐξέδυσαν αὐτὸν τὴν χλαμύδα, καὶ ἐνέδυσαν αὐτὸν, τὰ ἱμάτια αὐτοῦ Matt 27:31	οἱ ἄνδρες οἱ συνέχοντες τὸν Ἰησοῦν ἐνέπαιζον αὐτῷ Luke 22:63
they mocked him, they undressed him of the robe, and dressed him with his own clothes	the men who were holding Jesus were mocking him
(They spent some time mocking him, and eventually stopped; the aorist refers to the entire incident of mockery, however long or short.)	(The series of imperfects leads us to the aorist in v66.)
οὐκ εἰς κενὸν ἔδραμον Pol. *Phil.* 9.2	οἱ ὄνοι προδραμόντες ἔστασαν· πολὺ γὰρ τῶν ἵππων ἔτρεχον θᾶττον Xenophon, *Anab.* 1.5.2
they ran, not in vain	The donkeys ran ahead and stopped: because they ran much faster than the horses.
	(Here the imperfect explains the circumstance against which the previous statement makes sense: their donkeys were much faster than their horses.)
καὶ ἔγνων, τέκνα, ὅτι περὶ Ἰωσὴφ τοῦτό μοι συνέβη· καὶ μετανοήσας ἔκλαυσα, T. Sim. 2.13	ἔκλαιον δὲ πάντες, καὶ ἐκόπτοντο αὐτήν. ὁ δὲ εἶπε, Μὴ κλαίετε Luke 8:52
And I knew, children, that it was on account of Joseph that this had happened to me: so I repented and wept.	They were all weeping and mourning her. But he said, 'Stop weeping!'

If the action does have an endpoint, an aorist implies that the endpoint was reached.[5] (An imperfect draws you in to a point in time when the endpoint had not *yet* been reached; whether it went on to be completed or not isn't something that the imperfect tells you: **EM 6** 7.3.) Table 7.2 presents some examples.

---

[5] To describe a past action which has an endpoint but which was not successfully reached, one cannot use an aorist, but would need an imperfect, which would have a conative sense. *Contra* Wallace 561, 'the imperfect would be more natural, but not at all required'. He cites Fanning 257–8 [= 4.3.1, 2], which indeed doesn't seem to offer that restriction in discussing the uses of the aorist. However, it needs to be read in the light of Fanning 3.1.2.3, 3b, which explains the restrictions on aspectual function for different verb types: 'the aorist aspect with ACCOMPLISHMENTS [verbs with endpoints which take time] indicates that a process occurs and runs all the way to its termination or limit' (152–3).

Table 7.2 Verbs with Endpoint

Aorist of verb with endpoint	Imperfect of verb with endpoint
ἐνέπαιξαν αὐτῷ, ἐξέδυσαν αὐτὸν τὴν χλαμύδα, καὶ ἐνέδυσαν αὐτόν, τὰ ἱμάτια αὐτοῦ Matt 27:31 they mocked him, they <u>undressed</u> him of the robe, and <u>dressed</u> him with his own clothes (This means that they *successfully* removed the robe and *successfully* dressed him before whatever happened next; as my almost ironic use of '*successfully*' shows, there is nothing particularly significant about their achievement; the aorists simply tell us that it happened and keep the narrative moving.)	ταῦτα δὲ λέγουσα ἅμα <u>ἐνέδυε</u> τὰ ὅπλα … ἐπεὶ δὲ … ὁ Ἀβραδάτας **ὡπλίσθη** τοῖς ὅπλοις τούτοις … Xenophon, *Cyr.* 6.4.3 at the same time that she spoke these words, <u>she was dressing</u> [Abradatas] in his armour … now once Abradatas **was fully arrayed** in his armour … (The imperfect doesn't mean that she didn't manage to dress him, but that we're drawn into the action at a point where she was still doing it. The next thing is that he is fully armoured, expressed by an aorist. Her action did run to completion, but the imperfect draws us in to how she dressed him while speaking to him.)
Ἐγένετο δὲ αὐτῇ ἕκτος μήν, καὶ ἰδοὺ ἦλθεν Ἰωσὴφ ἀπὸ τῶν οἰκοδομῶν αὐτοῦ, καὶ εἰσελθὼν ἐν τῷ οἴκῳ αὐτοῦ εὗρεν αὐτὴν ὠγκωμένην Prot. Jas. 13.1 Now the sixth month [of Mary's pregnancy] happened, and look, Joseph came from his building work. He entered the house, and when he saw her swollen… (Joseph's act of coming home completed: the aorist implies that he reached his destination, as the following verb confirms.)	καὶ ἰδοὺ ἀνὴρ πρεσβύτης <u>ἤρχετο</u> ἐξ ἔργων αὐτοῦ ἐξ ἀγροῦ … καὶ **ἦρεν** τοὺς ὀφθαλμοὺς αὐτοῦ καὶ εἶδεν τὸν ὁδοιπόρον ἄνδρα ἐν τῇ πλατείᾳ τῆς πόλεως Judg 19:16–17 Look, an elder <u>was on his way</u> from his work, from the field … and **he lifted** his eyes and spotted the traveller in the town square … (Here the action of going home is interrupted: the elder stops to talk to the young man.)

5.1.2 Aorist of States

FURTHER READING: *CGCG* 33.30; vS 194I

An aorist of a state can refer to two different events.[6]

It can tell you that the subject was in that state for a while. The author will usually flag that with a time marker of some sort. As expected, the aorist covers

---

[6] Different verb types are explained in more detail when we cover the aspect in other moods: see **EM 8** 5.1.1.

the whole time of being in that state, including beginning and end, and presents it simply. This is the **default** or **global** aorist, as shown.[7]

> ἐπείνασα γάρ, καὶ ἐδώκατέ μοι φαγεῖν· ἐδίψησα, καὶ ἐποτίσατέ με Matt 25:35
> because I was hungry, and you gave me something to eat; I was thirsty, and you gave me something to drink
>> The context implies that these describe particular instances of hunger and thirst, rather than customary states.
>
> εὐηρέστησεν δὲ Ἐνὼχ τῷ θεῷ μετὰ τὸ γεννῆσαι αὐτὸν τὸν Μαθουσάλα **διακόσια ἔτη** Gen 5:22
> After he fathered Methuselah, Enoch was pleasing to God **for 200 years**.
>
> ταῦτα ἐποίησας καὶ ἐσίγησα 1 Clem. 35.9
> you did these things, and I kept silent
>> Note the difference with an equally surprising state of silence in Matt 26:63 ὁ δὲ Ἰησοῦς ἐσιώπα [imperfect]. The difference is that the imperfect sets the scene for what follows, while the aorist simply moves on to what follows.

Much more frequently, the aorist refers not to being in a state for a while, but to the action of *entering* into the state. It is this action which is viewed simply, as a whole. That's a natural fit for the aorist; it is labelled '**ingressive**' to distinguish it from 'being in a state' ('global' / 'default'). You can see these two uses of the aorist of states in Figure 7.2.

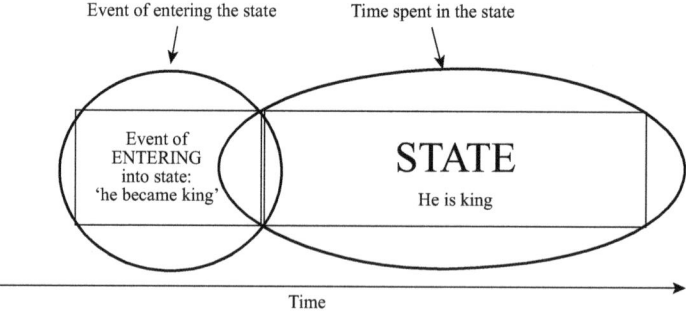

Figure 7.2 Aorist of States

---

[7] Some grammars refer to this as '**complexive**', reserving 'global' for actions rather than states. Since there really is no difference in what the aorist itself tells you, I use 'global' (or better, 'default') for both.

δῖ ὑμᾶς ἐπτώχευσε 2 Cor 8:9
on your account, he became poor

τότε ἰδὼν ὁ ἀνθύπατος τὸ γεγονὸς ἐπίστευσεν Acts 13:12
then, when the proconsul saw what had happened, he became a believer [= he believed]

... διάκονοι δι᾽ ὧν ἐπιστεύσατε ... 1 Cor 3:5
... servants through whom you became believers ...

> In these two examples, note how the aorist works for a single event 'he believed' and for many over a period of time 'you became believers'.

Ἐνώχ, διὰ τί ἐφοβήθης; 1 En. 21:9
Enoch, why have you become frightened [= are you afraid]?

> Note the need for a perfect tense in English, explained in **EM 7** 5.2.2.

ἐθεάσαντο αὐτάς ... καὶ ἐπεθύμησαν αὐτάς 1 En. 6:2
they caught sight of them ... and lusted after them [= became lustful]

εἶτ᾽ ἐκεῖ τοὺς μὲν ἐκβαλὼν τοὺς δὲ καταστήσας τῶν βασιλέων ἠσθένησε
Demosthenes, 1 *Olynth.* 13
After deposing some, and installing others, among the kings there, he became sick.

οἱ δ᾽ ὡς ἔγνωσαν ἠπατημένοι ... Thucydides, *P.W.* 2.4.1
And when they discovered [= 'they became aware'] that they had been deceived

A few verses apart we find two uses of ἐβασίλευσεν, one ingressive, the other default:

Ἐτῶν δὲ ἦν εἴκοσι πέντε Ἰωακεὶμ ὅτε ἐβασίλευσεν τῆς Ἰουδαίας καὶ Ἰερουσαλήμ 1 Esd 1:37
Ioakeim was twenty-five years old when he became king over Judea and Jerusalem
Ingressive

ἐβασίλευσεν ἐν Ἰσραὴλ καὶ Ἱερουσαλὴμ μῆνας τρεῖς 1 Esd 1:33
He was king in Israel and Jerusalem **for** three months
> **Default**: notice the explicit cue that it went on 'for three months', rather than merely beginning.

Note that βασιλεύω really is a state, and just means εἰμὶ βασιλεύς. It may be idiomatic to translate it in these two contexts as 'he was crowned' and 'he reigned'. Nonetheless, don't let that confuse you into thinking that the Greek verb refers to an action.

It is often argued that this 'ingressive' sense is transferred sometimes to actions, rather than states. However, this is to confuse the meaning of the context with the meaning of the tense. The aorist *always* includes the beginning of an action; that's not enough to say that a use is ingressive. It would need to *exclude* the middle and the end, which the aorist doesn't do.

The examples that get cited in grammars and commentaries are either aorists of states or else perfectly normal global aorists. An aorist will often describe an action that *begins* right after another action; that doesn't mean that the aorist tells you that the action is beginning, any more than the imperfect does in similar cases. The aorist tells you that the whole action happened:

> Καὶ ὡς ἤγγισεν, ἰδὼν τὴν πόλιν, ἔκλαυσεν ἐπ' αὐτῇ, λέγων ... Luke 19:41
> As he drew near, seeing the city, he wept over it, saying: ...
>> It is true that he 'began to cry' or even 'burst into tears', but the aorist describes the whole time of weeping, including the whole time that he spent speaking as he wept.

Any tense can tell you about an action that begins to happen, but that is not what that tense is telling you (as discussed for the imperfect in **EM 6** 7.5.3).

When Greek wants to tell you that an action (rather than a state) began, it will usually do so explicitly:

> καὶ ἄρξηται **τύπτειν** τοὺς συνδούλους Matt 24:49
> [the wicked servant] began to **strike** his fellow servants

5.1.3 Relative Past: Narrative vs Other Contexts

FURTHER READING: *CGCG* 33.13

We briefly discussed the difference between narrative and other contexts in **EM 6** 7.1. In narrative, aorists describe actions *prior to that point* in the narrative (and so prior to the next verb). In other contexts, such as speeches and letters, the aorist means that the action happened *prior to the time of speaking/writing*. These are examples of how the aorist can refer to a time which is past *relative* to some other time (the time of the narrative; the time of writing).

This *relative* past value of the aorist appears in various syntactical constructions. In indirect speech, the aorist refers to the past *relative* to the time of the original utterance. The same is true in some other easily predictable contexts. In all of these, English would use a pluperfect instead.

> εὗρον οὕτω καθὼς καὶ αἱ γυναῖκες εἶπον Luke 24:24
> they found it just as the women had said [aorist → pluperfect]

> ὃ ἔδωκεν Ἰακὼβ Ἰωσὴφ τῷ υἱῷ αὐτοῦ John 4:5
> which Jacob had given [aorist → pluperfect] to Joseph, his son

καὶ ἔγνων, τέκνα, ὅτι περὶ Ἰωσὴφ τοῦτό μοι <u>συνέβη</u>· καὶ μετανοήσας ἔκλαυσα, T. Sim. 2.13
And I knew, children, that it was on account of Joseph that this <u>had happened</u> [aorist → pluperfect] to me: so I repented and wept.

We have already seen this a little with *Joseph & Aseneth* chapters 1–3 in this and the previous chapter of the *Reader*. It is even more apparent in the unedited original, in Table 7.3. Bold indicates **aorists**, underlining <u>imperfects</u>, and double underline shows the two matching statements about time.

Table 7.3 *Joseph & Aseneth* Chapters 1–3

1:1 Ἐγένετο ἐν τῷ πρώτῳ ἔτει … **ἐξαπέστειλε** Φαραὼ τὸν Ἰωσὴφ …	**It came to pass** in the first year … Pharaoh **sent** Joseph **out** …
²Καὶ **ἦλθεν** Ἰωσὴφ τῷ τετάρτῳ μηνὶ τοῦ πρώτου ἔτους ὀγδόῃ καὶ δεκάτῃ τοῦ μηνὸς εἰς τὰ ὅρια Ἡλιουπόλεως.	Joseph **arrived** <u>in the fourth month of the first year on the eighteenth of the month at the region of Heliopolis.</u>
<u>Imperfects</u> introducing Heliopolis, Pentephres and Aseneth.	
⁹Καὶ **ἀπῆλθεν** ἡ φήμη τοῦ κάλλους αὐτῆς εἰς πᾶσαν τὴν γῆν ἐκείνην … καὶ <u>ἐμνηστεύοντο</u> and more <u>imperfects</u> …	The fame of her beauty **had gone out** into the whole of that land … and <u>they were wooing</u> …
¹¹Καὶ **ἤκουσε** περὶ αὐτῆς ὁ υἱὸς Φαραὼ ὁ πρωτότοκος καὶ <u>ἐξελιπάρει</u> and more <u>imperfects</u> …	Now the firstborn son of Pharaoh **had heard** about her <u>and had been begging</u> [his father]
¹³Καὶ **εἶπεν** αὐτῷ ὁ πατὴρ αὐτοῦ Φαραὼ … ¹⁴οὐχί …	But Pharaoh, his father, **had said to him**: 'No …'
2:1 Καὶ <u>ἦν</u> Ἀσενὲθ and more <u>imperfects</u> …	Now Aseneth <u>was</u> …
Her maidservants are introduced with <u>imperfects</u>.	
¹¹ <u>ἦσαν</u> ὁμήλικαι ὅτι ἐν μιᾷ νυκτὶ **ἐγεννήθησαν** σὺν τῇ Ἀσενὲθ … and more <u>imperfects</u> …	<u>they were of the same age because on one night</u> **they had been born** along with Aseneth …
¹⁶ ἐν ταύτῃ τῇ κλίνῃ ἐκάθευδεν Ἀσενὲθ μόνη, καὶ οὔτε ἀνὴρ οὔτε γυνὴ οὐδέποτε **ἐκάθισεν** ὑπ' αὐτῆς πλὴν τῆς Ἀσενὲθ μόνης	on this bed Aseneth used to sleep alone, and neither man nor woman **had** ever **sat** on it, except Aseneth alone
We know that the introduction and background are over when we read 3:1, which precisely places itself at the start of the action in 1:2, which was the last aorist we had seen before the background information began to be given with a sequence of imperfects:	
3:1 Καὶ **ἐγένετο** ἐν τῷ τετάρτῳ μηνὶ <u>ὀγδόῃ καὶ δεκάτῃ τοῦ μηνὸς</u> **ἦλθεν** Ἰωσὴφ εἰς τὰ ὅρια Ἡλιουπόλεως.	**It came to pass** <u>in the fourth month, the eighteenth of the month,</u> he **sent** Joseph into the region of Heliopolis.

5.2 Cautions about Aorist Labels

FURTHER READING: *CGCG* 30.1 n1

That's pretty much it for the aorist.

Descriptions of the various contexts for an element of grammar can often lead to fine distinctions that are very helpful for labelling our understanding of the wider sentence, but have little to do with that element of grammar itself. A good example is the various distinctions offered for aorists which are really just 'default aorists' of particular verbs in particular contexts. We have already seen this for the alleged 'ingressive' aorists (other than for states). Here are a few more.

5.2.1 Beware 'Consummative'

'Consummative' is another example of something which the aorist merely *implies*: the successful completion of an ongoing action. Where a 'consummative' sense is detected, that is supplied by the nature of the verb rather than the aorist. We have seen that the aorist of a verb with an endpoint *implies* that the endpoint was reached (**EH 7** 5.1.1). However, some verbs tell you, in and of themselves, that a prior action has come to a conclusion: I find *after searching*; I die *after becoming weaker*; I heal *after treatment*. Such verbs include εὑρίσκω, ἀπόλλυμαι, ἀποθνῄσκω, ἀποκτείνω, νεκρόω, ἐλευθερόω, ἰάομαι, καθαρίζω, λαμβάνω, πωλέω.[8]

The aorist is not particularly focussed on the success; the aorist εὗρον isn't a special 'consummative' aorist, as if it meant 'I have completed the process of finding'. It just means 'I found', even though it implies a prior process of seeking (ζητεῖν).

Πείθω is another such verb. It is the nature of πείθω 'I persuade' which focusses on completion or success; the aorist tense merely implies it:

> καὶ εἶπεν Δαυείδ πρὸς τοὺς ἄνδρας αὐτοῦ Μηδαμῶς ... καὶ ἔπεισεν Δαυείδ τοὺς ἄνδρας αὐτοῦ ἐν λόγοις, καὶ οὐκ ἔδωκεν αὐτοῖς ἀναστάντας θῦσαι τὸν Σαούλ 1 Kgdms 24:7–8
>
> But David said to his men: 'By no means ...' So David persuaded his men by his words, and did not allow them to get up and sacrifice Saul.
>
> In the context, the men have famously seen an opportunity for David to kill Saul by taking him unawares (v5); David tells them that he mustn't (v7), and in v8 we are told that he persuaded them. So ἔπεισεν does tell us that his words of v7 had their desired effect, and that his attempt to persuade was successful; however, the aorist is just a 'default' aorist: he persuaded them.

---

[8] Fanning 3.1.2.4. These verbs take no time, so when they are found in the present stem, they either refer to repeated actions or (in a descriptive context) to the necessary prior action: εὑρίσκω means 'I am searching [in order to find]'. They can, of course, occur in other contexts, such as historical present, gnomic, etc.

καὶ γὰρ <u>ἐδεήθη</u> τοῦ πατρὸς ἡμῶν Ἰωσὴφ ... καὶ οὕτως ἐβόα Ἰακώβ· Ὦ τέκνον Ἰωσήφ, ὦ τέκνον χρηστόν, <u>ἐνίκησας</u> τὰ σπλάγχνα Ἰακὼβ τοῦ πατρός σου. T. Benj. 3.6–7
For Joseph also <u>begged</u> his father ... and Jacob yelled like this: 'O Joseph, my child, O worthy child, you have <u>won over</u> the affections ['bowels'] of your father Jacob!'
The winning over means that the begging was successful. The aorist doesn't highlight the 'end of the winning over'. These verbs take no time but tell of an instantaneous transition: death to life; unpersuaded to persuaded; not yet victorious to victorious; ill to healthy; not in possession to possessing.

It would be better to say that νικάω is a verb with consummative meaning than to say that ἐνίκησας is a consummative aorist. See also Rev 5:5 in the next section. Accordingly, we don't list 'consummative' as a meaning of the aorist; the use of such a label involves thinking from English translation, rather than thinking about the meaning of the aorist in Greek.

5.2.2 Perfect in Greek vs English: 'Constative' Aorist

FURTHER READING: RIJKSBARON 8.3.1

Before we consider this translation issue, here is a quick reminder of three quite normal uses of the aorist in different contexts (Table 7.4).

Table 7.4 Uses of the Aorist

Narrative: a past action.	English past simple.
Narrative: a past action *relative* to a point in the past.	English pluperfect.
Direct speech or letter: an action completed by the time of speaking or writing.	English past simple *or* perfect.

In this section, we will consider why the English perfect is sometimes used when Greek uses an aorist; if you aren't yet confident about the perfect in Greek and English, you might want to come back to this section later.

If an action completes successfully (which an aorist would imply), that completion may or may not have ongoing consequences. The aorist doesn't tell us either way. It is the *perfect* system that draws attention to the consequences of a successful action.

ἢ ἀφ' ὑμῶν ὁ λόγος τοῦ Θεοῦ <u>ἐξῆλθεν</u>; 1 Cor 14:36
or was it from you that God's word <u>went out</u>?

ἐν παντὶ τόπῳ ἡ πίστις ὑμῶν ἡ πρὸς τὸν Θεὸν <u>ἐξελήλυθεν</u> 1 Thess 1:8
your faith in God <u>has gone out</u> in every place

In both cases there is a contextual ongoing relevance to the past event being achieved successfully: the going out of the word, and the going out of the Thessalonians' faith. However, it is only in the second example that the ongoing relevance is highlighted by the choice of tense: the perfect.

While we will discuss the Greek perfect in a later chapter, we need to understand why the English perfect is sometimes needed where Greek uses an aorist. These English translations are labelled 'constative'. Just like the 'durative present', this label says nothing about the Greek, and you only need it when you're thinking about translation rather than reading the Greek text.[9]

Imagine that you do the washing up at 10 am today. Here are some ways that you can describe that in English, at 3 pm, all using the English perfect tense:

1 I have washed up today.
2 I have washed up this week.
3 I have washed up this month.

However, you cannot say:

4 It is 3pm and I have washed up *this morning*.

Instead, you would need to use the past simple and say:

5 It is 3pm and I washed up *this morning*.

The English perfect only works when the time you're describing includes your present. Example 4 would work if it were still morning. But to talk about an action done in the morning when it is the afternoon and no longer morning, you need the past simple, as in example 5.

As in Greek, you will choose a perfect tense *to express that there is some ongoing relevance* to the action. That might mean changing other parts of the sentence so that the time of the action includes your 'now'. If it's the afternoon and you washed up this morning, and you want to highlight some ongoing relevance, then you can use any of examples 1, 2 or 3 and use the perfect. If, on the other hand, you don't want to highlight any ongoing relevance, you'll use example 5 and a past simple.

Now imagine that someone asks you, 'Have you ever washed up?' and you reply,

6 Yes, I have washed up.

You can use the perfect tense in English because the time which includes your 'now' is the whole of the past: 'ever'.[10]

---

[9] Be aware of some label confusion: 'constative' is used by some grammars to refer to 'global' (Wallace 557), and these grammars use 'effective' or even 'consummative' to describe what we are here calling 'constative' (Wallace 559).

[10] This is why *ENTG* points out that English uses the perfect for an action in the indefinite past (*ENTG* 16.3.2).

This is where English translation obscures what Greek tells you. In a non-narrative context, as we saw, the aorist implies that the event has happened by the time of speaking/writing. This forces us, in English, to use a perfect.

> Λάζαρος ἀπέθανε. John 11:14
> Lazarus <u>has died</u>.

Were the author writing in English from scratch, they could avoid the perfect by specifying the time of death as not including 'now':

> Lazarus <u>died</u> earlier.

Translators generally don't dare to add that kind of information. This means that the translation will convey a sense of ongoing relevance that the Greek author did not choose to highlight. Jesus isn't explaining that Lazarus is *now* dead; he already made that clear by using a perfect two verses earlier: κεκοίμηται 'he has fallen asleep'. He is now clarifying the misunderstanding of his metaphor: 'Lazarus isn't napping: he *died*'. However, that is ungrammatical English without some indication that the time of death is separate from 'now', so you need 'Lazarus has died'. Your privilege is to read the Greek text and thereby be freed from wrongly importing an emphasis on ongoing relevance into Jesus' statement. The ongoing relevance (that Lazarus continues to be dead) is quite clear throughout the context of the conversation, and there was therefore no need for it to be emphasised in John 11:14.

Most grammars will discuss the aorist in such a context and label it something like 'constative', to describe the successful completion of the action. However, it is just an aorist. Expressing this in English requires a perfect tense which expresses an ongoing relevance, but that doesn't mean that the Greek author intended that. There may or may not be an ongoing relevance, but the author did not draw attention to it by using an aorist; for that, Greek offers the perfect (see Table 7.5).

Table 7.5 Aorist vs Perfect

Aorist (agnostic re ongoing relevance)	Perfect (ongoing relevance)
ἰδού, ἐνίκησεν ὁ λέων ὁ ὢν ἐκ τῆς φυλῆς Ἰούδα Rev 5:5 Look: the lion who is from the tribe of Judah has conquered [aorist → perfect].	ἐν τῷ κόσμῳ θλίψιν ἔχετε· ἀλλὰ θαρσεῖτε, ἐγὼ νενίκηκα τὸν κόσμον. John 16:33 You will have affliction in the world: but be heartened: as for me, <u>I have conquered</u> [perfect] the world! (The future affliction at the hands of the *world* makes the past conquest of the *world* relevant now: it gives comfort.)

Table 7.5 (cont.)

Aorist (agnostic re ongoing relevance)	Perfect (ongoing relevance)
ἴδε, **νῦν** ἠκούσατε τὴν βλασφημίαν αὐτοῦ Matt 26:65 Look: **now** you have heard [aorist → perfect] his blasphemy (Notice how **νῦν**, not the aorist, draws attention to the success of the action.)	ἀκηκόαμεν περὶ σοῦ, ὅτι ... ἐπιτήδειος εἶ τοῦ εἶναι ἡμῶν φίλος. 1 Macc 10:19 We have heard [perfect] about you: that you are ... worthy to be our friend. (The past hearing is relevant in the present because it explains what they are about to ask of him.)

Sometimes the line between narrative and non-narrative is a fine one, and English gives you a way out because there is an implicit time, distant from 'now', at which the action happened. For example,

λόγων ὧν παρ' ἐμοῦ ἤκουσας [aorist] 2 Tim 1:13

is often translated with a perfect:

'words which you have heard from me [at any point up to now]'

But this instruction follows the narrative of Timothy's childhood and call to ministry, which could well have been the specific time when Timothy heard those words. Many translations treat that as an implied time in this verse, prior to the 'now' that would allow a past simple in English:

'words which you heard from me [at that point back then]'

'Constative' is not a type of aorist; it is an English translation that forces a sense of ongoing relevance where the Greek had none. All the Greek aorist tells you is that the action is over by the time in question.

5.2.3 Not Necessarily a Single Action

FURTHER READING: vS 199c

As we saw with the ongoing aspect of the present system, Greek tenses do not differentiate between a single action, a repeated action, or even a habit. The same is true of the 'simple' aspect of the aorist. What is being presented simply, as a complete whole, does not need to be a single action. Habits and repeated actions fit.

οἱ πατέρες ἡμῶν τὸ μάννα ἔφαγον ἐν τῇ ἐρήμῳ, καθώς ἐστι γεγραμμένον,
Ἄρτον ἐκ τοῦ οὐρανοῦ ἔδωκεν αὐτοῖς φαγεῖν. John 6:31
Our fathers ate the manna in the wilderness, as it stands written: 'He gave them bread to eat out of Heaven.'
Iterative – giving and eating of manna happened repeatedly over forty years.

Κατὰ πίστιν ἀπέθανον οὗτοι πάντες. Heb 11:13
All of these died in faith.
> Iterative – this refers to Abel, Noah, Abraham, Sarah, who died at very different times.

εἶδον τὰ ἔργα μου **τεσσαράκοντα ἔτη** Heb 3:9
they saw my works **for forty years**
> Iterative

ἐγὼ **πάντοτε** ἐδίδαξα ἐν τῇ συναγωγῇ καὶ ἐν τῷ ἱερῷ John 18:20
I **always** taught in the synagogue and in the temple
> Habitual

πάντοτε ὑπηκούσατε Phil 2:12
you **always** obeyed
> Habitual

ἆθλα γὰρ ἡμῖν οἱ πατέρες ἔθεσαν ῥαψῳδίας Plato, *Tim.* 21b
For our fathers set up recitation contests for us
> Iterative

ἐπεὶ δὲ **ἐδέησεν**, οὐ' πρὸς τὰ τιμήματα ὑμῖν ἐπεθήκαμεν ... ἀλλὰ μέρη φέρειν τῶν ἑκάστοτε καρπῶν ἐπετάξαμεν, Appian, *Bell. civ.* 5.4
But **whenever it was necessary**, we did not set these over you according to valuations ... but rather commanded that you bring a portion of your annual fruit,
> Customary

ἡ γυνὴ καὶ ἐθήλασεν τὸν υἱὸν αὐτῆς ἕως ἄν ἀπογαλακτίσῃ αὐτόν. 1 Kgdms 1:23
The woman suckled her son until she could wean him
> Habitual

Greek uses the present system to describe an action as ongoing, which includes actions that are not ongoing at that very moment, but which are in the process of being done repeatedly, habitually or customarily.

Greek uses the aorist system to describe the event simply, even if the event is a series of actions.

5.3 Less Obvious Contexts

5.3.1 English Idiom: Epistolary

When writing correspondence, we can sometimes draw attention to the act of writing. In English, we customarily do this from the point of view of the *writer*: the present tense. Greek does this too, but also has the option of referring to the action from the *reader's* point of view, for whom the event is past. Thus:

Ἴδετε πηλίκοις ὑμῖν γράμμασιν ἔγραψα τῇ ἐμῇ χειρί Gal 6:11
Look how large the letters are with which I am writing [aorist → present] with my own hand

This, again, is not a separate 'category' of aorist: it's just a default aorist in Greek, but English convention is different.

5.3.2 Gnomic

We have met the use of the present tense to express proverbially true, or perennially true, things: it is true *in the present* because it is *always* true. The NT occasionally uses the aorist as gnomic as well.[11]

> ἀνέτειλε γὰρ ὁ ἥλιος σὺν τῷ καύσωνι, καὶ ἐξήρανε τὸν χόρτον, καὶ τὸ ἄνθος αὐτοῦ ἐξέπεσε, καὶ ἡ εὐπρέπεια τοῦ προσώπου αὐτοῦ ἀπώλετο Jas 1:11
> for the sun rises [aorist] with its heat, and dries up [aorist] the grass, and its flower falls [aorist] and the beauty of its appearance dies off [aorist]

> Ἐπὶ τῆς Μωσέως καθέδρας ἐκάθισαν οἱ γραμματεῖς καὶ οἱ Φαρισαῖοι Matt 23:2
> the scribes and Pharisees sit [aorist] on the Seat of Moses

5.3.3 Present Mental States ('Dramatic' / Semitic)

FURTHER READING: FANNING 4.3.6; *CGCG* 33.32

Very rarely, the aorist is used to describe a present mental state. This might be a use of an old Greek 'dramatic' aorist (rather unexpectedly outside works of theatre!) or the result of Semitic influence.

> ἔγνων τί ποιήσω Luke 16:4
> I know what I will do.

5.3.4 Futuristic

This aorist describes a future event as though it had already happened. It is quite rare, and most potential examples are disputed. Purely as an illustration, some understand the aorists at the end of the *Magnificat* (Luke 1:51–4) as predicting the future:

> [51] ἐποίησε ... διεσκόρπισεν ... [52] καθεῖλε ... ὕψωσε ... [53] ἐνέπλησεν ... ἐξαπέστειλε ... [54] ἀντελάβετο ...
> he will do ... he will scatter ... he will abase ... he will exalt ... he will sate ... he will dismiss ... he will help ...

---

[11] In Classical Greek, the gnomic aorist had a subtly different meaning from the gnomic present (*CGCG* 33.31 n1), but that distinction doesn't hold in the NT.

The 'dramatic' and 'futuristic' uses of the aorist are not only very rare, but also controversial. If you read through the whole GNT, the Apostolic Fathers, the Greek OT and other contemporary literature, and never find one, that doesn't mean that you've done anything wrong. What's certain is that you've gained far more through that reading than by studying ten books *about* Greek.

5.4 Contexts of the Aorist System: Summary Table

Table 7.6 Contexts of the Aorist System

Context	Aorist tense
Default	Moses spoke to all the sons of Israel.
	they saw my works **for forty years** (an iterative situation)
	you always obeyed (a habitual situation)
	But **whenever it was necessary**, we commanded (a customary situation)
	the lion has conquered ('constative')
Ingressive (entry into states)	he became poor
Epistolary (letters)	I am writing with my own hand
Gnomic	Pharisees sit on the Seat of Moses
Futuristic	he will scatter the proud
Dramatic	I know what I will do

CHAPTER 8

Other Patterns of Nouns and Verbs
—
Aspect in the Infinitive

> **How to Use This Chapter**
>
> In this chapter, you meet no new grammatical principles, just new endings for different families of nouns and verbs. The rules you have met will save you a great deal of effort in this chapter.
> Read the sections of **Extra Help** below *before* you tackle the relevant section of *ENTG*. If you invested time in the **Extra Help** in Chapter 6, you will continue to reap the benefits in this chapter.
> In the **Extra Material**, we'll examine the significance of aspect in the 'other moods'. We'll see the general principles and how they apply to the infinitive.

1 BEFORE *ENTG* 8.1: VERB ENDINGS

Be encouraged: all the verb forms that you are about to meet are more regular, and easier to parse, than those you have met so far.

1.1 Indicative Endings

The same principles as we have seen with λύω still apply. The four tenses in *ENTG* 8.1.1 are shown in Table 8.1.

Table 8.1 Indicative Tenses

	Present stem: ῥυ-	**Aorist stem:** ῥυσα-	**Future stem:** ῥυσ-
Principal tense: No augment, principal endings	present		future
Historical tense: Augment, historical endings	imperfect	aorist	

1.1.1 Singular Endings

Regardless of principal or historical, the singular endings are built on the pattern of M-S-T (pronounced MiST in my classroom). Principal endings are μαι σαι ται; historical are μην σο το. (A little mnemonic: 'principal' tenses are also called 'primary' πραιmary αι.)

The thematic vowel follows the rules we have met already: it is ε, but switches to ο before μ/ν and to α in the aorist stem before any ending. See Table 8.2.

Table 8.2 Indicative Endings

	Present stem: ῥυ-	Aorist stem: ῥυσα-	Future stem: ῥυσ-
Principal tense: No augment, principal endings	ῥύ-ο-μαι ῥύ-ε-σαι ῥύ-ε-ται		ῥύσ-ο-μαι ῥύσ-ε-σαι ῥύσ-ε-ται
Historical tense: **Augment**, historical **endings**	ἐ-ρύ-ο-μην ἐ-ρύ-ε-σο ἐ-ρύ-ε-το	ἐ-ρύσ-α-μην ἐ-ρύσ-α-σο ἐ-ρύσ-α-το	

That table doesn't *quite* match *ENTG* 8.1.1, does it? We need one more rule, which will keep coming up.

1.1.2 Slippery Sigma

Sigma frequently causes trouble, as we have started to see (**EH 6** 5.2).

When stuck between two vowels in the ending of a verb, it will disappear and cause a contraction. We need to know some new rules of contract (review *ENTG* 2.2 for the ones you've already met):

$$\varepsilon + \alpha \rightarrow \eta$$
$$\alpha + o \rightarrow \omega$$

Remember also that if a diphthong ending in ι is lengthened, the ι becomes subscript.

This gives us the endings for the 2s that we find in *ENTG* 8.1.1, as in Table 8.3. Notice how easy this is when we remember that each tense is a combination of:

- a stem (indicating the **system**)
- with either principal endings or historical endings and augment (indicating the **time**).

Then it's just the same rules, which will keep reappearing: thematic vowels, contract and slippery sigma.

Keep remembering **M-S-T**.

Table 8.3 Second Singular Endings

	Expected	Sigma vanishes	Contraction	Iota subscript
Pres 2s:	ῥύ-εσαι →	ῥύ-ε+αι →	ῥύ-ηι →	**ῥύ-ῃ**
Fut 2s:	ῥύσ-εσαι →	ῥύσ-ε+αι →	ῥύσ-ηι →	**ῥύσ-ῃ**
Imperfect 2s:	ἐ-ρύ-εσο →	ἐ-ρύ-ε+ο →	**ἐ-ρύ-ου**	
Aor 2s:	ἐ-ρύσ-ασο →	ἐ-ρύσ-α+ο →	**ἐ-ρύσ-ω**	

1.1.3 Plural Endings

These are even easier, and are the same for both principal and historical endings. 1p and 2p are μεθα σθε (with thematic vowel as expected). 3p is always 3s with a ν before it, and then expected thematic vowel (remember, ε → o before μ, ν). Check that this works on the table of *ENTG* 8.1.1.

1.1.4 Embedding the Paradigms

Now apply the method we have used in earlier chapters.

> 1 Learn the rules for forming principal and historical middle endings.
> 2 Use these to write out the present and imperfect middle, without looking anything up.
> 3 Use the rules of Chapter 6 to write out the future from the present and the aorist from the imperfect, without looking anything up.
> 4 Check what you've written against the right pattern (*ENTG* 8.1.1), and use that to reinforce the rules.
> 5 Keep doing that until you never get it wrong.

1.2 Endings in the Other Moods

On the 'other moods of ῥυομαι' table in *ENTG* 8.1.1, you can see the familiar stems for the present (λυ plus ε/ο thematic vowel) and the aorist (λυσα). You can see that τε in active endings becomes σθε in the middle, both indicative and non-indicative. As with the active endings, 2p endings are the same for indicative and imperative.

The infinitives also use σθ, which makes it nice and easy to recognise the middle infinitive.

Helpfully, middle participles all have μεν: 'middle μεν'. This makes them very easy to spot. The masculine nominative singular/plural endings are the same as on λόγος: -μενος -μενοι.

Middle forms are more regular and easier to parse than active ones, including participles.

1.3 Building Your Verb

Verbs which are always middle, such as all the ones you will meet in this chapter, and any future verbs whose form you learn as -ομαι rather than -ω, can also have a stem ending with a contract ε, and they follow the exact same rules. They contract with thematic vowels as expected, and are lengthened when a sigma is added to the stem.

The table we built in **EH 6** 5.3 needs hardly any modification. The only difference is that the endings not only change based on mood and time, but also on voice. See Table 8.4.

Table 8.4 Building Your Verb

Preposition	Augment	Basic stem	Contract vowel	Suffix	Thematic vowel	Ending proper
Optional	Indicative only ἐ for past time	λυ- φιλ- ῥυ- ἀρν-	Optional ε (→η before σ)	σ fut/aor	ε (→ο before μ, ν) →α in aor	Different for: mood, voice and (indicative only) time

As ever, you can simply commit all these new endings to memory directly from the tables in *ENTG* 8.1.1. Alternatively, try to use the rules to reproduce the tables and keep doing that until you have learnt them.

1.4 Instead of *ENTG* 8.1.2–4: Middle Voice

The meaning of voice is explained in chapter 15 of *ENTG*. You should leave aside sections 8.1.2–4, and wait until the fuller treatment then instead. Here is what you need to know for now.

These are the middle voice endings, which we will later see on λύω and all other verbs. I have therefore added them to 'The Greek Verb So Far' for Chapter 8, in the **Online Material**.

Voice is a sub-column within the system columns on the table. All Greek verbs have two surnames. One is the system (present, aorist, etc.), the other is the voice (active, middle). This applies to all the moods, even the infinitive, as we see in *ENTG* 8.1.1.

1.4.1 Parsing

While you do not need to know what the middle is, or what voice is (until Chapter 15), it will get you into good habits for later if you incorporate voice into your parsing from now on.

For now, you *only* see these **middle** endings on verbs whose glosses are English **active** verbs, which is why you needn't know more about voice yet.

> Parse like this:
>
> > Does it have the endings we've learnt for λύω? **Active**.
> > Does it have the endings we're learning for ῥύομαι? Then:
> > > Is it in the aorist system or the future system? **Middle**.
> > > Is it in the present system? **Middle/Passive**.

Now tackle **Practice** 8.1.1 and 8.1.3.

1.5 (Optional) Before *ENTG* 8.2: Endings on εἰμί

These rules help us with the endings of εἰμί, which are much more regular than they seem.

1.5.1 Present

Table 8.5 Present Endings

Pres Act			Stem -εσ-		Pres mid/pass
	εἰμί	←	ἐσμι	←	λύομαι
	εἶ	←	ἐσσι	←	λύεσαι → λύῃ
	ἐστί(ν)	←	ἐστι	←	λύεται
λύομεν	→	ἐσμέν			
λύετε	→	ἐστέ			
λύουσι(ν)	→	εἰσί(ν)			

As you can see in Table 8.5, the stem in the present is **ἐσ-**. It does not take a thematic vowel.

The singular endings are the ones above, using M-S-T, with the ending ι (easy to remember because we're working out εἰμί) μι σι τι. That gives us ἐσμι ἐσσι ἐστι. The first two have a slippery sigma. Sigma really doesn't like to be before μ (**EH 11** 1.3). It will tend to vanish and cause whatever was before it to change its length. Here ε lengthens to a diphthong. So ἐ-σ-μι → ἐ-μι → **εἰ**-μι. The 2s has

sigma between two vowels, and vanishes, as in the 2s endings above. So ἐ-σσ-ι →
εἶ. The 3s is just what we expect: ἐσ-τι.

The plurals take the endings we have met in the present of λύω, again without the thematic vowels: ἐσ-μεν ἐσ-τε. The 3p, both in λύω and in εἰμί, involve some complicated changes because of slippery sigma which aren't worth learning, but you can see the similarity: λυ-ου-σι is the lengthened thematic vowel o followed by σι. εἰ-σι is the lengthened ε from the stem followed by σι.

1.5.2 Future

Table 8.6 Future Endings

ἔσομαι	λύσομαι
ἔσῃ	λύσῃ
ἔσται	λύσεται
ἐσόμεθα	λυσόμεθα
ἔσεσθε	λύσεσθε
ἔσονται	λύσονται

As you can see in Table 8.6, the stem in the future is ἐσ, just like the present. It *does* take a thematic vowel (except 3s). It uses the middle endings throughout.

1.5.3 Imperfect

The stem in the imperfect is ἐ, without the sigma, and augmented to ἠ, as expected. No thematic vowel. I'm afraid you just need to memorise the endings.

1.5.4 Participles

Notice that the whole participle of εἰμί is the ending on the present active participles of other verbs: λύ-**ων** λύ-**οντες**.

1.5.5 Embedding the Paradigms

Now apply the method we have used in earlier chapters.

1. Learn the rules for forming the tenses of εἰμί.
2. Use these to write out the imperfect and future, without looking anything up.
3. Check what you've written against the right pattern (*ENTG* 8.2), and use that to reinforce the rules.
4. Keep doing that until you never get it wrong.

Now tackle **Practice** 8.2.

2 BEFORE *ENTG* 8.3.1: NOUN ENDINGS

We saw in **EH 3** 2.2, that the endings of 1st declension feminine and 2nd declension masculine nouns are the same, except for the nominative singular and the genitive singular. Once you account for the thematic vowel, all other endings are the same.

With masculine 1st declension nouns, the same holds: you already know all these endings! See the table in 'Nouns So Far' for Chapter 8, in the **Online Material**.

1 The pl endings are the same as all other 1st declension nouns.
2 Acc sing is ν and dat sing is ι plus a lengthening of the thematic vowel – the same as all other masc and fem nouns so far.
3 However, these masculine nouns of the α declension ('α males', if you like) insist on keeping the nominative singular that we find on other masculine nouns: ς (like λογός).

This means that they don't use that ς ending for the genitive singular (unlike the α-declension nouns we've met so far). They get their genitive singular from λογός as well (ου). Notice:

4 For α-declension masc nouns in ης, it is ου, following the 2nd declension nouns. Προφήτης → προφήτου.
5 For α-declension masc nouns in ας, the ι-ρ-ε rule reappears, but in reverse. If the stem ends in ι-ρ-ε then the gen *isn't* α but ου. Ἠλίας → Ἠλίου.
6 Other α-declension masc nouns in ας just have α. Ἰούδας → Ἰούδα.

Their vocatives are always α. (Notice that it is always masculine nouns, regardless of declension, that have distinct vocatives.)

Notice that Ἰησοῦς (*ENTG* 3.3.5) follows the pattern of 1st declension masculine nouns, but using ο, rather than α, as the thematic vowel. Therefore, it is only irregular in the dative.

2.1 Vocab Memorisation Is Part of Parsing

You can begin to see why you need to memorise the nominative singular, the article and the genitive for nouns. That combination uniquely identifies the pattern of all the endings for each noun.

As you can also see, we now add more endings which can be ambiguous, and this reinforces the need to memorise vocab in a way that includes the article and genitive, so that you know which pattern you are following.

- -ας can be either acc pl of any 1st declension noun or gen sing of nouns that follow ἡμέρα or nom sing of nouns that follow Ἰούδας.
- -α can be nom sing of nouns that follow δόξα, voc sing of any masc 1st declension noun, gen sing of nouns that follow Ἰούδας or nom/acc pl of any neut noun.
- Knowing these patterns and your vocab can rule out ambiguity. If you see μαθητά, which of the above is it? If you have learnt μαθητής, ου, ὁ, then you know that it isn't the nom/acc pl of a neut noun (μαθητής, οῦ, ὁ is not

neut); you know that it isn't the gen sing (μαθητής, οῦ, ὁ); it isn't the nom sing (μαθητής, οῦ, ὁ); so it can only be the voc sing. You can only do that if you have learnt the word as vocab: μαθητής, οῦ, ὁ.
- Furthermore, -ας can be a verb ending, and knowing your vocab will narrow μαθητάς down to a noun.

2.1.1 Embedding the Paradigms

Now apply the method we have used in earlier chapters.

> 1 Make sure that you are thoroughly comfortable with the paradigm of λόγος and can effortlessly produce the paradigms of ἔργον, ἀρχή, ἡμέρα, δόξα as simple variations.
> 2 Learn the rules for forming προφήτης, Ἰούδας, Ἡλίας, Ἰησοῦς as simple variations.
> 3 Use these to write those paradigms out, without looking anything up.
> 4 Check what you've written against the right pattern (*ENTG* 8.3), and use that to reinforce the rules.
> 5 Keep doing that until you never get it wrong.

Now work through *ENTG* 8.3 and tackle **Practice** 8.3.
You are now ready for the **Greek Reading** and any end-of-chapter exercises that you normally do.

3 THE GREEK READING

The story so far ...

All the princes in the realm, even Pharaoh's firstborn, are besotted with Aseneth, but she has nothing but scorn for every suitor she claps eyes on. To avoid disappointment, her father (Pentephres)[1] has always kept men from seeing her. Joseph's tour of Egypt leads him to Heliopolis, where Pentephres is the priest and governor. Joseph asks to stay at his house and to be refreshed from the heat of the day. Pentephres is overjoyed, knowing Joseph to carry divine favour, and orders a banquet to be set. Aseneth, meanwhile, discovers that Pentephres has returned home from the family estates and is excited to see him. She dresses up, and we discover the trouble she takes to include all manner of Egyptian idolatry in her outfit.

4:1 καὶ ἐσπούδασε καὶ ἠκολούθησε τοῖς ὑπηρέταις ἐκ τοῦ ὑπερῴου αὐτῆς καὶ ἠσπάσατο τὸν Πεντεφρῆν. ² προσεκαλεῖτο ὁ Πεντεφρῆς τοὺς ὑπηρέτας αὐτοῦ, καὶ συνήρχοντο οἱ ὑπηρέται. θεωρήσαντες τὴν Ἀσενὲθ ἐλογίσαντο αὐτὴν εἶναι καλὴν

---
[1] We are finally able to give you the correct spelling of his name in Greek – see the vocabulary!

μεγάλην. ³ καὶ προσερχόμενοι ὁ Πεντεφρῆς καὶ ἡ γυνὴ τῇ Ἀσενὲθ ἐλάλησαν αὐτῇ δέξασθαι τὰ ἀγαθὰ τὰ ἐκ τοῦ ἀγροῦ αὐτῶν. ⁴ καὶ Ἀσενὲθ ἦν ἱλαρὰ ἐπὶ τοῖς ἀγαθοῖς καὶ ἐπὶ τῷ ἄρτῳ ἐπεὶ ἦσαν καλά. ⁵ καὶ ἐλάλησε Πεντεφρῆς τῇ Ἀσενὲθ λέγων·

Τέκνον.

ἈΣΕΝΕΘ·

Λάλησον, κύριε.

ΠΕΝΤΕΦΡΗΣ·

Κάθισον καὶ λαλήσω λόγους ἐντολῶν.

⁶ Καὶ ἐκάθισαν Ἀσενὲθ καὶ ἡ γυνὴ τοῦ Πεντρεφοῦ μετὰ αὐτοῦ.

ΠΕΝΤ·

Τέκνον.

ἈΣΕΝ·

Λέγε, κύριε.

ΠΕΝΤ·

⁷ ὁ Ἰωσὴφ ὁ ἀγαπητὸς τοῦ θεοῦ ἔρχεται πρὸς τὸν οἶκον σήμερον. καὶ ἔχει τὴν ἐξουσίαν ἐπὶ τῆς γῆς ὢν κύριος τῆς Αἰγύπτου. ⁸ ὁ Φαραὼ ἐποίησεν αὐτὸν εἶναι ὑπὲρ τοὺς ἀνθρώπους τῆς Αἰγύπτου. καὶ ἐργάζονται οἱ ὑπηρέται αὐτοῦ ὑπὲρ τοῦ Φαραώ. ⁹ ἤρξατο ζητεῖν τὸν ἄρτον. καὶ ἔσται ὁ τηρῶν ἄρτον. ¹⁰ ὁ ἐρχόμενος λιμὸς οὐκ ἐλεήσει, καὶ ἡ γῆ ἔσται ἔρημος. ἀλλὰ ὁ Ἰωσὴφ ῥύσεται τὴν Αἴγυπτον. ¹¹ καὶ ἐστιν Ἰωσὴφ προφήτης φιλῶν θεόν, καὶ παρθένος ὡς σύ. δέξαι αὐτὸν εἶναι νυμφίος καὶ ἔσῃ νύμφη αὐτοῦ.

¹² Καὶ ὡς ἤκουσεν Ἀσενὲθ τὸν λόγον, ἀνέβλεψε καὶ ἠρνήσατο προσέχειν.

ἈΣΕΝ·

¹³ Ὁ ἄνθρωπος ἦν τηρῶν πρόβατα ἐκ γῆς Χανάαν. ¹⁴ ἀλλὰ δέξομαι τὸν πρωτότοκον υἱὸν τοῦ Φαραώ. ¹⁵ αὐτῷ ἀκολουθοῦσιν οἱ ἄνθρωποι τῆς γῆς προσευχόμενοι καὶ προσκυνοῦντες αὐτῷ.

¹⁶ Τοὺς λόγους ἀκούσας Πεντεφρῆς οὐκ ἠθέλησεν ἔτι λαλῆσαι τῇ Ἀσενὲθ περὶ τοῦ Ἰωσήφ.

3.1 Vocabulary

ἀγρός, οῦ, ὁ – field
γυνή, ἡ – wife
ἐπεί – because
ἱλαρός, ά, όν – happy, cheerful
καθίζω – I sit down
λιμός, οῦ, ὁ/ἡ – famine
νύμφη, ης, ἡ – bride
νυμφίος, ου, ὁ – bridegroom
παρθένος, ου, ἡ / ὁ – virgin
Πεντεφρῆς, οῦ, ὁ – Pentephres (*ENTG* 8.3.1)
πρωτότοκος, ον – firstborn
  You are used to adjectives declining differently for masculine, feminine and neuter. Some adjectives use the masculine endings for the feminine as well, and you'll find them listed like this in dictionaries. Πρωτότοκος is the nominative singular agreeing with both masculine and feminine nouns, whereas πρωτότοκον agrees with neuter.
σπουδάζω – I hurry
σύ – you (nom sing)
ὑπερῷον, ου, τό – upper room
Χανάαν – Canaan (indeclinable)

4 ACCENTS

4.1 An Exception: Some Middle 2s Imperatives

FURTHER READING: PROBERT 83

While verb accents are generally recessive, an exception is the imperative middle 2s, which often takes a circumflex in its ending instead, on present stems (φοβοῦ, παραιτοῦ cf. the expected γίνου, συλλαμβάνου) and second aorists (ἐπιλαβοῦ, προσλαβοῦ, cf. the expected παράθου).

4.2 -σαι

You cannot see this in the paradigm of λύω, but accents will distinguish the aorist middle 2s imperative and the aorist active infinitive. This is because the imperative is recessive (as expected for a finite verb) whereas the infinitive is a noun, so follows different rules.

παίδευσαι imperative (2s aor act)
παιδεῦσαι infinitive (aor mid)

5 ASPECT IN THE INFINITIVE

You will be pleased to know that you're already familiar with the main ideas in the other moods, because we have seen them in the indicative:

- The nature of the action can affect the author's choice of aspect. Actions with an endpoint will naturally prefer the aorist, and those without one (including states) prefer the present (**EM 2** 5; **EM 6** 7 and especially **EM 7** 5.1).
- The aspects of the present and aorist lend themselves to a variety of situations. In *ENTG* we saw that 'ongoing' can include a single action in progress and also a habit (**EH 7** 1.1.1). Now we are aware that both the 'simple' aspect of the aorist and the 'ongoing' aspect of the present can lend themselves to various contexts. The aorist stem can be ingressive, the present stem can be gnomic, etc. (**EM 2** 5; **EM 6** 7; **EM 7** 5).

While we will treat each mood separately in its own chapter, these basic principles apply more broadly.

5.1 The Basic Approach: Aspect Choice and Situation Type

The basic point is worth grasping. If you ask: 'What does an aorist indicative or an imperfect indicative mean?', the answer in our previous chapters is that it *does* have one core sense, but it *applies* differently in different situations and depending on the meaning of the verb. For example, an **aorist** indicative means that an action is being referred to simply, as a whole. An **aorist** indicative *of a verb with an endpoint* implies that the endpoint was reached; by contrast, an **imperfect or present** indicative of verb with an endpoint implies that the endpoint was not reached. Similarly, in the other moods, the aorist and present stems have that same core meaning (an action presented simply, an action presented as ongoing, respectively) and an application of that meaning to different situations.[2]

---

[2] In the last century or so, classicists have held one of two positions on aspect in the other moods. In one view, the present and the aorist each communicate something positive, with the present indicating something like 'ongoing' and aorist indicating something like 'completion'. So Gildersleeve, 11.19; Kühner-Gerth 389.6; Schwyzer-Debrunner II:252, 257–62. The other view sees the present as telling you something (such as 'ongoing') but the aorist as being the default, communicating nothing at all. So Goodwin 1272; Smyth 1859–60, 1864–5.

Neither view will account for all cases: some of these grammars make allowances for the nature of the verb (states, endpoint verbs, etc.) to explain exceptions. More recently,

We have dealt with different types of situations in passing throughout the **Extra Material** in Chapters 2, 6 and 7, but this is a good moment to gather the threads together.[3]

5.1.1 A Summary of Situation Types

FURTHER READING: *CGCG* 33.8; FANNING 3.1.1

Firstly, some actions **have an end in view**, so that you can say 'job done' once it has been reached. We have called these verbs '**with an endpoint**'.[4] Ἀνάγω – 'I lead up, I restore, I offer up' comes to an end when the object has reached the 'up' destination, or been fully restored, or been offered. If you get halfway there, the action is obviously incomplete.

Secondly, some actions **do not have an end** in view. We have called these verbs '**without an endpoint**'.[5] Ἄγω – you can lead someone along indefinitely, and at some point you might stop. Ἄγω by itself would never be seen as *incomplete*; it just happened for a while and then stopped.

Finally, are we really talking about 'doing' something, or just describing a 'state of being'? If the verb involves **no change and is effortless**, then it is a '**state**'.[6] The most obvious is εἰμί – 'I am'.[7]

See Table 8.7 for some examples.

Table 8.7 Verb Types

States	Without an endpoint	With an endpoint
πλουτέω 'I am rich' (many such Greek verbs describe states of being, and we have no English verb equivalent, so we use 'I am X')	διδάσκω 'I teach' λέγω 'I speak' τηρέω 'I guard, keep' (notice the implied effort, as opposed to ἔχω)	πείθω 'I persuade'. It will take time to make the arguments, but at some point, I have won you over. ἐκβάλλω 'I cast out'. It isn't over as long as 'it' is still inside.

---

this has led to a third view: the nature of the verb affects the choice of aspect. This seems to be gaining in popularity. It is central to Fanning, and you can see it more recently both in grammars of Classical Greek (*CGCG* 33.8–10 and the primer by JACT, *Reading Greek: Grammar and Exercises* §200) and of NT (Köstenberger 238–44 and the fourth edition of *ENTG*). That is the view that we will take below.

[3] This description of different verb types is known as their 'lexical aspect'; what we usually call 'aspect' (the properties of the different verb systems) is '*grammatical* aspect'.
[4] Technically known as 'telic'.
[5] Technically known as 'atelic'.
[6] Technically known as 'stative'.
[7] In the **Extra Material** in Chapters 2, 6 and 7 we have *very occasionally* seen other properties of verbs, but all that was needed to understand their interaction with aspect was common sense. For example, if an event takes no time (like knocking at a door once), then the present stem can't refer to the ongoing single knock but to a sequence of knocks.

Table 8.7 (cont.)

States	Without an endpoint	With an endpoint
κυριεύω 'I am master' (the verb describes the state of *being* the κύριος, and by extension the act of ruling; likewise βασιλεύω, 'I am king', 'I rule')	φιλέω 'I love' (cf. πιστεύω)	τύπτω 'I hit'
	ἐπακούω 'I listen' (cf. ἀκούω)	προσκόπτω 'I strike, I stumble'
κατοικέω 'I dwell'	περιβλέπω 'I look around' (cf. βλέπω, ὁράω)	βάλλω 'I throw'
ἀκούω 'I hear' (cf. the more active ἐπακούω)	λογίζομαι 'I consider' (cf. γινώσκω, οἶδα)	εὑρίσκω 'I find'
βλέπω, ὁράω 'I see' (cf. περιβλέπω)	ζητέω 'I look for'	
γινώσκω, οἶδα 'I know' (cf. λογίζομαι)		
πιστεύω 'I believe' (cf. φιλέω)		
ἔχω 'I have'		

Here are three important caveats.

First, this isn't about verbs in isolation, but about entire *situations*: verbs in specific contexts. This is why we generally refer to 'situations without endpoint' rather than 'verbs without endpoint'. Ἔχω by itself doesn't imply a change or that any effort is required. However, in some contexts, someone might be trying to deprive you of what you have, so that it takes effort to *hold on to* it. Ἔχω in such a context would refer to an action, not merely to remaining passively in a state.

> ἀπῆλθε ποιῆσαι πόλεμον … τῶν **τηρούντων** τὰς ἐντολὰς τοῦ Θεοῦ καὶ <u>ἐχόντων</u> τὴν μαρτυρίαν τοῦ Ἰησοῦ Χριστοῦ Rev 12:17
> he went to wage war … against those who **keep** God's commands and <u>hold on to</u> the testimony of Jesus Christ.
> Ἔχω is just as active here as **τηρέω**.

Similarly, compare διδάσκω (no endpoint) with με ἱππεύειν διδάσκεις (you teach me horse-riding, Xenophon, *Cyr.* 1.3.7) or διδάξετε αὐτὴν τοὺς υἱοὺς Ἰσραήλ (teach [the song] to the children of Israel, Deut 31:19). Ἄγω has no endpoint in itself, but you can supply one: ἤγαγον means 'they led it *here*' in Matt 21:7. This is why the examples below discuss *situations* (rather than *verbs* by themselves) with/without an endpoint.

Second, words can have different senses, and sometimes a verb might fit different categories depending on the sense. Κρατέω usually refers to an action without an endpoint (to hold on to something, using effort), but by extension it can also mean to seize or arrest someone (which has an endpoint).

Third, we're asking how the Greek language conceives of situations, which might be quite different from English. For example, some verbs refer to what you do in your mind; in Greek some of them are viewed as active, others as states. English often views them differently. We're not learning a formula, but learning a language, and once you get beyond the 'Elements' that means getting to know individual words and how they work. The task is to read plenty of Greek texts and develop a nose for them.

This is why we can say that the aorist has a single meaning, despite the various situations which we distinguished in **EM 7** 5. The aorist means that the author presents an event simply, as a complete whole. If that action has an endpoint, that obviously means that the *complete* action reached the endpoint. If it lacks an endpoint, then we mean that the action happened for a while, and it presents *that whole while* simply. Sometimes, for states, the complete event is the *entry* to the state (the 'ingressive' aorist: **EM 7** 5.1.2). These all have a single meaning in common: the event is presented from start to finish as a simple whole. The variation in meaning is because that one meaning has different implications for different types of verbs.

5.1.2 In Summary: Aspect and Situation Type

FURTHER READING: FANNING 6.1.1–6.1.2

The type of situation affects the author's choice of system, as in the indicative.

> **In Summary**
> For **actions that have a natural endpoint, the aorist is the default system: it is what an author will use unless there is something special to highlight**. The use of the present in such a situation presents it *pointedly* as 'in progress' (**EM 2** 5.1.1) for some reason.
>
> For **actions that *do not* have a natural endpoint, the present is the default system**. The use of an aorist infinitive means that an endpoint has been supplied, perhaps implicitly.
>
> For **states, the present is the default system**. The aorist is likely to be *ingressive* or, more rarely, to refer to a period of time in the state (**EM 7** 5.1.2).

This means that even an apparently pointed contrast between aorist and present might not be significant at all:

> ... εἴτε διὰ ζωῆς, εἴτε διὰ θανάτου. ἐμοὶ γὰρ τὸ <u>ζῆν</u>, Χριστός· καὶ τὸ <u>ἀποθανεῖν</u>, κέρδος. Phil 1:20–1
> ... whether by means of life or of death. For as far as I'm concerned, <u>to live</u> is Christ, and <u>to die</u> is gain.

The options open to Paul are life or death. 'To live' is a state, so the present infinitive is what we'd expect for remaining in the state of life. 'To die' is a verb with a natural endpoint, so the aorist is expected. This means that there is nothing being contrasted.[8]

The rest of this section will treat the different situation types in turn: ones with endpoint, without endpoint, and states.

5.2 Situations with Endpoint

5.2.1 Default: Aorist

If a situation has an endpoint, an author will use the aorist by default. The aspect of the aorist presents the action as a whole, which naturally fits an action that has an endpoint. It's when the present is used that you need to ask why. We'll begin with some examples of aorists (the default), and then examples of the present (the departure from the default).

For **actions that have a natural endpoint, the aorist is the default system**:

> ἦλθον δὲ καὶ τελῶναι βαπτισθῆναι. Luke 3:12
> Tax collectors also came to be baptised.
>> They didn't come to attempt to be baptised, or to go through part of a baptism only. The aorist is the default for situations with an endpoint, so that's as expected.
>> If the author had departed from that and used a present stem, we would ask why: perhaps it would refer to a repeated or habitual situation.
>
> See also: Luke 3:21 (infinitive and adverbial participle βαπτισθῆναι, βαπτισθέντος); 2 Clem. 8.3 (infinitive ἐξελθεῖν).

5.2.2 Pointed: Present

The use of the *present* in a situation with an endpoint presents it pointedly as 'in progress, not yet finished'. The various reasons for departing from the aorist correspond to the various contexts in which an author uses ongoing aspect, as seen in the present and imperfect indicative (**EM 2** 5 and **EM 6** 7).

This might be simply to refer to a point when the action was in progress ('descriptive' **EM 2** 5.1.1):

> τὰ δὲ κύματα ἐπέβαλλεν εἰς τὸ πλοῖον, ὥστε αὐτὸ ἤδη γεμίζεσθαι. Mark 4:37
> the waves were breaking into the boat, so that it was already filling up.

---

[8] S. M. Baugh, *Introduction to Greek Tense Form Choice in the Non-Indicative Moods* (PDF Edition), 18–19; available at https://dailydoseofgreek.com/wp-content/uploads/sites/2/2015/09/GreekTenseFormChoice-Baugh.pdf.

Or it might refer to a repeated action, such as a habit or custom (**EM 2** 5.1.3):

> ἐν τῷ εἰσπορεύεσθαι τὸν κύριόν μου εἰς οἶκον Ῥεμμὰν προσκυνῆσαι ἐκεῖ ... 4 Kgdms 5:18
> when my master <u>goes into</u> the house of Rimmon, to worship there ...
>
> ἐντέταλται τῷ Ἰσραὴλ <u>προσφέρειν</u> δάμαλιν Barn. 8.1
> he commanded Israel <u>to offer</u> a heifer

5.3 Situations without Endpoint

If a situation has no endpoint, the author will use a present by default. The 'ongoing' aspect of the present system, referring to the action in progress, not including its end, fits a situation where there is no natural end to be reached. If you see a verb without an endpoint in the *aorist* infinitive, an endpoint has been supplied; it might be implicit, and the choice of aorist might be your only clue that it is there.

Actions that *do not* have a natural endpoint use the present stem.

As we have seen, a verb might not have an endpoint but can be used in a context that supplies one (**EM 8** 5.1.1). Some more examples can be found in Table 8.8.

Table 8.8 Endpoints in Context

Verb without an endpoint	The same verb in a situation with a supplied endpoint
μετέβη ἐκεῖθεν τοῦ <u>διδάσκειν</u> καὶ <u>κηρύσσειν</u> ἐν ταῖς πόλεσιν αὐτῶν Matt 11:1 He went down from there to <u>teach</u> and <u>preach</u> in their cities.	ἃ **ἤκουσας** ... **ταῦτα** παράθου πιστοῖς ἀνθρώποις, οἵτινες ἱκανοὶ ἔσονται καὶ ἑτέρους <u>διδάξαι</u> 2 Tim 2:2 *The things that you heard* ... hand **these** on to faithful men, who are able also <u>to teach</u> others. *This isn't teaching in general, but the passing on of a specific body of instruction, which can therefore be completed. See also Acts 11:26, 20:20.*
ἐργάζεσθαι and φυλάσσειν Gen 2:15	ἐργάσασθαι Isa 28:24 φυλάξαι Exod 22:7

To illustrate the warning about verbs which can have different senses (**EM 8** 5.1.1), Table 8.9 shows κρατέω with and without an endpoint, each time using the expected aspect.

Table 8.9 κρατέω with and without an Endpoint

τοῦ κρατεῖν χεῖρα αὐτοῦ. Ezek 21:11	ἐξῆλθον κρατῆσαι αὐτόν Mark 3:21
to <u>hold</u> it with his hand.	they left <u>to seize</u> him

5.4 States

States don't have an endpoint, so they use the present stem. Unlike the verbs in the previous section, you cannot supply an endpoint to a state. However, as we have seen in the indicative, the aorist of states is frequently used *ingressively*, to refer to the entry to the state. It can also be used (rarely) to refer to a period of time in the state (**EM 7** 5.1.2).

5.4.1 Default: Present

For **states, the present is the default system.**

> δὸς ἡμῖν, κύριε, <u>ἐλπίζειν</u> ἐπὶ τὸ ... ὄνομά σου. 1 Clem. 59.3
> Grant us, Lord, <u>to hope</u> on ... your name.

5.4.2 Ingressive: Aorist

Aorists, of entry to the state ('ingressive'):

> Θέλεις δὲ <u>γνῶναι</u>, ὦ ἄνθρωπε κενέ, ὅτι ...; Jas 2:20
> Do you want <u>to come to know</u>, you witless man, that ... ?

5.4.3 Past Period in the State: Aorist

The aorist can also refer to a period of being in the state (**EM 7** 5.1.2):

> ... ὥστ' ἀναμνησθῆναι τοιαῦτα συμβεβηκότα ... ἢ <u>ἐλπίσαι</u> γενέσθαι ... Aristotle, *Rhet.* 2h.7.1
> [when he is affected] with the result that he remembers such things having befallen ... or <u>he expects</u> them to happen ...
> The *aorist* infinitives describe specific periods of remembering, ἀναμνησθῆναι, or <u>expecting</u>, ἐλπίσαι.

5.5 Avoiding Over-Exegesis

Before analysing the aspect of a verb, it is worth checking that the author had a real choice. Here are some situations where there is little or no choice (**EM 8** 5.5.1–5.5.4) and a reminder not too read the wrong thing into an aorist (**EM 8** 5.5.5).

5.5.1 Indirect Speech

In indirect speech, infinitives, participles and (in older Greek) optatives are used instead of indicative tenses. Rather than analyse the author's choice of aspect of the infinitive, you need to reconstruct the original (or implied) speech, and then analyse the resulting finite verb instead (**EM 10** 6.3).

5.5.2 Purpose

Infinitives of purpose are overwhelmingly aorist, even when the situation has no endpoint:

> Παρακαλῶ οὖν ὑμᾶς ... ἀξίως <u>περιπατῆσαι</u> τῆς κλήσεως ἧς ἐκλήθητε
> Eph 4:1
> So I urge you <u>to walk</u> worthily of the calling by which you were called

> ἐν τῷ εἰσπορεύεσθαι Μωυσῆν εἰς τὴν σκηνὴν τοῦ μαρτυρίου <u>λαλῆσαι</u> αὐτῷ Num 7:89
> When Moses entered the tent of witness <u>to speak</u> with him

5.5.3 Complements of Certain Verbs

FURTHER READING: FANNING 6.1.3.1

When an infinitive is the complement of a verb of desire or command, the aspect of the infinitive should generally be interpreted along the same grounds as an imperative (see **EM 11** 5).[9] However, other verbs appear to affect the aspect of their complement.

Examples:

Ἄρχομαι always takes present complementary infinitives. This makes sense, since whatever you are beginning is obviously being presented as in progress. That means that we shouldn't spend time wondering why the aorist hasn't been used even though the verb has an endpoint.

> **Ἤρξατο** δὲ πρὸς τὸν λαὸν <u>λέγειν</u> τὴν παραβολὴν ταύτην Luke 20:9
> **He began** <u>to tell</u> this parable to the people
> > 'This parable' supplies the endpoint to the verb, but still the present infinitive is used.

Μέλλω almost always takes a present infinitive.[10]

5.5.4 Translated Hebrew

FURTHER READING: JOBES & SILVA 113–27; HORROCKS 4.7.8

Sometimes, a translation of the OT into Greek can be bound more by the underlying Hebrew syntax than normal Greek grammar.

---

[9] Rijksbaron 33.1 (ii).
[10] In older Greek, you could use μέλλω to indicate the aspect of the future, by choosing the stem of the complementary infinitive (Rijksbaron 9n3). That subtlety seems to have died out by the NT period.

5.5.5 Repetition in the Aorist Stem

In the indicative tenses, we stressed that Greek doesn't make a sharp distinction between a single action and a series of actions (including habits and customs). One of the reasons an author will use the **present** stem is precisely to tell you that the action was repeated, habitual, etc. However, the **aorist** stem doesn't inherently *deny* that an event involved a sequence of actions. It just presents an event (including a sequence of actions, a habit, a custom) as a simple whole, without interest in its inner workings (**EM 7** 5.2.3).

> ἐγὼ **πάντοτε** ἐδίδαξα ἐν τῇ συναγωγῇ καὶ ἐν τῷ ἱερῷ John 18:20
> I **always** taught in the synagogue and in the temple

We need to bear this in mind in the other moods as well. The aorist can refer to repeated events, albeit more rarely:

> ἐξουσίαν ἔχουσιν … πατάξαι τὴν γῆν **πάσῃ πληγῇ, ὁσάκις** ἐὰν θελήσωσι Rev 11:6
> they have authority … to strike the earth **with every plague, as often** as they should want.
> 'As often as …' tells us that the aorist infinitive refers to an iterative situation, not to a single act of striking.

> καὶ λαβὼν τοὺς **πέντε ἄρτους** … καὶ κλάσας ἔδωκε τοῖς μαθηταῖς τοὺς ἄρτους Matt 14:19
> having taken the **five loaves** … after breaking [**the loaves**] he gave them to the disciples
> At least five actions are referred to as a simple whole by the aorist participle.
> See also: Matt 13:24; 21:2–6; 26:60; Exod 12:23; Eccl 3:5; 1 Clem. 61.3; 2 Clem. 8.3.

Don't throw your hands up and conclude that Greek can mean *anything*. It can't. Whether you are dealing with a single event or a sequence is something that you determine from the context: that is true in the indicative and in the other moods. The aspect of the verb is about how you view that event (regardless of whether it is a single one or a sequence).

CHAPTER 9

Pronouns and Conjunctions
—
Accusative Case; Conjunctions

> **How to Use This Chapter**
>
> In this chapter, you meet two new classes of words. Pronouns work very much like adjectives; please make sure you are completely happy with the adjective endings so far. You will also meet short words that show how sentences relate to each other: conjunctions.
>
> Everything in the **Extra Help** in this chapter is optional, and if this is your first time learning Greek, you might want to skip it for now and just work through the chapter of *ENTG* and then the **Greek Reading** below. If you do want to include the **Extra Help**, please work through the sections below, which will guide you through this chapter of *ENTG*.
>
> In the **Extra Material** you will meet the major contexts in which the accusative case can appear. We go a bit further with accents. We go a little bit further on the principle of reading with understanding, as opposed to translating; we'll use the conjunctions in this chapter as examples.

1 BEFORE *ENTG* 9.1: READING WITH UNDERSTANDING

The single aim of *ENTG* is stated on page 1: 'To help you learn enough Greek to read the New Testament.' With this focus on *reading*, we need to note that the NT has been translated many times and always competently. *ENTG* is not a course in translation but in reading with understanding, and there is a difference.

It is obvious to you by now that Greek cannot be transposed into English one word at a time.

> ὁ ἄνθρωπος ὁ καλός
> 'the man the beautiful' makes no sense at all

Much of the information contained in English word order is given over to cases in Greek. Think of the difference between these two:

> ὁ ἄρτος αὐτοῦ
> 'the bread of him' isn't English.

As we read Greek, we work from the rules of Greek to work out meaning. That's our aim. If we want to express that meaning into English, we then go through the rules of English to put it into a coherent sentence, as shown in Figure 9.1.

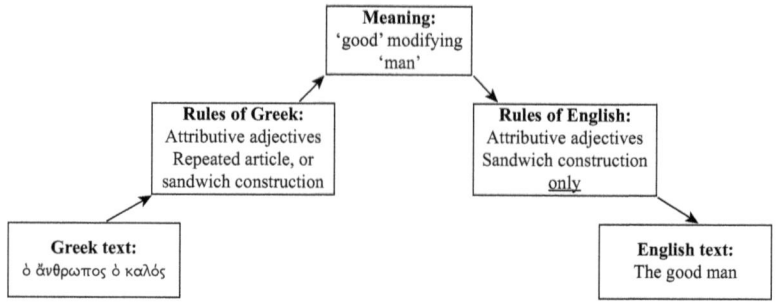

Figure 9.1 From Greek to English Meaning

Not 'the man the beautiful' but 'the beautiful man'; not 'the bread of him' but 'his bread'. The difference is down to understanding what the Greek words tell us, and then how to say that in English.

In this chapter of *ENTG*, you will need to pay attention to the rules of Greek for some new words. In **EM 9** 5, I'll give you a little window into how you will eventually want to think about some of the Greek words you will meet in this chapter. These are just to illustrate the principle: it pays to understand how certain individual words *work* rather than memorising an English equivalent.

The way to understand how Greek works better is to read plenty of Greek texts. At this stage, you have your hands full, while you're still having to think slowly about parsing the various words in a sentence, so reading is quite a struggle. The simplified and made-up texts you're using so far will help you get into a habit of reading; once you complete *ENTG* your most important way of growing in Greek is reading *Greek*. Become a confident reader before you become an exegete. The point of these notes on οὗτος, ἐκεῖνος and contrastive pronouns is to illustrate what you will eventually want to aim for: not replacing Greek words with glosses from a flashcard, but seeing how words work together.[1]

You can choose whether to use or skip each section of this **Extra Help** independently: they don't depend on each other, and nothing in later chapters depends on them.

1.1 Embedding the Paradigms

Work through *ENTG* 9.1, stopping before **Practice** 9.1.1. Now use the method we have used in earlier chapters.

---

[1] If you'd like to take this further by thinking about conjunctions as well, you'll find notes in **EM 9** 5.

1. Make sure that you are thoroughly comfortable with the paradigm of λόγος and can effortlessly produce the paradigms of ἔργον, ἀρχή, ἡμέρα, δόξα as simple variations.
2. Make sure you can write out the endings of any adjective based on the above endings.
3. Remember that the neut sing nom/acc ending is -ον except on the article and on pronouns, where it is -ο. Note the very helpful rules in the **Notes** in *ENTG* 9.1.1.
4. Use the above to write out the paradigms of both pronouns, without looking anything up.
5. Check what you've written against the right pattern, and use that to reinforce the rules.
6. Keep doing that until you never get it wrong.

Complete **Practice** 9.1.1.

Work through *ENTG* 9.1.2 and complete **Practice** 9.1.2 before reading on below.

1.2 After *ENTG* 9.1: οὗτος and ἐκεῖνος

English will sometimes *but not always* use 'this' or 'that' when Greek uses οὗτος or ἐκεῖνος. This is where reading the Greek text gives you cues as a reader which get lost in translation.

The author will use the difference between οὗτος or ἐκεῖνος to help you. For example, having had various characters or ideas in a story, he might use οὗτος to refer to the most recent one or ἐκεῖνος to refer to a less recent one.

For example, Matt 27:58, having mentioned several characters' reactions to the crucifixion, and most recently Joseph of Arimathea, says:

'οὗτος approached Pilate …'

In John 2:21, Jesus has been speaking, then some others speak. John uses ἐκεῖνος to tell us that he is explaining the words of *Jesus*, not those of the most recent speaker:

ἐκεῖνος δὲ ἔλεγε περί …

You'll see several examples in the opening of John, where English word order doesn't allow you to show what John makes quite clear:

Θεὸς ἦν ὁ λόγος. οὗτος ἦν ἐν ἀρχῇ …
The word was God. [The word] was in the beginning …
The most recently mentioned person is referred to by οὗτος, and that's ὁ λόγος, which doesn't work in English (where God has to go at the end of the previous sentence).

ὄνομα αὐτῷ **Ἰωάννης**· οὗτος ...
his name was **John**. This one [John, as opposed to the Word] ...
> English doesn't like 'this one' but would prefer 'he', which is more ambiguous than the Greek text.

Work through *ENTG* 9.2 and complete all exercises, including the **Half-Way Practice**.

1.2.1 Predication with οὗτος and ἐκεῖνος

ENTG 9.1.2 (ii) tells us that οὗτος and ἐκεῖνος, when they are attributive modifiers, go in 'predicative word order'. See my warning about what this means in **EH 5** 1.3.2.

However, to express predication, you also use predicative word order. You'll have to decide whether you're seeing 'this man' or 'this is the man':

ἐλάλησας τὰ ἀγαθὰ **ταῦτα** 1 Chr 17:26
you spoke **these** good things
> Obviously attributive, because the sentence has another verb, ἐλάλησας.

οὗτοι οὐκ εἰσιν θεοί Jer 16:20
these are not gods
> Obviously predicative, because it has εἰμί.

τοῦτο θέλημα Θεοῦ 1 Thess 5:18
this [is] God's will [θέλημα, vocab in chapter 12]
> Predicative, because there is no other verb in the sentence.

Work through *ENTG* 9.3, but stop before **Practice** 9.3, and read on here.

1.3 After *ENTG* 9.3: Contrastive Pronouns

You might wonder why there seem to be two forms of the 1st person singular pronoun, except in the nominative. In fact, there are also two forms for the 2nd person singular pronouns. Please see the fully accented tables in the **Online Material**.

The unmarked forms are the default forms, with no particular emphasis. The contrastive forms always have the accent, and in the 1st person also begin with ἐ.

These accented forms are used:

- whenever they follow a preposition (almost always, but there are exceptions). No special emphasis is implied.
- otherwise, to indicate a contrast of some form. This is when they become interesting. They make it clear that it is *I* or *you*, as opposed to someone else, or as opposed to expectation.
- Since the nom form is always implied by the verb ending anyway, the *unmarked* nom sing forms cannot exist. ἐγώ / σύ always clarifies or highlights the fact that I/you are the subject, as opposed to someone else.

This is an example where accents really make a clear and easy difference to reading.

The possessive *adjectives* (*ENTG* 9.3.3), on the other hand, are always accented and always emphasise the possessive relationship.

1.3.1 Word Order with Pronouns

Pronouns can generally appear before or after the phrase they modify, or even in sandwich construction.

> τὸν πατέρα ὑμῶν Matt 5:16
> your heavenly father
>
> μου τοὺς λόγους Matt 7:24
> my words
>
> τὸν ὑμῶν ζῆλον 2 Cor 7:7
> your zeal

Where the meaning is altered by word order, *ENTG* will alert you to it (e.g. 9.2.1 on αὐτός). Where a pronoun is more restricted in how it can appear, you don't need to know this: you just need to be able to read it in the forms where it does appear.

Complete **Practice** 9.3.

Work through *ENTG* 9.4, but stop before **Practice** 9.4, and read on here.

1.4 Conjunctions (*ENTG* 9.4) and Other Little Linking Words

These little words aren't best understood by English equivalents. An author will use them to guide your understanding of how two portions of Greek relate to each other. We need to understand what they tell the reader, not replace them with English equivalents. Eventually, see this in **EM 9** 5.

For now, be aware that my translations of the **Greek Readings** will often interpret these conjunctions in ways that aren't captured by the glosses you've learned. This is especially true of καί and δέ, which might vanish in translation altogether.

Complete **Practice** 9.4 before reading on here.

2 THE GREEK READING

The story so far ...

Aseneth's parents sing the virtues of their imminent guest, Joseph. He is righteous, beloved by God, second only to Pharaoh in power, the national keeper of grain who will rescue Egypt from the looming famine. Aseneth replies that he was, in fact, a Canaanite keeper of sheep (see Gen 46:34) and that she would rather marry Pharaoh's firstborn, a true prince. Her father drops the subject. Yet that is only the story so far!

5:1 Καὶ εὐηγγέλισεν ὑπηρετῆς τοῦ Πεντεφροῦ λέγων·

[2] Ὁ Ἰωσὴφ πρὸ τῶν θυρῶν τῆς οἰκίας ἡμῶν ἐστιν.

[3] Καὶ ὁ Πεντεφρῆς ἀπέλυσε τὴν Ἀσενὲθ ἀπὸ τοῦ προσώπου αὐτοῦ. [4] ἐκείνη οὖν ἀπὸ τοῦ ὑπερῴου αὐτῆς ἔβλεψε θεωρῆσαι τὸν Ἰωσήφ. [5] ἐκεῖνος γὰρ εἰσήρχετο εἰς τὴν οἰκίαν. [6] ἐξήρχετο ἄρα ἀσπάζεσθαι τὸν Ἰωσὴφ ὁ Πεντεφρῆς καὶ ἡ γυνὴ αὐτοῦ καὶ ὁ οἶκος αὐτοῦ. [7] καὶ ἤνοιξαν τὰς θύρας τῆς οἰκίας καὶ εἰσήρχετο ὁ Ἰωσὴφ ἐν τῷ ἅρματι τοῦ Φαραώ. [8] ἤρχετο ὁ Ἰωσὴφ εἰς τὴν οἰκίαν ὅτε ἔκλεισαν τὰς θύρας ὀπίσω αὐτοῦ. [9] ἄλλοι δέ, εἴτε ἄνθρωπος εἴτε τέκνον, συνήρχοντο ἔξω, διότι οἱ στρατιῶται ἔκλεισαν τὰς θύρας. [10] προσεκύνησαν μὲν ὅ τε Πεντεφρῆς καὶ ἡ γυνὴ αὐτοῦ καὶ ὁ οἶκος αὐτοῦ τῷ Ἰωσήφ. [11] ἡ δὲ Ἀσενὲθ μήποτε προσεκύνησε τῷ ἀνθρώπῳ εἴτε ἐκείνῳ εἴτε ἄλλῳ. [12] ἀλλὰ ἦν ὁ Ἰωσήφ, ἔχων ἱμάτιον καινόν. [13] καὶ θεώρησας αὐτοὺς ὁ Ἰωσὴφ ἀπὸ τοῦ ἅρματος καὶ ἀσπασάμενος αὐτοὺς ηὐχαρίστησεν αὐτοῖς.

ἸΩΣΗΦ·

[14] Πεντεφρᾶ, ἐδόξασας ἐμὲ σὺ καὶ ὅλος ὁ οἶκός σου. εὐχαριστῶ σοι.

([15] οἱ ὑπηρέται ἔλεγον πρὸς ἀλλήλους·

[16] Πόσος ἐστὶν οὗτος;

[17] ἐπεὶ αὐτὸς ἦν μέγας ὡς δένδρον.)

ΠΕΝΤΕΦΡΗΣ·

[18] Κύριε, οἱ σοὶ δοῦλοί ἐσμεν. [19] αἴτησόν με κἀγὼ ποιήσω. [20] τὰ ἐμὰ σά ἐστιν. [21] συνάγομεν ἀρνία πολλά σοι καὶ τοῖς ἀνθρώποις σου. [22] ἀλλὰ ἀποκάλυψον ἡμῖν μυστήριον· ποῖον ποτήριόν ἐστι τοῦτο;

²³ Ἐπεὶ εἶχεν ποτήριον.

ἸΩΣΗΦ·

²⁴ Τὸ μὲν ποτήριον ἦν τοῦ Φαραὼ νῦν δέ ἐστιν ἐμὸς ἀλλὰ ἔσται γε σός.

2.1 Vocabulary

ἅρματι – chariot (neut dat sing)
ἅρματος – chariot (neut gen sing)
γυνή, ἡ – woman

θύρα, ας, ἡ – door / gate
κλείω – I close
ὑπερῷον, ου, τό – upper room

3 ACCENTS

3.1 New Enclitics and Proclitics

FURTHER READING: VS 54B

In **EH 9** 1.3, we saw the 1st and 2nd person personal pronouns have unmarked and emphatic forms, with the unmarked ones lacking an accent. The unaccented forms are *enclitic*, so throw their accent back onto the previous word (**EM 5** 3.1).

Γε and τε are also enclitic.

Enclitics are usually post-positive ('timid words' *ENTG* 9.4.1), such as γε and τε. *Not* all post-positives are enclitic: γάρ and μέν.

4 ACCUSATIVE

FURTHER READING: VS 149–57; WALLACE 176–205

In **EM 3** and **EM 4** we met a variety of contexts in which Greek authors can use a dative and genitive, with the genitive being quite vague and open-ended. The accusative is even more straightforward than the dative. We meet its few contexts now.

4.1 Reminder: Beware of the Labels

FURTHER READING: *CGCG* 30.1

As with other cases (**EM 3** 5.1), the accusative doesn't mean a variety of things, but has a meaning that lends itself to various situations. You don't necessarily need to pin every accusative with one of the labels below. Resist the urge to invent new types of accusative which say more about our exegetical interest than about the accusative itself.

4.2 Direct Object

This is the main context you have met so far.

4.2.1 Direct Object

ἐπέγνων[2] τὸν κύριον ἡμῶν Ἰησοῦν Χριστόν Acts Pil., Prologue.
I recognised our <u>Lord Jesus Christ</u>.
> Remember that all cases can occur in apposition, as here: κύριον with Ἰησοῦν Χριστόν.

4.2.2 Verbs with Double Accusative

In English, as in Greek, many verbs helpfully distinguish a more direct object from a more indirect one. Some, however, take two direct objects, and the learner of the language must learn to work out which is which.

Some act on a person and on a thing, in an obviously different way:

<u>δικαιοσύνην</u> διδάξας ὅλον <u>τὸν κόσμον</u> 1 Clem. 5.7
having taught <u>righteousness</u> to <u>the whole world</u>.

ἐνέδυσάν <u>με</u> τὸν <u>χιτῶνα</u> Dio Chrysostom, *Ven.* 7.62
they clothed <u>me</u> <u>with the tunic</u>

Others connect one thing with another, as a *complement* of the object:

ἐκάλεσε τὸ <u>ὄνομα</u> αὐτῆς <u>Ζέλφαν</u> T. Naph. 1.11
She called her <u>name</u> <u>Zilpah</u>

ὁ ποιῶν <u>τοὺς ἀγγέλους</u> αὐτοῦ <u>πνεύματα</u> Ps 103:4
the one making his <u>angels</u> <u>spirits</u>

4.2.3 Infinitives

An infinitive is a verbal noun: a noun giving the idea of the verb. The infinitive can be the object of sentences. When the infinitive has its own object, that object will be in the accusative.

καὶ τότε ἄρξῃ ... <u>τὸν ἔσχατον τόπον</u> κατέχειν Luke 14:9
then you will begin ... to take <u>the last place</u>

When it has a subject, that too will be in the accusative. This is because the infinitive, and its subject, are the object of the sentence, as in English, 'Tell *him* to come' not 'Tell *he* to come.'

εἴπωμεν <u>πῦρ</u> καταβῆναι; Luke 9:54
should we tell <u>fire to come down</u>?

---

[2] For help parsing this: *ENTG* 11.1.6 (i).

This means that it can be ambiguous, even when there is obviously both a subject and an object. It will mostly be obvious which meaning makes sense, but not always:

διὰ τὸ ἔχειν **με** ἐν τῇ καρδίᾳ ὑμᾶς Phil 1:7
'because you hold **me** in such affection'[3] or
'because I have you ...'[4]

4.3 Adverbial Accusative (Rare)

The accusative appears in the contexts below rather rarely. Instead, Greek usually expresses the manner of an action using adverbs, certain prepositions, participles (EM 14 4.2.2), the dative (EM 4 4.2.1), or the noun τρόπος 'manner'. Here are some examples:

Καὶ ἐβαρεῖτο ὁ υἱὸς Φαραὼ καὶ ἐλυπεῖτο σφόδρα δι' Ἀσενὲθ καὶ ἔπασχε κακῶς.
Pharaoh's son was depressed, he was grieved greatly because of Aseneth, and he suffered badly.
Using adverbs.

κατὰ ἄνθρωπον λέγω Gal 3:15
I am speaking humanly
Using a preposition: 'according to a person', as a human

ὁ σπόρος πῶς καὶ τίνα τρόπον γίνεται; 1 Clem. 24.4
How and in what way does the sowing come about?
Using τρόπος

κατὰ πάντα τρόπον πᾶσιν ἀρέσκειν Ign. Trall. 2.3
to please everyone according to every way
Combining τρόπος and a preposition

4.3.1 The 'Internal' Object

Consider a sentence like: 'He landed a blow on him', 'She made her way to town', or 'They walked a funny walk.' The 'objects' in each sentence aren't a 'thing' that you can buy in a shop or find lying around. They only exist during the action. They are really a description of the action: *how* it happened. They do the work of an adverb, like *quickly*. 'Did he hit him *lightly*?' 'No, he hit him *with a blow*; he landed *a punch*.'

---

[3] Gerald F. Hawthorne, *Philippians* (WBC 43; Dallas: Word, 2004), 26.
[4] J. B. Lightfoot, *Saint Paul's Epistle to the Philippians* (London: Macmillan, 1913), 84.

This is called the 'internal object' and was the original use of the accusative case, from which the 'direct object' eventually grew.[5]

> ποιμένες **φυλάσσοντες** φυλακάς Luke 2:8
> shepherds **keeping** watch
>
> **παρήλθομεν** ἔρημον ὁδόν Μωάβ Deut 2:8
> **we walked** the way of the Moab desert
>> The accusative describes how they walked. They didn't do something to a pre-existing 'way' (there wasn't one), but made their way in the desert. They had to endure desert conditions.

There isn't always a hard dividing line between internal object and direct object. For example:

> οἰκίας καλὰς **κατοικήσας** Philo, *Sacrifices* 55
> **having inhabited** beautiful houses
>> This could mean that they did something to the houses (the direct object), namely, inhabit them. From the context, the sense seems adverbial, describing the style of their living: in *beautiful houses* (internal object).

4.3.2 Manner

From that internal object grew the more general idea: the accusative telling you the manner in which you perform an action.[6] It is therefore adverbial. It is no coincidence that many Greek adverbs look like accusative neuter singulars of an adjective, since that's exactly what they are.

> ἀνθρώπινον λέγω Rom 6:19
> I'm speaking humanly [in the manner of people]
>
> ὁ Θεὸς ἡμᾶς τοὺς ἀποστόλους ἐσχάτους ἀπέδειξεν 1 Cor 4:9
> God has displayed us apostles last [in the manner of being at the tail end]
>
> πιστὸς ἀρχιερεὺς τὰ πρὸς τὸν Θεόν Heb 2:17
> a faithful chief-priest in the things that concern God
>> τά turns the following preposition and all that it governs into a noun (**EH 5** 1.4.3).
>>
>> That accusative phrase doesn't *limit* the faithfulness of the priest, as though he was faithless in other things (that would be an accusative of **reference/respect**); it *describes* his faithfulness.

---

[5] This is sometimes labelled 'cognate accusative', because the verb and internal object can be cognate (they feared a great fear Mark 4:41; he was amazed with great amazement Rev 17:6). However, this tells you nothing useful at all.
[6] Cf. the instrumental dative, referring to manner (**EM 4** 4.2.1).

Often the sense of manner comes through some modifier on the accusative:

> βαπτισθέντες τὸ βάπτισμα **Ἰωάννου** Luke 7:29
> having been baptised <u>with **John's** baptism</u> [in the manner of how John baptises, 'baptised John's way']
>
> ἐκαυματίσθησαν οἱ ἄνθρωποι καῦμα **μέγα** Rev 16:9
> the men were scorched <u>with a **strong** heat</u>
>> Notice that, while the verb and noun are cognates (ἐκαυματίσθησαν καῦμα), this is *not* an 'internal object', because the heat really does exist in the real world, whether they got scorched by it or not.

The label 'cognate' accusative distracts from what the accusative is telling you, which can be internal (Luke 4:8, above), manner (the two examples above), or even (as in the following) direct object:[7]

> Ἀναβὰς εἰς ὕψος <u>ᾐχμαλώτευσεν αἰχμαλωσίαν</u>, καὶ <u>ἔδωκε δόματα</u> Eph 4:8
> After ascending on high, <u>he led captivity captive</u>, and <u>gave gifts</u>

4.3.3 Reference / Respect

> αὐξήσωμεν εἰς αὐτὸν τὰ πάντα Eph 4:15
> let us grow into him <u>in every way</u> [or in everything]
>> An accusative of 'manner' implies '*how* we grow is in every way that we can grow'.
>> That's obviously quite close to:
>> 'let me tell you what the command to grow refers to: its scope is "everything"; grow without leaving anything out'.

This 'accusative of reference or respect' does the same job as the 'dative of reference or respect': it tells you what the sentence applies to (**EM 4** 4.2.6). The dative is much more common as a way of expressing this:

> φρόνιμος γίνου ὡς ὁ ὄφις ἐν πᾶσιν Ign. *Pol.* 2.2
> Be as shrewd as the serpent <u>in all things</u>
>
> εἰ γὰρ τὸ δοκεῖν ταῦτα ἐπράχθη … κἀγὼ τὸ δοκεῖν δέδεμαι Ign. *Smyrn.* 4.2
> for if these things happened <u>in appearance</u> … then I too am bound <u>in appearance</u>
>> The second half shows that it means '*merely* in appearance'.

---

[7] Discussions of different types of cognate accusative seem to be telling us more about English idiom than Greek, and missing the significance of the accusatives that are cognate with their verbs for a variety of reasons (e.g. Smyth 1563–70).

This sense of the accusative (and dative) is limiting, compared with the accusative (and dative) of *manner*, which further describes something which is true in general. Compare 1 Cor 4:9 above, which has the accusative of manner ἐσχάτους. The statement is true without it: 'God has displayed us apostles.' It adds the manner in which it happened, 'last'. An accusative of reference, if removed, renders the sentence false: 'I too am bound' isn't true. It is only true that 'I too am bound in appearance'.

> πάντα ὑμῖν γνωριοῦσι τὰ ὧδε Col 4:9
> he will make known to you everything <u>as far as here is concerned</u>
> > He won't reveal everything in the universe, just the local matters.

The difference in meaning between accusative of manner vs respect can sometimes be quite important, but we must remember that the author simply used *an accusative*. We're deciding what it means based on other factors, not deciding 'what kind of accusative' it is. The label follows the exegesis, not the other way round:

> οὗτοι ἀνθίστανται τῇ ἀληθείᾳ, ἄνθρωποι κατεφθαρμένοι <u>τὸν νοῦν</u> 2 Tim 3:8
> These oppose the truth,
> > men corrupted <u>as far as their mind goes only</u> [**respect**] or
> > men corrupted, <u>specifically</u>, corrupted <u>by the way that they think</u> [**manner**]

4.3.4 Measure

Whereas the dative of place or time identifies the area or time period (Tuesday rather than Wednesday), and the genitive tells you that it was part of that time (at some point during the night), the accusative usually *fills* the time or space. That's an extension of the sense above, telling you when the statement is true. 'I mowed the lawn' is a true statement when qualified by 'throughout Saturday morning'.

> ἀλλ' ἔδωκεν ἑαυτὸν εἰς τὴν ἔρημον κἀκεῖ ἔπηξε την σκηνὴν αὐτοῦ, καὶ ἐνήστευσεν <u>ἡμέρας τεσσαράκοντα καὶ νύκτας τεσσαράκοντα</u> Prot. Jas. 1.4
> but he handed himself over to the desert, and pitched his tent there, and fasted <u>forty days and forty nights</u>

> ἐληλακότες οὖν ὡς <u>σταδίους εἰκοσιπέντε ἢ τριάκοντα</u> John 6:19
> having rowed about <u>twenty-five or thirty stades</u>

However, as Deut 2:8 above shows, the accusative of a region or time can also have a sense of **manner**, or just be an **internal object**; it won't fill the region or time in that case.

As ever, if using simply an accusative would be too ambiguous, or if the author wants to emphasise this meaning more strongly than merely by using an accusative of space, they can rephrase it to make the point: ὅλην τὴν Γαλιλαίαν the *whole* of Galilee (Matt 4:23).

We will now compare the accusative of measure with the other cases in time and space (**EM 9** 4.4).

4.4 Time and Space and Cases

FURTHER READING: *CGCG* 30.56

We have now seen, separately, how three cases apply to time and space: the partitive genitive (**EM 3** 5.2.6), the locative dative (**EM 4** 4.3.1) and the accusative of measure (**EM 9** 4.3.4). Let's look at them side by side in Table 9.1.

Table 9.1 Time and Space and Cases

Case	Region	Time period
Dative (locative) Identifies one among the options.	Where	When
Accusative (measure) Tells you the extent in space or time.	How far	How long
Genitive (partitive) Tells you which region this time or space *is a part of*.	Within which region	Within which time

Time:

> ὁ Παῦλος ... εἶπε, Παραγγέλλω σοι ... ἐξελθεῖν ἀπ' αὐτῆς. καὶ ἐξῆλθεν αὐτῇ τῇ ὥρᾳ. Acts 16:18
> Paul ... said, 'I command you ... to come out of her.' And it came out in that very hour.
>
> καὶ ἐρρέθη πρὸς Ἀβράμ ... πάροικον ἔσται τὸ σπέρμα σου ἐν γῇ οὐκ ἰδίᾳ ... ταπεινώσουσιν αὐτοὺς τετρακόσια ἔτη. Gen 15:13
> And it was told to Abram: ... your seed will dwell in a land not their own ... and they will abase them for 400 years.
>
> ἢ μεσονυκτίου, ἢ ἀλεκτοροφωνίας, ἢ **πρωὶ** Mark 13:35
> [for you do not know when he will return] whether during the middle of the night, or during the rooster's crowing, or **at daybreak**

Space:

> οἱ δὲ ἄλλοι μαθηταὶ τῷ πλοιαρίῳ ἦλθον John 21:8
> the other disciples came in the boat
>
> καὶ ἀνεβιβάσθη ὁ βάτραχος, καὶ ἐκάλυψεν τὴν γῆν Αἰγύπτου. Exod 8:6
> The frog [i.e. the plague of frogs] was brought up, and it covered the land of Egypt

> κηρύσσων ἐν τῇ ἐρήμῳ τῆς Ἰουδαίας Matt 3:1
> preaching in the desert of Judaea [i.e. within Judaea]

5 CONJUNCTIONS: UNDERSTANDING THEIR FUNCTION, NOT LEARNING GLOSSES

FURTHER READING: RUNGE, *DGGNT*, CHAPTER 2

Remember: the way to understand how Greek works better is to read plenty of Greek texts. Become a confident reader before you become an exegete. These brief notes illustrate the aim of reading: not replacing Greek words with glosses from a flashcard, but seeing how words work together.

A **γάρ** B: tells you that B **explains** A. 'For' or 'because' usually work. However, you cannot say 'γάρ B, A', unlike English, 'because of the weather, we'll stay indoors'. Γάρ always *follows* what is explained, and precedes the explanation. 'For' in English is also (and more commonly nowadays) a preposition, whose meanings have nothing to do with γάρ: 'I brought it *for* you'.

> Unlike **γάρ, διά** + acc ('because') can precede what it explains: in Matt 13:6, διὰ τὸ μὴ ἔχειν ῥίζαν ('because of its not having roots') precedes 'it dried up'.

A **ἀλλά** B: tells you that **rather** than A, B **instead**. 'But' is often a good fit. However, 'but' in English also has a different job, meaning 'except': 'there *but* for the grace of God go I'. You cannot use **ἀλλά** to mean 'except', only to mark a contrast.[8]

A **δέ** B: tells you 'I, the author, am **moving on** from A to B.' **Don't** simply translate it as 'but'. The author tells you that he is, in some way, making progress. It is up to you to discern in what sense there is a shift in meaning, subject, topic, etc. (As *ENTG* 9.4.3 tells you, when combined with the article it marks a shift in subject.)

> **μέν** A **δέ** B: I'm telling you in advance that I'll say A and then *move on* with δέ to B. μέν can signal the start of a longer list of items, with δέ moving from one to the other each time. For example, Eph 4:11 has four items in a list, headed by μέν and divided from each other by three δέ.

Even more open-ended is **καί**. A **καί** B tells you: 'A is **associated** with B, but I'm not saying how.' **Don't** simply replace with 'and'. The author is just telling the reader that there is some connection to be inferred between A and B. In Mark's Gospel, it functions basically like punctuation, dividing sentences from each other.[9] In other

---

[8] Remember to learn ἀλλά with the stress on the final α, not the first one: *ENTG* 9.2.3; don't worry about the difference between ἀ and ἀ – see **EM 1** 3.3.
[9] The original version of *Joseph & Aseneth*, like Mark's Gospel, is very fond of using καί as the equivalent of punctuation, but in the **Reading** below, I'll sprinkle other connectives throughout the passage for the sake of practice.

passages, the range of published translations is bewildering, including: 'and, also, but, even, then, so, *comma*, or, with, now', and many more. Καί does not mean any of these: it means, 'Dear reader, I leave you to work out the connection between A and B.' That's our job as readers, and that's why competent translators do not stick to one or two glosses but work out the connection each time in context. A very common connection is, of course, that covered by 'and' in English.

> τε A καί B: τε is to καί as μέν is to δέ. It tells you that it will start a list of items, each joined by καί. When there are only two items, English can capture this with 'both … and'. However, that's often an overtranslation, and it doesn't work when there are more items in the list, such as Gen 37:10, 'I, and your mother, and your brothers.'
>
> *Redundant* καί: tells you 'what's more' (*ENTG* 9.4.4).

γε – this postpositive puts what has just been mentioned in sharp focus, but this can have opposite meanings: it can **intensify** it, such as English 'indeed'; or it can **play it down**, such as English 'at any rate'. It combines with many other connectives, such as εἴ γε … 'if <u>really</u> …'.

A οὖν B is particularly interesting. You can frequently get away with thinking that it means 'therefore'. However, in narrative that often doesn't work (John 4 is a good passage to skim and see this). Runge offers us an explanation that incorporates those cases: A οὖν B means 'there is a close connection between A and B such that B develops A'. In a logical argument, that will often mean that 'A implies B' ('therefore'). In a narrative, it will often mean that A is concluded, and B is next. In narrative, sometimes A does cause B, and you can say 'therefore'; other times, you want something more neutral, like 'thus' or 'so'. However, just as δέ doesn't mean 'and / but', οὖν doesn't mean these English equivalents, but tells you 'B develops A and is very closely connected with it'.

With all the above, we need to work out what the Greek text means, and then work out how to put that into English. Replacing these connective words with English equivalents will not do that, any more than replacing each of ὁ ἄνθρωπος ὁ ἀγαθός with 'the man the good'.

Be aware, especially, that good English renderings will not necessarily provide any equivalent word for a conjunction if the context already conveys their meaning. For example:

> ἄλλοι **δὲ** ἔλεγον, Οὔ, **ἀλλὰ** πλανᾷ τὸν ὄχλον. John 7:12
> 'No,' others said, 'he is leading the people astray.'
>> Most English translations omit the δέ entirely (it is obvious that we are moving on from one set of people to another); about half omit the ἀλλά (the use of 'no' already flags up the impending contrasting opinion).

5.1 Examples in Combination

In Gal 4, we have combined uses of δέ ἀλλά καί μέν οὖν and γάρ. Published translations by no means replace these with standard glosses. Verse 1 uses δέ to express moving on, followed by λέγω; even quite literal translations have nothing of 'but' in them, rather conveying that Paul is now explaining what he has previously written. (He is moving on from the one to the other.)

In v7, the sequence ἀλλά ... δέ ... καί most commonly becomes 'but ... *and* ... *then*' not 'but ... but ... and'.

In v8, the combination of ἀλλά ... μέν does not yield 'but on the one hand'; instead, we find translations such as 'formerly', or even no equivalent at all. This is because the contrast is obvious enough as it is. On the other hand, the δέ which answers this μέν (start of v9) is then translated as a strong 'but'.

Let each of these connectives make you think about what the author is doing; don't reach for the English in your flashcards.

CHAPTER 10

Complex Sentences
—
Indirect Discourse; 'Little Words'

> **How to Use This Chapter**
> Work through this chapter of *ENTG*, section by section, completing exercises as you go. As you complete each section, read **Extra Help** below for that section.
> In the **Extra Help**, you will see how *relative clauses* are similar to the 'branches' we have met, and find some help with morphology. After a little more help with indirect statements, you will find help with some of the 'little' words in vocab that can be so hard to learn.
> In the **Extra Material** you will meet other ways of expressing indirect speech and some patterns that help us to learn a lot of these 'little words'.

1 TREES AND SUPER-BRANCHES: THE RELATIVE

1.1 After *ENTG* 10.1.1

1.1.1 Review of Tree and Branches

Heed the warning in *ENTG* that you need to be perfectly happy with how basic sentences work so far, which directs you to chapters 2, 3 and 4.

Remember that we tackle any Greek sentence by identifying the elements of the trunk, by parsing them. Everything else is a branch, which modifies something within that trunk. We can connect two trees, using the connective words of Chapter 9.

1.1.2 The Relative Clause

We now meet the most flexible modifier of all: the relative. It can take a whole other tree (with all its trunk, branches and twigs) and turn it into a branch off another tree. That branch is called the 'relative clause', and the trunk of the tree is called the 'main clause'.

The best way to get to grips with the relative pronoun is to do as many English-to-Greek exercises as you have time for. As we discussed in **EH 9** 1, you need to avoid thinking of English words to replace the relative pronoun, and instead learn thoroughly how the pronoun works in Greek.

It may help you to do it in two stages: write two Greek sentences, and replace the noun with the right form of αὐτός. If you then replace αὐτός with the relative pronoun in the same gender, case and number, you can combine the sentences into one. Take the first example in *ENTG* 10.1.3:

ὁ κύριος ἔπεμψεν <u>τὸν ἄγγελον</u>.   <u>ὁ ἄγγελος</u>   ἔβλεψεν τὴν θάλασσαν.
↓

ὁ κύριος ἔπεμψεν <u>τὸν ἄγγελον</u>.   <u>αὐτός</u>   ἔβλεψεν τὴν θάλασσαν.
↓

ὁ κύριος ἔπεμψεν <u>τὸν ἄγγελον</u>,   <u>ὅς</u>   ἔβλεψεν τὴν θάλασσαν.

The relative pronoun is simply *the ending* of that form of αὐτός, always with a rough breathing and an accent.

1.2 After *ENTG* 10.1.2

1.2.1 Morphology and Accent of the Relative

Accents occasionally help you by distinguishing two otherwise identical words, such as the 2nd person singular pronouns in the last chapter. As *ENTG* tells you, accents distinguish the article from the relative pronoun in a couple of cases.

The difficulty is that accents change in context: a word without an accent can receive one from the word that follows it. Also, the accent at the end of a word can appear either as ὅ or as ὁ. You can see this by comparing the table in *ENTG* 10.1.2 with the accented table in the **Online Material** of this chapter.

What this means is that rules in *ENTG* for telling such pairs of words apart work nine times of out ten. However, by learning the very basic rudiments of accents, you can pick up the other one out of ten. This is why we give you those basics in the **Extra Material**.[1]

Once you grasp that, the relative is very easy. It's easiest to work from the relative to the article.

> The **relative** *always* has an accent and *always* begins with a rough breathing. The relative pronoun has the same endings as αὐτός.[2]
>
> The **article** is *nearly always* identical, except turning the rough breathing into a τ. The exceptions are:

---

[1] All you need for this is found in **EM 5** 3.1 (how accents are thrown to previous words) and **EM 1** 3.3 (the switch from ὅ to ὁ).

[2] Remember that the neuter nominative (and accusative) singular ending sometimes has a *v*. The *v* is always and only missing on the article and on relative pronouns. That's why the relative pronoun endings are the same as the article and the pronoun, but differ from nouns, adjectives and participles in that one detail.

- the nominatives of the masculine/feminine lose the accent and keep the rough breathing.
- the masculine singular nominative loses the final ς.

See the table in the **Online Material** for this chapter. (The table in *ENTG* is missing most accents, because it only shows them where it makes the indispensable difference.)

1.2.2 When the Relative Is Ambiguous

Notice the first example in *ENTG* 10.1.3. You end up with a masculine singular relative pronoun, so you look for a masculine singular antecedent in the main clause. However, there are two: κύριος and ἄγγελος. How do you decide which it is? The basic principle is that authors like to be understood and know when they are being ambiguous. Generally, the *most recently mentioned* candidate is most likely (ἄγγελος), unless common sense tells you something else.

1.2.3 Embedding the Paradigms

Use the method we have used in earlier chapters.

1. Make sure that you are thoroughly comfortable with the paradigm of λόγος and can effortlessly produce the paradigms of ἔργον, ἀρχή, ἡμέρα, δόξα as simple variations.
2. Make sure you can write out the article in full based on the above endings. (Remember that the neut sing nom/acc ending is -ον except on the article and on pronouns, where it is -ο.)
3. Use the rules in the section above to write out the paradigm of the relative pronoun in full, without looking anything up.
4. Check what you've written against the right pattern (*ENTG* 10.1.2 or the fully accented version in the **Online Material**), and use that to reinforce the rules.
5. Keep doing that until you never get it wrong.

2 AFTER *ENTG* 10.3: INDIRECT STATEMENTS

As *ENTG* 10.3 warns you, we need to think about the verbs when we turn *direct* statements into *indirect* statements. The good news is that there is nothing Greek to learn here: it is English which is difficult, but you already know English!

As in English, so in Greek, the **person** of the verbs takes the perspective of the person reporting the statements, not the person who spoke originally.

> Bob says to Peter: '*I* saw *you*, Peter.'
> Peter then says to Alice: 'Bob said that *he* had seen *me*.'

You've been getting this right all your life, and there is nothing new here.

In English, the **time** of the verbs is also told from the perspective of the person *reporting* the statements, not the person who spoke originally. Greek, on the other hand, uses the perspective of the *original* speaker. This makes Greek very easy to understand: whatever the tense of the indirect statements, that is also the tense of the original statements. What could be easier? Now that you've understood the Greek, you just put it in English, as you have been doing all your life. See the examples in *ENTG* 10.3.

The rules in English are: the shift in tense only happens when the speech being reported was in the past, not the present or future. If what was said or thought in the past is still true now, then you do not have to shift tense either. ('Last Tuesday, I said that I *was* hungry' vs 'Last Tuesday, I said that Wales *is* beautiful.')

2.1 Tackling Indirect Statements

Approach indirect statements in Greek as follows. This is simply an application of our general principle: work out what the Greek means from the rules of Greek; then use the rules of English to put that into English (**EH 9** 1).

> 1 Is the verb introducing it (*say, think, consider, warn*) past? If not, just translate normally.
> 2 If it's past, turn the Greek indirect statement into a Greek direct statement. Easy! You leave all the tenses the same in Greek.
> ἔλεγεν αὐτῷ ὅτι ἀγαθός ἐστι
> →
> ἔλεγεν αὐτῷ· Ἀγαθός εἶ
> 3 Translate *that* into English
> 'She said to him, "*You are* good."'
> 4 Turn that *English* direct statement into an *English* indirect statement:
> 'She said to him *that he was* good.'
> No knowledge of Greek required!

The only trick with indirect speech, and indeed with direct quotations, in Greek is knowing when they end, since this is not marked by the end of quotation marks or anything like it (see *ENTG* 10.3 on John 3). The **Reading** below will give you plenty of practice.

There are other ways of introducing indirect statements, and different rules for indirect questions and commands; these are described in **EM 10** 6 below, since they do not form part of *ENTG*.

3 AFTER *ENTG* 10: A LITTLE VOCAB HELP WITH 'LITTLE WORDS'

Lots of us find it jolly hard to keep track of little words that indicate connections rather than things. We knew διά (Chapter 4), but have recently added διό and διότι (Chapter 9) and now a new use for ὅτι. These are in fact linked, and this can help us to remember which is which.

διά + acc means '**because**'.

Now add the relative pronoun in the accusative singular (ὅ). διά ὅ means 'because of which'. What precedes explains what follows, much like οὖν or 'therefore'. διά ὅ → δι' ὅ → **διό therefore**.

So **διά** and **διό** are opposites: what precedes either *explains* (**διά**) or *is explained by* (**διό**) what follows.

διότι = διὰ τοῦτο, ὅτι (ὅτι in the sense of *that*), 'it is because of this, that ...', '**because**' (= **διά**)

More help with little words is available in **EM 10** 7, rather than here, because it includes words that you have not yet met. These are related to ones that you have met, and looking at them now could save you some memory work.

3.1 Getting to Know Words: An Example

In **EH 9** 1, you saw the need to get to know how words work beyond learning a couple of glosses, and that this comes from plenty of reading.

Here is another example: διότι can have completely opposite meanings. We have just seen how it means 'because'. However, it can also work like this:

διότι = διὰ τοῦτο *because of which*, '**therefore**' (= **διό**)

Not only do words have a variety of contexts in which they can appear with different shades of meaning, but sometimes they can have entirely opposite meanings (like the English words 'cleave' and 'draw [the curtains]'). Your privilege as a reader of the text is to work out what you think the author meant in any given case.

You don't need to know this second meaning of **διότι** (or the others it has): I mention it here to illustrate the need to *read* Greek and get to know the language.

4 THE GREEK READING

The story so far ...
Joseph approaches Pentephres' house, riding Pharaoh's chariot, and looking rather regal. Pentephres' whole family assemble to meet him, and bow prostrate before him, while the slaves close the gates on the gathering crowd outside the house. Joseph greets the family and thanks them for their reception. Aseneth had excused herself

from the reception committee and watched Joseph from her upper-room window. We were left to wonder what she made of him.

6:1 καὶ ἐθεώρησεν ἡ Ἀσενὲθ τὸν Ἰωσὴφ ἡμέρας. ὅτε ἔβλεψε τὸ καινὸν ἱμάτιον ὃ εἶχεν, ἐθαύμασεν. καὶ εὐθὺς ἔτρεμεν ὅλον τὸ σῶμα αὐτῆς. ² ἔλεγεν γὰρ ἐν ἑαυτῇ· Μὴ θεωρήσει ἐμὲ ὁ Ἰωσὴφ ὁ υἱὸς θεοῦ, διότι ἐλάλουν κακὰ ἐγὼ περὶ αὐτοῦ; ³ οὐχί· δεῖ οὖν κρύψαι, ἀλλὰ ποῦ; ποῦ κρύψω ἐμαυτὴν ἀπὸ τοῦ προσώπου αὐτοῦ; καθὼς γὰρ βλέψεί με ὧδε, οὕτως βλέψεί με ἐκεῖ. ⁴ ἐπιστεύσεν δὲ αὐτὴ ὅτι ἐκεῖνος μήποτε καθεύδει ἀλλὰ βλέπει τοὺς κρυπτοὺς ὅπου εἰσίν. ⁵ ἔδοκουν γὰρ οἱ ὑπηρέται ὅτι αὐτὸς βλέπει πάντοτε διὰ τὴν ἐξουσίαν τὴν μεγάλην ἣν ἔχει. ⁶ καὶ ἔκραξεν ἡ Ἀσενὲθ ὅτι Πάτερ, οὐ καλῶς ἐφιλήσας ὅτε ἐλάλησάς μοι τὴν ἀλήθειαν λέγων ὅτι Ὁ ἀγαπητὸς τοῦ θεοῦ ἔρχεται ταύτῃ τῇ ὥρᾳ; ⁷ καὶ ἔκραξε πάλιν· Καὶ νῦν ἐλέησόν με κύριε, θεὲ τοῦ Ἰωσήφ, διότι ἐλάλησα ἐγὼ λόγους πονηροὺς ἐν ἀγνοίᾳ. ⁸ οὐχὶ γὰρ ἐλάλησα ὅτι ὁ τηρῶν πρόβατα ἐκ γῆς Χαναὰν ἔρχεται; ⁹ καὶ οὐκ ἐλάλησα· Ἀλλὰ δέξομαι τὸν πρωτότοκον υἱὸν τοῦ Φαραώ; ¹⁰ νῦν δὲ ὁ ἥλιος ἐκ τοῦ οὐρανοῦ ἤγγισε πρὸς ἡμᾶς ἐν τῷ ἅρματι ἐκείνῳ καὶ ἤδη ἐστὶν ἐν τῇ οἰκίᾳ ἡμῶν σήμερον. ¹¹ οἱ δὲ ὑπηρέται ἤκουσαν τοὺς λόγους οὓς ἡ Ἀσενὲθ ἐλάλησεν. καὶ ἐμαρτύρησαν λέγοντες ὅτι Σὺ οὔτε δίκαια οὔτε γε ἀγαθὰ ᾖς ὅτε ἠρνήσω δέξασθαι αὐτόν. ¹² καὶ ἐλάλησας πονηρὰ περὶ αὐτοῦ ὅτε οὐκ ἐλογίζη ὅτι ὁ Ἰωσὴφ υἱὸς ἀληθινὸς θεοῦ ἐστι. ¹³ ἡ δὲ Ἀσενὲθ ἔλεγεν ἐν ἑαυτῇ·Ναί. ἀλλὰ νῦν θέλω ἀπέρχεσθαι. ¹⁴ θέλω εἶναι χωρὶς τῆς οἰκίας μου ἕνεκα τοῦ Ἰωσήφ. ἐπεί θέλω δουλεύειν ἔμπροσθεν τῷ Ἰωσὴφ ᾧ θεὸς λέγει. ¹⁵ πλὴν ἔξεστί μοι περιπατεῖν ἔμπροσθεν τοῦ Ἰωσὴφ ὃν ἠρνησάμην; ὃν ἠρνησάμην, ἡγούμενός μου ἔσται; ἢ ἀπολύσεί με ἐκεῖθεν;

4.1 Vocabulary

ἄγνοια, ας, ἡ – ignorance
ἅρματι – chariot (neut dat sing)
δουλεύω – I serve (cf. δοῦλος)
ἥλιος, ου, ὁ – the sun (Ἡλιου-πόλις city of the sun)
κρύπτω – I hide

κρυπτός, ἡ, όν – hidden
πάτερ – father (voc)
πρωτότοκος, ον – firstborn
σῶμα – body (neut nom/acc sing)
τρέμω – I tremble

5 ACCENTS: MORE ENCLITICS

We add some relative pronouns to the list of enclitics (**EH 10** 1.2.1).

6 INDIRECT DISCOURSE

ENTG covers one way of expressing *statements* indirectly (**EH 10** 2); there are others, and there are different rules for indirect questions and commands.

6.1 General Principles

Keep four general principles in mind, which apply to all of these.

1. The **time** of the indirect statement is relative to the time of the *original* statement, unlike English, which gives the time relative to the *reporting* of the statement (**EH 10** 2).
2. The **persons** of the indirect statement are relative to the *reporting* of the statement, as in English (**EH 10** 2).
3. When the verb of the original statement is put in an 'other mood', the system of the new verb indicates **time**, relative to the time of the *original* statement, as explained below.
4. Be clear on the difference between the verb which announces indirect speech ('said', 'thinks', 'commands') and the verb within the indirect speech ('he drank', '*open* the door!', 'shall I *go*?', 'what time *is* it?').

Keep using the method in **EH 10** 2.1, adapting for the rules that apply in each case.

I am not giving you every little rule that you would need if you were going to turn English into Greek. For example, you don't need to know when to use οὐ vs μή: whichever you see, you know it's a negation.

6.2 Systems Indicate Relative Time

Present system: same time as the verb introducing the statement.
Aorist system: time prior to the verb introducing the statement.
Future system (EM 21 1.3): time subsequent to the verb introducing the statement (which might well be in the past now).
Perfect system (EH 16 1.1): a relevance that is ongoing at the time of the verb introducing the statement.

6.3 Indirect Statements

FURTHER READING: VS 274

6.3.1 ὅτι

ENTG gives you by far the most common means of expressing indirect statements in the GNT. However, there are others. These include not only the content of 'speech bubbles' (she said 'X') but also 'thought bubbles' (she thought 'X').

6.3.2 ὡς (= ὅτι)

Simply replace ὅτι with ὡς, with exactly the same rules.

Ὑμεῖς ἐπίστασθε **ὡς** ἀθέμιτόν ἐστιν ἀνδρὶ Ἰουδαίῳ ... Acts 10:28
You yourselves know **how** it is unlawful for a Jewish man ...

6.3.3 Infinitive

In English if I believe the statement 'he is a good student', I will say:

    I consider *that he is* a good student

or

    I consider *him to be* a good student

The verb goes in the infinitive ('is' → 'to be'), and its subject goes in the accusative ('he' → 'him').
    Likewise in Greek.

Ξένων δαιμονίων **δοκεῖ** καταγγελεὺς εἶναι Acts 17:18
He appears to be a preacher of foreign spirits.

The system indicates time *relative* to the verb which reports the statement (**EM 10** 6.2).

ᾔδεισαν τὸν Χριστὸν αὐτὸν εἶναι Luke 4:41
they knew him to be the Christ

implicit direct statement (what they knew):
'he is the Christ'
αὐτός ἐστιν ὁ Χριστός
= they knew <u>that he was</u> the Christ. Present infinitive relative to past verb.

ἀλλὰ διὰ τῆς χάριτος Κυρίου Ἰησοῦ Χριστοῦ **πιστεύομεν** <u>σωθῆναι</u>, καθ' ὃν τρόπον κἀκεῖνοι. Acts 15:11
but through the grace of the Lord Jesus Christ, **we believe** that <u>we</u> <u>have been saved</u> [aorist: past, relative to present verb], just in the same way as they.

δόξαντες τῆς προθέσεως <u>κεκρατηκέναι</u> ἄραντες ἆσσον παρελέγοντο τὴν Κρήτην. Acts 27:13
thinking <u>themselves to have obtained</u> their target, weighing anchor, they were sailing along Crete.
= **they thought** that <u>they</u> <u>had obtained</u> [perfect: prior, with ongoing relevance, relative to past verb, so English pluperfect] their target ...

ὤμοσε μὴ <u>εἰσελεύσεσθαι</u> εἰς τὴν κατάπαυσιν αὐτοῦ Heb 3:18
he swore that <u>they would not enter</u> his rest
[future infinitive, relative to a past verb]

Unlike English, if the subject of the statement is the same person who holds the opinion (*I* consider that *I* am good), the subject is left out of the indirect statement.

δοκεῖτε ἐν αὐταῖς ζωὴν αἰώνιον <u>ἔχειν</u> John 5:39
you think <u>yourselves to have</u> eternal life through these
= '**you think** that <u>you</u> <u>have</u> eternal life'

If the subject is the same and does appear, it will be nominative (not accusative) and always additionally emphatic.

ηὐχόμην γὰρ **αὐτὸς** <u>ἐγὼ</u> ἀνάθεμα <u>εἶναι</u> ... ὑπὲρ τῶν ἀδελφῶν μου Rom 9:3
For **I would wish** that <u>I</u> **myself** <u>were</u> accursed ... on behalf of my brothers.

δοκῶ δὲ **κἀγὼ** Πνεῦμα Θεοῦ <u>ἔχειν</u>. 1 Cor 7:40
I consider that <u>I</u> **as well** <u>have</u> God's Spirit

Note that the infinitive in indirect discourse is different from the complementary infinitive, even with verbs of similar meaning. The complementary infinitive puts the subject in the accusative, and the aspect of the infinitive is not a matter of relative time.

> ἠθέλησεν ὁ Ἰησοῦς ἐξελθεῖν εἰς τὴν Γαλιλαίαν John 1:43
> Jesus **wanted** to leave for Galilee.
>> The implied thought isn't 'I will leave' [future infinitive] but 'I **want** to leave' [aorist infinitive]. The infinitive is completing the main verb θέλω, so it's a complementary infinitive, not an infinitive of indirect speech.

6.3.4 Supplementary and Complementary Participle

This use is very rare in the NT, and we discuss it with other participles in **EM 14** 4.4. The key distinction with other forms of indirect speech is that the indirect statement is seen as *true*.

6.4 Indirect Commands / Wishes

> FURTHER READING: VS 273D

You have a choice:

1. Introduce the reported command with ἵνα (or equivalent), and put the command in the subjunctive (*ENTG* 17.3.2).
2. Turn the verb into an infinitive. You know that it's a command, not a statement, because the indirect speech is introduced by a verb of commanding.

Either way, you retain the system of the original direct command, which must be analysed according to the rules for imperatives (**EM 11** 5).

> Ἐρωτῶ οὖν σε, πάτερ, ἵνα πέμψῃς αὐτὸν εἰς τὸν οἶκον τοῦ πατρός μου Luke 16:27
> So **I ask** you, father, that you would send him into the house of my father.
>> No change in person or time needed.
>> Present subjunctive comes from a present imperative.
>> Implied command, 'Send him' πέμπε.
>> The choice of aspect must be analysed as an imperative.

> ἠρώτα αὐτὸν Φαρισαῖός τις ὅπως ἀριστήσῃ παρ' αὐτῷ. Luke 11:37
> A certain Pharisee **was inviting** him that he should dine with him
>> Change of person needed: that he (Jesus) should dine.
>> Aorist subjunctive comes from an aorist imperative.
>> Implied command: 'Dine' ἀρίστησον.
>> The choice of aspect must be analysed as an imperative.

Notice how English would more naturally want an infinitive: 'I **ask** you to send …' 'He **invited** him to dine.' Greek can do this:

> ἠρώτησεν αὐτὸν ἀπὸ τῆς γῆς ἐπαναγαγεῖν ὀλίγον. Luke 5:3
> **he asked** him <u>to push off</u> a little from the land.
> > Change of person needed.
> > Aorist infinitive comes from an aorist imperative.
> > Implied command: 'Push off' ἐπάναγε.
> > The choice of aspect must be analysed as an imperative.

6.5 Indirect Questions

FURTHER READING: VS 273D

You keep the same mood as the original question. The same rules about person and relative time apply as always.

> **Ἐπερωτηθεὶς** δὲ ὑπὸ τῶν Φαρισαίων, <u>πότε ἔρχεται</u> ἡ βασιλεία τοῦ Θεοῦ, ἀπεκρίθη ... Luke 17:20
> **When he was asked** by the Pharisees <u>when</u> God's Kingdom <u>was coming</u>, he answered ...
> > Ἔρχεται is relative to a past tense verb introducing the question.
> > Implied question: 'When <u>is it coming</u>?' <u>πότε ἔρχεται</u> unchanged, but tense changed in English.

> Πιλᾶτος ... **ἐπηρώτησεν** <u>εἰ ὁ ἄνθρωπος Γαλιλαῖός ἐστι</u> Luke 23:6
> Pilate ... **asked** <u>whether</u> the man <u>was</u> Galilean
> > Implied question: 'Is he Galilean?' ἐστι unchanged, but tense changed in English.

> πάλιν οὖν **ἠρώτων** αὐτὸν καὶ οἱ Φαρισαῖοι, <u>πῶς ἀνέβλεψεν</u>. John 9:15
> So the Pharisees **were asking** him again <u>how he had regained sight</u>.
> > Implied question: 'How have you regained sight?' πῶς ἀνέβλεψες. Tense unchanged, but person changed. Person and tense changed in English.

If the question doesn't make sense out of context, but refers to something outside of itself, such as 'What is <u>this</u>?', you still almost always do the above. A few authors retain an older rule, which is to put the verb in the question into the *optative* (**EM 21** 1.1).
Compare Mark (normal) and Luke (optative):

> καὶ ἐθαμβήθησαν πάντες, ὥστε **συζητεῖν** πρὸς αὐτούς, λέγοντας, Τί <u>ἐστι</u> τοῦτο; Mark 1:27
> They all became amazed, so that **they were asking** among themselves: 'What <u>is</u> this?'

> **διελογίζετο** ποταπὸς <u>εἴη</u> ὁ ἀσπασμὸς οὗτος. Luke 1:29
> **she was wondering** what sort of greeting this <u>could be</u>.
> > Implied question: 'What sort of greeting <u>is</u> this?'

6.6 Indirect Discourse: Summary Table

Table 10.1 Indirect Discourse Summary

Original or implicit speech being reported	Syntax of indirect discourse	
	Introduced with	Verb becomes
Indirect statement	ὅτι	same mood
	ὡς	same mood
	–	infinitive
	–	participle
Indirect command / desire	ἵνα	subjunctive
	–	infinitive
Indirect question	–	same mood
	–	optative

7 EXTRA HELP WITH LITTLE WORDS

The bewildering number of 'little words' with connective or adverbial use can be simplified slightly by recognising some patterns.

By Chapter 10 we have met:

> ἐκεῖ – *over there*
> ἐκεῖνος – *the one* over there (Chapter 9)
> ἐκεῖθεν – *from* over there

The suffix -θεν is an ancient case ending which indicates 'from'. So we also have

> ποῦ – where?
> **πόθεν** – *from* where? (by metaphorical extension: 'why?'; cf. the English expression 'where did you get that idea *from*?')

Beyond the vocab in *ENTG*, you will be able to guess the meaning of these common NT words:

> ἄνωθεν – from above
> ἔξωθεν – from outside
> ἔσωθεν – from inside
> ἐντεῦθεν – from here
> μακρόθεν – from a great [distance], 'from afar'
> κἀκεῖθεν – and from there

We have also learnt various question words, indefinite words, demonstratives and relatives. They are related in a predictable pattern.

π **indicates a question** (ποῦ *where?*)
π **without the accent is indefinite** (που *somewhere*)
the relative pronoun does what you would expect,
> either in combination with π: **ὅπου**, if the relative is quite general 'wherever …'
> or by itself ὅ: **οὗ**, if the relative refers to a specific one 'the place where …'

τ indicates *demonstrative* (as in **τοῦτο**- *this one*)

Many of these combinations are dying out by NT times, so this table presents those that you will find in the GNT. The few that don't follow the pattern are in italics. What's more, the fine distinctions in meaning are often ignored by authors in the NT period and beyond, but it is still useful to see these relationships as an easier way to learn all these bewilderingly similar words, as in Table 10.2.

For example, in the previous section, we saw πότε used in an indirect question, because the expected ὁπότε has died out (Luke 17:20), but we also saw πῶς in an indirect statement, even though ὅπως is available (John 9:15).

Table 10.2 Correlative Words

When used:	Question		Indefinite	Relative			Demonstrative
	(Direct and indirect)	(Indirect)		General		Specific	
formation:	π	ὁπ	π enclitic	ὁπ		ὁ	τ
Example:	Who?	Who is the one who?	Someone	Someone who …		The one who	This one
location	ποῦ; where? to where?	ὅπου; where?	που somewhere	ὅπου wherever your treasure is …		οὗ the place where the child was	–
kind	ποῖος; what kind?	ὁποῖος; what kind?	–	ὁποῖος I don't care what kind they were		οἷος you know what kind of men	τοιοῦτος many such parables
time	πότε; when?	–	ποτέ when you turn you were at one time lost	–		ὅτε when he had finished	τότε then

Table 10.2 (Cont.)

When used:	Question (Direct and indirect)	Question (Indirect)	Indefinite	Relative General	Relative Specific	Demonstrative
amount	πόσος; *how much?*	–	–	–	ὅσος *I have heard how much was done*	τοσοῦτος *where will we find so much bread?*
place from	πόθεν; *where from?*	–	–	–	ὅθεν *my house from where I came*	–
manner	πῶς; *how?*	ὅπως; *how?* cf. ὅπως + subj [ENTG 17.3.2], which is far more common	πως *somehow*	ὡς *in such a way* often comparative, paired with οὕτως; and many other uses	–	οὕτως *in this way*
person, thing	τίς; *who?*	–	τις *Someone*	ὅστις *Someone who …*	ὅς *the one who*	οὗτος *this one* ἐκεῖνος *that one*

CHAPTER 11

Special Verbs
—
Consolidation Greek Readings
—
Aspect in Imperatives

> **How to Use This Chapter**
>
> **You are about to pass the half-way mark: congratulations!**
> Work through this chapter of *ENTG*, section by section, completing exercises as you go. As you complete each section, read **Extra Help** below for that section.
>
> In **Extra Help** we will reap the benefits of the rules we have learnt to see how the irregular verbs in this chapter are easy to understand. We will also introduce the easiest way of learning all irregularities of any verb: **Principal Parts**.
>
> In the **Extra Material** we will continue to examine the significance of aspect in the 'other moods'. We'll apply the general principles to the imperative. You will also see how accents help distinguish some of the irregular forms that we meet in this chapter.
>
> Chapter 11 marks the half-way point of this course. As in Chapter 6, we therefore offer the additional **Greek Reading B** to help you consolidate Chapters 1–11. What's more, **Greek Reading C** is an *entire* book of the GNT: the letter to Philemon.
>
> As usual, **Greek Reading A** has some notes and plenty of questions, focussed on this chapter and recent chapters, to embed this recent content. However, in **Greek Readings B** and **C**, I won't ask you questions, but supply notes and many references to relevant sections of *ENTG* and **Extra Help** throughout Chapters 1–11. Working through these **Readings** and following up the notes will cause you to review pretty much everything you have studied so far, hopefully in a fun way. They are ideal if you have a mid-year exam to revise for, and/or a long inter-semester break during which you need to keep your Greek fresh.

1 VERB ENDINGS

This chapter is full of good news!

As in Chapter 8, there is no new grammar, just new morphology. You will now discover why, in our **Readings** so far, I have never been allowed to say 'Joseph arrived' or 'Aseneth will eat'. Greek has irregular verbs.

The great news is that Greek irregular verbs behave in very regular and predictable patterns, so there is very little to memorise.

The way we have learnt to lay out our verb table, and the rules of thematic vowels, endings and 'slippery sigma' will make everything in this chapter a doddle.

1.1 After *ENTG* 11.1.1: Second Aorists

These really couldn't be simpler. Look at 'The Greek Verb So Far' for Chapter 8, in the **Online Material**. Find the aorist stem: two columns.

Wherever you are in that stem, you take the endings from the *exact same place* in the present stem. Just look to the left along the same row. Check that this works with the examples in Table 11.1.

Table 11.1 Parsing Second Aorists

Parsing of 2nd **aor**	Ending
Aor act inf	**Pres** act inf -ειν
Aor mid imperative 2p	**Pres** mid imperative 2p -εσθε
Aor act pl masc nom ptcpl	**Pres** act pl masc nom ptcpl -οντες
Aor ind act historical tense (a.k.a. 'aorist tense') act 2s	**Pres** ind act historical tense (a.k.a. 'imperfect tense') act 2s -ες

Even though it's easy to understand, don't feel discouraged when you forget this. Much more experienced readers are still getting this wrong regularly when we read fast.

Heed the warnings in *ENTG*:

- You must memorise the 2nd aorist stems (on which more below). For example, notice the table for βάλλω in *ENTG* 11.1.3: if you don't know how many λ there are in the aorist stem, then aorist and present will look identical to your eye.
- You need to know the aorist stem of 2nd aorists, but learning the indicative means the augment is already included: see the two aorist columns in *ENTG* 11.1.3.
- Beware of the 'mixed forms', which are few but very common (*ENTG* 11.1.6 (ii)).

For your encouragement, many English words derive from second aorist stems, not from the regular present stem: *path*etic comes from παθ-, not πασχ-;

likewise many Greek nouns: a disciple is a μαθητής from μαθ- not μανθαν-; the first book of the Bible is ΓΕΝΕΣΙΣ not ΓΙΝΕΣΙΣ.

1.1.1 A Cheeky Addition

While this is (rightly) not in *ENTG*, please add to your list of 2nd aorists: τρέχω 'I run' with second aorist ἔ-δραμ-ον.

1.2 (Optional) After *ENTG* 11.1.6: Root Aorists

If you have mastered thematic vowels for verbs (**EH 6** 3.1), this section will help you further; otherwise, skip ahead to **EH 11** 1.3.

All these endings are ones that we have already met or will meet eventually. These verbs have a different aorist stem and add the endings straight to it without the sigma and the thematic vowel: they are therefore called *root aorists*.

The aorist stems are γνο- and βα-. In the vocab you also meet χαίρω, which is a root aorist (χαρ-).

Indicative: Adding the thematic vowel (ε/ο) and the historical indicative endings (ν ς – μεν τε σαν) produces the aorist indicative. NB: ο + ε/ο contracts to ω; α + ε/ο contracts to η.

Plural imperative: as ever, the same as the 2p indicative.

Participle: the endings remain the aorist endings ας and ντες. NB: ο + α contracts to ου; α + α contracts to long α.

That leaves only the singular imperative and infinitive to learn. We will meet those again, so it's worth doing now.

1.2.1 Contracts

Notice that the order of the vowels in contraction matters: we have previously met ε + ο → ου, e.g. φιλοῦμεν. What we have met now is ο + ε → ω, e.g. ἔγνως.

Some handy rules:

1. Any contraction involving any form of ο sound will contract to a form of ο sound.
2. If α and ε sounds contract, whichever comes first wins.
3. If the same sound contracts with itself, you get a long version of the same.

1.2.2 Review of Historical Endings

As you know, the historical endings are mostly the same regardless of which system we are in, and the differences are down to how thematic vowels behave (**EH 6** 3.1). The exception we have met so far is that the imperfect 1s ending is ν, while the aorist 1s is a silent and invisible letter which merely changes the thematic vowel to α. There is also an alternative form of the 3p, which we have met as ν so far (in both imperfect and aorist); the alternative is σαν, which we meet on the root aorists above, and will meet again. There are no other historical endings to meet – ever! See Table 11.2.

Table 11.2 Historical Endings

1s	ν / [silent invisible]
2s	ς
3s	–
1p	μεν
2p	τε
3p	ν / σαν

1.3 (Optional) After *ENTG* 11.2: Liquid Verbs

Two things will help us make sense of liquid verbs.

1 **Slippery sigma** strikes again – multiple times!
2 We are used to taking the present stem as our starting point, and then understanding how the future and aorist stems change. With liquid verbs, the present stem changes as well: we can't always get the future or aorist from it. The simplest answer, as we will see, is to learn the three stems for each verb.

As *ENTG* explains, you can't pronounce σ comfortably after μ ν ρ λ in the middle of a word. This causes three different changes in the present, aorist and future.

1.3.1 Future

The **future** stem adds an ε to break up the μ ν ρ λ from the σ: it attaches -εσ- to the stem. Then slippery sigma strikes: being stuck between two vowels in a verb ending, it disappears, leaving the vowels either side to contract. That leaves the same endings as ε contracts, plus a different accent.[1] (Notice that this is not the same as ε contract verbs, which lengthen the ε to η before the σ.)

σπέρ - σει → σπερ - έσει → σπερ - έ σ ει → σπερ - εῖ → σπερεῖ

1.3.2 Aorist

Here is a new way that slippery sigma causes changes: after certain consonants, it vanishes and lengthens the vowel before that consonant.

---

[1] This change in accent is completely predictable from the basic rules of verb accents (**EM 2** 3.1).

This is what happens in the aorist.

σπερ - σα → σπερ - σα → σπειρ - α → σπειρα

1.3.3 Present

Notice that we started with σπερ even though the present is σπειρ. That's because the same lengthening often happens in the **present** stem of liquid verbs (for reasons that we do not need to get into). You can then see the original stem in the future: σπερ-.

Other times, the present stem has doubled its liquid consonant, and you see the original single consonant in the future and aorist: ἀγγέλλω ἀγγελῶ ἤγγειλα.

The changes are small and easily recognisable: as you compare the three stems, a vowel changes length and/or a consonant doubles. The aorist always lengthens its vowel and makes no other changes. The present and future may or may not lengthen their vowel, and may or may not do it at the same time. The present may or may not double its consonant. See the examples in Table 11.3.

Table 11.3 Liquid Stem Examples

Original stem σπερ- ἀρ-	Pres: vowel lengthens	σπειρ- αἰρ
	Fut: no change	σπερ-
	Aor: vowel lengthens	σπειρ- ἄρ- (notice how the aor and pres have lengthened differently. When we add the augment in the aor we get ἦρ- not ᾖρ-.)
Original stem ἀγγελ-	Pres: consonant doubles	ἀγγελλ-
	Fut: no change	ἀγγελ
	Aor: vowel lengthens	ἀγγειλ-
Original stem μεν- κριν- (short ι)	Pres: no change	μεν- κριν-
	Fut: no change	μεν- κριν-
	Aor: vowel lengthens	μειν- κρῑν- (long ι, which you generally won't notice)

When learning liquid verbs as vocab, you also need to learn their future and their aorist stem.

1.4 After *ENTG* 11.2: Voice Changes

Notice the entry for ἔρχομαι in *ENTG* 11.1.3. The always-middle verb **ἔρχομαι** has a 2nd aorist **ἦλθον**. **-ον** is the active ending, not the middle (-μην). In *ENTG* 11.2.1, notice that ἀποθνῄσκω has active endings in the present and aorist, but middle in the future. Some verbs change their voice in different stems. We also need to learn these changes as vocab.

Is it beginning to sound as though there are a lot of different irregularities to learn? There is a time-honoured way of making this ever so easy.

1.5 After *ENTG* 11.2: How to Remember It All: Principal Parts

If you've learnt, or taught, English as a second language you will know that all the irregularities of English verbs can be dealt with by learning three words for each verb. If you learn 'hang, hung, hung' you know all there is to know.

Greek is similarly kind: all the possible irregularities we've discussed are dealt with by learning three words for each verb. Look again at 'The Greek Verb So Far' for Chapter 8, in the **Online Material**. The three sets of columns with different colours represent the three stems: present, aorist and future. Each stem is perfectly regular: if a liquid verb has a doubled consonant in one form of the present stem, it has it in all forms. If a second aorist takes middle endings, it does so throughout the aorist stem. You can therefore handle all second aorists, root aorists, liquid verbs, contract verbs, and anything else just by learning those three stems.

These are called the **Principal Parts**, and they are numbered: the 1st is the present, the 2nd is the future, and the 3rd is the aorist: λύω λύσω ἔλυσα. There are six in total, and we will meet the other three in later chapters. Accordingly, there is a revised verb table online, even though it is identical to the one in Chapter 8, except that it indicates the Principal Parts.

If you are using the vocab resources that I provide online, you will see that the verbs all have their Principal Parts listed. A dash means that the verb does not exist in that stem. Bold indicates that this Principal Part is listed at the back of *ENTG*; I therefore recommend memorising it. I strongly recommend, from now on, learning verbs along with these Principal Parts. At a minimum, you must learn the irregular future and aorist stems in Chapter 11 as vocab.

1.5.1 Compounds

Almost without exception, compound verbs have the same Principal Parts as the simple forms, just with the preposition added.

1.5.2 Aorist Stem

The Principal Parts are, by convention, always the 'top left' of their column: the 1s of the active of the highest indicative tense in that column. Therefore the 3rd Principal Part is the aorist *indicative* 1s (ἔλυσα), which of course includes the augment. What you really need to know is the stem itself, without the augment (*ENTG* 11.1.5), which you sometimes need to learn separately.

1.5.3 Imperfect

I also recommend learning the imperfect separately. In the vocab, I present verbs as though they had seven Principal Parts, with the imperfect being the 2nd one: λύω ἔλυον λύσω ἔλυσα … .

Firstly, a handful of verbs do have irregular imperfects, like ἔχω → εἶχον (*ENTG* 6.7 **Note**).

Secondly, even when the imperfect does what it should and follows the present stem, it can still be a bit of a trick to tell it apart from its irregular aorist, so learning them both is helpful.

1.5.4 Examples

Notice how these Principal Parts (plus imperfect) mean you can handle any irregularity at all:

ἔχω, εἶχον, ἕξω, ἔσχον

tells you all you need for this most irregular verb. Any dictionary will tell you these forms before it even tells you what the word means.

Which of the changes does a particular liquid verb take? Just learn the Principal Parts:

σπείρω, ἔσπειρον, σπερῶ, ἔσπειρα
μένω, ἔμενον, μενῶ, ἔμεινα

Does a 2nd aorist use mixed forms? Does the future or aorist change voice? Does the future or aorist look completely different? Just learn the Principal Parts:

λέγω, ἔλεγον, ἐρῶ, εἶπον / εἶπα
ἀποθνῄσκω, ἀπέθνῃσκον, ἀποθανοῦμαι, ἀπέθανον

Be encouraged: as you start to learn Principal Parts of various verbs, you'll spot patterns. As with all vocab learning, the most important Principal Parts will stick in your mind, as you keep meeting them in your reading of Greek texts. On which note, enjoy the **Readings** below with the notes and questions online.

2 THE GREEK READING

The story so far …

Aseneth has caught sight of Joseph and takes leave of all her senses. Instead of rejecting him as a husband, she is so overawed by his magnificence that she wishes that he would *accept her as a slave!*

2.1 Reading A

7:1 Καὶ εἰσῆλθεν ὁ Ἰωσὴφ εἰς τὴν οἰκίαν τοῦ Πεντεφροῦ καὶ προσήνεγκαν αὐτῷ μονῷ ἄρτον διότι οὐ ἤσθιε μετὰ τῶν Αἰγυπτίων, ὅτι σκάνδαλον ἦν αὐτῷ τοῦτο. ² καὶ εἶπεν ὁ Ἰωσὴφ τῷ Πεντεφρῇ λέγων·

> Ἰδού· τίς ἐστιν ἡ γυνὴ ἐκείνη ἣν εἶδον ἐκεῖ; παράγγειλον αὐτῇ ἀπελθεῖν. οὐκ ἀποστελεῖτε αὐτήν; ἢ μενοῦμεν καὶ κρινοῦμεν αὐτήν; παραγγελεῖτε αὐτοῖς ἆραι αὐτήν;

³ Ἔπαθε γὰρ ὁ Ἰωσὴφ διὰ τὰς γυναῖκας τῶν Αἰγυπτίων. ἔμελλον γὰρ καθεύδειν μετ' αὐτοῦ. ⁴ καὶ πολλαὶ τῶν Αἰγυπτίων, ὅσαι ἐθεώρησαν τὸν Ἰωσήφ, ἔπασχον ἐπὶ αὐτῷ. ἀποστόλους ἄρα ἀπέστελλον πρὸς αὐτόν. καὶ πεσόντες προσεκύνουν αὐτῷ καὶ προσέφερον αὐτῷ δῶρα. ⁵ καὶ πάντοτε ἠρνεῖτο παραλαβεῖν ταῦτα ὁ Ἰωσὴφ ἀλλὰ ἐξέβαλλε τοὺς ἀποστόλους λέγων ὅτι οὐχ ἁμαρτήσει ἐνώπιον τοῦ θεοῦ Ἰσραήλ. ⁶ τὸ γὰρ πρόσωπον τοῦ Ἰακὼβ πρὸ ὀφθαλμῶν εἶχεν πάντοτε ὁ Ἰωσὴφ καὶ ἐμνημόνευε τὰς ἐντολὰς τοῦ Ἰακὼβ καὶ τῆς Ῥαχὴλ διότι εἶπαν·

> Φεύγετε, τέκνα, ἀπὸ τῆς γυναικὸς τοῦ ἑτέρου.

⁷ Διὰ τοῦτο εἶπεν Ἰωσήφ· παράγγειλον αὐτῇ ἀπελθεῖν. ⁸ καὶ εἶπεν αὐτῷ ὁ Πεντεφρῆς·

> Κύριε, ἐκείνη ἣν εἶδες οὐκ ἐγένετο ἡ γυνὴ τοῦ ἑτέρου ἀνθρώπου, ἀλλὰ θυγάτηρ ἡμῶν ἐστιν. καὶ ἄνθρωποι ἄλλοι οὔτε ἔγνωσαν οὔτε εἶδον αὐτὴν ἀλλὰ σὺ μόνος σήμερον ἰδὼν ἔγνως αὐτήν. ⁹ αἰτήσω οὖν αὐτὴν καταβῆναι, ἡ γὰρ θυγάτηρ ἡμῶν ἀδελφή σού ἐστιν.

¹⁰ Καὶ ἐχάρη ὁ Ἰωσὴφ καὶ παρήγγειλεν αὐτοῖς καταγαγεῖν αὐτὴν λέγων·

¹¹ Ἔξεστιν αὐτῇ καταβῆναι, ὅτι ἀδελφή μού ἐστι καὶ φιλήσω αὐτὴν ὡς ἀδελφήν μου.

2.1.1 Vocabulary

Αἰγύπτιος, ία, ιον – Egyptian
γυνή – woman, wife (nom fem sing; γυναῖκας acc pl)
δῶρον, ου, τό – gift
θυγάτηρ – daughter (fem nom sing; θυγατέρας acc pl)

μνημονεύω – I remember, keep in mind
σκάνδαλον – scandal
τίς …; – who …?

3 HALF-WAY CONSOLIDATION

Since we're half-way through the *Reader*, we will consolidate and review Chapters 1–11 by reading more of *Joseph & Aseneth*, and then a whole NT book (Philemon). Now that you understand how to handle irregular verbs (Chapter 11), this becomes much easier!

In the notes, I will generally not ask you questions, but point you to where you should look and revise if you're unsure how to handle a point of Greek. Unlike the questions in the **Readings** so far, I haven't limited myself to matters that are either recent or particularly hard. Rather, I have tried to help review as much of *ENTG* as possible with constant cross-references.

If you have a mid-way exam to face, use **Reading B** for revision. Enjoy!

3.1 Reading B: More *Joseph & Aseneth*

The story so far …

Joseph has spotted Aseneth watching him from the upper room. He has a history of being accosted by the wives of Egyptian men (quite famously in Genesis 39). He has always followed his parents' command: stay away from other men's wives! Therefore, he has asked for her to be ejected from the house, but Pentephres explains that this is his daughter, who has kept herself from all men, and indeed Joseph is the first man to come to know her (or even see her). He offers to invite her down and be to Joseph as a sister. Joseph readily agrees.

3.1.1 *Joseph & Aseneth* 8–9

8:1 Καὶ ἀνέβη ἡ γυνὴ τοῦ Πεντεφροῦ εἰς τὸ ὑπερῷον καὶ ἤγαγεν τὴν Ἀσενέθ πρὸς τὸν Ἰωσὴφ καὶ εἶπεν ὁ Πεντεφρῆς τῇ θυγατρὶ αὐτοῦ Ἀσενέθ·

Ἄσπασαι τὸν ἀδελφόν σου, διότι καὶ αὐτὸς παρθένος ἐστὶ ὡς καὶ σὺ σήμερον, καὶ μισεῖ ἀλλοτρίας ὡς καὶ σὺ ἀλλοτρίους.

² Καὶ εἶπεν Ἀσενὲθ τῷ Ἰωσήφ·

Χαῖρε, κύριε, μακάριε ὑπὸ τοῦ θεοῦ τοῦ ὑψίστου.

Καὶ εἶπε πρὸς αὐτὴν Ἰωσήφ·

Χαῖρε, ἀδελφή μου.

³ Καὶ εἶπε Πεντεφρῆς τῇ Ἀσενέθ· πρόσελθε καὶ φίλησον τὸν ἀδελφόν σου. ⁴ ἡ δὲ προσῆλθε φιλῆσαι τὸν Ἰωσήφ, ἀλλὰ ὁ Ἰωσὴφ εἶπεν·

⁵ Ὁ δίκαιος ὃς εὐλογεῖ τῷ στόματι αὐτοῦ τὸν θεὸν τὸν ἀληθινόν, καὶ ὃς ἐσθίει τὸν τῆς ζωῆς ἄρτον, καὶ ὃς πίνει τὸν μακάριον ποτήριον, οὐ φιλήσει ἀλλοτρίαν, ἢ εὐλογεῖ τῷ στόματι αὐτῆς εἴδωλα νεκρὰ καὶ κωφά, καὶ ἢ ἐσθίει ἐκ τοῦ ἄρτου αὐτῶν, καὶ ἢ πίνει ποτήριον τοῦ θανάτου.

⁶ Καὶ ὅτε ἤκουσεν ἡ Ἀσενὲθ τοὺς λόγους τοῦ Ἰωσήφ, ἔκραξε καὶ οἱ δοῦλοι ἰδόντες ἐφοβοῦντο. ⁷ καὶ θεώρησας αὐτὴν ὁ Ἰωσὴφ ἠλέησεν αὐτήν, ὅτι ὁ Ἰωσὴφ ἦν ἐλεῶν καὶ προσκυνῶν τῷ κυρίῳ. προσηύξατο λέγων·

⁸ Κύριε ὁ θεὸς τοῦ Ἰσραήλ, ὁ ὕψιστος, ὁ καλέσας με ἀπὸ τοῦ θανάτου εἰς τὴν ζωήν, σὺ κύριε εὐλόγησον τὴν παρθένον ταύτην. ⁹ ἆρον τὴν καρδίαν αὐτῆς τὴν νεκρὴν καὶ ποιῆσον καρδίαν καινὴν ἐν αὐτῇ.

¹⁰ Ἐκήρυξεν οὖν τῇ Ἀσενὲθ λέγων·

¹¹ Νυνὶ ἐσθίεις τὸν τῆς ζωῆς ἄρτον σὺ καὶ δέξῃ τὸν ποτήριον τῆς εὐλογίας.

9:1 Καὶ ἐχάρησαν χαρὰν μεγάλην ἐπὶ τῇ εὐλογίᾳ τοῦ Ἰωσὴφ καὶ ἀνῆλθεν

Ἀσενὲθ εἰς τὸ ὑπερῷον αὐτῆς καὶ ἔπεσεν, διότι ἦν αὐτῇ χαρὰ καὶ φόβος πολύς,

ὅτε ἤκουσε τοὺς λόγους τούτους παρὰ τοῦ Ἰωσήφ, οὓς ἀπήγγειλεν αὐτῇ ὑπὲρ

τοῦ θεοῦ.

²καὶ κατέλιπεν τοὺς θεοὺς αὐτῆς δι' οὓς ἀποθανεῖται. ³καὶ ἔφαγεν ὁ Ἰωσήφ. ⁴

καὶ εἶπε Πεντεφρῆς πρὸς τὸν Ἰωσήφ·

Μεῖνον, κύριε, σήμερον.

Ὁ δὲ Ἰωσὴφ εἶπεν·

⁵Οὐχί, ἀλλὰ δεῖ μοι ἀπελθεῖν σήμερον, διότι ἐστὶν ἡ ἡμέρα ἐν ᾗ ἤρξατο ὁ

θεὸς ποιῆσαι τὰ ἔργα αὐτοῦ, καὶ τῇ ἡμέρᾳ τῇ ὀγδόῃ εὑρήσετέ με πάλιν.

3.1.2 Vocabulary

From now on, verbs that you have learnt, but which appear in Principal Parts that *ENTG* has not told you to memorise, are given as vocab.

ἀλλότριος, α, ον – belonging to another; strange; foreign (note the word play in 8:1)
γυνή – woman (nom fem sing)
εἴδωλον, ου, τό – idol (**εἶδον**: an idol was something that was *seen*)
εὐλογία, ας, ἡ – blessing
εὑρίσκω – Principal Parts: 2. εὑρήσω; 3. εὗρον
θυγάτηρ – daughter (fem nom sing; θυγατρί dat sing)

καταλείπω – Principal Parts: 2. καταλείψω 3. κατέλιπον
μισέω – I hate
ὄγδοος, η, ον – eighth
παρθένος, ου, ὁ / ἡ – virgin
στόμα – mouth (neut sing nom/acc; στόματι dat sing)
ὑπερῷον, ου, τό – upper room
ὕψιστος, η, ον – most high
φιλέω – you have learnt 'I like, love'; it also means 'I kiss'
φοβέομαι – I fear

3.2 Reading C: Philemon (Yes, a Whole GNT Book!)

For your encouragement, let's look at a decent chunk (a whole book, in fact) of NT Greek. If you have a mid-year holiday, use this **Reading C** to avoid forgetting all the Greek that you've worked so hard to acquire!

I have filled the notes with cross-references to sections of *ENTG* or this *Reader* that explain a point, even if it is a very easy point. If you review those sections as you come across them in the notes, you'll revise a good deal of what you've learnt. I hope you will have fun by meeting the topics of *ENTG* through a text rather than through a textbook.

The text is annotated, but not simplified.[2] Be aware that more modern translations will be based on a slightly different Greek text.[3] However, I have supplied a translation in the **Online Material**, which will remove that problem, but will also help you check your work where English idiom requires changes.[4] As an unedited Greek text, it contains not only material from later chapters in *ENTG*, but also more advanced uses of elements that we have already met, and which you would study in later years. Don't worry, then, if you can't see how to go from a wooden translation to what you find in a printed Bible. (Don't fear: in Chapter 12 and onwards, *Joseph & Aseneth* will still be simplified for you as before.)

As ever, for your encouragement, vocab that you will come to learn in *ENTG* is in bold. Points of grammar that you haven't yet met are glossed for you, and I indicate which chapter of *ENTG* covers that point.

ΠΑΥΛΟΥ Η ΠΡΟΣ ΦΙΛΗΜΟΝΑ ΕΠΙΣΤΟΛΗ

¹ Παῦλος δέσμιος Χριστοῦ Ἰησοῦ καὶ Τιμόθεος ὁ ἀδελφός, Φιλήμονι τῷ ἀγαπητῷ καὶ συνεργῷ ἡμῶν, ² καὶ Ἀπφίᾳ τῇ ἀγαπητῇ, καὶ Ἀρχίππῳ τῷ συστρατιώτῃ ἡμῶν, καὶ τῇ κατ' οἶκόν σου ἐκκλησίᾳ· ³ χάρις ὑμῖν καὶ εἰρήνη ἀπὸ Θεοῦ πατρὸς ἡμῶν καὶ Κυρίου Ἰησοῦ Χριστοῦ.

⁴ Εὐχαριστῶ τῷ Θεῷ μου, πάντοτε μνείαν σου ποιούμενος ἐπὶ τῶν προσευχῶν μου, ⁵ ἀκούων σου τὴν ἀγάπην, καὶ τὴν πίστιν ἣν ἔχεις πρὸς τὸν Κύριον Ἰησοῦν καὶ εἰς πάντας τοὺς ἁγίους, ⁶ ὅπως ἡ κοινωνία τῆς πίστεώς σου ἐνεργὴς γένηται ἐν ἐπιγνώσει παντὸς ἀγαθοῦ τοῦ ἐν ὑμῖν εἰς Χριστὸν Ἰησοῦν. ⁷ χαρὰν γὰρ ἔχομεν πολλὴν καὶ παράκλησιν ἐπὶ τῇ ἀγάπῃ σου, ὅτι τὰ σπλάγχνα τῶν ἁγίων ἀναπέπαυται διὰ σοῦ, ἀδελφέ.

---

[2] F. H. A. Scrivener, *The New Testament in Greek* (Cambridge: Cambridge University Press, 1881; in the public domain). I have edited the text only by comparison with other editions, but not to make it simpler (unlike *Joseph & Aseneth*).
[3] I have chosen this edition purely pragmatically: it is out of copyright.
[4] See my notes at the start of the translation to this text in the **Online Material**.

⁸ Διὸ πολλὴν ἐν Χριστῷ παρρησίαν ἔχων ἐπιτάσσειν σοι τὸ ἀνῆκον, ⁹ διὰ τὴν ἀγάπην μᾶλλον παρακαλῶ, τοιοῦτος ὢν ὡς Παῦλος πρεσβύτης, νυνὶ δὲ καὶ δέσμιος Ἰησοῦ Χριστοῦ. ¹⁰ παρακαλῶ σε περὶ τοῦ ἐμοῦ τέκνου, ὃν ἐγέννησα ἐν τοῖς δεσμοῖς μου, Ὀνήσιμον, ¹¹ τόν ποτέ σοι ἄχρηστον, νυνὶ δὲ σοὶ καὶ ἐμοὶ εὔχρηστον, ¹² ὃν ἀνέπεμψά σοι, αὐτόν, τοῦτ' ἔστι τὰ ἐμὰ σπλάγχνα, προσλαβοῦ· ¹³ ὃν ἐγὼ ἐβουλόμην πρὸς ἐμαυτὸν κατέχειν, ἵνα ὑπὲρ σοῦ διακονῇ μοι ἐν τοῖς δεσμοῖς τοῦ εὐαγγελίου· ¹⁴ χωρὶς δὲ τῆς σῆς γνώμης οὐδὲν ἠθέλησα ποιῆσαι, ἵνα μὴ ὡς κατὰ ἀνάγκην τὸ ἀγαθόν σου ᾖ, ἀλλὰ κατὰ ἑκούσιον. ¹⁵ Τάχα γὰρ διὰ τοῦτο ἐχωρίσθη πρὸς ὥραν, ἵνα αἰώνιον αὐτὸν ἀπέχῃς· ¹⁶ οὐκέτι ὡς δοῦλον, ἀλλ' ὑπὲρ δοῦλον, ἀδελφὸν ἀγαπητόν, μάλιστα ἐμοί, πόσῳ δὲ μᾶλλον σοὶ καὶ ἐν σαρκὶ καὶ ἐν Κυρίῳ. ¹⁷ εἰ οὖν ἐμὲ ἔχεις κοινωνόν, προσλαβοῦ αὐτὸν ὡς ἐμέ. ¹⁸ εἰ δέ τι ἠδίκησέ σε ἢ ὀφείλει, τοῦτο ἐμοὶ ἐλλόγει·

¹⁹ ἐγὼ Παῦλος ἔγραψα τῇ ἐμῇ χειρί, ἐγὼ ἀποτίσω· ἵνα μὴ λέγω σοι ὅτι καὶ σεαυτόν μοι προσοφείλεις. ²⁰ ναί, ἀδελφέ, ἐγώ σου ὀναίμην ἐν Κυρίῳ· ἀνάπαυσόν μου τὰ σπλάγχνα ἐν Κυρίῳ.

²¹ Πεποιθὼς τῇ ὑπακοῇ σου ἔγραψά σοι, εἰδὼς ὅτι καὶ ὑπὲρ ὃ λέγω ποιήσεις.

²² ἅμα δὲ καὶ ἑτοίμαζέ μοι ξενίαν· ἐλπίζω γὰρ ὅτι διὰ τῶν προσευχῶν ὑμῶν χαρισθήσομαι ὑμῖν.

²³ Ἀσπάζονταί σε Ἐπαφρᾶς ὁ συναιχμάλωτός μου ἐν Χριστῷ Ἰησοῦ, ²⁴ Μᾶρκος, Ἀρίσταρχος, Δημᾶς, Λουκᾶς, οἱ συνεργοί μου.

²⁵ Ἡ χάρις τοῦ Κυρίου ἡμῶν Ἰησοῦ Χριστοῦ μετὰ τοῦ πνεύματος ὑμῶν. ἀμήν.

3.2.1 Vocabulary

ἀδικέω – I wrong (+ acc of person wronged)
ἅμα – 'at the same time' (in the sense of 'also')
ἀνάγκη, ης, ἡ – compulsion
ἀναπαύω – I refresh
ἀναπέμπω – I send back
ἀναπέπαυται – 'have been refreshed' (perfect tense: Chapter 16)
ἀποτίνω – I pay compensation
Ἀπφίᾳ – personal name (fem dat sing)
Ἀρίσταρχος – proper noun
Ἀρχίππῳ – personal name (masc dat sing)
ἄχρηστος – useless
βούλομαι – I want
γεννάω – I beget (easily confused with the aor stem of γίνομαι γεν-); in the form in this text, the contract α behaves just like a contract ε (6.8 note i).
γνώμη, ης, ἡ – assent
Δημᾶς – proper noun
δέσμιος, ου, ὁ – prisoner
δεσμός, οῦ, ὁ – bond (cf. δέσμιος above)
εἰδώς – knowing (treat as a present ptcpl; Chapter 18)
ἑκούσιος, ια, ιον – voluntary
ἐλλογέω – I charge to someone's account (+ dat of person charged)
ἐλπίζω – I hope
ἐνεργής – effective (nom sing fem; Chapter 13)
Ἐπαφρᾶς – proper noun
ἐπιγνώσει – knowledge (dat sing fem; Chapter 13)
ἐπιτάσσω – I command: (+ dat of person commanded).
ἑτοιμάζω – I prepare

εὔχρηστος – useful
ἐχωρίσθη – he was separated (pass voice, Chapter 15) cf. χωρίς
ἵνα ... ἀπέχῃς – so that you might have him back
ἵνα ... διακονῇ – in order that ... he might serve (subjunctive, Chapter 17)
ἵνα ... ᾖ – in order that ... it might be (Chapter 17)
κατέχω – I keep
κοινωνία, ας, ἡ – participation
κοινωνός – companion
Λουκᾶς – proper noun
μάλιστα – most of all
μᾶλλον – rather, more
Μᾶρκος – proper noun
μνεία, ας, ἡ – remembrance
ὀναίμην – 'I wish to enjoy, or to have some benefit from' (optative, EM 21 1.1).
Ὀνήσιμος, ου, ὁ – Onesimus
ὅπως ... γένηται – so that ... might become (Chapter 17)
οὐδέν – nothing (*ENTG* 13.4)
πάντας ... – all of (masc acc pl; Chapter 13)
παντός ... – of every ... (masc / neut gen sing)
παράκλησιν – encouragement (fem acc sing; Chapter 13)
πατρός, ὁ – father (gen sing; Chapter 12)
πεποιθώς – from πείθω; this is a 'perfect participle' (Chapters 15–16); translate as 'I am persuaded'
πίστιν – faith (fem acc sing; Chapter 13)
πρεσβύτης, ου, ὁ – an old(er) man
προσευχή, ῆς, ἡ – prayer

προσλαμβάνω – I welcome
προσοφείλω – I owe (in some extra way beyond ὀφείλω)
πνεῦμα, ατος, τό – spirit
σαρκί – flesh (fem dat sing; Chapter 12)
σπλάγχνον, ου, τό – bowels, but metaphorically equivalent to 'heart' in English
συναιχμάλωτος, ου, ὁ – fellow-prisoner
συνεργός, όν – helper, fellow-worker (adjective; takes masc endings in the fem)
συστρατιώτης, ου, ὁ – one who fights alongside you
τάχα – possibly
τι – something (neut sing acc; Chapter 12)
τὸ ἀνῆκον – 'that which is a duty'; a neut ptcpl (Chapter 14)
ὑπακοή – obedience
Φιλήμονι – personal name (masc dat sing)
χάρις, ἡ – grace (nom sing; Chapter 12)
χαρισθήσομαι – 'I will be restored' (Chapter 15)
χειρί – hand (fem sing dat; Chapter 12)
ξενία, ας, ἡ – the duty of hospitality and/or its practical details

4 ACCENTS OF LIQUID FUTURES

Further Reading: Probert 84

Just as with contract verbs, the accents are placed before the contractions happen. If the rise and fall happen within the contracted vowels, they form a circumflex (**EM 7** 4.1).

σπέρ - σει → σπερ - έσει → σπερ - έ + ει → σπερ - εῖ → σπερεῖ

An exception: a handful of *second* aorist verbs have a final accent in the 2s imperative: ἐλθέ, ἰδού, εἰπέ. This doesn't happen with their compounds: εἴσελθε.

5 ASPECT IN IMPERATIVES

Further Reading: *CGCG* 38.30, 41; Fanning 5; Kühner-Gerth 389.6C

5.1 The Core Sense

In every mood, the difference between the present and aorist systems is aspect. Outside the indicative, this does not interact with time to give tenses. As we saw with the infinitive (**EM 8** 5), the aorist imperative refers to an event simply, whereas the present imperative refers to an event 'ongoingly'.

As with the infinitive, the type of situation (state, action with/without an endpoint) affects the author's choice. Where the choice is pointed (choosing a present imperative when the action has an endpoint), some element of the 'ongoing' aspect of the present stem is being highlighted. These are included in the uses of the indicative tenses (present and imperfect indicative). We will see which are most commonly used below.

5.1.1 Equivalent Expressions to Imperatives

Throughout this chapter, 'imperative' applies also to the other forms of expressing a desire or instruction: subjunctive in aorist prohibitions, hortatory subjunctive, optative in wishes and desires, subjunctive and infinitive in indirect commands. An author will choose the aspect of these on the same basis as when the imperative is used.

5.2 Situation Type

As you might expect, the situation type (i.e. what kind of thing you're being commanded to do) affects the author's choice of aspect.

5.2.1 Situations without Endpoints (Including States)

The present imperative is used when the situation has no endpoint:[5]

> Σιώπα [present imperative] Mark 4:39
> Be quiet!

When a verb without an endpoint uses an aorist imperative, we need to find the endpoint that is supplied, which might be implicit:

> ὃ εἰς τὸ οὖς **ἀκούετε**, κηρύξατε [aorist] Matt 10:27
> preach **what you hear** with your ear
> > Once you have preached the whole message (**what you heard**) you've completed the action.

5.2.2 Situations with Endpoints

For a verb (or action) with an endpoint, the aorist imperative is the default. It means that you're telling them to do the action to completion, not just do it for a while:

> Κύριε, σῶσον ἡμᾶς, ἀπολλύμεθα Matt 8:25
> Master, rescue us, we are dying!
> > This doesn't mean 'do some work towards rescuing us'; he has to put them out of peril and into safety.

Where a situation has an endpoint, and the imperative is *present*, we should look for one of the nuances of the present system which can be emphasised by the indicative present and imperfect. Most commonly, for imperatives, the 'ongoing' aspect will usually mean:

---

[5] You might expect stative verbs to use the aorist to command you to enter the state (as an ingressive aorist, cf. EM 7 5.1.2; EM 8 5.4.2); however, they seem to use the present instead.

- make a habit of it (cf. habitual **EM 2** 5.1.3; **EM 6** 7.2.2)
- *keep doing* something that you're already doing (cf. descriptive **EM 2** 5.1.1; **EM 6** 7.2.1)
- do it urgently or emphatically (cf. futuristic **EM 2** 5.2.3)
- get started with the action (cf. inceptive **EM 6** 7.3.4).

5.3 The Present Imperative

These are the nuances from the present stem that are often intended when an author uses the present imperative *of an action that has an endpoint.*[6]

5.3.1 Habitual

The 'ongoing' sense will most often mean that a command is not only applicable to the present situation, but is to become a habit or custom (cf. habitual present and imperfect **EM 2** 5.1.3; **EM 6** 7.2.2).

> θησαυρίζετε [present] δὲ ὑμῖν θησαυροὺς ἐν οὐρανῷ Matt 6:20
> <u>deposit</u> treasure for yourselves in heaven

> εὐλογεῖτε [present imperative] τοὺς διώκοντας ὑμᾶς Rom 12:14
> <u>bless</u> those who persecute you
>> Even though each individual act of blessing has an endpoint, the present imperative makes it a habit, to be done every time the situation arises.

We can see a nice contrast with the Lord's Supper. The command to eat and drink at the Last Supper was a one-off:

> Λάβετε φάγετε ... Πίετε [all aorists] Matt 26:26–7
> <u>Take</u> <u>eat</u> ... <u>drink</u>

but it was also instituting something to be done habitually thereafter as the Lord's Supper:

> τοῦτο ποιεῖτε [present] εἰς τὴν ἐμὴν ἀνάμνησιν Luke 22:19
> <u>do</u> this for the sake of my remembrance

---

[6] These nuances can be implied, of course, with actions that do not have an endpoint, but the use of the present stem doesn't emphasise the fact in those cases. For example:

> Ὡς οὖν παρελάβετε τὸν Χριστὸν Ἰησοῦν τὸν Κύριον, ἐν αὐτῷ περιπατεῖτε [present] ... καθὼς ἐδιδάχθητε. Col 2:6–7
> Therefore, as you received Christ Jesus the Lord, <u>continue walking</u> in him ... just as you were taught.

ἐσθιέτω καὶ ... πινέτω [both present] 1 Cor 11:28
he should <u>eat</u> and <u>drink</u>

5.3.2 Continue to ...

The present imperative can be used for actions already in progress (cf. descriptive present and imperfect EM 2 5.1.1; EM 6 7.2.1):

> καὶ εἶπεν αὐτῷ Λάλησον [aorist]
> ...
> καὶ εἶπεν αὐτῷ Βηρσάβεε <u>Λάλει [present]</u> 3 Kgdms 2:14–16
> [Batsheba] said to him, 'You may speak.'
> ...
> And Batsheba said to him, 'You may speak on.'

Here it has the sense of resuming an interrupted action:

> πρῶτον διαλλάγηθι τῷ ἀδελφῷ σου, καὶ τότε ἐλθὼν <u>πρόσφερε</u> τὸ δῶρόν σου. Matt 5:24
> First become reconciled with your brother, then come and <u>offer</u> your gift.

5.3.3 Urgent/Emphatic

In the indicative, the aspect of the present system can point to an action that is just beginning or about to begin: the **futuristic** present can refer to a future action as either *imminent* or more *certain*.

Obviously, commands tend to refer to actions that are future anyway, and many of those in contexts where the command is to be done right away. An aorist imperative works fine in those circumstances. The present imperative is used to *stress* one or both of those points.

1 *without delay*, do this (cf. futuristic present, with imminent sense: EM 2 5.2.3)

2 *emphatically* do this (cf. futuristic present, with vivid sense: EM 2 5.2.3)

The emphatic clamour of the crowd before Pilate, that he should take Jesus away (αἴρω) is given by John with two aorist imperatives:

> οἱ δὲ ἐκραύγασαν, Ἆρον ἆρον, σταύρωσον αὐτόν. John 19:15
> But they screamed: '<u>Take him away! Take him away!</u> [2 x aorist] Crucify him!'

In Luke, on the other hand, we get more of Pilate's attempts to persuade the crowd, which causes them to yell with more urgency:

> ἀνέκραξαν δὲ παμπληθεί λέγοντες, Αἶρε τοῦτον Luke 23:18
> But they shouted as one: 'Take this one away [present]'
> It has the sense of 'Enough talk: away with him!'

The emphatic or urgent sense can be ironic:

> Λέγετέ μοι, οἱ ὑπὸ νόμον θέλοντες εἶναι ... Gal 4:21
> Come on then, tell me: you who want to be subject to the law ...

Sometimes a command/petition will be given with an aorist, and then if there is some objection or perceived danger that it won't be granted, it is restated with a present:

> Ἀναστὰς πορεύθητι [aorist] ἐπὶ τὴν ῥύμην τὴν καλουμένην Εὐθεῖαν, καὶ ζήτησον ἐν οἰκίᾳ Ἰούδα Σαῦλον ὀνόματι, Ταρσέα.
> ...
> Πορεύου [present], ὅτι σκεῦος ἐκλογῆς μοι ἐστίν οὗτος ... Acts 9:11–15
> Get up and go to the street called Straight, and seek out a Tarsean named Saul in Judas' house.
> ...
> Get going, because that man is my chosen instrument ...

> εἴ τι δύνασαι, βοήθησον [aorist] ἡμῖν
> ...
> Πιστεύω, Κύριε, βοήθει [present] μου τῇ ἀπιστίᾳ. Mark 9:22–4
> if you are able to do something, help us
> ...
> I do believe, Master, help my unbelief!

> γυνὴ Χαναναία ... ἐκραύγασεν αὐτῷ ... Ἐλέησόν [aorist] με, Κύριε ...
> ...
> ἡ δὲ ἐλθοῦσα προσεκύνει αὐτῷ λέγουσα, Κύριε, βοήθει [present] μοι. Matt 15:22–5
> A Canaanite woman ... yelled at him ... 'Show mercy to me, Master ...!'
> ...
> But she came and prostrated herself before him, saying, 'Master, help me!'

5.3.4 Immediative

FURTHER READING: *CGCG* 38.30; SCHWYZER-DEBRUNNER II: 340–1; MURAOKA 28DFC, 28HA(III)

In the indicative, the aspect of the present system can point to an action that is just beginning or about to begin, and which will take some time. The present imperative can highlight one or other of these:

1 *Now* is the time to get started with the action, as opposed to earlier (cf. **inceptive** imperfect **EM 6** 7.3.4).
2 Start this *process which will take some time*.

> ἕως ἄρτι οὐκ ᾐτήσατε οὐδὲν ἐν τῷ ὀνόματί μου· **αἰτεῖτε** [present], καὶ λήψεσθε. John 16:24
> **Until now, you haven't** asked for anything in my name: <u>start asking</u> [i.e. ask from now on], and you will receive.

When you have been warned in advance that you will need to do something (perhaps with an aorist imperative), the present imperative tells you that now is the time to do it.

> Ἄνθρωπός τις ἐποίησε δεῖπνον μέγα, καὶ <u>ἐκάλεσε</u> πολλούς· καὶ ἀπέστειλε τὸν δοῦλον αὐτοῦ **τῇ ὥρᾳ τοῦ δείπνου** εἰπεῖν τοῖς κεκλημένοις, Ἔρχεσθε [present], ὅτι **ἤδη** ἕτοιμά ἐστι πάντα. Luke 14:16–17
> A certain man laid on a great feast and <u>invited</u> many; **at the time of the feast** he sent his servant to say to those who had been invited: '<u>Come</u>, because everything is ready **now**.'

You might tell someone to do a series of one-off things that are needed before they can proceed with something more lengthy. You will make that final action, which is the point of the whole thing, a present imperative. Its immediative sense means 'now you can start the process'.

> εἶπε τε ὁ ἄγγελος πρὸς αὐτόν, <u>Περίζωσαι</u> [aorist] καὶ <u>ὑπόδησαι</u> [aorist] τὰ σανδάλιά σου. ἐποίησε δὲ οὕτω. καὶ λέγει αὐτῷ, <u>Περιβαλοῦ</u> [aorist] τὸ ἱμάτιόν σου, καὶ **ἀκολούθει** [present] μοι. Acts 12:8
> The angel told him: '<u>Get dressed</u> and <u>put on</u> your sandals.' He did so. He told him: '<u>Wrap up</u> with your cloak and **follow me**.'

The 'immediative' sense can simply highlight that the action will be a process, taking time, and perhaps with multiple steps. While this is quite rare, it is worth bearing it in mind as an option:

> ἀσπάζου [present] τοὺς φίλους **κατ' ὄνομα**. 3 John 15
> <u>Greet</u> the brothers **each individually** ['according to name'].

> Ἑτοιμάσατε [aorist] τὴν ὁδὸν Κυρίου·
>   εὐθείας ποιεῖτε [present] τὰς τρίβους αὐτοῦ. Luke 3:4
> <u>Prepare</u> the Lord's way
>   <u>Make</u> his lanes straight.
> The first command refers to the whole thing that must be done; the second refers to it in its constituent parts, as a process of straightening individual roads.

5.3.5 A Note on Verbs of Motion

Modern grammars helpfully list certain verbs (including many verbs of motion) as breaking the pattern: these verbs sometimes use present imperatives to issue obviously one-off commands: πορεύομαι, ἔρχομαι, περιπατέω, ὑπάγω, ἀκολουθέω, φέρω, ἐγείρω, αἱρέω, θαρσέω and γινώσκω.[7]

By and large, we're talking about a small number of exceptional uses for each verb. It may be that most, if not all, of these are in fact explained by the urgent/emphatic or 'immediative' senses above.[8]

Start doing this lengthy process now:

> λέγει αὐτῷ, **Ἀκολούθει [present]** μοι. καὶ ἀναστὰς ἠκολούθησεν αὐτῷ. Mark 2:14
> He said to him: '**Follow** me.' So he got up and followed him.

A series of one-off things that are needed before you can proceed with something more lengthy:

> Ἐγερθεὶς [aorist participle for imperative][9] παράλαβε [aorist imperative] τὸ παιδίον καὶ τὴν μητέρα αὐτοῦ, καὶ **φεῦγε [present]** εἰς Αἴγυπτον Matt 2:13
> Get up, take the child and his mother, and **flee** to Egypt

Without delay:

> ἕως πότε ἀνέξομαι ὑμῶν; φέρετέ [present] μοι αὐτὸν ὧδε. Matt 17:17
> Until when shall I put up with you? Bring him to me here!

Such uses of ὑπάγω seem to function like the English 'go and *do*', as an idiom for urgency:

> **Ὕπαγε [present]**, φώνησον [aorist] τὸν ἄνδρα σου, καὶ ἐλθὲ [aorist] ἐνθάδε. John 4:16
> **Get going**, call your husband, then come here.

5.4 The Aorist Imperative

5.4.1 Simple

The aorist commands an action to be done to the completion of its endpoint. It is the default for situations with an endpoint. Even where an action involves multiple steps or is to be repeated, the aorist presents the whole as a simple summary (cf. **EM 7** 5.2.3; see further **EM 11** 5.5).

---

[7] Fanning 5.3–4; vS 212e; Köstenberger 242–3.
[8] Θαρσέω and γινώσκω are states, so there is nothing to explain (**EM 11** 5.2.1).
[9] **EM 14** 4.2.5.

A command to do an action once, completely:

> εἴσελθε [aorist] εἰς τὴν πόλιν Acts 9:6
> enter the city

In a context of habitual instructions for life, the aorist can stand out as an order to do something *once and for all*, which will have enduring consequences:

> ἀλλ' ἐνδύσασθε [aorist] τὸν Κύριον Ἰησοῦν Χριστόν Rom 13:14
> but clothe yourselves with the Lord Jesus Christ
> > An action with an endpoint. It is definitive and won't need to be repeated, but has life-long consequences.
>
> ἀσπάσασθε [aorist] ἀλλήλους ἐν ἁγίῳ φιλήματι 2 Cor 13:12
> greet each other with a holy kiss
> > The previous verse has five present imperatives, describing a new life of mutual reconciliation. This aorist imperative commands the starting point for that new, reconciled life: 'kiss and make up', not just 'kiss and forget', but also not 'keep greeting each other with kisses'.

The aorist can be a summary view of a whole series of commands, as Matt 19:17, then expanded in v19:

> εἰ δὲ θέλεις εἰσελθεῖν εἰς τὴν ζωήν, τήρησον [aorist] τὰς ἐντολάς …
> τίμα [present imperative] τὸν πατέρα σου καὶ τὴν μητέρα Matt 19:17–19
> if you wish to enter life, keep the commandments …
> > honour your father and your mother.

An aorist can therefore point to an action that takes a long time or even requires multiple actions; the aorist describes the desired endpoint, in summary:

> μαθητεύσατε πάντα τὰ ἔθνη Matt 28:19
> make all nations into disciples

5.4.2 Prayers

Petitions in prayers are almost exclusively aorists:

> ἁγιασθήτω … ἐλθέτω … γενηθήτω … δός … ἄφες Matt 6:9–12
> may it be hallowed … may it come … may it become … give … forgive

This makes Luke's version of the petition for bread striking:

> τὸν ἄρτον ἡμῶν τὸν ἐπιούσιον δίδου [present imperative] ἡμῖν **τὸ καθ' ἡμέραν** Luke 11:3
> our daily bread keep giving us **day by day**

5.5 Generic Situations: Present or Aorist?

If an aorist works for a single situation, it works also in the sense of 'every time that this situation arises, do this once'.

> Ὅταν δὲ νηστεύητε ... ἄλειψαί [aorist] σου τὴν κεφαλήν, καὶ τὸ πρόσωπόν σου νίψαι. [aorist] Matt 6:16–17
> **Whenever** you fast ... <u>anoint</u> your head and <u>wash</u> your face.

The problem is that a present also works:

> ὅταν ποιῇς δοχήν, κάλει [present] πτωχούς ... Luke 14:13
> **whenever** you lay on a feast, <u>invite</u> the poor ...

When the context is more implicit, we have the same problem. The *Didache* uses aorist, even though it is *entirely* given over to lifestyle issues and customs for each believer and each church:

> Περὶ δὲ τοῦ βαπτίσματος, οὕτω βαπτίσατε [aorist] Did. 7.1
> Concerning baptism, <u>baptise</u> like this ...
>   Not, 'perform one baptism', but 'this is how you perform baptisms'.

Many NT epistles use present imperatives for habits, and reserve the aorist along the lines of **EM 11** 5.4.1 (e.g. Romans, Corinthians and Galatians). Nonetheless, it is well-known that 2 Timothy, James and 1 Peter are full of *aorist* imperatives which are obviously teaching habits and lifestyles, not specific one-off commands.[10]

If we were only interested in the question, 'Is this a command to do something once only, or a command for a new lifestyle?', then the answer is clear enough from the context. However, you want to learn to read Greek and understand the choices authors make. I humbly confess that I cannot explain why an author has these options: when an author has already made a 'habitual' sense clear by context, what is added by choosing a present over an aorist?

It may be that the aorist is truly just a default and is entirely 'unmarked'. It doesn't tell you what the present imperative tells you, but *neither does it deny it*.[11] That still doesn't tell us *why* an author would choose one over the other in these situations.

What this does mean is that we need to be aware of that 'summary' use of the aorist, and not insist that an aorist commands only a single action to be done once:

---

[10] A thorough discussion is offered by Fanning 5.3–4.
[11] This is more often true in Greek than in English. For example, the perfect indicative tells you something which the aorist doesn't, but the aorist doesn't deny it (whereas the English past simple does deny what an English perfect means); the Greek middle voice tells you something, but the active voice doesn't deny it (whereas English active voice denies the passive voice). We will see these in Chapters 15 and 16.

ἐν φόβῳ **τὸν τῆς παροικίας ὑμῶν χρόνον**[12] ἀναστράφητε [aorist]
1 Pet 1:17
behave in fear **throughout the time of your exile**

ἔδωκεν αὐτοῖς δέκα μνᾶς, καὶ εἶπε πρὸς αὐτούς, Πραγματεύσασθε [aorist] **ἕως ἔρχομαι** Luke 19:13
he gave them ten minas, and said to them: 'Do business **until I return.**'

Ὦ Τιμόθεε, τὴν παραθήκην φύλαξον [aorist] 1 Tim 6:20
O Timothy, guard what has been entrusted.
A summary of all the *present* imperatives in the letter.

5.6 Prohibitions

If there is debate about aspect, there is even more about aspect in the other moods; the imperative is particularly contested and difficult; but that's just a warm-up act for the uncertainty that surrounds *prohibitions*. If our interest is only in whether something is prohibited as a one-off rather than permanently forbidden, then we must decide the issue quite apart from the form of the imperative, as the four examples in Table 11.4 illustrate.

Table 11.4 Prohibitions

	μή + pres imperative	μή + aor subjunctive
Don't do it this time:	Μὴ κλαίετε· οὐκ ἀπέθανεν, ἀλλὰ καθεύδει. Luke 8:52 Don't cry: she hasn't died, but is sleeping.	Ἰωσὴφ, υἱὸς Δαβίδ, μὴ φοβηθῇς παραλαβεῖν Μαριὰμ τὴν γυναῖκά σου Matt 1:20 Joseph, David's son, don't be afraid to take Mary as your wife.
Never do this:	μὴ κρίνετε … . μὴ καταδικάζετε Luke 6:37 Do not judge … Do not condemn.	Μὴ μοιχεύσῃς, μὴ φονεύσῃς, μὴ κλέψῃς, μὴ ψευδομαρτυρήσῃς … Luke 18:20 Do not commit adultery, do not murder, do not steal, do not commit perjury …

5.7 As Readers / As Writers

To summarise what we have seen, when a writer is issuing a prohibition, it isn't clear what lies behind the choice of aspect. As readers, therefore, we should avoid saying much about it.

---
[12] Accusative of time, EM 9 4.4.

When issuing commands, a writer seems to be tied to the following rules:
- In prayers you must generally use the aorist.
- If the verb is a state or an action without an endpoint, you must use the present imperative.
  - If you want to alert the reader that there is an implicit endpoint, use the aorist.
- If the verb or situation has an endpoint, then:
  - you can *always* use the aorist, with nothing particular implied or denied.
  - If you want to highlight something pointed, then you use a present to indicate:
    - The command is a habit.
    - The command is something your reader is already doing.
    - The command is to be obeyed urgently or emphatically.
    - The command is a process to be started now, or to be started as soon as some prerequisite commands are obeyed ('get up and *go*').
    - Simply to point out that the command is a process.

Note that there are two ways of expressing that something should be made a habit:

- Make it clear in the context (and use either present or aorist).
- Rather less clearly, use a present imperative and hope the reader understands why.

This means that, as readers, we reason as follows:

- If it's a prayer, and aorist, that's expected. If it's present, that's interesting.
- If the situation has no endpoint and is a present imperative, that's what we expect.
- If the situation has an endpoint and
  - is an aorist imperative, that's what we expect. None of the following is denied by this aorist.
  - is a present imperative, then consider what point the author might be making:
    - habit
    - continuation
    - urgency / emphasis
    - getting a process started
    - just telling you that the action is a process.

> Note especially that commands to do something habitually are most clearly expressed by context; don't jump to the conclusion that a present imperative is commanding a habit, or that an aorist imperative is a one-off.

5.8 The Need for Perspective

Here's a humbling thought:

> the decisive factor [aspect] hadn't been noticed until the middle of the 19th C., despite the fact that, even today, every native Greek speaker has a living and subtle feel for [differences in aspect], even in cases where the foreigner cannot detect any difference.[13]

A great deal has happened in the last century, and especially the last four decades, concerning aspect in ancient Greek. Nothing in this *Reader* will be the final word on anything, and this is especially true of the aspect of the other moods, and even more in this chapter on the imperative.

What, then, is the benefit of studying aspect in the other moods, and even in the imperative?

First, you will avoid over-exegeting. You will see that, generally, the author's choice of aspect matches what you can already see from context. There is then little need to comment on aspect.

Second, aspect *will* help you to correct your understanding of the context: if aspect clashes with what you were expecting, the author might not be saying what you thought they were saying.

Third, understanding the limits of our current knowledge about aspect in the other moods will help you to read with due humility. You needn't spend time correcting *all* who have gone before and have 'misread' this imperative or that subjunctive. At the same time, even when reading the most honoured of experts, it will help you to be aware that their conclusions might be based on a view of aspect that is less widely held today.

---

[13] Schwyzer-Debrunner II:255.

CHAPTER 12

The Third Declension, Part 1

> **How to Use This Chapter**
>
> In the next three chapters we get some respite: we learn how to use one set of new endings. One sequence of eight sounds is all you really need for the next three chapters!
>
> Work through this chapter of *ENTG*, section by section, completing exercises as you go. As you complete each section, read **Extra Help** below for that section.
>
> In **Extra Help** we will see how nouns and adjectives are formed when their stems do not end in α or ο. This gives us the opportunity to practise the idea of **agreement**.
>
> The **Extra Material** in this chapter is a just a trivial pointer about accents.

1 THREE CHAPTERS OF *ENTG* WITH JUST EIGHT ENDINGS

1.1 After *ENTG* 12.2 (before *ENTG* 12.2.1)

The great news is that everything in the next three chapters of *ENTG* (12–14) hinges on learning one simple set of endings. Learn them now, and your life will never be the same again.

[ς], α, ος, ι, ες, ας, ων, σι(ν)

Up until now, we have dealt with nouns that have a *thematic* vowel, either α (1st declension) or ο (2nd declension), and we have seen that they have one set of endings in common.

There is only one other family of nouns, and these do not have a thematic vowel. They are known as *consonant* declension, or 3rd declension. Their stems end in a consonant (this chapter) or in vowels which behave like consonants (next chapter). Their endings, which you have just learnt, bolt directly onto the consonants that end their stem.

As with all nouns, the neuter (**EH 3** 2.1):

- copies the masc in gen and dat
- has the same ending in the nom and acc
- has α as the pl nom and acc ending.

1.1.1 How to Learn Nouns

You need to learn three things for any noun as vocab:

> 1 the nominative
> 2 the genitive (which gives you the stem, from which you work out the other forms)
> 3 the article (which gives you the gender).
>
> (On the dative plural, see 1.2.1 below.)

1.1.2 Super-Simple Rules

Be ready to see any of these changes in the nominative singular, compared with the stem:

1 The ending might be ς (which might combine into ξ, ψ).
2 The ending might be blank, and the stem might lose its final consonant.
3 A vowel in the stem might change its length.

The rules marked 'optional' in 1.2 and 1.3 below explain when and why each of these happen, but if you're ready to recognise the above changes, you'll be able to parse these nouns fine.

1.2 (Optional) After *ENTG* 12.2.1

1.2.1 Slippery Sigma Again

As *ENTG* 12.2.1 explains, a slippery sigma applies to the dative plural. You can see that the combinations described there are what we have seen with liquid verbs (**EH 11** 1.3.1).

As an aside, we can now explain the 3p of the present indicative active. The ending proper is ντσιν. The thematic vowel ε becomes ο before a ν: -ο-ντσιν. The οντ+σ combination behaves as described in *ENTG* 12.2.1: οντ+σ → ουσιν. The τ is lost, and the preceding vowel is lengthened half-way.

$$\lambda\acute{\upsilon}\text{-}\epsilon\text{-}\nu\tau\sigma\iota\nu \rightarrow \lambda\acute{\upsilon}\text{-}o\nu\tau\text{+}\sigma\text{+}\iota\nu \rightarrow \lambda\acute{\upsilon}\text{-}o\upsilon\sigma\text{+}\iota\nu \rightarrow \lambda\acute{\upsilon}o\upsilon\sigma\iota\nu$$

1.2.2 The Masculine/Feminine Singular Nominative Ending

ENTG 12.1 n2 rightly warns you that the deep rules here might be more trouble than they're worth; for those of you who find such things helpful, here goes.

There are two options for the masculine singular endings. After the stem you put:

- *either* a **σ**
  - Remember that in certain combinations it will be spelt ξ or ψ, of which you're reminded in **Key Grammar** *ENTG* 12.2.1: νυκτ- + σ → νύξ
  - Remember that after certain letters, the σ will simply remove the preceding letter, and lengthen the preceding vowel, *ENTG* 12.2.1: ποδ- + σ → πούς
- *or* a **blank** ending with a **change of preceding vowel length**,
  ἀστέρ- + – → ἀστήρ.

However, Greek words can only end in one of three consonants: σ, ρ, ν (SiReN).¹ Remember that ξ and ψ do indeed end in σ. When a blank ending leaves the stem ending in any other consonant, it is simply removed: ἀρχοντ- + – → ἄρχων. As above, the blank ending causes a vowel lengthening.

1.3 (Optional) After *ENTG* 12.3

1.3.1 The Neuter Singular Nominative Ending

The ending is almost always blank. There may or may not be change in vowel length.

πυρ- + – → πῦρ

SiReN applies:

αἵματ- + – → αἷμα
φωτ- + – → φῶς [A rare example of the ς ending.]

1.4 Embedding the Paradigms

Now apply the method we have used before.

> 1 Memorise the sequence of eight endings: [ς], α, ος, ι, ες, ας, ων, σι(ν). Don't stop when you get it right. Stop when you can no longer imagine getting it wrong.
> 2 Learn the rules in *ENTG* 12.2 and 12.3 for adding these to masc/fem and neut stems.
>   ◦ Optionally, learn the additional rules in 1.2.2 and 1.3.1.

---

[1] Apart from foreign names (Ἰωσήφ), the only two exceptions are ἐκ and οὐκ / οὐχ; however, ἐκ is really ἐξ (which does end with an s); οὐκ / οὐχ are variants of οὐ (Smyth 133a).

3   Check that you can write out the whole paradigm of: πνεῦμα, -ματος, τό; χάρις, -ιτος, ἡ and αἰών, -ῶνος, ὁ.
4   Check what you've written against the patterns in *ENTG* or the table in 'Nouns So Far' for Chapter 12, in the **Online Material**, and use that to reinforce the rules.
5   Keep doing that until you never get it wrong.

If you can do this, then the heavy lifting in Chapters 13 and 14 (as well as 12) is already behind you: well done!

1.5   After *ENTG* 12.4: How to Learn Adjectives

Adjectives need to be able to modify nouns of all three grammatical genders, which is why we learn the nominative singular ending they take in each of the masculine, feminine and neuter. With consonant declension adjectives, we also need to learn their stem, which means learning the genitive singular. Look at the table in *ENTG* 12.4, and check that you can decline these fully for all genders, cases and numbers by learning:

1   the masc/fem nom sing
2   the neut nom sing
3   the gen sing

πλείων, πλεῖον, πλείονος.

And watch out for slippery sigma in the dative plural – as above.

Likewise for the pronoun τις, just learn **τις** (m/f nom sing), **τι** (neut nom sing), **τιν-ος** (gen sing).

Check that you can reproduce the tables in *ENTG* 12.2–5 from these rules.

You needn't memorise the *slightly* irregular family nouns (*ENTG* 12.2.2) as long as you can parse them from their endings. Try writing them out as though they were regular and notice that the endings all work fine.

1.5.1   Agreement

Remember that agreement is always in *parsing*, not in appearance. A *consonant* declension stem adjective can qualify an *o* declension noun, and vice versa. The endings won't look alike, but the parsing will match: ἀδελφοῦ πλείονος 'a greater brother [genitive]'; ἀγαθὸν πνεῦμα 'a good spirit [accusative]'.

That really is it: commit [ς], α, ος, ι, ες, ας, ων, σι(ν) to memory as though it were your phone number and practise using it soon in the **Greek Reading** below.

1.6 After *ENTG* 12: Little Notes on Vocab

1.6.1 ὅστις

ὅστις combines the relative pronoun ὅς and the indefinite pronoun τις, and *both* inflect. The neuter singular is normally printed as two separate words. See Table 12.1.

Table 12.1 ὅστις

	Masc	Fem	Neut
Sing	ὅστις	ἥτις	ὅ τι
Pl	οἵτινες	αἵτινες	ἅτινα

Can you use the rules above to decline ὅστις in full?

1.6.2 τί

τί is often short for διὰ τί: because of what? Or simply '**why?**' (Cf. note in *ENTG* 12.5.)

1.6.3 τίς vs τις

You really need to know some wider rules of accents to tell the difference between the interrogative (τίς τί) and indefinite (τις τι), because words will give their accents to nearby words (explained in **EM 12** 3).

Without those rules, you can say for certain that **if** it has two syllables, **and if** the accent is on the first, it is interrogative, **but if** on the second *only*, then indefinite (see the table in the **Online Material**). If it has one syllable and no accent, it is indefinite. If it has the accent, you can't tell.

2 THE GREEK READING

The story so far ...

Aseneth has been introduced to Joseph. He is cordial enough to her as a sister, but will not even give her the customary kiss of greeting, citing his devotion to the living God and her idolatry. He prays for her to turn from her idols and be renewed inwardly. Finally, he leaves the house, promising to return after seven days.

From now on, the 'verse' numbers match the original text, which means that some will be quite short and others missing altogether.

10:1 τότε ὁ πατὴρ καὶ ἡ μήτηρ ἀπῆλθον, ² ἀλλὰ ἡ θυγάτηρ ἦν μόνη καὶ ἔκλαιεν ἕως νυκτός· καὶ ἄρτον οὐκ ἔφαγεν καὶ ὕδωρ οὐκ ἔπιεν. ⁵ ἔκλεισε γὰρ τὴν θύραν καὶ ἔκραξε τῷ στόματι καὶ φωνῇ μεγάλῃ. ⁶ καὶ ἤκουσέ τις τῶν γυναικῶν τὴν φωνὴν τῆς κυρίας αὐτῆς καὶ ἤγειρε τὰς δούλας καὶ ἦλθον, ἀλλὰ εὗρον ὅτι ἔκλεισεν Ἀσενὲθ τὴν θύραν. ⁷ καὶ ἠκροάσαντο τῆς φωνῆς τῆς Ἀσενέθ, εἶπον οὖν· Διὰ τί σὺ πάσχεις, κυρία μου; καὶ τίνες εἰσίν αἱ σπιλάδες; ἄνοιξον ἡμῖν καὶ βλέψομέν σε. ⁸ ἤκουσεν δὲ Ἀσενὲθ τὰ ῥήματα καὶ εἶπεν αὐταῖς· Ἐστι πῦρ πολὺ ἐν τῷ σώματί μου. διὸ οὐ θέλω ἀνοῖξαι νῦν ὑμῖν, διότι οὐκ ἔχουσι θέλημα αἱ χεῖρες, οὔτε ἐν σαρκὶ οὔτε ἀπὸ τοῦ πνεύματος. ἀλλὰ ἀπέλθατε ἑκάστη ὑμῶν εἰς τὸν κοιτῶνα αὐτῆς. ⁹ ἤνοιξεν δὲ Ἀσενὲθ τὴν θύραν καὶ ἀπῆλθεν εἰς ἄλλον τῶν κοιτώνων αὐτῆς, ὅπου ἦσαν τοὺς κόσμους αὐτῆς, καὶ ἐξήνεγκε χιτῶνα μείζονα. ¹⁰ οὗτος γὰρ ἦν ὁ χιτὼν ὃν ἐνεδύσατο ὅτε ἀπέθανεν ὁ ἀδελφὸς αὐτῆς. ¹¹ καὶ ἐξεδύσατο Ἀσενὲθ τὰ ἐνδύματα αὐτῆς καὶ ἐνεδύσατο τὸν χιτῶνα καὶ ἔλυσε τὰ ψέλια ἐκ τῶν χειρῶν αὐτῆς. ¹² καὶ ἔλαβε τοὺς χιτῶνας αὐτῆς καὶ ἔβαλεν αὐτοὺς ἐν ταῖς χερσίν διὰ τῆς θυρίδος τοῖς πένησι. ¹⁵ καὶ ἔλυσε[2] τοὺς θεοὺς αὐτῆς ὑπὸ τοὺς πόδας, ¹⁶ μετὰ δὲ ταῦτα ἔλαβε σάκκον καὶ ἐνεδύσατο καὶ ἔπεσεν ἐπὶ τὴν γῆν. ¹⁷ καὶ ἔκλαιε τὴν νύκτα, καὶ νὺξ ἐγένετο ἡμέρα. ¹⁸ ὅτε ἐγένετο φῶς εἶδεν Ἀσενὲθ καὶ ἰδοὺ· ἦν ἡ γῆ ὑπὸ αὐτὴν ὡς πηλὸς διὰ τὰ δακρύα καὶ τὸν ἱδρῶτα αὐτῆς. ¹⁹ διὸ ἔπεσε πάλιν Ἀσενὲθ ἐπὶ τὴν γῆν ἕως νυκτός. ²⁰ καὶ οὕτως ἐποίησεν Ἀσενὲθ ἑπτὰ ἡμέρας καὶ οὐκ ἔφαγεν.

---

[2] λύω here in the sense of 'tear apart'.

2.1 Vocabulary

ἀκροά-ομαι – I listen to (+ gen of what I listen to)
δάκρυον, ου, τό – tear
δούλη, ης, ἡ = female δοῦλος
ἐκφέρω – I bring out
ἐκδύω – I take clothes off someone [mid: I take clothes off myself; I undress]
ἔνδυμα, τος, τό – clothing
ἐνδύω – I put clothes on someone [mid: I put clothes on myself; I dress]
ἑπτά – (indeclinable) seven
θύρα, ας, ἡ – door
θυρίς, ίδος, ἡ – window
ἱδρώς, ῶτος, ὁ – sweat

κλαίω – I weep
κλείω – I close
κοιτών, ῶνος, ὁ – bedroom
κοσμος, ου, ὁ – adornments, cosmetics
 [NB: from which also 'order' and from that '[the well-ordered] universe']
κυρία, ας, ἡ = female κύριος
πηλός, οῦ, ὁ – mud
πένης, ητος, ὁ – a poor person (cf. *pen*ury).
σάκκος, ου, ὁ – sackcloth
σπιλάς, άδος, ἡ – peril
χιτών, ῶνος, ὁ – tunic
ψέλιον -ου, τό – bracelet

3 ACCENTS

3.1 Question Words

FURTHER READING: PROBERT 76

ENTG introduces τίς as a question and τις (enclitic) as an indefinite pronoun (**EH 12** 1.6.3).

This is one example of a set of word groups where the enclitic is indefinite, but the accented form is a question: see these in the context of their word groups in **EM 10** 7.

On the rules governing enclitics and proclitics, which you need if you want to be sure whether you're dealing with a question or not *in context*, see **EM 1** 3; **EM 2** 3.2; **EM 5** 3.

Note also that τί and τίς *never* change their acute to a grave.

CHAPTER 13

The Third Declension, Part 2
Nominative Case

> **How to Use This Chapter**
>
> This is the second of three chapters on the third declension noun endings. One sequence of eight sounds is all you really need: and you learnt those in the last chapter!
>
> Work through this chapter of *ENTG*, section by section, completing exercises as you go. As you complete each section, read **Extra Help** below for that section.
>
> In **Extra Help** we will see how nouns and adjectives are formed when their *consonant* stems end in a contract vowel.
>
> In the **Extra Material** you will meet the very few contexts for the nominative, and use them to think about when sense overrules strict grammar. There is also a short note on accents.

1 *ENTG* 13

1.1 The Good News: Same Endings as Last Chapter

In Chapter 12 we learnt one simple set of endings:

[ς], α, ος, ι, ες, ας, ων, σι(ν)

In this chapter we discover that some nouns add a contract vowel to their stems. Remember that φιλ-έ-ω takes the same endings as λύ-ω, once you know how to handle contract vowels. Similarly, these nouns take the same endings, once we account for contract vowels.[1]

The only different ending is that the accusative singular is sometimes ν (like α- and ο- declension nouns).

With that one difference in place, all that we are going to see in Chapter 13 are the same endings. It may seem as though there are several different families with different endings, but really it is just the one set: [ς], α, ος, ι, ες, ας, ων, σι(ν).

---

[1] These aren't really contract vowels, but involve a set of complicated changes that we needn't know about (as *ENTG* points out). The result is easiest to explain as though they were contract vowels. For details, see vS 40–1.

1.2 Nouns with Contract Stems

The main thing is to be familiar enough to **recognise them**.

You may find it easiest to try to learn them thoroughly, or you may prefer to be ready to recognise endings with some flexibility. Your choice. If you try to learn them, the method we have used throughout for related endings will serve you well here: apply the eight endings we have learnt, plus the rules below, and keep doing that until you never get the paradigms wrong.

Whichever approach you choose, in the sections below, I will describe the peculiarities of each ending and show you how they really are just the same eight endings every time. Even when you meet highly irregular 3rd declension nouns, or authors who break the rules, you will still be able to parse them accurately.

Whereas in Chapter 12, we saw that you can't predict the nominative singular, the nouns in this chapter fall into a couple of families, and each family always has exactly the same nominative singular ending.

1.2.1 -ος, ους, τό

These end the stem in ε. That ε contracts predictably with the usual endings. We follow the universal rules of the neuter:

1 nom = acc
2 the nom pl is α.

See the table of ἔθνος, ους, τό in *ENTG* 13.2.1. Notice the new rule of contraction: ε + α → η.

1.2.2 -εύς, -έως, ὁ (*ENTG* 13.1)

Its stem ends in ε, like the neuter, but its contraction is less regular, and an υ appears at the start and end of the paradigm.

The ε is *always* visible. Sometimes it contracts, sometimes it doesn't, but an ε will remain (underlined below). Let's see how the familiar endings behave here:

βασιλεύς	–
βασιλεῦ	
βασιλέα	α added to stem
βασιλέως	ος added to ε; instead of contracting, ο lengthens (and ε remains)
βασιλεῖ	ι as expected
βασιλεῖς	ε + ες → εις as expected
βασιλεῖς	ε + ας → εις, rather than the expected ης (this preserves the ε)
βασιλέων	ων as expected, but without contraction (this preserves the ε)
βασιλεῦσι(ν)	σι(ν) as expected, but υ reappears

1.2.3 -ις, -εως, ἡ / ὁ (Almost All ἡ) (*ENTG* 13.1)

Nearly identical to -εύς, -έως, ὁ, with two differences:

1 There is no υ anywhere.
2 In the sing nom and acc, ε becomes ι.

πόλις	–
πόλι**ν**	**ν** after a vowel
πόλε**ως**	same as βασιλεύς
πόλε**ι**	"
πόλ**εις**	"
πόλ**εις**	"
πόλε**ων**	"
πόλε**σι(ν)**	" (without the υ)

As long as you can recognise that εως is a strange version of ε+ος, and εις a strange contraction of ε+ας, you can parse all of this just fine.

1.2.4 Easier Than Chapter 12

In Chapter 12 we met 3rd declension nouns where the nominative singular could be *anything*. These contract ones are totally predictable, even in their nominative singular:

> -ος, -ους, τό goes exactly like ἔθνος
> -εύς, -έως, ὁ goes exactly like βασιλεύς
> -ις, -εως, ἡ/ὁ goes exactly like πόλις

That's it!

Put another way, to decline a third declension noun fully, you just need to know the nominative, and whether it behaves like ἀστήρ, ἔθνος, πόλις or βασιλεύς. For that, you need the genitive, which will give you the stem, from which you construct all other forms.

> ἀστέρ**ος** → ἀστέρ-
> ἔθν**ους** → ἔθνε-
> πόλε**ως** → πόλε-
> βασιλέ**ως** → βασιλέ**υ**

1.2.5 Others Are Easy to Spot

There are, inevitably, irregular nouns. However, all of them follow the basic pattern of endings [ς], α, ος, ι, ες, ας, ων, σι(ν) plus some contractions or changes to the stem. For example:

- See the completely regular endings on ἰχθύς in Table 13.1 (also found in *ENTG* 13.1).

- See νοῦς in Table 13.1 (also found in *ENTG* vocab) and check that its endings are recognisable.
- Look back at the 1st and 2nd pl pronouns in *ENTG* 9.3.1.

You will be able to recognise and parse all irregular 3rd declension nouns without any difficulty.

1.2.6 Summary

Check that you can see how [ς], α / ν, ος, ι, ες, ας, ων, σι(ν) is here in every column, except where the neuter plural nom/acc is α in σῶμα and ἔθνος.

Table 13.1 Consonant Declension Nouns

–	ἀστήρ	σῶμα	ἰχθύς	ἔθνος	πόλις	βασιλεύς	νοῦς	Μωϋσῆς
						βασιλεῦ		Μωϋσῆ
α/ν	ἀστέρα	σῶμα (1)	ἰχθύν	ἔθνος (1)	πόλιν	βασιλέα	νοῦν	Μωϋσῆν
ος	ἀστέρος	σώματος	ἰχθύος	ἔθνους	πόλεως	βασιλέως	νοός	Μωϋσέως
ι	ἀστέρι	σώματι	ἰχθύϊ	ἔθνει	πόλει	βασιλεῖ	νοΐ	Μωϋσῇ / Μωϋσεῖ
ες	ἀστέρες	σώματα (2)	ἰχθύες	ἔθνη (2)	πόλεις	βασιλεῖς		
ας	ἀστέρας	σώματα (1)	ἰχθύας	ἔθνη (1)	πόλεις	βασιλεῖς		
ων	ἀστέρων	σωμάτων	ἰχθύων	ἐθνῶν	πόλεων	βασιλέων		
σιν	ἀστέρσιν	σώμασιν	ἰχθύσιν	ἔθνεσιν	πόλεσιν	βασιλεῦσιν		

(1) acc = nom for all neut nouns
(2) nom pl = α for all neut nouns

1.3 Adjectives

Adjectives with contract vowels are even easier (more regular) than nouns. See the table in *ENTG* 13.2.2. As *ENTG* 13.3 explains, we now meet adjectives called **3-1-3**.

> So you just need to know:
>
> 1 the stem is παν-
> 2 the masc nom sing is πᾶς
> 3 the neut nom sing is πᾶν
> 4 one more thing: the fem nom sing is πᾶσα
> 5 from there, it's the same rules as usual. The fem stem doesn't end in ι-ρ-ε so it goes like δόξα. The masc/neut just follow the 3rd declension.
>
> With that in mind, can you practise writing out πᾶς?
> Then do the same for the adjectives in *ENTG* 13.4.

1.4 The 3rd Declension Is EASY

Please don't be discouraged: if you're thinking that there are too many endings, they really are just slight variations on [ς], α, ος, ι, ες, ας, ων, σι(ν). That's all there is to learn.

1.5 That's It for Nouns!

There are no more noun endings: congratulations! Pick up any page of the GNT and you will be able to recognise every ending on every noun, adjective and anything else that declines for gender, case and number.

2 THE GREEK READING

The story so far ...

Joseph has left the house and promised to return after seven days. For seven days and nights, Aseneth has kept herself in seclusion, fasting and attired for repentance, and has wept to the point of turning the ground under her into mud.

11:1–12:1 Ἐγένετο δὲ τῇ ὀγδόῃ ἡμέρᾳ καὶ Ἀσενὲθ ἦρε μίαν τῶν χειρῶν αὐτῆς πρὸς τὰ ὄρη καὶ εἶπε· ² Κύριε ὁ θεὸς τῶν αἰώνων, ὁ ποιήσας πάντα· σύ ἐγερεῖς πάντας ἐν τῇ ἀναστάσει. ⁴ κύριε, ὁ θεός μου, πρὸς σὲ κράζω, ἄρα πρόσεχε τῇ δεήσει μου, σοὶ γὰρ ἀποκαλύψω πάσας τὰς ἁμαρτίας μου.

⁷ᵃ Ἥμαρτον, βασιλεῦ μού, ἐνώπιόν σου, ἐγώ, ἡ θυγάτηρ ἱερέως, σοὶ προσφέρω τὴν δέησίν μου. ⁷ᵇ ῥῦσαί τὸ σκεῦος σου ἀπὸ τῆς ἐκδικήσεώς σου, διότι ἐγὼ πρὸς σὲ ἔφυγον ὡς τέκνον ἐπὶ τὸν πατέρα αὐτοῦ καὶ τὴν μητέρα. ⁷ᶜ ἰδού· πάντα τὰ μέλη μου ἀσθενά. καὶ οἱ ὀφθαλμοί μου οὐ βλέπουσιν οὐδὲν εἰ μὴ τὸ σκότος.

¹⁰ᵃ Ἀλλὰ σύ, κύριε, ῥῦσαί με τῇ χάριτι κατὰ τὸ μέγα ἔλεός σου καὶ κατὰ τὸ πλῆθος τῶν οἰκτιρμῶν σου. ¹⁰ᵇ ἰδὲ τὴν θλῖψιν ἐν τῇ ἐμῇ συνειδήσει καὶ μὴ εἰσέρχου εἰς κρίσιν μετὰ τοῦ δούλου σου. ¹¹ οὐ γὰρ ἔστι μοι ἄλλη ἐλπὶς εἰ μὴ ἐπὶ σοί.

¹³:⁸ Καὶ ἰδοὺ ἐγὼ ἑπτὰ ἡμέρας οὐδὲν οὐκ ἔφαγον. ⁹ ἀλλά, κύριε, σύγγνωθί μοι, ὅτι οὐκ εἶχον γνῶσιν ἐν τῷ νοΐ ὅτε ἥμαρτόν, καὶ ἐλάλησα τὰ κακὰ κατὰ τοῦ βασιλέως μου Ἰωσήφ. ¹⁰ᵃ οὐ γὰρ ἔγνων ἐγὼ ὅτι υἱός σοῦ ἐστι, κύριε, διότι εἶπόν μοι οἱ ἄνθρωποι ὅτι Ἰωσὴφ ποιμένος ὁ υἱός ἐστιν ἐκ τοῦ ἔθνους Μωϋσέως, ¹⁰ᵇ καὶ ἐπίστευσα αὐτοῖς καὶ διὰ τοῦτο ἐλάλησα ἐν τῷ στόματί μου περὶ αὐτοῦ πονηρά, διότι οὐκ ἔγνων ὅτι υἱός σοῦ ἐστιν. ¹¹ τίς γὰρ τῶν ἀνθρώπων ἐστὶ τοιοῦτος δίκαιος καὶ τίς ἄλλος ὑπάρχει ἅγιος ὡς Ἰωσήφ; ἀλλὰ ἐγὼ φιλῶ αὐτὸν ὑπὲρ τὴν ψυχήν μου. ¹² καὶ νῦν θέλω εἶναι δούλη αὐτῷ τὰ ἔτη ἅπαντα τῆς ζωῆς μου.

2.1 Vocabulary

δέησις, εως, ἡ – urgent prayer to God
δούλη, ης, ἡ = female **δοῦλος**
ἐκδίκησις, εως, ἡ – punishment
ὄγδοος, η, ον – eighth

οἰκτιρμός, οῦ, ὁ – compassion, mercy
ποιμήν, ένος, ὁ – shepherd
συγγινώσκω – I agree with (+ dat)

3 ACCENTS

3.1 -εως

FURTHER READING: PROBERT 123

Unlike verbs, I don't recommend trying to learn the rules for accents on nouns. You already know the rules telling us where an accent *can* go on a noun; the rules of where they *do* go vary declension by declension, and are even more variable within 3rd declension nouns, which come in different accent families.

What you do need to notice is that the nouns in -ις -εως break the rule of limitation (**EM 1** 3.4) in their genitive singular and genitive plural:[2]

πόλεως   rule of limitation would expect πολέως
πόλεων   rule of limitation would expect πολέων

---

[2] See vS 40 for the explanation.

4 NOMINATIVE

There is hardly any news when it comes to the nominative. When you read Greek, you will almost certainly never be left wondering what the author meant (unlike, say, with the genitive). It is simply worth pointing out some uses where the nominative isn't the subject or complement, so that you're not surprised when you encounter them.

We'll take the opportunity to think about how languages use the 'wrong' grammar where it helps understanding.

4.1 Contexts for the Nominative

FURTHER READING: vS 147; WALLACE 36–64

4.1.1 Pendent (a.k.a. 'Nominative Absolute')

Imagine saying: 'I saw the teacher this morning.' The direct object of the sentence is 'the teacher'. In Greek, it would be accusative: τὸν διδάσκαλον.

For clear communication, we sometimes want to make sure that our hearer remembers this teacher whom we're talking about, before we go on to say 'I saw him'. 'Do you remember the chap we met on the bus yesterday? Remember that he was a physics teacher, because he found Greek too hard? Well, I saw him this morning.' ('Him' is still the direct object, and accusative in Greek: αὐτόν.)

Sometimes, we do the same thing by bringing 'teacher' to the front of the sentence, before then putting 'him' where it belongs: 'The teacher we met yesterday, who teaches physics: I saw him this morning.' This time, 'him' is the direct object (αὐτόν). 'The teacher', though, is hanging loose at the front of the sentence. It isn't the subject (that's *I* saw). It's there to make sure that you call to mind who the 'him' is, who is coming later in the sentence.

> ὁ γὰρ Μωσῆς[3] οὗτος, ὃς ἐξήγαγεν ἡμᾶς ἐκ γῆς Αἰγύπτου, οὐκ οἴδαμεν τί γέγονεν **αὐτῷ**. Acts 7:40
> For, this Moses, who led us out of Egypt – we don't know what has happened **to him**.

As opposed to: 'We don't know what has happened **to this Moses** [**τῷ Μωσῇ τούτῳ** dat], who led us out of Egypt.' The reason for bringing Moses to the front, as a 'pendent nominative', is rhetorical: whether for clarity or (in this case) to show contempt, or to downplay his significance.

Greek word order is often described as 'for emphasis', without much explanation. As you can see here, words are often put in an order that helps you follow

---

[3] Variant spelling of Μωϋσῆς.

along with what is being said: 'Remember Moses – that's who I'm about to talk about.'

Another way to put this is that the topic you're speaking about isn't the same as the grammatical subject of the sentence. Your topic is Moses, but he's grammatically the indirect object, not the subject; a pendent nominative helps to clarify that 'I want you to think about Moses now.'

4.1.2 Address (Replacing Vocative)

You already know that many classes of nouns have a vocative which looks the same as the nominative. Here, we're thinking about something slightly different: where you might expect a vocative, but the nominative is used instead. This often happens when the name is qualified in some way, which makes the vocative impossible (e.g. with the article).

> Οὐά, ὁ καταλύων τὸν ναόν, καὶ ἐν τρισὶν ἡμέραις οἰκοδομῶν, σῶσον σεαυτόν Mark 15:29–30
> Ha! [You] destroyer of the sanctuary, and [you who] were going to rebuild it in three days: save yourself!

4.1.3 Appellation (Naming Someone)

When you're giving someone their name, or telling someone else what their name is, the name might be the direct object of the sentence. However, it's a little ridiculous to use anything other than the nominative, when you're trying to communicate what their name is. This applies to lists of names or titles as well.

> καὶ **ἐκάλουν** αὐτὸ ἐπὶ τῷ ὀνόματι τοῦ πατρὸς αὐτοῦ **Ζαχαρίαν** [acc].
> καὶ ἀποκριθεῖσα ἡ μήτηρ αὐτοῦ εἶπεν, Οὐχί, ἀλλὰ **κληθήσεται** Ἰωάννης [nom]. Luke 1:59–60
> They were about to name him Zechariah [accusative as expected], after his father's name. But his mother replied: 'No. Rather, he will be called John [nominative, stating what his name will actually be].'

4.2 Agreeing with the Sense, Not the Parsing

FURTHER READING: VS 265; 289E; 289F

As with the 'nominative of appellation', authors don't always stick to strict rules of grammar, but will make sense instead. 'I saw a flock of birds, and they were circling.' What I saw was a single flock, so surely the verb should be singular: 'it [the flock] was circling'. No, the point is that 'the birds were circling', and this overrules the pedantic expectation. The verb *agrees* with the *sense* of what you're talking about (birds, plural), rather than with the strict parsing of the words (one flock, singular).

You will see this most often where relative pronouns don't behave: the relative will keep the case of the 'antecedent' rather than the case it should have in its own clause, or else the 'antecedent' itself will look ahead and take the case that the relative pronoun has, rather than the case the noun should have in its own clause. Don't force what the 'grammar' should be into changing a meaning that is clear enough.

The principle here is that *authors want to help you understand them* more than they want to be pedantic.

CHAPTER 14

Participles
—
Participles

> **How to Use This Chapter**
>
> This chapter goes further with participles and is the final of three chapters using the third declension noun endings. One sequence of eight sounds is all you really need – and you learnt those in Chapter 12!
>
> In **Extra Help** you will see that there is little new to learn, and that you can reap the benefits of previous chapters by combining your understanding of participles (Chapter 7) with your grasp of how all adjectives decline (including Chapters 12 and 13). You can now parse and understand all present and aorist participles, without putting more effort in than reviewing what you have already learnt.
>
> Begin with the '**Before You Start**' section below, which will take the fear out of participles and then guide you through Chapter 14 of *ENTG*.
>
> In the **Extra Material** you'll think further about what Greek authors communicate when they choose to use a participle.

1 BEFORE YOU START: REVIEW

1.1 Parsing Participles

There is virtually nothing new in this chapter. If you understood participles in Chapter 7, and if you have been keeping up with 1st, 2nd and 3rd declension nouns, you already know almost everything in this chapter of *ENTG*. Only half a page remains, and it is an easy half a page.

I've stressed before that learning paradigms will make future material much easier. Nowhere is this more true than with participles. Glance at the whole page of endings in *ENTG* 14.2 (make sure you're sitting down first). There is *not a single new* ending here: participles simply recycle adjective paradigms. You need to be completely happy with 2-1-2, 3-1-3 and 3-3 adjectives. These are utterly trivial, provided you're completely happy with 1st, 2nd and 3rd declension nouns. If you're behind on Chapters 12–13, or the noun endings in *ENTG* 3.3.4, stop and nail those *now*.

Please check that you can turn the following vocab entries into full paradigms:

δίκαιος, αία, ον
πᾶς, πᾶσα, πᾶν, παντός

If you can't, review *ENTG* chapters 5, 12 and 13, and **EH 12** 1.1.1, **EH 12** 1.5 and **EH 13** 1.3.

Now try writing out these new adjectives, which you haven't met yet:

ῥυόμενος, η, ον
ῥυσάμενος, η, ον
λύων, λύουσα, λῦον, λύοντος
λύσας, λύσασα, λῦσαν, λύσαντος

If you did that correctly, you have written out the endings on *ENTG* 14.2; that's all there is to the endings of participles! Relax and enjoy.

1.2 Participles as Adjectives

You can now decline and parse a participle; but why are there so many of them?

The participle is an adjective and therefore has to agree with nouns in any gender, case and number.

The meaning of the participle is that of a verb, but verbs always have two surnames: system and voice. The verb can be present or aorist, active or middle. That gives us four combinations of verbal meanings: four adjectives.

The good news is that you parse each feature independently. The stem of the verb tells you whether you have an aorist or present participle really easily. Even easier, whether you have -μεν- in the middle ('middle men') tells you the voice.

After that, you just parse like any other adjective.

1.3 The Meaning of Participles

As discussed in **EH 7** 2, participles are simply adjectives and can do whatever an adjective can do. However, back then, all the participles were nominative. In this chapter, we see participles in the other cases too.

Once again, if you understand adjectives, and you understand what we have already covered about participles, there is very little new in this chapter.

By way of review, then:

1.3.1 Attributive

ἡ ἐρχομένη βασιλεία – the coming kingdom
ὁ προφήτης ὁ ἐρχόμενος – the coming prophet

1.3.2 Nominal

ὁ ζητῶν εὑρίσκει – the one who seeks finds

1.3.3 Predicative

ἐγώ εἰμι ὁ ἀναγαγὼν ὑμᾶς – I am <u>the one who brought</u> you <u>up</u>

1.3.4 Adverbial (Qualifying the Action)

περιπατῶν Ἰησοῦς εἶδεν δύο ἀδελφούς – Jesus, while walking, saw two brothers

> Remember that the participle can turn an entire sentence into an adjective by bringing its object, indirect object and any modifiers with it. It can graft an entire 'tree' as a 'branch' of another tree.

Now proceed through *ENTG* chapter 14, referring to the sections below.

2 PARTICIPLES

2.1 After *ENTG* 14.4.2: Adverbial Uses

You are already used to handling these implied connections in English, though it is becoming less common. Pick a random page in *Lord of the Rings* and you'll find a participle with an implied causal, concessive, instrumental, or other meaning. Browse through the 1662 Book of Common Prayer and you'll see that you are naturally expected to understand the connection between 'we worthily *lamenting* our sins' and 'may obtain forgiveness' or between 'we *being defended*' and 'pass our time in rest and quietness'.

Pretty much any use of the participle in Greek is intelligible from a wooden English translation; if you want to become familiar with the full menu of options (which isn't long), see **EM 14** 4.2.2.

2.2 After *ENTG* 14.4: Parsing

You might like to try the **Parsing Puzzle (Vocab Is Part of Parsing)** in the **Online Material** for this chapter.

3 THE GREEK READING

The story so far …

Aseneth has pleaded with God that her insulting words towards Joseph were spoken in ignorance, not knowing that Joseph was upright, divine and her king. She acknowledges her guilt and begs for forgiveness. She wants to be taken on as a slave in Joseph's house and spend the rest of her life there.

14 ⁴ καὶ προσερχομένος πρὸς αὐτὴν πρεσβύτερος ἐκ τοῦ οὐρανοῦ ἐφώνησεν

αὐτήν· Ἀσενέθ. ⁵ ἡ δὲ εἶπεν· Τίς ὁ φωνήσας με; ⁷ ὁ δὲ εἶπεν· Ἐγώ εἰμι ὁ ἄρχων

πάσης τῆς στρατιᾶς τοῦ κυρίου· ἔγειρε ἐπὶ τοὺς πόδας σου καὶ προφητεύσω σοι.

The heavenly elder reassures Aseneth and replaces her apparel of penitence with glorious garments.

15 ¹ ἡ δὲ ἦλθε πρὸς τὸν πρεσβύτερον. καὶ ἰδὼν αὐτὴν ὁ πρεσβύτερος

λέγει αὐτῇ· ² Θάρσει, Ἀσενέθ, ἤκουσε γὰρ κύριος τὰ μετανοοῦντα ῥήματά

σου. ⁴ ἀπὸ οὖν τῆς σήμερον ἔσῃ ἡ ἐσθίουσα ἄρτον ζωῆς. ⁵ καὶ λαβών σε

ὁ Ἰωσὴφ εἰς γυναῖκα αὐτὸς ἔσται σου ἀνήρ. ⁶ καὶ ἐν σοὶ φεύξονται ἔθνη

πολλὰ μετανοήσαντα τῷ θεῷ. ⁷ διότι ἡ μετάνοιά ἐστι παιδίον τοῦ θεοῦ

καὶ αὕτη παρακαλεῖ τὸν θεὸν ὑπὲρ σοῦ πᾶσαν ὥραν καὶ ὑπὲρ πάντων

τῶν μετανοούντων, καὶ αὕτη φυλάξει τοὺς φιλοῦντας αὐτὴν εἰς

τὸν αἰῶνα.

¹² Καὶ ἀκούσασα ἡ Ἀσενέθ τοῦ πρεσβυτέρου ἐχάρη. καὶ ἔπεσεν εἰς τοὺς πόδας

αὐτοῦ λέγουσα αὐτῷ· ¹³ Εὐλογητὸς κύριος ὁ θεός, ὁ ἀποστείλας σε καὶ ὁ

ῥυσάμενός με ἐκ τοῦ σκότους. ¹⁴ λαλήσω, κύριε, εἰ εὗρον χάριν ἐνώπιόν σου.

Aseneth invites the heavenly elder to sit and speak with her over some food. He provides food miraculously, including honeycomb. A swarm of bees surround Aseneth and weave a festal robe around her, leaving her looking resplendent.

17 ⁴ᵃ Καὶ εἶπε τῷ πρεσβυτέρῳ Ἀσενέθ· Εἰσί, κύριε, σὺν ἐμοὶ ἑπτὰ παρθένοι

διακονοῦσαι μοι καὶ χαριζομέναι ταῖς χερσίν. ⁴ᵇ κἀγὼ φιλοῦσα αὐτάς, καλέσω

αὐτάς. ἀλλὰ εὐλογήσεις αὐτάς, κἀμὲ εὐλογήσας;

⁵ᵃ Ὁ δὲ εἶπεν· Κάλεσον. καὶ ἐκάλεσεν αὐτὰς Ἀσενέθ. τότε ἀκούσασαι ἤγγισαν.

καὶ εὐλόγησεν αὐτὰς ὁ πρεσβύτερος λέγων· ⁵ᵇ Εὐλογήσει ὑμᾶς εἰς τὸν αἰῶνα ὁ θεὸς ὁ ὑποτάξας τοῦτον τὸν παῖδα τὸν βλασφημήσαντα τοῦ ἀρχιερεώς.

⁵ᶜ ἀκούσασαι δὲ ταῖς ὠσὶν καὶ διαλογιζόμεναι ἐν ἑαυταῖς τὴν παράκλησιν τοῦ πρεσβυτέρου ἐμίσουν παντὰ τὰ ἁμαρτωλά. ⁶ ὁ δὲ ἀπῆλθεν ἐξ ὀφθαλμῶν αὐτῶν, αἱ δὲ εἶδον ἅρμα πυρὸς ἀναβαῖνον εἰς τὸν οὐρανόν.

3.1 Vocabulary

ἁμαρτωλός, όν – sinful (you have learnt this as a noun, which is simply a nominal use of the adjective: ὁ ἁμαρτωλός, the sinful person, i.e. the sinner)
ἅρμα, ατος, τό – chariot

ἑπτά – **seven (indeclinable)**
θαρσέω – I am of good courage
μετάνοια, ας, ἡ – repentance, penitence
παρθένος, ου, ἡ – virgin
στρατιά, ᾶς, ἡ – army

4 PARTICIPLES

4.1 Reminders

4.1.1 Participles Are Adjectives

Remember that participles are adjectives, with the meaning of a verb. They can therefore be used like all other adjectives: attributive (to modify a part of a sentence); nominal (with the implied noun 'person / woman / thing'); predicative (as the complement of a sentence). Review **EH 14** 1.3 and **EH 7** 2 on these points. Here are just some simple examples:

> αἰτείτω παρὰ τοῦ διδόντος Θεοῦ πᾶσιν ἁπλῶς Jas 1:5
> he should ask of the God who gives generously to all
>   Attributive.

> δεήσεις τε καὶ ἱκετηρίας πρὸς τὸν δυνάμενον σῴζειν αὐτὸν ἐκ θανάτου Heb 5:7
> prayers and entreaties to the one who was able to save him from death
>   Nominal.

Predicative participles without forms of εἰμί aren't in the GNT; those *with* εἰμί can, of course, be understood as periphrastic instead (**EH 20** 1.3).

> ἦν γὰρ ἡ καρδία αὐτῶν πεπωρωμένη Mark 6:52
> for their hearts had been hardened
>   Periphrastic pluperfect.

4.1.2 Indirect Discourse

We have met this in **EM 10** 6.3.4, but we see further **EM 14** 4.4.

4.1.3 Periphrastic

See **EH 20** 1.3.

That leaves adverbial participles, which we will spend most of this section considering.

4.2 Understanding Adverbial Participles

FURTHER READING: WALLACE 623-39; vS 231-2; B-D-R 417-25

We need to ask three sets of questions about each adverbial participle in a sentence:

1 Why has the author relegated these verbs to participles while keeping another one as the main verb?
2 What is the significance of the choice of aspect of each participle?
3 Is there an implied logical connection between each participle and the main verb?

4.2.1 Why an Author Uses Adverbial Participles

FURTHER READING: RUNGE, *DGGNT* CHAPTER 12; *CGCG* 60.32

In English, we're quite happy to use multiple verbs in the same mood in a row, within one sentence. For example:

'He <u>called</u> them, they <u>left</u> their father and <u>went off</u>.'

Greek avoids having multiple finite verbs in the same mood. Authors prefer to leave just one finite verb in a sentence and turn the rest into participles. This gives the Greek author the opportunity to gather together various actions and tell us which is the main event (the main verb), relegating the other verbs to a supporting role (adverbial participles).

> **ἐκάλεσεν** αὐτούς· καὶ <u>ἀφέντες</u> τὸν πατέρα αὐτῶν ... **ἀπῆλθον** ὀπίσω αὐτοῦ. Mark 1:20
> **he called** [aorist indicative] them, and <u>they left</u> [aorist participle] their father ... and **went off** [aorist indicative] after him.

Trying to capture this in English translations is very awkward stylistically, and also opens the door to all manner of unintended misunderstandings. It really pays to read the Greek, not to think in terms of translation. Consider the options available to Mark in the short passage above.

Mark could have had three main verbs, in separate sentences.

> ἐκάλεσεν [aorist indicative] αὐτούς. καὶ ἀφῆκαν [aorist indicative] τὸν πατέρα αὐτῶν. καὶ ἀπῆλθον [aorist indicative] ὀπίσω αὐτοῦ.
> **He called** them. **They left** their father. **They went off** after him.

He could have chosen just one of the three to be the main verb, and relegated the others to participles, in any of these ways:

> ἐκάλεσεν [aorist indicative] αὐτούς, ἀφέντες [participle] τὸν πατέρα αὐτῶν, ἀπελθόντες [participle] ὀπίσω αὐτοῦ.
> **He called** them, so that leaving their father they went off after him.

> καλέσας [participle] αὐτούς, ἀφέντες [participle] τὸν πατέρα αὐτῶν, **ἀπῆλθον** [aorist indicative] ὀπίσω αὐτοῦ.
> After he called them, leaving their father, **they went off** after him.

> καλέσας [participle] αὐτούς, **ἀφῆκαν** [aorist indicative] τὸν πατέρα αὐτῶν, ἀπελθόντες [participle] ὀπίσω αὐτοῦ.
> Having called them, **they left** their father, going off [participle] after him.

That would put the focus on the calling, the leaving or the following, as the main action. Notice how it's impossible to capture the focus on the one main verb in English, and you have to insert some logical connection ('so that ...' 'after ...') to make sense of it, but that introduces ideas which aren't in the Greek text.

However, Mark chose none of these, but gave us two main verbs and one participle:

> **ἐκάλεσεν** αὐτούς· καὶ ἀφέντες τὸν πατέρα αὐτῶν ... **ἀπῆλθον** ὀπίσω αὐτοῦ. Mark 1:20
> **he called** [aorist indicative] them, and they left [aorist participle] their father ... and **went off** [aorist indicative] after him.

Thus, there are two main actions: the call and the departure. Leaving their father is not the main result of the calling, but a further detail to the real response. 'He called and they went off after him (and left their father).' Various logical connections are possible, such as 'despite the fact that it meant leaving their father' or 'only after they left their father'. However, Mark didn't give us those connections explicitly; what he did give us was a clear indication of which are the main events and which are secondary.

We often go looking for the very thing the author left out: those logical connections. When we don't find one, we create categories like 'attendant circumstance'. We will return to this below, but the point is to notice what the Greek tells you, rather than focus on what it doesn't: the main verbs are the main point.

4.2.2 Various Intuitive Connections

FURTHER READING: B-D-R 425; vS 231c; WALLACE 622–40

There will often be some implied connection between the participle and the main verb. Sometimes the author intends you to understand that connection, sometimes not. This is purely a matter of interpretation, unless a connecting word makes the relationship explicit: καί, καίπερ, καίτοι, ἅμα, εὐθύς, ὡς.[1]

Generally, start with the assumption that the point is just 'time', and then ask yourself whether there is something more precise to be inferred (examples below) or even *less* than that to be inferred (the 'stylistic' use EM 14 4.2.4).

The general point in EH 14 2.1 stands: pretty much any use of the participle in Greek is intelligible from a wooden English translation.[2] For example, in these English translations, the underlined English participle corresponds to one in Greek. The common labels which we use when we infer a particular connection are given in brackets afterwards:

> <u>Having received</u> the bond from Jason and the others, they dismissed them. Acts 17:9
> **Once they** <u>had received</u> **(but not before!)** the bond … they dismissed them. **[temporal]**

> <u>wanting</u> to justify himself, he said to Jesus … Luke 10:29
> **because** <u>he wanted</u> to justify himself, he said to Jesus **[causal]**

> <u>testing</u> him he was saying this. John 6:6
> he was saying this, **in order to** <u>test</u> him **[purpose]**

> calling God his own Father <u>making</u> himself equal with God. John 5:18
> calling God his own Father **with the result that** <u>he was making</u> himself equal with God. **[result]**

> One thing I know, that <u>having been</u> blind, I see. John 9:25
> One thing I know, that **despite** the fact that <u>I was</u> blind, I see. **[concessive]**

> nothing <u>received</u> with thanksgiving is rejected. 1 Tim 4.4
> nothing is rejected, **on condition that** <u>it is received</u> with thanksgiving. **[conditional]**

---

[1] B-D-R 425.
[2] You can practise this by looking up some older English on the internet, which you'll find full of participles that you're expected to grasp intuitively. For example, the 1662 Book of Common Prayer, or the Westminster Shorter Catechism, or the 1901 American Standard Version, in such passages as Eph 1:3–14.

> So they went off rejoicing. Acts 5:41
> So they went off, and **the manner of their going was that** they were rejoicing as they went. [**manner**][3]

> and that believing you may have life in his name. John 20:31
> and that **by means of** believing you may have life in his name. [**means**][4]

> Notice a *very* common participle of **means** with the verb λέγω, which is the result of Hebrew influence. This is called '**redundant**' (or '**pleonastic**'), because a verb of speaking makes the participle superfluous; a colon and quotation marks will do fine in translation.

> οἱ δὲ **ἐπεφώνουν**, λέγοντες, Σταύρωσον, Luke 23:21
> but they **were shouting**: 'Crucify!'

As we have seen, adverbial participles have been chosen *not* to be the main verb. They aren't the main point, but they do serve the main point. Because of this connection, they will often answer questions that you might have about the main verb: 'What caused the action?' (**causal**); 'What makes the action unexpected?' (**concessive**); 'How was the action possible?' (**means**), etc.

As we have warned with tenses and cases, so with participles: Greek grammar doesn't tell you whether a participle is '**causal**' or '**concessive**', or any of these connections.[5] For example:

> Ἰωσὴφ δὲ ὁ ἀνὴρ αὐτῆς, δίκαιος ὤν, καὶ μὴ θέλων αὐτὴν παραδειγματίσαι, **ἐβουλήθη** λάθρᾳ ἀπολῦσαι αὐτήν. Matt 1:19
> Joseph, her husband, being a just man, and unwilling for her to be shamed, **sought** to divorce her secretly.
> Did he do this *despite* being a just man or *because* he was a just man? Matthew doesn't tell you. The story so far has three main verbs, supported by various participles: 'the birth happened as follows ... she was found ... Joseph sought ...'. The main point is his resolve to divorce Mary; cue the angel: the next main verb is 'he appeared' (supported by various participles).

I cannot stress this point enough:

> The circumstantial [adverbial] participle **expresses simply circumstance or manner in general**. It may imply various other relations, such as *time, manner, means, cause, purpose, concession, condition*, etc. But it is **often impossible to assign a participle exclusively to any one of**

---

[3] A participle of manner is another way of woodenly capturing a Hebrew idiom indicating emphasis, alongside the 'cognate' dative of manner. See the example of Matt 13:14 in **EM 4** 4.2.2.
[4] Also known as *instrumental* (*ENTG* 14.4.2).
[5] Runge, *DGGNT* 244 n6; Wallace 639–40; vS 231c.

4 Participles

these relations (which are purely logical), nor can all the delicate relations of the participle be set forth in systematic form.[6]

The force of these circumstantial [adverbial] participles **does not lie in the participle itself, but is derived from the context**. Unless attended by some modifying adverb, the context often does not decide whether the participle has a temporal, a causal, a conditional, a concessive force, etc.; and some participles may be referred to more than one of the above classes.[7]

The reason these connections are not front and centre is that the participles are not the main show: they support the main verb. It is the main verbs that lead you through the events in the narrative, or the stages in the argument.

4.2.3 Time

You would expect the same relationship which we have met before between the aspect of the participle and relative time (**EM 10** 6.2):

Present system: same time as the main verb.
Aorist system: time prior to the main verb.
Future system (**EM 21** 1.3): time subsequent to the main verb (which might be in the past now).
Perfect system (**EH 16** 1.1): a relevance that is ongoing at the time of the main verb.

These relationships in time are seen in Figure 14.1.

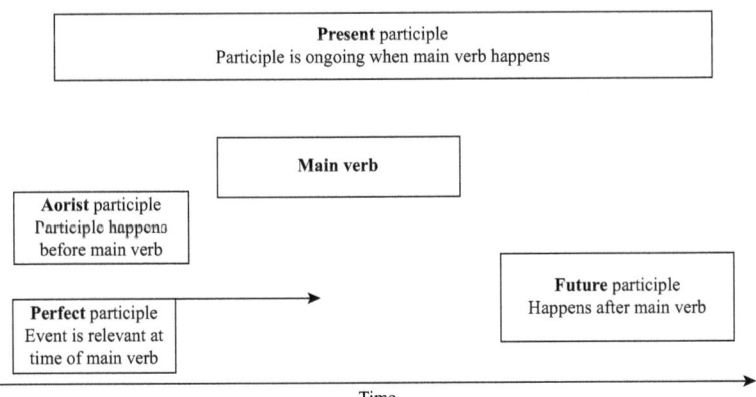

Figure 14.1 Participles and Time

---

[6] Herbert Weir Smyth, *A Greek Grammar for Colleges* (New York: American Book Company, 1920), §2060; italics original, bold added.
[7] Ibid., §2069; bold added.

Examples:

> ὃν οὐκ ἰδόντες **ἀγαπᾶτε** 1 Pet 1:8
> whom **you love** not <u>having seen [aorist]</u>

> εἰς Δαμασκὸν **ἐπορευόμην**, <u>ἄξων [future participle]</u> καὶ τοὺς ἐκεῖσε ὄντας ... ἵνα **τιμωρηθῶσιν [subjunctive]** Acts 22:5
> **I went** to Damascus <u>with the intention of taking</u> also those who were there ... with the intention that **they should be punished**.
> Notice how the <u>future participle</u> and the more familiar ἵνα + **subjunctive** do the same job.

> ἵνα **γένηται** ἡ προσφορὰ τῶν ἐθνῶν εὐπρόσδεκτος, <u>ἡγιασμένη [perfect]</u> ἐν Πνεύματι Ἁγίῳ Rom 15:16
> with the intention that the gentiles' offering **should become** pleasing, <u>having been sanctified</u> by the Holy Spirit
> The <u>perfect participle</u> expresses the **cause** of the main event, and it points out that the past act of sanctification has some ongoing relevance: in this case, because they remain sanctified.

Here are a couple of tweaks:

<u>Relationship of Relative Time to Adverbial Connection</u>

FURTHER READING: WALLACE 626

If the action of the participle happens as a **result** or intended result (**purpose**) of the main verb, then it follows it in time. The natural choice would be a future participle, but this is rare in Koine Greek, so we usually find present participles.

> οἱ Φαρισαῖοι καὶ Σαδδουκαῖοι <u>πειράζοντες [present participle]</u> **ἐπηρώτησαν** αὐτόν Matt 16:1
> The Pharisees and Sadducees, <u>with the intention of testing</u>, **asked** him
> The present participle indicates that the intention of testing was there while they were asking him.

In the opposite case, where the action of the participle precedes the main verb in time (**causal, conditional** and **concessive**), you will normally find an aorist or perfect participle:

> ἵνα ... **κερδηθήσωνται** <u>ἐποπτεύσαντες [aorist participle]</u> τὴν ἐν φόβῳ ἁγνὴν ἀναστροφὴν ὑμῶν. 1 Pet 3:1–2
> so that ... **they should be won over** <u>because they observe</u> your pure conduct in reverence.
> The idea is that they will be won over because they have first observed the conduct: the participle is the cause of the main event, and so prior to it in time.

ἐγὼ οὐδὲν ... <u>ποιήσας</u> ... **παρεδόθην** εἰς τὰς χεῖρας τῶν Ῥωμαίων Acts 28:17
Even though <u>I had done nothing</u> ... **I was handed over** into the hands of the Romans.

πῶς ἡμεῖς **ἐκφευξόμεθα** τηλικαύτης <u>ἀμελήσαντες</u> σωτηρίας; Heb 2:3
How can we **escape** [future indicative] if we <u>neglect</u> [aorist participle] such a salvation?

The sense being: 'If in the future we were to neglect such a salvation, then after that, how could we expect to get away with it?'

However, any of the adverbial connections can be simultaneous (rather than prior or subsequent), and therefore use a present participle:

<u>συλλέγοντες</u> τὰ ζιζάνια, **ἐκριζώσητε ἅμα** αὐτοῖς τὸν σῖτον Matt 13:29
<u>by gathering up</u> [present] the weeds, **you would uproot** the grain **at the same time** as them

The gathering of the weeds would be the **cause** of uprooting the grain, but they happen simultaneously, rather than one after the other.

<u>Perfects with Present Meaning</u>

When a verb in the perfect loses sight of the anterior event (such as οἶδα, ἕστηκα, EM 16 4.4.2), it functions like a present participle, focussed entirely on the *ongoing* effect.

ἡ δὲ γυνὴ φοβηθεῖσα καὶ τρέμουσα, <u>εἰδυῖα</u> [perfect participle οἶδα] ὃ γέγονεν ἐπ' αὐτῇ, **ἦλθε** Mark 5:33
the woman **came** frightened and trembling, <u>knowing</u> what had happened to her

<u>Coincident Participles</u>

FURTHER READING: *CGCG* 33.59–60; 52.5; RIJKSBARON 38

When it comes to participles of *means* or *manner*, the participle might be simultaneous or it might precede the main verb, depending on the details. However, sometimes you're really talking about a *single* event, rather than two related events. 'He taught him *by singing*' (**means**) is only a single event: the singing *was* the teaching. 'She went along *skipping*' (**manner**) is a single event: the skipping *was* the going. This means that if the main verb is aorist, the participle will be aorist too, not because it is prior to the main verb, but because it is the same event. See Figure 14.2.

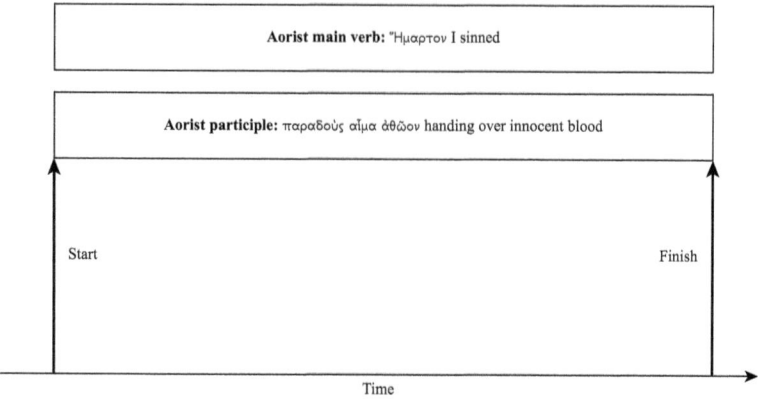

Figure 14.2 Coincident Participles

> **Ἥμαρτον** παραδοὺς αἷμα ἀθῷον Matt 27:4
> **I sinned** [by] handing over innocent blood.
>> It's one event, not two. The participle is the **means** by which the event happened. He didn't first hand over, and then sin afterwards.
>
> Βαρνάβας δὲ καὶ Σαῦλος **ὑπέστρεψαν** ἐξ Ἰερουσαλὴμ ... συμπαραλαβόντες καὶ Ἰωάννην. Acts 12:25
> Barnabas and Paul **returned** from Jerusalem ... bringing along John.
>> Bringing John isn't the means of their return but is a further description of how they did it. It's the **manner** of their return. Nonetheless, it's the same event, so both verb and participle are aorist.
>
> See also Acts 12:4; 15:8; Eph 1:13; 1 Tim 1:19.

4.2.4 Author's Choice of Verb(s) to Turn into Participles

FURTHER READING: RUNGE, *DGGNT* CHAPTER 12; *CGCG* 60.32

As we have seen (**EM 14** 4.2.1), adverbial participles serve a main verb. The author *chose* which of these verbs to keep as the main verb, and which to turn into a participle. This is probably significant.

One recent suggestion is that participles which come before the verb (i.e. to the left in the sentence) are relegated in importance. They give background to the action: what are the circumstances of the action (time, location, events leading up to it or concurrent with it)?[8] Turning these into participles puts the focus on

---

[8] Runge, *DGGNT* chapter 12. This is part of a wider pattern: not only adverbial participles (including genitive absolutes) but also temporal clauses and other modifiers ('branches')

the main verb. Participles that come later (i.e. to the right of the main verb in the sentence) are spelling the action out in more detail: what does doing the action look like or require or result in? Unlike participles put on the left, they are not less important, but they are less prominent.

The main verb is the main thing: the point of it all. If adverbial participles tend to answer questions about the circumstances of the main verb (*why? when? despite what? with what intention?*), that's because the main verb is the idea around which the participles orbit. 'Why did *the main verb* happen?' is what a causal participle tells you.

In the example of Mark 1:20 (**EM 14** 4.2.1), the point is that when Jesus summoned them, they answered. They didn't respond by leaving their father, but by following Jesus. What they walked away from is shocking (think of the Prodigal Son!), but Mark puts it in the background: it is what they did in order to follow Jesus. But they followed Jesus.

With imperatives, this is particularly helpful, since the main verb identifies the main objective, while the participles give commands related to that main objective. For example:

> **στῆτε [imperative, aorist active ἵστημι]** οὖν περιζωσάμενοι τὴν ὀσφὺν ὑμῶν ἐν ἀληθείᾳ, καὶ ἐνδυσάμενοι τὸν θώρακα τῆς δικαιοσύνης, καὶ ὑποδησάμενοι τοὺς πόδας ἐν ἑτοιμασίᾳ τοῦ εὐαγγελίου τῆς εἰρήνης Eph 6:14–15
> **Stand up**, therefore, <u>having fastened</u> your belt (which is truth), and <u>having got dressed with</u> the breastplate (which is righteousness), and <u>having shod</u> your feet with the preparedness which comes from the gospel of peace.

The aim is **to stand**. Notice that the aorist participles must precede *in time*, but they follow the verb *in the sentence*. Had they been written to the left, they would have been relegated to background: perhaps what was needed in order to stand up. Since they are to the right of the verb, they explain the main point further. They supply detail about how the action is to proceed. 'This is how I want you to stand up: I want you to be standing in your armour.'

In summary, see Table 14.1.

Table 14.1 Position of Participles

Participles to the **left** of the main verb: relegated, **background circumstances**.	**Main verb:** the **main** point.	Participles to the **right** of the verb: **expand** on the main point.

---

are put before the verb to set the scene: the time, place or circumstances for the main action (*CGCG* 60.32). For an older view to the contrary: Smyth 2147a.

Example:

> ὑμεῖς δέ, ἀγαπητοί, τῇ ἁγιωτάτῃ ὑμῶν πίστει <u>ἐποικοδομοῦντες</u> ἑαυτούς, ἐν Πνεύματι Ἁγίῳ <u>προσευχόμενοι</u>, ἑαυτοὺς ἐν ἀγάπῃ Θεοῦ **τηρήσατε**, <u>προσδεχόμενοι</u> τὸ ἔλεος τοῦ Κυρίου ἡμῶν Ἰησοῦ Χριστοῦ εἰς ζωὴν αἰώνιον. Jude 20–1
> As for you, beloved, <u>building yourselves up</u> by your most holy faith, <u>praying</u> by the Holy Spirit, **keep** yourselves in God's love, <u>looking forward</u> to the mercy of our Lord Jesus Christ for the sake of eternal life.

All of these are commands: you can't opt out of 'praying' or 'looking forward to'. But they are linked: the point of it all is the main verb **keep**. Even though all the participles are present, which means that they happen at the same time, some are before and some after the verb in the sentence. Those before provide background: you must carry on building yourselves up and praying, but why? To keep yourselves in God's love. What will keeping yourselves in God's love look like? It is something you do while looking forward to mercy and eternal life.

This doesn't remove the adverbial connections that we've discussed earlier: 'praying' and 'building' might be the *means* of 'keeping'; 'looking forward' might be the *manner* of 'keeping'. What it does is put 'keeping' central: it makes you ask how each participle is connected to *that*.

4.2.5 Stylistic [Attendant Circumstance]

FURTHER READING: WALLACE 640–4

Greek prefers to have just one main verb in a sentence and turn the rest into participles. We have seen that the choices which the author must make provide information: the main verb, the participles to the left and to the right, each tell us something. There might well be further logical connections between each participle and the main verb (the adverbial connections in **EM 14** 4.2.2). However, if we insist on finding such a connection in each participle, we get into trouble. In fact, grammarians have had to invent a label for participles where no such connection is to be found; this is to defend against the idea that there *must* always be an intended connection: 'attendant circumstance'. I prefer to call these 'stylistic', to remind us of why they are participles in the first place.

This means that, often, there is no intention to communicate any of the possible relationships between the participles and the main verb which were listed in **EM 14** 4.2.2.

With imperatives, this is especially important to grasp.

> **στῆτε [imperative, aorist active ἵστημι]** οὖν <u>περιζωσάμενοι</u> τὴν ὀσφὺν ὑμῶν ἐν ἀληθείᾳ, καὶ <u>ἐνδυσάμενοι</u> τὸν θώρακα τῆς δικαιοσύνης, καὶ <u>ὑποδησάμενοι</u> τοὺς πόδας ἐν ἑτοιμασίᾳ τοῦ εὐαγγελίου τῆς εἰρήνης Eph 6:14–15

> **Stand up**, therefore, <u>having fastened</u> your belt (which is truth), and <u>having got dressed with</u> the breastplate (which is righteousness), and <u>having shod</u> your feet with the preparedness which comes from the gospel of peace.

This doesn't mean: '*only if* you happen to fasten … then stand up'. Nor is it simply, 'stand up, *after* you fasten … whenever that might be'. It is a command to do all of those: '**stand up, fasten … get dressed … put on your feet …**'. A string of imperatives (i.e. finite verbs in the same mood) has been replaced with a single verb and participles, for stylistic reasons (**EM 14** 4.2.1). The aorist participles tell you that you must do all of those things (fastening, etc.) *and then* stand up. In English you would have to express each participle as an imperative. Reading *Greek*, however, you want to notice which one is the main verb. You also want to notice two different things: which happens first (the aspect of the participles), and which are background (to the left of the verb). English might come close with:

> **Stand up**, but to do that, first **fasten** … and **get dressed** … and … **put on your feet** ….

4.2.6 Summary: Reading Adverbial Participles

Before we cover some final details in the sections below, let's review what you want to look for when reading adverbial participles.

1. Look for the main verb. Let the main verbs guide your reading of the narrative or argument (**EM 14** 4.2.1).
2. Take participles to the left as background (**EM 14** 4.2.4).
3. Take participles to the right as expanding on the main verb (**EM 14** 4.2.4).
4. Let the chosen stem of the participles tell you how they relate in time to the main verb (**EM 14** 4.2.3).
5. Consider the *possibility* that the author wants you to infer some logical connection between a participle and the main verb, from the list in **EM 14** 4.2.2.
6. Consider any of the possible nuances associated with the aspect of the participle (**EM 14** 4.3).
7. Notice the impossibility of conveying all this in translation, and feel the delight of reading Greek.

4.2.7 Adverbial Participles Not Connected to the Subject

Adverbial participles can relate to some part of the sentence other than the subject.[9] The sense of time and possible adverbial connection with the main verb still apply.

---

[9] This isn't quite the same thing as saying that the adverbial participle isn't nominative: genitives absolute can relate to the subject of the sentence, and the subject of an infinitive can be

Διὸ οὐκ ἀμελήσω **ὑμᾶς** ἀει ὑπομιμνῄσκειν περὶ τούτων, καίπερ
εἰδ**ότας**, καὶ ἐστηριγμέν**ους** ἐν τῇ παρούσῃ ἀληθείᾳ. 2 Pet 1:12
Therefore I will not fail to keep reminding **you** always about these
things, even though you know them, and remain firmly established in the truth that is with you.
Notice how the adverbial connection of '**concessive**' is made
explicit with καίπερ.

Here is a bit more practice:

Βοῦν ἀλοῶ**ντα** οὐ φιμώσεις. 1 Tim 5:18
An **ox** while it is treading out [the grain] you shall not muzzle.

μὴ ξενίζεσθε **τῇ** ἐν ὑμῖν **πυρώσει** πρὸς πειρασμὸν ὑμῖν γινομέν**ῃ** 1 Pet 4:12
don't be surprised **by the trial-by-fire** among you, when it comes to
you to test you

ὀλίγον παθ**όντας** αὐτὸς καταρτίσαι **ὑμᾶς**. 1 Pet 5:10
after **you** have suffered a little, he will restore **you**.

ἀπέστειλεν **αὐτὸν** εὐλογοῦ**ντα** ὑμᾶς Acts 3:26
he sent **him** [with the intention of] blessing you
That is, he sent **him** *so that* **he** would bless you

τὴν ἴσην δωρεὰν ἔδωκεν αὐτοῖς ὁ Θεὸς ὡς καὶ **ἡμῖν**, πιστεύ**σασιν** ἐπὶ
τὸν Κύριον Ἰησοῦν Χριστόν Acts 11:17
God gave to them the same gift as also to **us**, when **we** put our trust in
the Lord Jesus Christ
Or is it 'when *they* put their trust …'? The ambiguity is telling.

ἄλλοι δὲ εἶπον ὅτι **τὸν Λάζαρον** τεθνηκ**ότα** ἤγειρεν Acts Pil. 8.1
Others said that he had raised **Lazarus** after **he [Lazarus]** had died.

4.2.8 Genitive Absolute

FURTHER READING: WALLACE 654–5; VS 230D

This is an adverbial participle like any other, whether its subject is the subject of the main verb, another element of that main clause, or someone else entirely. The sense of time, possible aspectual nuances and possible adverbial connections with the main verb still apply. The genitive absolute usually gives background circumstances to the action, which is why it is usually written to the left of the verb.

Historically, the whole point of the genitive absolute was that the participle had a subject which was *not* already a member of the sentence (the 'proper'

---

qualified by an adverbial participle even when the subject is accusative (e.g. Matt 15:31 ὥστε τοὺς ὄχλους θαυμάσαι, βλέποντας … with the result that the crowd was amazed, seeing …).

genitive absolute). If the subject of the genitive absolute phrase were already in the sentence, then the participle would agree with *that* instead. In our literature, it has become common to use the genitive absolute even if the subject is a member of the sentence (the 'improper' genitive absolute).

> ἀνδρὸς οὐκέτ' ὄντος, ἀλλ' ἤδη σκιᾶς,
> θαρσῶν **ὑβρίζεις** Sophocles, *Aj.* 1257–8.
> The man no longer existing, but already a wraith,
> > you, being bold, **insult** us.
> > A proper genitive absolute: 'The man' isn't in the main sentence, and that's why he's the genitive subject of a genitive preposition.
> The sense of time (contemporaneous) and the adverbial connection (concessive) are there, and are there also with the present participle of manner (θαρσῶν), but the main thing is to highlight the main point, which is 'you insult'. Thus:
> 'Even though the man no longer exists and is already a wraith, you insult us boldly nonetheless.'

> Καὶ ἔτι αὐτοῦ λαλοῦντος, ἰδού, Ἰούδας εἷς τῶν δώδεκα **ἦλθε** Matt 26:47
> While he was still speaking, look, Judas (one of the Twelve) **arrived**

> Καὶ γὰρ ἐλθόντων ἡμῶν εἰς Μακεδονίαν οὐδεμίαν **ἔσχηκεν** ἄνεσιν ἡ σὰρξ ἡμῶν, 2 Cor 7:5
> For, when we arrived in Macedonia, our flesh **had** no rest at all.
> > Notice that 'we' is not the same as 'our flesh' and so requires the genitive absolute.

> Καὶ διαπεράσαντος τοῦ Ἰησοῦ ἐν τῷ πλοίῳ πάλιν εἰς τὸ πέραν, **συνήχθη** ὄχλος πολὺς ἐπ' **αὐτόν** Mark 5:21
> After Jesus had crossed over in the boat again to the other side, a large crowd **gathered** to **him**.
> > Notice that Jesus is in the sentence: αὐτόν; this is an improper genitive absolute.

4.2.9 A Quick Reminder: The Article

Remember that adverbial participles *never* have the article, whereas adjectival participles will follow the usual rules for adjectives. This means that if the noun has no article, the line between attributive and adverbial modifier isn't always clear. Sometimes the adverbial sense is made clear by conjunctions that tell you how they relate to the main verbs, such as καίπερ or ὡς.

4.3 Aspect of Participles: Nuances

Here are some illustrative examples where the kind of nuances you get with aspect can be in play with participles. Notice that these also apply to participles that aren't adverbial.

αἰτείτω παρὰ τοῦ διδόντος Θεοῦ πᾶσιν ἁπλῶς Jas 1:5
he should ask of the God who gives generously to all
> Habitual, customary or even characteristic.

τοὺς ἅπαξ φωτισθέντας, γευσαμένους ... μετόχους γενηθέντας ...
γευσαμένους ... καὶ παραπεσόντας ... Heb 6:4–6
those who have once been enlightened, have tasted ... have become
> partakers ... have tasted ... and have fallen away ...
> Aorists of actions with endpoints, telling us that the action completed successfully.

ὑμεῖς γὰρ οὐκ εἰσέρχεσθε, οὐδὲ τοὺς εἰσερχομένους ἀφίετε εἰσελθεῖν
Matt 23:13
For you yourselves do not enter, neither do you allow those who *are trying to* enter to enter.
> Conative.

τοὶ μὲν σὺν γένει φίλῳ Ἀτρέος Ἑλέναν κομίζοντες,
οἱ δ' ἀπὸ πάμπαν εἴργοντες Pindar, Ol. 13.59
While some, with the aid of Atreus' dear race, *are trying to* recover Helen,
yet others *are trying* to repel them by all possible means.
> Conative.

Εἰ σὺ εἶ αὐτὸς ὁ διαστρέφων τὸν Ἰσραήλ; 3 Kgdms 18:17
Is it you, the troubler of Israel?
> Habitual to the point of being an ironic title.

καὶ ἐθεασάμην πῦρ διατρέχον καὶ οὐκ ἀναπαυόμενον ... ἡμέρας καὶ
νυκτός ... ... τὸ πρὸς δυσμὰς πῦρ τὸ ἐκδιῶκόν ἐστιν πάντας
τοὺς φωστῆρας τοῦ οὐρανοῦ. 1 En. 23:2–4
And I saw a fire that was running and wasn't stopping [descriptive present] ... night and day ... ... It is the Western fire that chases [characteristic present] all the luminaries of heaven.

ὁ πιστεύσας [aorist] καὶ βαπτισθεὶς σωθήσεται Acts Pil. 14.1
The one who has come to believe and been baptised will be saved.
> Ingressive aorist of a state.

ζήσασα [aorist] **ἔτη** μετὰ ἀνδρὸς **ἑπτά** Luke 2:36
having lived with a husband **for seven years**
> Aorist of a state that lasted some time in the past.

καὶ τότε θυμωθεὶς [aorist] νομίζει δικαίως ὀργίζεσθαι [present]. T. Dan. 4.4
And then, having got angry, he imagines [himself] to be angry righteously.
> The aorist participle is ingressive, while the present infinitive refers to the state that he is still in.

4.3.1 Aspect Is Not Situation Type: It Interacts with It

Here is a reminder by way of cautionary example. Aspect is not a simple matter of the *nature* of the action. NT studies went through a phase of insisting on a straight correspondence between the choice of stem and the nature of the action (or *Aktionsart*), as though an aorist must refer to a simple action (rather than referring to an action simp*ly*) and the present to an action that must be somehow repeated or extended (rather than referring to the action *as* ongoing).[10] We have seen plenty of examples to the contrary in previous chapters.

Consider this participle:

Θεὸς ὁ δικαιῶν. Rom 8:33
God is the one who justifies.

This (nominal) participle is present, and that could be for any of the reasons we have seen. It is probably habitual: it identifies God alone as the one who justifies. What it *doesn't* do is tell us that the nature of the verb δικαιόω 'justify' is somehow a long drawn-out process, *pace*: 'the present tense once again reminding us that God's justifying action is not a once-for-all event (at conversion or whenever), but an ongoing sustaining'.[11] Plenty of processes which take time use an aorist to indicate that it is complete (if they have an endpoint) or ended (if they don't); plenty of processes that do not take time will take a present to indicate repetition, for example. We have seen examples of these in the indicative tenses (e.g. present EM 2 5.4 and imperfect EM 6 7.5.2) and in the other moods in previous chapters. Whether δικαιόω is a one-off event or not cannot be established from the present participle in Rom 8:33.

4.4 Supplementary / Complementary

FURTHER READING: *CGCG* 52.8–28; WALLACE 645–6; VS 234

We turn now to a few ways that a participle can complete the sense of a main verb.

The various uses below have this in common: the participle presents something as *actual* and *real*. By contrast, with complementary infinitives, you can *wish* to do something, or be *allowed* to do something, or be *required* to do something, but it might not happen. A supplementary **participle** means that the action *does happen*. Similarly, with other forms of indirect speech, you can *think* or *believe* or *perceive* something but be quite wrong about it, whereas the supplementary **participle** says that you think *correctly*.[12]

---

[10] A relatively recent summary of the history of understanding aspect in NT studies is offered by Christopher J. Thomson, 'What Is Aspect? Contrasting Definitions in General Linguistics and New Testament Studies', *GVR*, 38–48.

[11] James D. G. Dunn, *Romans 1–8*, Word Biblical Commentary 38A (Dallas: Word, 1988), 503.

[12] Be aware that different grammars use (or don't use) 'complementary' and/or 'supplementary' to refer to some or all of the uses in this section.

We are familiar with verbs that take a *complementary* infinitive, to complete the sense of the verb: you have to desire *something*, and the infinitive tells you the action you desire, for example. We still find some remnants of a Classical usage, where certain verbs use a participle instead.

These include verbs that describe an action as *starting* or *ending* or *continuing*.

> **ἐπέμενον** ἐρωτῶντες αὐτόν John 8:7
> **they kept** asking him
>> Note that they were *actually* asking him: it wasn't a desire or an attempt.

> οὐ **παύσῃ** διαστρέφων τὰς ὁδοὺς Κυρίου τὰς εὐθείας; Acts 13:10
> Won't you **stop** twisting the Lord's straight ways?
>> They were *actually* twisting them.

These also include verbs of perception, where the participle describes the action of the person or thing that is perceived.

> **εἶδε** τὸ Πνεῦμα τοῦ θεοῦ καταβαῖνον ὡσεὶ περιστερὰν καὶ ἐρχόμενον ἐπ' αὐτόν Matt 3:16
> **he saw** the Spirit of God descending as a dove and arriving on him.
>> The use of the complementary participle tells us that what he saw actually happened.

> **ὄψεσθε** τὸν υἱὸν τοῦ ἀνθρώπου καθήμενον ἐκ δεξιῶν τῆς δυνάμεως καὶ ἐρχόμενον ἐπὶ τῶν νεφελῶν τοῦ οὐρανοῦ. Matt 26:64
> **you will see** the son of man seated at the right hand of power, and coming on the clouds of heaven.
>> They won't imagine it: it will be happening when they see it.

You can see that it isn't much of a stretch to turn 'you will see the son seated' into 'you will see *that* the son *is* seated'. In fact, these are simply examples of indirect discourse. We have met various forms of indirect speech and other indirect implied statements, involving a variety of options in **EM 10** 6.3.4. Participles are used to express what is done to propositional content (whether knowing it, grasping it, revealing it, responding to it emotionally) when that content is *true*.

> Μαρία ἡ Μαγδαληνὴ ... **βλέπει** τὸν λίθον ἠρμένον ἐκ τοῦ μνημείου. John 20:1
> Mary Magdalene ... **saw** that the stone had been removed from the tomb.
>> She didn't see 'the removed stone' – that would be attributive and would have the repeated article: τὸν λίθον τὸν ἠρμένον.
>> Neither did she merely see that the stone had been removed (regardless of whether she saw accurately or not). The *supplementary* participle means that John is telling you that Mary saw the stone and that *it had in fact* been removed.

The value of understanding this form is that the event or idea is perceived as *true*.¹³ I have translated more freely to capture this idea:

ἐγὼ γὰρ **ἔγνων** δύναμιν ἐξελθοῦσαν ἀπ' ἐμοῦ Luke 8:46
for I **noticed** ['I came to know']¹⁴ power going out from me
That is, that *power* was going out from me – the content of the knowledge (that power was going out) is accurate.

ἀκούομεν γάρ τινας περιπατοῦντας ἐν ὑμῖν ἀτάκτως, 2 Thess 3:11
for **we have got wind of the fact that** some are living among you idle

Ἐχάρην λίαν ὅτι **εὕρηκα** ἐκ τῶν τέκνων σου περιπατοῦντας ἐν ἀληθείᾳ
2 John 4
I had great joy because **I discovered** some of your children living by the truth

ἐὰν γάρ τις **ἴδῃ** σὲ τὸν ἔχοντα γνῶσιν ἐν εἰδωλείῳ κατακείμενον ...
1 Cor 8:10
for if someone **were to observe you** (who have knowledge) feasting in the temple of an idol ...
This doesn't mean that they *are* feasting at the moment, but that if they *did* and then someone (accurately) saw them ...

καὶ πᾶν κτίσμα ... **ἤκουσα** λέγοντας, Rev 5:13
and **I heard** every creature ... while they were saying

ἀλλ' ἢ μετὰ ἀνδρὸς εὐσεβοῦς ἐνδελέχιζε,
ὃν ἂν **ἐπιγνῷς** συντηροῦντα ἐντολάς, Sir 37:12
Conversely, persist with a pious man,
[if] **you recognise** that he keeps the commandments,

... τὸν ἐπουράνιον θεὸν **ἐγνωκότες** ἀσφαλῶς ὑπερησπικότα τῶν
Ἰουδαίων ... 3 Macc 7:6
... **having discovered** that the heavenly God certainly shielded the Judaeans ...

4.4.1 Comparing the Options

Notice the difference between normal indirect speech and three sorts of participles: attributive, adverbial and supplementary.

---

¹³ Beware of confusing the options in Greek and in English. Whether you translate 'you will see the son of man seated' or 'you will see *that* the son of man is seated' is just a matter of English style, reflecting no difference in Greek meaning. However, whether the Greek indirect discourse uses a supplementary participle or some other form of discourse is the difference between the perception being true or not.
¹⁴ Ingressive aorist of a state (**EM 7** 5.1.2; **EM 8** 5.1.1).

He saw *that* the Spirit was descending.
>This would use the quite normal forms of indirect speech, such as ὅτι and a present tense of καταβαίνω.

He saw *the descending* Spirit.
>This would be an *attributive* participle: τὸ Πνεῦμα **τὸ** καταβαῖνον (note the repeated article). This would mean that, of all the spirits he might have seen, he saw the one that was descending.

He saw the Spirit *descending*.
>This is the supplementary participle: τὸ Πνεῦμα __ καταβαῖνον (note the lack of article). It tells us that he saw the Spirit, and it tells us what it was that he saw the Spirit doing, and that it was true, not merely his perception.

He saw the Spirit *while he was descending*.
>This is adverbial and is (syntactically) indistinguishable from the supplementary participle above: τὸ Πνεῦμα __ καταβαῖνον (note the lack of article). It would tell us *when* or *why* or *despite what*: he saw the Spirit not before and not after he was descending; he saw the Spirit because the descent rendered him visible; he saw the Spirit despite the fact that descending makes him less easy to see. If an author intended that, he would probably use a conjunction to make this adverbial sense clear.

CHAPTER 15

The Passive and Voices
—
The Middle Voice

> **How to Use This Chapter**
>
> Follow the instructions throughout the **Extra Help** below, which will tell you when to work through various sections of *ENTG*. The instructions below are for the fourth edition of *ENTG*. If you have the third edition, please check the **Online Material**, which has different instructions for you for this chapter.
>
> In **Extra Help** you will see that we can save a lot of effort because of the way that we have understood the Greek verb so far.
>
> In the **Extra Material** you'll think further about the middle voice.

1 BEFORE YOU START

This chapter of *ENTG* is quite straightforward. If you have been following the way that I have been teaching you to understand the verb, the new material slots in effortlessly. We have learnt that every verb belongs to a system (the major column in our verb table) and has a voice (the minor columns in our table). All we are doing now is adding one more voice (the passive) to two of the systems (the aorist and future): that is, adding a sub-column to two columns. Glance briefly, in the **Online Material**, at 'The Greek Verb So Far' for Chapter 14 and compare it with 'The Greek Verb So Far' for Chapter 15.

You won't regret making sure that you're quite solid on the verb. Write out the full paradigm of the verb, active and middle, that we've learnt up to Chapter 14. Check your answer against 'The Greek Verb So Far' for Chapter 14, in the **Online Material**. Did you get it perfectly right (apart from accents)? If so, read on. If not, repeat until perfect. Keep testing yourself with your study buddy and/or some software.

Now read *ENTG* 15.1.

2 PASSIVE AND MIDDLE VOICES

2.1 After *ENTG* 15.1: The Passive in Every Verb Form

Once you understand what the passive voice means, everything in *ENTG* 15.2–4 is already apparent from the way we have laid out the verb.

Instead of 15.2, you can easily see that the passive exists separately in the future and aorist systems, and therefore in every tense and mood of those systems. In the present system, it is the same as the middle. This is why I asked you in Chapter 8 to parse verbs in -ομαι as 'middle' in the future and aorist systems, but as middle/passive in the present system (**EH 8** 1.4.1). I also warned you back there that you would eventually see those endings on verbs in -ω.

2.1.1 The Passive Stem (6th Principal Part)

The passive gives us a new **stem** which is shared by the aorist and future passives. (Until now, a stem and a system have always been the same.) This stem is the 6th Principal Part (**EH 11** 1.5). (We will meet the 4th and 5th in the next chapter.)

The stem simply adds a θ to the end of the basic stem, and the thematic vowel is η. The future, as expected, adds a σ to this. It can't connect directly to the θ, so another η joins them; the σ is followed by the normal thematic vowel. See Table 15.1.

Table 15.1 Stems and Thematic Vowels

	Stem	Thematic vowel	
Present stem	-λυ-	ε/ο	
Future stem	-λυ-σ-	ε/ο	
Aorist stem	-λυ-σ-	α	
Aorist passive stem	-λυ-θ-	η	(1)
Future passive stem	-λυ-θησ-	ε/ο	(2)

(1) The η becomes short (ε) before vowels and before ντ (this happens in the other moods).
(2) Notice that η is there for both aorist and future, but for different reasons: thematic vowel in aorist, part of the longer stem in the future.

This means that you don't need a new lesson in how to tell the moods and tenses apart in the passive voice. They work just like all the other ones.

As for its meaning in those different tenses and moods, the same principles apply as always: you don't need to learn the 'passive' separately in each tense or mood or system. Keep remembering:

1 what each system tells you (present: presented as ongoing; aorist: presented simply; future: future action)
2 what the augment does in the indicative (absent: time isn't shifted; augment: past time)
3 what the voices tell you (indicative vs imperative vs participle).

2.1.2 The Passive Endings

You already know that the passive is identical to the middle in the present system. You therefore already know the present passive endings, from Chapter 8. What more is there to know?

1 The **future passive** takes **middle endings**. Check that this explains what you see on our verb table.
2 The **aorist passive** takes **active endings**. They are historical, as expected.[1]
3 You have one new adjective to learn: the aorist passive participle. Check that you can write out the table in the footnote in *ENTG* 15.5 completely by learning this: λυθείς, λυθεῖσα, λυθέν,[2] λυθέντος. (If not, review **EH 14** 1.1.)

2.1.3 Embedding the Paradigms

Now apply the method we have used throughout.

1 Write out the entire aorist passive column for λύω from scratch, without looking anything up, by:
   ○ using the aorist passive stem -λυθ-
   ○ using the η thematic vowel
     ▪ *either* memorising the endings (or having memorised them from root aorists in Chapter 11)
     ▪ *or* knowing the rules from Chapter 11 for root aorists.
2 Keep doing that until you never get it wrong.
3 Write out the entire future passive column for λύω from scratch, without looking anything up, by:
   ○ using the future passive stem -λυθησ-
   ○ using the middle endings which you already know.
4 Keep doing that until you never get it wrong.

2.1.4 Thlippery Theta

Theta at the end of a stem is even more creative than σ. It can behave normally, or disappear completely, or add itself to a consonant and change that consonant. As ever, the principle is simply that some combinations are impossible to pronounce comfortably at speed.[3] You can either memorise the table in **Key Grammar** in *ENTG* 15.5.2, or just be ready for certain stems to look odd in the passive. Learning Principal Parts of verbs is a great help here, since it builds up your instincts.

---

[1] Remember that there is a little bit of flexibility in the historical endings: see the table in **EH 11** 1.2.2.
[2] The η has shortened before vowels and before ντ. However, the neuter nominative singular has no ending after the ντ; you can't end a Greek word with any consonant other than σ ρ ν (SiReN, **EH 12** 1.2.2), so the τ disappears, just as it does with nouns ending in ματ.
[3] It may help you to remember that θ is shorthand for τ +' (a *t* sound with aspiration). Pronouncing one consonant *without* an aspiration and then immediately another *with* aspiration is harder than aspirating them both. That's why any version of π (φ, β) becomes the aspirated φθ and any version of κ (χ, γ) becomes the aspirated χθ. However, when it comes to versions of τ (ζ, τ, δ, θ) becoming θ, it would create the difficult θθ, so σθ happens instead.

Now tackle *ENTG* **Practice** 15.5.1 and 15.5.2.
Now read *ENTG* 15.5.3 and then return here.

2.2 After *ENTG* 15.5.3: Irregular Stems

Whatever happens because of a θ in the aorist passive, the same happens in the future passive: you simply add the -ησ- to whatever the aorist passive did. We can see this in Table 15.2, using examples from *ENTG* 15.5.3.

Table 15.2 Irregular Stems

Present stem	Aorist passive	Future passive
ἀκούω	ἠκού**σθ**ην	ἀκου**σθή**σομαι
βάλλω	ἐβλ**ήθ**ην	βλη**θή**σομαι
ἀποστέλλω	ἀπεστάλην	ἀποσταλή**σ**ομαι
λέγω	ἐρρ**ήθ**ην	ῥη**θή**σομαι

2.2.1 Building Your Verb

Table 15.3 builds on that from **EH 8** 1.3. *Nothing else* changes: the augment, prepositions, contract vowels, thematic vowels, endings proper: all the principles we have learnt hold good.

Table 15.3 Building Your Verb

Preposition	Augment	Basic stem	Contract vowel	Suffix	Thematic vowel	Ending proper
optional	ἐ for past time (indicative)	λυ- φιλ- ῥυ- ἀρν-	optional ε (→η before σ or θ)	σ fut/aor	ε (→ο before μ, ν) α in aor	Varies with mood, voice and (indicative only) time
				θ in aor pass θησ in fut pass	η in aor pass (→ε before ντ or vowel)	

Now tackle *ENTG* **Practice** 15.5.3 and the **Half-Way Practice**, then return here.

If you have the fourth edition of *ENTG*, you can optionally read *ENTG* 15.6 and 15.7; if you have the third edition, skip them.

Now work through the section below.

2.3 Instead of (or after) *ENTG* 15.6 and 15.7: From Parsing to Meaning

The key is to know what kind of verb you're looking at. There are two types of verb:

1 Verbs you've learnt as -ω (λύω, ποιέω, εσθίω), which *can be active*.
2 Verbs you've learnt as -ομαι (ἔρχομαι, δέχομαι, λογίζομαι), which *can never be active*.

When you see a middle or passive ending on a verb, if the verb *can* be active (λύω, ἁγιάζω), then it means whatever you learnt for that verb, but in the *passive*.

| λύω I am untying | λύομαι I am being untied | ἐλύθην I was untied |
| ἁγιάζω I am sanctifying | ἡγιάζομαι I am being sanctified | ἡγιάσθην I was sanctified |

When you see a middle or passive ending on a verb, if the verb *cannot* be active (ῥύομαι, ἀποκρίνομαι), then don't worry about the voice. It means whatever you learnt for that verb.[4]

If you want to check why this really simple decision works, see tables 15.2 and 15.5.

2.3.1 For Verbs Like λύω (Which Can Be Active)

Table 15.4 Active Verbs

	Active form	Middle form	Passive form
Present system	the gloss you've learnt	passive meaning	
Aorist/future	the gloss you've learnt	rare – look up the verb	passive meaning

2.3.2 For Verbs Like ῥύομαι (Which Are Never Active), Even Easier

Table 15.5 Never-Active Verbs

	Active form	Middle form	Passive form
Present system	can't happen	the gloss you've learnt	
Aorist/future	can't happen	the gloss you've learnt	the gloss you've learnt

---

[4] When they're aorist or future, they will be either middle or passive. These 'never-active' verbs *don't* have separate meanings in the middle and the passive. You only need to know which way the verb goes if you're *writing* Greek (hence the list of verbs that go passive in *ENTG* 15.7).

2.3.3 The Rare True Middles

If you follow the simple table above, you will occasionally come up with a result that makes no sense, for example, an aorist/future of a verb that can be active, but is *middle* (not passive). In that case, you want to look up that verb in a lexicon.

As a taster for more advanced material, ENTG 15.6.1 points out that some verbs use their middle to be 'reflexive', where the subject is the object. Make that your first guess when you come across a verb that *can be active* (you've learnt it as -ω not as -ομαι) and either:

> is middle (in the aorist or future systems)
> or
> is middle/passive (in the present system) but that
>   passive makes no sense.

Now tackle *ENTG* **Practice** 15.7.

3 THE GREEK READING

The story so far ...

A heavenly man has come down to Aseneth to assure her that God has heard her plea for mercy and given her new and eternal life, and that Joseph will marry her. He has blessed her and her beloved maidens, and made a dramatic exit.

18:1 Καὶ ἰδοὺ ἐπορεύθη παῖς τοῦ Ἰωσὴφ λέγων· Ἰδοὺ ὁ Ἰωσὴφ ὁ φιλούμενος ὑπὸ τοῦ θεοῦ πορεύεται σήμερον πρὸς ὑμᾶς. ²ᵃ ἄρα ἐκάλεσεν Ἀσενὲθ δοῦλον, ὑπὸ οὗ ἡ οἰκία ἐκελεύετο, καὶ εἶπεν· ²ᵇ Ἑτοίμασόν μοι δεῖπνον καλόν, ὅτι ἀσθενῶ διότι ἐφοβήθην ἀλλὰ νῦν ὁ Ἰωσὴφ ὁ περισσεύων τῇ δόξᾳ τοῦ θεοῦ ἐπιστρέφει πρὸς ἡμᾶς. ³ ὑποστρέψασα δὲ Ἀσενὲθ εἰς τὸν κοιτῶνα αὐτῆς ἐβάστασέ τι ἔνδυμα. καὶ τοῦτό ἐστι φαῖνον ὡς ἀστήρ. καὶ ἐνεδύσατο τὸ ἔνδυμα τὸ ἔχον λίθους ἁγιασθέντας. ⁶ ἀλλὰ ἐκρύβη ἡ κεφαλὴ αὐτῆς μὴ γνωρίσθεισα μηδενί. ⁷ᵃ καὶ εἶπε τῷ παιδὶ αὐτῆς· Ἔκχεόν μοι ὕδωρ. ἄρα ἐνίψατο Ἀσενὲθ ἐν τῷ ὕδατι. τότε ἦν τὸ πρόσωπον αὐτῆς ὡς ὁ ἥλιος καὶ οἱ ὀφθαλμοὶ αὐτῆς ὡς ἀστέρες φαίνοντες.

⁷ᵇ Οὕτως ἐτέλεσε ὅλος ὁ φόβος ὁ τῆς Ἀσενὲθ καὶ οὐκέτι ἐλυπήθη.

19:1a Καὶ ἦλθε παῖς κηρύσσων· Ἰδοὺ Ἰωσὴφ ἥκει. ἡ δὲ ἀπεκρίθη λέγουσα·

¹ᵇ Γαμηθήσομαι τῷ Ἰωσήφ. ἐκπορεύθη οὖν Ἀσενὲθ σὺν τοῖς ἑπτὰ παισίν.

¹ᶜ ἐβούλοντο γὰρ ἀσπάζεσθαι τὸν Ἰωσὴφ τὸν ἰσχύοντα Αἰγύπτου.

²ᵃ ὡς δὲ εἶδεν αὐτὴν Ἰωσήφ, εἶπε πρὸς αὐτήν· ²ᵇ Ἔγγισον πρός με, διότι μοὶ εὐηγγελίσθην περὶ σοῦ ἐξ οὐρανοῦ. ²ᶜ καὶ πάντα τὰ περὶ σοῦ ἐλαλήθη μοι.

³ ἐνηγκαλίσατο δὲ Ἰωσὴφ τὴν Ἀσενὲθ ἐν ταῖς χέρσιν αὐτοῦ, καὶ ἡ Ἀσενὲθ τὸν Ἰωσὴφ καὶ ἠσπάσαντο ἀλλήλους κλαίοντες πολὺν χρόνον καὶ ἀνεπαῦθη τὰ πνεύματα αὐτῶν.

3.1 Vocabulary

ἀναπαύω – I refresh, revive
δεῖπνον, ου, τό – feast
ἐναγκαλίζομαι – I hug
ἔνδυμα, ατος, τό – garment
ἑπτά – seven
ἥλιος, ου, ὁ – sun
κοιτών, ῶνος, ὁ – bedroom

κρύπτω – I cover, hide; Principal Parts: 1 κρύπτω, 2 κρύψω, 3 ἔκρυψα, 6 ἐκρύβην
**νίπτω –
active: I wash something/someone (+ acc);
middle: I wash myself**

4 THE MIDDLE VOICE

CGCG 35.1; Rutger Allan, 'Middle', *EAGLL*; Rutger Allan, 'Mediopassive', *EAGLL*

We can understand the active and passive voices, because English has them too. The middle is harder.[5] The temptation for English readers is to assume it means nothing: not only does the middle not have an English equivalent, but the meaning in Greek is so subtle that we doubt it really tells us much. We need to resist thinking about English, and instead understand the Greek meaning of the middle.

> The middle voice says: the *subject* is *affected* by the action.

---

[5] The middle voice is common among European languages, but not in English. Speakers of French, Spanish, German, Italian and others have a distinct advantage when it comes to understanding the Greek middle.

4.1 Verbs Which Can Be Active

FURTHER READING: RUTGER ALLAN, 'MIDDLE', *EAGLL*

As we have seen (**EH 15** 2.3), the choice to use the middle or passive voice is only significant on verbs which can be active: verbs which we learn (or find in a lexicon) ending in -ω.

We have seen that when you find them in the middle/passive, you should guess at a passive meaning (where the subject is acted on, rather than performing the action). What happens when that guess doesn't work? In stems that have a separate middle and passive, you expect to see them in the passive. What happens when you find them in the middle? In those cases, we are dealing with a true middle meaning: the *subject is affected*.

The two common ways that the subject is affected are the direct reflexive and the indirect reflexive.

4.1.1 Direct Reflexive

FURTHER READING: *CGCG* 35.11–12

We have already met the direct reflexive (**EH 15** 2.3.3): the subject performs the action and is also the direct object: I wash, I dress.

This meaning is limited to a very small number of verbs, usually of grooming. Other verbs cannot make themselves 'directly reflexive' by using the middle, but only by using the reflexive pronoun. This is much like English, where only a few verbs are understood to be reflexive without an object ('I wash' means 'I wash myself') and any others need the pronoun ('I watch' doesn't mean 'I watch myself'):

> ὅταν εἰσπορεύωνται εἰς τὴν σκηνὴν τοῦ μαρτυρίου, νίψονται ὕδατι
> ... Ex 30:20
> Whenever they enter the tent of testimony, they will wash with water ...
>
> πρόσεχε σεαυτῷ μή ποτε θῇς διαθήκην τοῖς ἐνκαθημένοις ἐπὶ τῆς γῆς
> ... Ex 34:12
> Watch yourself so that you don't establish a covenant with those who dwell in the land ...

4.1.2 Indirect Reflexive

FURTHER READING: *CGCG* 35.8–10

The indirect reflexive means that the subject performs the action *and has a special interest in the action*; typically, the subject performs the action *for his or her own benefit*. This is what English speakers will find hard to grasp, because it seems insubstantial. It is certainly hardly ever worth bringing out in translation, but that's precisely where Greek gets interesting: where the Greek text tells you something that English doesn't.[6]

A couple of English uses of the reflexive can come close, such as 'I buy *myself* an ice-cream' means 'I buy an ice-cream *for my own enjoyment*', and cf. US idioms such as 'Have *yourself* a merry little Christmas'.

4.1.3 Look the Verb Up

It happens quite often that verbs have specialised meanings in different voices, which you couldn't guess. You need to look the verb up. For example:

ἅπτω	I kindle, light	ἅπτομαι	I touch
ἄρχω	I rule	ἄρχομαι	I begin
αἱρέω	I take	αἱρέομαι	I choose

Such specialised meanings were more common in older Greek, such as:

| γράφω | I write | γράφομαι | I indict |
| αἰτέω | I ask | αἰτέομαι | I beg |

4.1.4 Consider the Possible Meaning of Middle Forms

ENTG 15.6.1 advises you that some Atticising authors use middle forms to tell you nothing more than: 'I'm doing something that older Greek used to do, but I don't mean what it once meant.' It's pure style, and the middle means the same as the active.

I advise you to consider the possibility that they were indeed using the middle for stylistic reasons, but nonetheless meaning what the middle means. The subject is *somehow* affected. If Acts uses active ποιέω and occasionally makes it middle, and if James in a very short passage uses both active and middle of αἰτέω, it might mean something. At the very least, look the verb up in a lexicon to see whether a separate middle meaning is listed.

4.2 Verbs Which Are Never Active

> FURTHER READING: RUTGER ALLAN, 'MEDIA TANTUM', *EAGLL*; RUTGER ALLAN, 'PASSIVA TANTUM', *EAGLL*; *CGCG* 35.20–32; RACHEL AUBREY, 'MOTIVATED CATEGORIES, MIDDLE VOICE, AND PASSIVE MORPHOLOGY', *GVR*, 563–625

You already know all you need to about this. If you find language interesting, or if you're left unsettled by the strangeness of these verbs, read on.

---

[6] It is very similar to the 'ethical dative' in that respect (**EM** 4 4.1.6).

4.2.1 Families of Middle-Only Meanings

FURTHER READING: RUTGER ALLAN, 'MIDDLE', *EAGLL*, 2:441; RACHEL AUBREY, 'MOTIVATED CATEGORIES, MIDDLE VOICE, AND PASSIVE MORPHOLOGY', *GVR*, 613

Verbs which *cannot* be active are not arbitrary. There is a range of ways in which the 'subject-affected' meaning of the middle can apply.[7]

- Indirect reflexive, as discussed. Ἐργάζομαι doesn't mean 'I work for myself' but 'I work for some indirect benefit, such as wages'. However, the verb remains middle even when there is no such sense of reward in view, such as when God is the subject, in Acts 13:41.
- Speech acts. Ἀρνέομαι 'I refuse' (and it clearly affects me, since I therefore do not do whatever it is that I've refused). It might not be obvious how some such verbs affect their subject, but you will see that they belong to the family of speech acts.
- Acts of the mind. Λογίζομαι 'I reckon': the outcome of that thought process is a conclusion in my mind. It affects my mind.
- Perception. If I taste something (γεύομαι), then I'm clearly receiving the effect (or even benefit) of tasting.
- Direct reflexive, as discussed.
- Reciprocal. Μάχομαι means 'I fight you, and of course the implication is that you fight me back, which affects me.' However, even when it means 'I fight', not 'we fight each other', it's still middle (2 Tim 2:24).
- Group motion. Συνέρχομαι means 'we gather ourselves together', which affects the subject, as all verbs of motion do.
- Motion. If I walk from A to B (ἔρχομαι), I'm performing the action, and I'm also clearly affected by the action: I get moved from A to B.
- States or processes (as opposed to acts) of mind. Μιμνήσκομαι 'I remember'.
- Spontaneous process. Γίνομαι 'I come into being'; ἰάομαι 'I get better' (I heal).

4.2.2 Middle-Only, Not 'Deponent'

The label 'deponent' carries with it the idea that the endings of a verb (middle) don't match the meaning (active). This confuses meaning with translation: the *English* glosses which we learn for verbs like πορεύομαι and γεύομαι are active *in English*: I walk and I taste. But in *Greek*, the subject of the action is affected by the action (**EM 15** 4.2.1). They *are* middle in meaning, not only in form.

Verbs which are never active (put another way, which are middle-only) fall into one of the families of meaning we have just listed. Notice that it isn't obvious for any particular verb, and certainly not for every single use of any verb, *how* the

---

[7] For the list and other examples, see Rutger Allan, 'Middle', *EAGLL*; for an analysis of how these relate to each other, Aubrey, 'Motivated Categories'.

subject is affected. What we can see is that the general meaning of the family is a meaning which affects the subject.

However, these are not meanings which you can guess at when an -ω verb becomes middle. If you see λυομαι it cannot mean 'we release in a way which gathers us together'; 'we release each other'; 'I release, but only as a mental process', or 'I release but only as a speech-act'. When you see an -ω verb in the middle voice, you can guess at direct or indirect reflexive; when you see it in the passive voice, you can guess at passive; when those guesses don't make sense, you must look the verb up.

4.2.3 Active Does Not Deny Middle

FURTHER READING: *CGCG* 35.1

The middle voice tells you that the verb is subject-affected. However, an active verb does *not deny* that the verb is subject-affected. Just as the perfect tells you something, but the aorist does not deny that, so the middle voice tells you something, but the active voice doesn't deny it.

This is why you can have verbs with nearly identical meanings, some of which are active, and some are middle: βαίνω and χωρέω but ἔρχομαι and πορεύομαι. Active does not deny subject-affectedness; middle asserts it. That is why you can have verbs in any of the families of meaning listed above, and yet they are active.

Notice how some verbs have Principal Parts that are a mixture of different verbs *in different voices*: ὁράω becomes ὄψομαι with no change in meaning. As above, verbs of perception affect the subject; the middle in ὄψομαι tells us that; the active in ὁράω *does not deny* it.

This is why these verbs are not 'deponent'; they have a middle meaning in Greek.

4.3 Verbs Which Are Always Passive

FURTHER READING: RACHEL AUBREY, 'MOTIVATED CATEGORIES, MIDDLE VOICE, AND PASSIVE MORPHOLOGY', *GVR*, 563–625

4.3.1 The Passive Is Middle

The Greek passive is just a subset of the middle. It is one of the ways that the subject of the action is affected by the action. In the list of categories above, you might notice that the subject is less and less active in performing the action as you go further down the list. The top end is the direct reflexive: the subject fully engages in the action, and is also the object. The passive is just the final step in the opposite direction: the subject *doesn't perform* the action at all, but is simply the object.

This is why the present and perfect stems do not distinguish between the middle and the passive voice: the passive is just a type of middle. This also explains 'passive deponents', as we will see next.

4.3.2 The Choice of Middle or Passive Endings

When verbs are never active, they take the middle/passive endings. But when they go into a stem which distinguishes between middle and passive, they must choose. Some go middle, and some go passive.

What is happening is a slow shift across the centuries. The θ passive arrived late to the verb, and was initially just a marker of 'passive meaning' in the future and aorist. In other words, it marked that extreme end of the range of middle meanings which we saw in **EM 15** 4.2.1.

Eventually, that θ ending crept its way along that range of meanings from the true passive, up through slightly more active meanings: spontaneous processes (γίνομαι; ἰάομαι), states of mind (μιμνῄσκομαι), etc. It no longer marked the *passive* exclusively, but was used for verb types where the subject is less active. Over time, it worked its way further up that list, until eventually the future and aorist stems completely lost the σ endings; they use θ for the whole range of middle, from 'indirect reflexive' to 'passive'. Everything that is marked by σ in the present and perfect is marked by θ in the aorist and future.

In the age of the NT, that gradual process was still happening, and that's why some verbs which are never active choose σ middle endings, and others choose the θ endings. As we have seen, you don't need to notice or worry about that choice; if a verb is never active, it has the same meaning, regardless of whether the endings are 'middle' or 'passive'.

This is why I tell you in **EH 15** 2.3.2 that for verbs which are never active, you only need the one meaning you've learnt, regardless of whether it is middle, passive or middle/passive. That's because that meaning is *already* middle in Greek, and the passive includes the middle.

When in doubt, look the verb up.

CHAPTER 16

The Perfect
—
Consolidation Greek Reading
—
The Perfect System

> **How to Use This Chapter**
>
> Follow the instructions throughout the **Extra Help** below, which will tell you when to work through various sections of *ENTG*. The instructions below are for the fourth edition of *ENTG*. If you have the third edition, please check the **Online Material**, which has different instructions for you for this chapter.
>
> In this chapter, we meet the final verb system that *ENTG* covers: the perfect. In **Extra Help** you will see how easy it is to understand this new system using the pattern we have followed so far for the verb.
>
> From now on, each chapter will offer a **Greek Reading B**. These are unedited passages from the GNT: be encouraged!
>
> We are three-quarters of the way through this *Reader*, so **Greek Reading C** is an extended passage from *Joseph & Aseneth* for consolidation.
>
> In the **Extra Material** you'll discover the range of uses of the perfect system.

1 BEFORE YOU START: THE PERFECT SYSTEM

We have met three systems: present, aorist and future. Each exists in the various voices. They have one or more stems. They communicate aspect. That aspect then interacts with time to form the indicative tenses, or remains timeless in the other moods.

The perfect system is no different. This is the final system introduced by *ENTG* and nearly completes the verb.

As ever, the notes below do not depart from what *ENTG* teaches you. However, if you have followed along with how this *Reader* teaches the verb (in terms of systems), then the material below builds on that, whereas *ENTG* 16.1 builds on how *ENTG* has taught the verb. The end result is, of course, the same.

1.1 After *ENTG* 16.1: Combinative Aspect

I will explain how the aspect of the perfect relates to our discussion of aspect of the other systems:

16 The Perfect

> A **prior** event with some **ongoing relevance**.

See Figure 16.1.

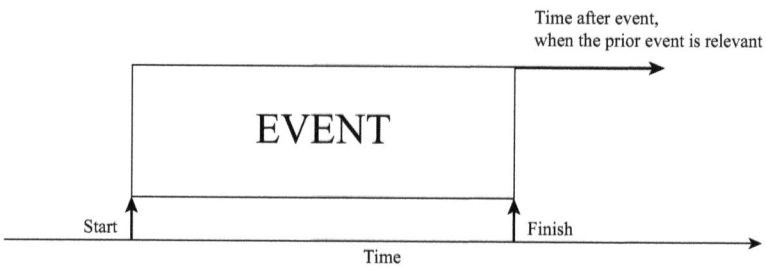

Figure 16.1 Aspect of the Perfect

The prior event is presented 'simply' like the aorist; the ongoing relevance is presented as ongoing, like the present. No one-word label is ideal. *ENTG* calls this '**combinative**'.[1] This is not a description of its aspect per se, but it alerts us to the fact that the perfect combines certain ideas from two different tenses.

'Ongoing relevance' needs to be viewed as broadly as possible. Some authors talk about 'effect' or 'state', but the relevance can be subtle.

In English, if a child says to a parent, 'I have tidied my room' (rather than just 'I tidied my room'), the ongoing relevance could be:[2]

- The room remains tidy.
- The room is ready for guests.
- You can now see the floor.
- I'm too tired to do another chore.

But it could also be relevant in less direct ways:

- You don't need to tidy the room. Or you don't need to remind me to tidy it. (Consequence, rather than a state or an effect.)

---

[1] Common labels include: 'anterior', 'stative', 'perfect' (as opposed to 'perfective'). All of these capture something helpful, but not the full picture. Likewise, 'combinative'.

[2] In modern US English, the perfect aspect is being lost, and the 'past simple' is used instead of the perfect tense. Ongoing relevance is often left to be inferred by the hearer from context, or communicated by 'yet' or 'already'.

- I have earned my pocket money. I have duly done my chore for today, even though the room no longer looks tidy, because I've had a play date. (None of the states, effects or consequences in the previous list of bullets remain, but it has clear relevance.)

The 'ongoing relevance' is something which the speaker expects the hearer to understand, but it might not be obvious to someone overhearing the statement.

> Whenever a verb is put in the perfect system, ask what ongoing relevance the author is pointing out.

1.2 Before *ENTG* 16.2

ENTG explains the formation of the perfect thoroughly in this section, but first let's get a simple overview of how it fits with the verb as we have learnt it so far. Of course, feel free to skip this and learn the perfect endings in any way that works for you.

Remember that each system is identified by one or more stems. The stems of the perfect involve *reduplication*. The first consonant of the stem is repeated and the letter ε is inserted. λυ- becomes λελυ-; ποι- → πεποι-, etc.

Like the present, the perfect system has no separate passive, but just the active and the middle/passive. However, these two stems are slightly different.

The **active stem** reduplicates and then adds a κ and changes the thematic vowel to α in the same way as the aorist. λυ- → λελυκα; ποι- → πεποικα. This is the **4th Principal Part** (EH 11 1.5).

The **middle/passive stem** reduplicates and does *not* add anything, and even loses the **thematic vowel**. λυ- → λελυμαι; ποι- → πεποιμαι. This is the **5th Principal Part** (EH 11 1.5).

Now that we have all the systems, stems and Principal Parts, we can recap the Greek verb in Table 16.1.

Table 16.1 Principal Parts

System: (aspect)	Present (ongoing)	Aorist (simple)		Future (no aspect)		Perfect (combinative)	
Stem:	present stem -λυ-	aorist stem -λυσα-	passive stem -λυθ-	future stem -λυσ-	passive stem -λυθ-	perfect active stem -λελυκα-	perfect mid/pass stem -λελυ-
Voice:	A and M/P	A and M	P	A and M	P	A	M/P
PP:	1st	3rd	6th	2nd	6th	4th	5th

All forms of the perfect are built on one of the two perfect stems (the 4th and 5th Principal Parts). Let's see how.

1.2.1 The Perfect Indicative

As expected, the perfect indicative takes the meaning of the perfect system (ongoing relevance of a prior event) and adds *time* to form tenses. First, we meet the *principal* tense, called the 'perfect tense'.[3]

There are only four sets of verb endings: principal indicative tenses, historical indicative tenses, the imperative and the infinitive. All other verb forms borrow these (subjunctive, optative), or use adjective endings (participles).

Let's start with the perfect middle/passive. The perfect indicative **middle/passive** builds on the perfect middle/passive stem (reduplication, *no* κα). It takes the *principal* middle endings (**EH 8** 1.1), as expected. However, there is *no* thematic vowel. This means that there is no slippery sigma in the 2s, so the true ending -σαι appears, unlike in the present tense εσαι → ῃ (**EH 8** 1.1.2). This is easier to learn and recognise than the middle/passive endings we've met so far!

Embed this in the usual way by writing out the perfect indicative middle/passive, using the rules above and the endings you already know, checking against 'The Greek Verb So Far' for Chapter 16, in the **Online Material** (or *ENTG* 16.2).

The perfect indicative **active** builds on the perfect active stem (reduplication and κα). It takes the principal endings, as you would expect for a principal tense – but it is more regular than the principal endings you have seen so far. The perfect is easier to learn. Remember that the present indicative active *singular* endings have done something strange to their thematic vowels. Once you account for that, remembering that the thematic vowel of the perfect changes to α, you can see that the endings are the same. (Table 16.2.)

Table 16.2 Perfect Endings

	Present indicative active	Principal active ending	Perfect indicative active
1s	λύω	–	λέλυκα (1)
2s	λύεις	ς	λέλυκας
3s	λύει	–	λέλυκε(ν) (2)
1p	λύομεν	μεν	λελύκαμεν
2p	λύετε	τε	λελύκατε
3p	λύουσι(ν)	σι(ν) (3)	λελύκασι(ν)

(1) Converts thematic vowel as though there were an ending, like the aorist active indicative 1s.
(2) No ending, so no change to thematic vowel, like the aorist active indicative 3s.
(3) Sometimes the ending is ν (the historical, rather than principal, ending), as in the answers to exercise A11: ἑώρακαν vs ἑωράκασιν.

---

[3] In 'The Greek Verb So Far' for Chapter 16, in the **Online Material** (or *ENTG* 16.2), you can now see that the systems are lazily named after whichever tense is highest in its column! This causes confusion, especially because there is nothing 'present' about the 'present system'.

1 Before You Start: The Perfect System 267

Embed this in the usual way by writing out the perfect indicative active, using the rules above and the endings you already know, checking against 'The Greek Verb So Far' for Chapter 16, in the **Online Material** (or *ENTG* 16.2).

What does the perfect indicative mean? It is a <u>present</u> tense. Even though it refers to a past event, the <u>ongoing relevance</u> of that event is ongoing *now*.

> The perfect tense is a **present** tense: it tells you of the **present relevance** of a past event.

See Figure 16.2.

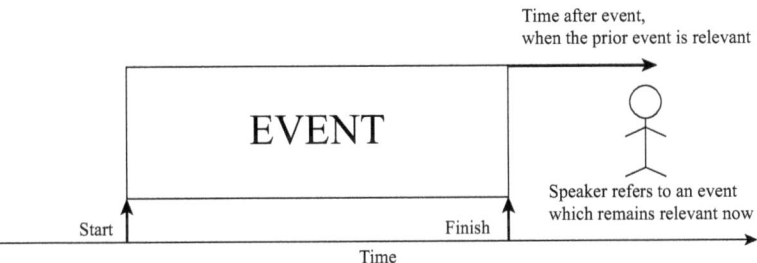

Figure 16.2 Perfect Indicative

ENTG covers the historical perfect tense later in the chapter.

1.2.2 The Perfect Participle

As you know, a participle is an adjective. The verb has two surnames: system and voice. That means that we now have two more adjectives: both perfect, but one active and one middle/passive (**EH 14** 1.1–2). They are:

    λελυκώς, -υῖα, -ός, λελυκότος
    λελυμένος, -η, -ον

Notice 'middle men' as usual. Make sure you can write out the perfect participles in full, from the above.

Now work your way through *ENTG* 16.2 and stop just before 16.2.2.

1.2.3 Before *ENTG* 16.2.2: Slippery Everything

You have met 'slippery sigma' and 'thlippery theta'. The perfect stem is even more prone to unexpected changes. Rather than try to predict them all, learning the

Principal Parts of a number of common verbs will give you a feel for the kind of thing that happens (they are in the vocab online and in the back of *ENTG* as 'Principal Parts'). There are rules and patterns which you could learn, but you've got enough on your plate.[4] For now, go with your gut.

Proceed to *ENTG* 16.2.2 and **Practice** 16.2 and **Half-Way Practice**.

Then proceed to *ENTG* 16.3 and stop before 16.3.2.

1.3 Before *ENTG* 16.3.2

ENTG 16.3.2 is very helpful and important. It points forward to the kind of **Extra Material** throughout this *Reader*, usually covered in second-year classes, that moves beyond one single meaning for each tense and case. Digest it carefully.

However, remember the difference between aspect and the nature of the event (**EH 6** 2.1; **EH 6** 4.2). The difference between the aorist and perfect isn't to do with the event being complete. The difference is that:

- the aorist *does not* imply anything about the present
- the perfect *does* imply a *present relevance*.

Proceed to *ENTG* 16.3.2 and **Practice** 16.3.

1.4 Before *ENTG* 16.4: The Historical Perfect Tense (Pluperfect)

The meaning of the perfect stem is:

> A **prior** event with some **ongoing relevance**.

In the indicative, combining with time, we get the principal tense, called the 'perfect indicative tense':

> The perfect tense is a **present** tense: it tells you of the **present relevance** of a past event.

What if we combine the aspect of the perfect system with past time? Then the *ongoing relevance* is in my past; the prior event is *prior to that relevance*.

'By the time we reached the bridge, *it had collapsed*.'

We call this tense the pluperfect.[5]

> The pluperfect tense is a **past** tense: it tells you of the **past relevance** of a prior event.

---

[4] See vS 72 or Mounce, *Morphology* 32, 45–6.
[5] *ENTG* tells you that there is no pluperfect outside the indicative. This isn't news to you: it is an indicative tense, the combination of the perfect system with past time. When the other moods use the label 'present' or 'aorist', that is not a tense, but a *system*. There is no pluperfect system.

1 Before You Start: The Perfect System

See Figure 16.3 on the pluperfect. You might find it helpful to compare with Figure 16.2 (p. 267).

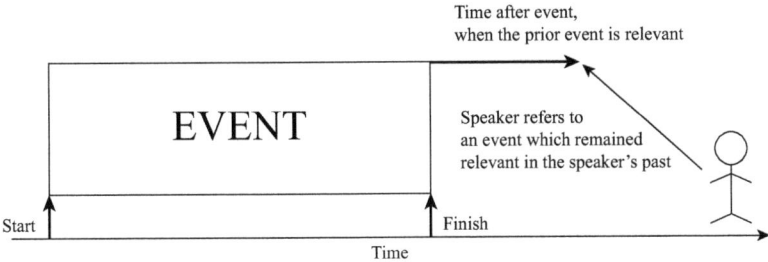

Figure 16.3 Pluperfect Indicative

1.4.1 Forming the Pluperfect

This is as expected. You build on the same stem: the perfect active, or the perfect middle/passive.

You add the augment, because it is a historical tense.

In the active, the thematic vowel is replaced by ει, and you use the **historical active** endings (**EH 11** 1.2.2).

In the middle/passive, there is no thematic vowel, and you use the **historical middle** endings.

The augment is sometimes left out, but you will be able to parse this accurately, nonetheless. As you can see in Table 16.3, the four combinations of time and voice are uniquely identified by **reduplication plus the information in the table**.

Table 16.3 Indicatives in the Perfect System

	Active	Middle/Passive
Principal (perfect tense)	κα suffix	principal middle endings
Historical (pluperfect tense)	κει suffix	historical middle endings[6]

Embed these by using the rules above to write out the pluperfect indicative, both active and middle/passive, checking against 'The Greek Verb So Far' for Chapter

---

[6] The middle 1p and 2p endings are identical; theoretically, a perfect middle 1p or 2p could be a pluperfect that hasn't got the augment; remember that authors make themselves clearly understood, and context is unlikely to let you down.

16, in the **Online Material** (or *ENTG* 16.4). Keep going until you don't get it wrong.

Now work through *ENTG* 16.4 and tackle **Practice 16.4**.

2 THE GREEK READINGS

2.1 Reading A: *Joseph & Aseneth* 20–1

The story so far …

Joseph's return is announced, and Aseneth makes herself ready, armed with confidence because of the heavenly assurance she received from her mysterious visitor. When Joseph sees her, he explains that he too has been told all about her from Heaven, and they embrace. But chastely …

(Be encouraged: the unedited chapters 20–1 of Joseph & Aseneth *are almost entirely within your reach, needing only a dozen words of vocab and hardly any grammar; I have edited it to provide you with practice on voice, participles and the perfect system, rather than to make the text intelligible.)*

20:1 Καὶ εἶπε πρὸς αὐτὸν Ἀσενέθ· Κύριε, εἴσελθε εἰς τὸν οἶκόν μου. κρατήσασα δὲ τὴν χεῖρα αὐτοῦ εἰσήγαγεν αὐτὸν εἰς τὴν οἰκίαν αὐτῆς. ² καὶ ᾔτηκει ὕδωρ νίψαι τοὺς πόδας αὐτοῦ. λέγει δὲ Ἰωσήφ· Κέκληκας μίαν τῶν διακονούσων σοι; ³ ἀλλὰ ἀπεκρίθη Ἀσενέθ· Οὐχί, κύριε, διότι αἱ χεῖρές μου χεῖρές σου καὶ οἱ πόδες σου πόδες μου. διὸ οὐ νίψει ἄλλη τοὺς πόδας σου. ἄρα ὁ Ἰωσήφ οὐκ ἐνίψατο.

⁴ καὶ Ἰωσήφ κατεφίλησε τὴν χεῖρα αὐτῆς καὶ Ἀσενέθ κατεφίλησε τὴν κεφαλὴν αὐτοῦ.

⁵ᵃ Ἐλθόντες δὲ οἱ γονεῖς τῆς Ἀσενέθ ἐκ τῆς χώρας εἶδον τὴν Ἀσενέθ καθεζομένην μετὰ τοῦ Ἰωσήφ καὶ ἐνδεδυμένην γάμου στολήν. ⁵ᵇ διὸ ἐχάρησαν καὶ ἐδόξασαν τὸν θεόν. καὶ προσενέγκαντες προσευχάς τε καὶ θυσίας ἔφαγον καὶ ἔπιον.

⁶ εἶπε δὲ Πεντεφρῆς πρὸς Ἰωσήφ· Ἐγὼ κέκληκα πάντας τοὺς ἄρχοντας τῶν φυλῶν καὶ ποιήσω ὑμῖν γάμους. ⁷ ἀλλὰ ἀπεκρίθη Ἰωσήφ ὅτι· Ἀπαγγελῶ

τῷ Φαραὼ περὶ τῆς Ἀσενέθ, διότι αὐτός ἐστι πατήρ μου. μὴ γὰρ οὖσα ἡ

παρουσία τοῦ Φαραώ, δοκήσει ὅτι πεφρονήκαμεν τὴν πορνείαν.

21:1 Ἰωσὴφ οὖν ἀπῆλθε πρὸς τὸν Φαραώ. ²ᵃ καὶ ἀπέστειλεν ὁ Φαραὼ καὶ

ἐκάλεσε τὸν Πεντεφρῆν καὶ τὴν Ἀσενέθ. ²ᵇ ἐτεθαυμάκει γὰρ ὁ Φαραὼ ἐπὶ τῇ

ἀκοῇ τῆς Ἀσενέθ. ⁴καὶ εἶπεν· Εὐλογηθῆτε ὑπὸ τοῦ θεοῦ τοῦ Ἰωσήφ.

⁵ καὶ ἐπίστρεψεν αὐτοὺς Φαραὼ ἐπὶ ἀλλήλους καὶ κατεφίλησαν ἀλλήλους.

⁶ ἐποίησε δὲ Φαραὼ γάμους αὐτῶν καὶ δεῖπνον ὡς ἑορτὴ ἡμέρας ἑπτά. ⁷ καὶ

ἐκήρυξε λέγων· Πᾶς ἄνθρωπος πάσης κώμης ὃς ποιήσει ἔργον ἐν ταῖς ἑπτὰ

ἡμέραις τοῦ γάμου θανάτῳ κακῷ ἀποθανεῖται. ⁸ ὅτε δὲ ὁ γάμος καὶ τὸ δεῖπνον

ἐτελέσθησαν, εἰσῆλθεν Ἰωσὴφ πρὸς Ἀσενέθ. καὶ συνέλαβεν Ἀσενὲθ ἐκ τοῦ

Ἰωσήφ. καὶ ἐτέχθησαν ὁ Μανασσῆ καὶ ὁ Ἐφραίμ.

2.1.1 Vocabulary

ἀποθνήσκω – Principal Parts: 2.
ἀποθανοῦμαι, 3. ἀπέθανον, 4.
ἀποτέθνηκα
γάμος, ου, ὁ – sing: marriage; pl:
wedding.
γονεύς, έως, ὁ – parent
δεῖπνον, ου, τό – banquet
εἰσφέρω – I bring in
καθέζομαι – I am sitting
καταφιλέω – I kiss

νίπτω –
active: I wash something/someone
(+ acc);
middle: I wash myself
στολή, ῆς, ἡ – gown
συν-λαμβάνω = συλλαμβάνω – I
conceive
τίκτω – I give birth; Principal Parts:
2. τέξομαι, 3. ἔτεκον, 4. τέτοκα,
6. ἐτέχθην

2.2 Reading B: John 3:3–13

In each chapter from now on, we will have a short reading from the GNT. Unlike Joseph & Aseneth, they will be unedited (apart from occasional punctuation), with vocab and annotations for anything that you cannot yet know. Be encouraged: there is little vocab here which you don't know, and only a couple of bits of grammar, which you'll cover in the next few chapters.
As with Philemon in Chapter 11, notes point you to prior material.

³Ἀπεκρίθη ὁ Ἰησοῦς καὶ εἶπεν αὐτῷ· Ἀμὴν ἀμὴν λέγω σοι, ἐὰν μή τις γεννηθῇ ἄνωθεν, οὐ δύναται ἰδεῖν τὴν βασιλείαν τοῦ Θεοῦ.

⁴λέγει πρὸς αὐτὸν ὁ Νικόδημος, Πῶς δύναται ἄνθρωπος γεννηθῆναι γέρων ὤν; μὴ δύναται εἰς τὴν κοιλίαν τῆς μητρὸς αὐτοῦ δεύτερον εἰσελθεῖν καὶ γεννηθῆναι;

⁵ἀπεκρίθη ὁ Ἰησοῦς, Ἀμὴν ἀμὴν λέγω σοι, ἐὰν μή τις γεννηθῇ ἐξ ὕδατος καὶ Πνεύματος, οὐ δύναται εἰσελθεῖν εἰς τὴν βασιλείαν τοῦ Θεοῦ.

⁶τὸ γεγεννημένον ἐκ τῆς σαρκὸς σάρξ ἐστι· καὶ τὸ γεγεννημένον ἐκ τοῦ πνεύματος πνεῦμά ἐστι. ⁷μὴ θαυμάσῃς ὅτι εἶπόν σοι· Δεῖ ὑμᾶς γεννηθῆναι ἄνωθεν. ⁸τὸ πνεῦμα ὅπου θέλει πνεῖ, καὶ τὴν φωνὴν αὐτοῦ ἀκούεις, ἀλλ' οὐκ οἶδας πόθεν ἔρχεται καὶ ποῦ ὑπάγει· οὕτως ἐστὶ πᾶς ὁ γεγεννημένος ἐκ τοῦ πνεύματος.

⁹ἀπεκρίθη Νικόδημος καὶ εἶπεν αὐτῷ· Πῶς δύναται ταῦτα γενέσθαι;

¹⁰ἀπεκρίθη ὁ Ἰησοῦς καὶ εἶπεν αὐτῷ· Σὺ εἶ ὁ διδάσκαλος τοῦ Ἰσραήλ, καὶ ταῦτα οὐ γινώσκεις; ¹¹ἀμὴν ἀμὴν λέγω σοι ὅτι ὃ οἴδαμεν λαλοῦμεν, καὶ ὃ ἑωράκαμεν μαρτυροῦμεν· καὶ τὴν μαρτυρίαν ἡμῶν οὐ λαμβάνετε. ¹²εἰ τὰ ἐπίγεια εἶπον ὑμῖν καὶ οὐ πιστεύετε, πῶς ἐὰν εἴπω ὑμῖν τὰ ἐπουράνια, πιστεύσετε; ¹³καὶ οὐδεὶς ἀναβέβηκεν εἰς τὸν οὐρανόν, εἰ μὴ ὁ ἐκ τοῦ οὐρανοῦ καταβάς, ὁ υἱὸς τοῦ ἀνθρώπου ὁ ὢν ἐν τῷ οὐρανῷ.

2.2.1 Vocabulary

ἄνωθεν – from above, again
δύναμαι – I am able [requires a complementary infinitive]

γεννάω – I beget, give birth to [parse it as though it were γεννέω]
γέρων, οντος, ὁ – old man

ἐπίγειος, ον – earthly (ἐπί + γῆ)
ἐπουράνιος, ον – heavenly (ἐπί + οὐρανός)
κοιλία, ας, ἡ – womb

πνέω – I blow (*move like wind*, or *exhale*)
ὁράω – **Principal Parts: 2. ὄψομαι, 3. εἶδον, 4. ἑώρακα, 6. ὤφθην**
οὕτως – in this way [cf. EM 10 7]

3   CONSOLIDATION: THREE-QUARTERS OF THE MATERIAL COVERED!

Since we're three-quarters of the way through the *Reader*, we will consolidate and review Chapters 1–16 by reading more of *Joseph & Aseneth*.

In the notes, I will generally not ask you questions, but point you to where you should look and revise if you're unsure how to handle a point of Greek. Unlike the questions in the **Readings** so far, I haven't limited myself to matters that are either recent or particularly hard. Rather, I have tried to help review as much of *ENTG* as possible with constant cross-references.

If you have a mid-semester exam to face, use **Reading C** for revision. Enjoy!

3.1   Reading C: *Joseph & Aseneth* 22–3

The story so far …

Joseph and Aseneth have married and produced Manasseh and Ephraim, and are set to live happily ever after. Right?

(Transliterate any proper nouns that you don't recognise.)

22:1 Καὶ ἐγένετο μετὰ ταῦτα καὶ ἐτελέσθη τὰ ἑπτὰ ἔτη τῆς εὐθηνίας. ² ὡς δὲ ἐλαλήθη τῷ Ἰακὼβ τὰ περὶ Ἰωσὴφ τοῦ υἱοῦ αὐτοῦ, εἰσῆλθεν εἰς Αἴγυπτον σὺν πάσῃ τῇ οἰκίᾳ αὐτοῦ ἐν τῷ δευτέρῳ μηνὶ μιᾷ καὶ δέκα τοῦ μηνός, καὶ κατῴκησεν ἐν γῇ Γεσέμ. ³ καὶ εἶπεν Ἀσενὲθ πρὸς Ἰωσήφ· Πορεύσομαι καὶ ὄψομαι τὸν πατέρα σου, διότι ὁ πατήρ σου Ἰσραὴλ πατήρ μού ἐστιν. ἄρα εἶπεν αὐτῇ Ἰωσήφ· Πορευσόμεθα. ⁴ ἦλθεν δὲ Ἰωσὴφ καὶ Ἀσενὲθ ἐν γῇ Γεσέμ καὶ ἤγγισαν αὐτοῖς οἱ ἀδελφοὶ Ἰωσὴφ καὶ προσεκύνησαν ἐπὶ τὴν γῆν. ⁵·καὶ ἐλθόντες πρὸς Ἰακὼβ εὐλογήθησαν ὑπὸ αὐτοῦ καὶ κατεφίλησεν αὐτούς.

⁶ καὶ μετὰ ταῦτα ἔφαγον καὶ ἔπιον. ⁷ ἐπορεύθησαν δὲ Ἰωσὴφ καὶ Ἀσενὲθ εἰς τὸν οἶκον αὐτῶν καὶ προέπεμψαν αὐτοὺς Συμεὼν καὶ Λευίς, διότι ἐφθόνουν οἱ μισοῦντες. ⁸ καὶ ἐκράτησεν Ἀσενὲθ τὴν χεῖρα Λευί, διότι ἐφίλει αὐτὸν ὡς ἄνδρα προφήτην καὶ φοβούμενον τὸν κύριον, ⁹ διότι αὐτὸς ἔβλεπε ῥήματα γεγραμμένα ἐν τῷ οὐρανῷ καὶ ἀνεγίνωσκεν αὐτὰ καὶ ἀπεκάλυπτεν αὐτὰ τῇ Ἀσενέθ. 23:1 Ἀλλὰ ἰδὼν τὴν Ἀσενὲθ ὁ υἱὸς Φαραὼ ὁ πρῶτος ἐμίσει. ² καὶ προσεκαλέσατο τὸν Συμεὼν καὶ τὸν Λευὶ ἀποστέλλων ἀγγέλους ἔχοντας ἐπιστολήν.

³ᵃ διὸ ἦλθον πρὸς αὐτὸν καὶ λέγει αὐτοῖς ὁ υἱὸς Φαραώ· ³ᵇ Γινώσκω ὅτι ἐστὲ ἄνδρες δυνατοὶ ὑπὲρ πάντας ἀνθρώπους καὶ ἐν ταῖς χερσὶν ὑμῶν ἀνῃρέθη ἡ πόλις τῶν Σικιμιτῶν ³ᶜ καὶ ἐν ταῖς δυσὶ μαχαίραις ὑμῶν ἀπέθανον δώδεκα χιλιάδες ἀνδρῶν τῆς περιτομῆς· ⁴ᵃ παρακαλῶ δὲ ὑμᾶς ἐν τῇ ἀσθενείᾳ μου· ⁴ᵇ ἰδοὺ λάβετε χρυσίον πολὺν καὶ ἀργύριον καὶ δώδεκα θρόνους καὶ δέκα παῖδας καὶ τέσσαρας οἴκους, ⁴ᶜ καὶ ποιήσατε μετ' ἐμοῦ ἔλεος, ⁴ᵈ διότι ἐσκανδαλίσθην ἐγὼ ὑπὸ τοῦ ἀδελφοῦ ὑμῶν Ἰωσήφ, ⁴ᵉ διότι ἔλαβεν αὐτὸς τὴν Ἀσενὲθ εἰς γυναῖκα.

⁵ᵃ ἆρα νῦν ὀμνύετε ἀποκτεῖναι Ἰωσὴφ ἐν τῇ μαχαίρῃ. ⁵ᵇ τότε χήρα ἔσται καὶ μετὰ χρόνον τῆς ὑπομονῆς λήψομαι τὴν Ἀσενὲθ εἰς γυναῖκα, ⁵ᶜ καὶ ἔσεσθε ὑμεῖς ἀδελφοί ἀγαπητοί μου εἰς τέλος. ⁶ᵃ εἰ δὲ κωλύετέ μου τὰ ῥήματα, ἀποκτενῶ ὑμᾶς. ⁶ᵇ καὶ ταῦτα λέγων ἔλαβε τὴν μαχαίραν αὐτοῦ. ⁷ Ὁ δὲ Συμεὼν θέλων ἀποκτεῖναι τὸν υἱὸν Φαραὼ ἐλάμβανε τὴν ἑαυτοῦ μαχαίραν. ⁸ᵃ ἀλλὰ ἔγνω Λευὶς τὴν ἀσθένειαν Συμεὼν καὶ ὅτι πειράζεται, ⁸ᵇ διότι Λευὶς ἦν προφήτης καὶ ἑωράκει πάντα τὰ μέλλοντα. ⁹ᵃ εἶπεν οὖν Λευὶς πρὸς αὐτόν· ⁹ᵇ Ἡμεῖς ἀνδρὸς

δικαίου παῖδές ἐσμεν, ⁹ᶜ καὶ οἱ δίκαιοι οὐ ποιοῦσι κακὸν ἀντὶ κακοῦ τῷ πλησίον αὐτῶν.

¹⁰ᵃ Καὶ εἶπε Λευὶς πρὸς τὸν πλησίον αὐτοῦ τὸν υἱὸν Φαραὼ ἱλαρῷ τῷ προσώπῳ· ¹⁰ᵇ Διὰ τί σύ, κύριέ μου, λαλεῖς τὰ ῥήματα ταῦτα ἐνώπιον ἡμῶν; ¹⁰ᶜ καὶ ἡμεῖς ἐσμεν ἄνδρες δουλεύοντες τὸν θεὸν καὶ Ἰωσήφ ἐστιν ἀγαπητὸς τοῦ θεοῦ. ¹¹ᵃ πῶς οὖν ποιήσομεν τὸ πονηρὸν τοῦτο; ¹¹ᵇ καὶ νῦν ἄκουσον ἡμῶν καὶ φύλαξαι μὴ λαλῆσαι ἔτι περὶ τοῦ Ἰωσήφ ταῦτα τὰ ῥήματα. ¹³ᵃ τότε δέ λαβόντες τὰς μαχαίρας αὐτῶν εἶπον· Οὐχ ἑώρακας τὰς μαχαίρας ταύτας; ¹³ᵇ ἐν αὐταῖς ἐξεδίκησε κύριος ὁ θεὸς τὴν ἁμαρτίαν τῶν υἱῶν Ἰσραήλ, ¹³ᶜ ἣν ἐποίησαν Σικιμῖται κατὰ τῆς ἀδελφῆς ἡμῶν Δῖνα, ¹³ᵈ ἣν ἠδίκησεν Συχὲμ ὁ υἱὸς Ἐμμώρ.

¹⁴ᵃ ὅτε δὲ εἶδεν ὁ υἱὸς Φαραὼ τὰς μαχαίρας αὐτῶν ἐφοβηθεὶς ἔκραξεν· Οὐαί μοι. ¹⁴ᵇ καὶ κλαίων ἔπεσεν ἐπὶ πρόσωπον ἐπὶ τὴν γῆν ὑπὸ τοὺς πόδας αὐτῶν.

¹⁵ᵃ Λευὶς δέ τε καὶ Συμεὼν ἤγειραν αὐτὸν λέγων· ¹⁵ᵇ Μὴ φοβοῦ, πλὴν φύλαξαι μὴ λαλῆσαι κατὰ τοῦ ἀδελφοῦ ἡμῶν ῥῆμα πονηρόν. ¹⁶ οὕτως ἐξῆλθον ἀπ' αὐτοῦ καταλείποντες αὐτὸν κλαίοντα καὶ φοβούμενον.

3.1.1 Vocabulary

ἀδικέω – I wrong
ἀναιρέω – I destroy
ἀντί: in the place of (+ gen)
ἀργύριον, ου, τό – silver
δυνατός, ή, όν – powerful
ἐκδικέω – I avenge
εὐθηνία, ας, ἡ – plenty
ἱλαρός, ά, όν – cheerful

καταφιλέω – I kiss
λαμβάνω – I take; Principal Parts: 2. λήμψομαι
μήν, μηνός, ὁ – month
ὁράω – I see; Principal Parts: 2. ὄψομαι; 3. εἶδον 4. ἑώρακα
πλησίον, ὁ⁷ – neighbour
προπέμπω – I accompany

---

⁷ You would expect either πλησίος, ὁ or πλησίον τό. What we have here is an adjective (πλησίος α ον), meaning 'adjacent', which then became the adverb πλησίον, meaning

τελέω – Principal Parts: 2. τελέσω; 3 ἐτέλεσα; 4 τετέλεκα; 5 τετέλεσμαι; 6 ἐτελέσθην

φθονέω – I am jealous
χρυσίον, ου, τό – gold

4 MORE ON THE PERFECT SYSTEM

4.1 The Perfect Indicative: History

FURTHER READING: SCHWYZER-DEBRUNNER II:263

A quick overview of how the perfect tense evolved over time will help us to understand two things:[8]

- Why the perfect combines features of the aorist (past event, simple aspect) and the present (present relevance).
- Why some verbs in the perfect don't have the standard meaning 'past event with ongoing relevance'.

Originally, the perfect tense only applied to states, rather than actions: it was the present tense for states. There was no reference to any past event: it purely referred to the present state.

Secondly, a natural extension of that meaning came about: 'I am hot because I have been heated' or 'I am king because I have been crowned'. It remained a present tense, and only of states, but it referred to a prior event that had led to the present state: 'I have been crowned', 'I have been heated'.

Thirdly, the requirement that the verb be a state loosened. It could be used of any verb at all, and it simultaneously referred to a past event and to some ongoing present relevance. This is the meaning that it has most often in the Greek of the NT and for centuries either side (including Classical Greek and the early Greek Fathers). It is the meaning presented in *ENTG* and in **EH 16** 1.

Fourthly, the sense of ongoing relevance was lost, and it came simply to refer to a past event, with simple aspect. It became identical to the aorist, and eventually disappeared from the language as redundant.

There was a gradual shift from one pole (present relevance) to another (past event). The meaning you're most familiar with has the perfect holding on to both poles. See Table 16.4 and Figure 16.4.

'adjacent'. From that evolved the indeclinable noun we have, meaning 'one who is adjacent', that is, 'neighbour'.

[8] This overview skips over all manner of intermediate stages, because they are not relevant to the meanings of the perfect that remain. A fuller account, which includes the intermediate stages very compactly, is Schwyzer-Debrunner II:263 (I am indebted to Dean Anderson for pointing me to it); the same evolution, in more or less detail, is found in the following: Rutger Allan, 'Tense and Aspect in Classical Greek', *GVR*, 110–13; Klaas Bentein, 'Perfect', *EAGLL*, 3:47–9; Robert Crellin, 'The Semantics of the Perfect', *GVR*, 440–54. Not all agree on whether the first stage existed in Greek; making the case that it existed at least in the parent language of Greek: Sihler §510.

4 More on the Perfect System

Table 16.4 Evolution of the Perfect

Age when the meaning begins to appear	Stage	Past event	Present relevance	Paraphrase
pre-Classical	1	-	present state	I am in the state
Classical	2	prior event resulting in: →	present state	I have entered the state
Koine	3	prior event resulting in: →	any ongoing relevance	The event has happened
Post-NT	4	past event only	-	The event happened

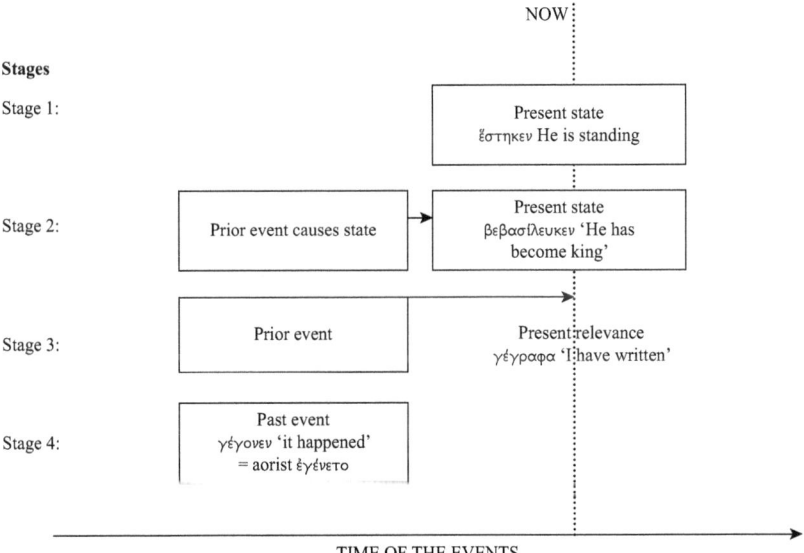

Figure 16.4 The Four Historical Stages of Meaning of the Perfect Compared

The first two of these stages leave us some fossils, and we meet them in the GNT. The fourth stage may or may not have begun by the time of the GNT. The third stage remains by far the most common.

4.2 Main Uses and Contexts of the Perfect Indicative

FURTHER READING: VS 200; FANNING 4.5; MURAOKA 28E; CGCG 33.34–33.38

Be aware that Classical grammars have labels for the stages we've described above which clash with the syntax labels used in NT grammars.

4.2.1 Default Perfect

FURTHER READING: FANNING 4.5.1; B-D-R 341; VS 200A; CF. WALLACE 577

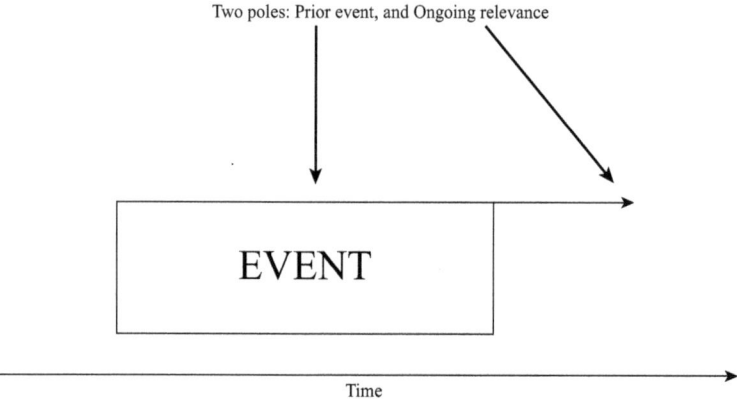

Figure 16.5 Default Perfect

This is the standard and most common meaning, as described in *ENTG* and in **EH 16** 1. It is the third of the stages in **EM 16** 4.1. A completed prior event with ongoing relevance (see Figure 16.5). Like the aorist, the subject has performed or experienced the action. Unlike the aorist, the focus is some present relevance of that action. The nature of that relevance needs to be inferred by the reader. In the examples below, I'll insert (what I think) the relevance is in italics. Notice that in each example below, there is some **explicit consequence**, but it only works once you've worked out the *implicit ongoing relevance*.

> ἡ πίστις ὑμῶν ἡ πρὸς τὸν Θεὸν <u>ἐξελήλυθεν</u>, **ὥστε** μὴ χρείαν ἡμᾶς ἔχειν λαλεῖν τι. 1 Thess 1:8
> Your faith in God <u>has gone out</u>, **so that** there is no need for us to say anything.
> The perfect tells you two things: 1. It went out in the past. 2. There is an ongoing relevance, which you need to work out. You could guess at various possibilities, but the rest of the sentence gives a big clue, so that we can paraphrase:

4 More on the Perfect System

'Your faith in God has gone out *with the ongoing relevance that people have heard about it,* **so that** *there is no need for us to say anything.*'

Οὐ γὰρ προσεληλύθατε ψηλαφωμένῳ ὄρει ... ἀλλὰ προσεληλύθατε Σιὼν ὄρει ... καὶ αἵματι ῥαντισμοῦ κρείττονα λαλοῦντι παρὰ τὸ Ἄβελ. **βλέπετε** μὴ παραιτήσησθε τὸν λαλοῦντα. Heb 12:18–25
For you have not come to a mountain that can be handled ... but you have come to Mt Zion ... and to the sprinkled blood that speaks better than Abel *and you are still there, in his presence, and Jesus (rather than Moses) is still speaking to you (from Zion, not Sinai).* **See to it** *that you do not reject the one who speaks* [*i.e. Jesus, not Moses*].

καὶ αἱ βοαὶ τῶν θερισάντων εἰς τὰ ὦτα Κυρίου Σαβαὼθ εἰσεληλύθασιν. Jas 5:4
And the cries of those who harvest have come to the ears of the Lord of Hosts *which means that he is conscious of the injustice and will act on it* [*explaining why the start of the paragraph tells the guilty to weep* **because** *of the judgment that is coming for their crimes*]

γέγραφα δὲ πρὸς αὐτὸν τὰ ὑπογεγραμμένα. παρακαλῶ **οὖν** ὑμᾶς ... συντηρεῖν τὴν οὖσαν εὔνοιαν εἰς ἐμὲ καὶ τὸν υἱόν. 2 Macc 9:25–6
I have written to [my son] the things written here *which means that he knows what I want him to do, which are the things causing your good will towards me.* **Therefore**, I exhort you ... to keep your existing good will towards not only me, but also my son.

Sometimes the relevance is entirely inferred from the wider setting or the nature of the people involved. This is especially obvious in judicial contexts (where responsibility is the relevance) or logical arguments (where a premise is relevant as building to the conclusion):

Ἵνα τί ἀποθνήσκει; τί πεποίηκεν; 1 Kgdms 20:32
Why should he die? What has he done?
The issue is judicial culpability for what he has done.

ὃ ὠφείλομεν ποιῆσαι πεποιήκαμεν. Luke 17:10
that which we were required to do, we have done *which means we have discharged our responsibility and are eligible for a reward.*[9]

πεπλήρωκεν ἐντολὴν δικαιοσύνης· ὁ γὰρ ἔχων ἀγάπην μακράν ἐστιν πάσης ἁμαρτίας. Pol. Phil. 3.3

---

[9] In this particular context, the point is that they have *only* done what was required and therefore *don't* deserve a reward.

He has fulfilled the righteous commandment *and therefore has earned the righteousness required*: for whoever has love, is far from all sin.¹⁰

Οὐ πεποιημένης δὲ τὰς τριήρεις, γέγραφεν δοῦναι τὴν δωρειάν Demosthenes, *Andr.* 22.16
But despite the fact that the triremes hadn't been constructed, he wrote to pay the cost.

The first perfect (a participle, probably with concessive sense) has obvious relevance: you should only pay when the work has been done, so to pay *when it hasn't* been is corruption.

The second perfect shows that the official who paid is *now guilty* of corruption, because he paid. (Notice that English won't allow a perfect here: **EM 16** 4.3.3.)

τῆς μὲν γραφῆς ἠκούσατε ἣν ἐγραψάμην ἄνδρες δικασταί· δεινότατα γὰρ ἔργων δέδρακε Aristophanes, *Vesp.* 907–9 (simplified)
Hear the indictment that I have prepared,¹¹ gentlemen of the jury: for he has committed the most heinous of deeds.

τὸν ἀγῶνα τὸν καλὸν ἠγώνισμαι, τὸν δρόμον τετέλεκα, τὴν πίστιν τετήρηκα· λοιπὸν, ἀπόκειταί μοι ὁ τῆς δικαιοσύνης στέφανος 2 Tim 4:7–8
The good fight I have fought, the race I have completed, the faith I have kept: as for the rest, the crown of righteousness is reserved for me.

ἀπεκρίθη ὁ Πιλάτος, Ὅ γέγραφα, γέγραφα. John 19:22
Pilate answered: 'What I have written, I have written.'

The first perfect is relevant because it is what they are reading on the inscription above the cross. The second one is relevant because it means 'case closed', which Pilate can do by virtue of his authority.

Notice that the prior event is viewed with 'simple' aspect, like the aorist. That means that, if the event is an action with an endpoint, the use of the perfect implies that the endpoint was reached.

Ἰδοὺ λαὸς ἐξελήλυθεν ἐξ Αἰγύπτου, Num 22:5
Look: a nation has exited out of Egypt.

To leave a place has an endpoint: once you're no longer there. This perfect tells us both that the exit was successful and that it remains relevant, as the rest of Balak's message to Balaam will show.

---

¹⁰ What is in view is that no one would do that, but for the sake of argument, that is the logic.
¹¹ Note the 'constative' English idiom for the aorist (**EM 7** 5.2.2).

4.2.2 Resultative Perfect (with Verbs of Result)

FURTHER READING: FANNING 3.1.2.4.4.C; B-D-R 342;
MICHAEL AUBREY, 'THE GREEK PERFECT', *LNTG*, CH. 3;
CGCG 33.34; RIJKSBARON 10.1; CF. WALLACE 574–6

You know that some verbs describe states, rather than actions: ὑγιαίνω 'I am in good health'. However, some verbs which do describe actions *produce a state*, either in the subject or the object. Ἰάομαι 'I heal' changes the state of its object, and that new state is described by ὑγιαίνω 'I am in good health'. Examples include: ἀπόλλυμαι, ἀποθνῄσκω, ἀποκτείνω, ἐλευθερόω, εὑρίσκω, ἰάομαι, καθαρίζω, λαμβάνω, νεκρόω, πωλέω (as discussed in EH 7 5.2.1).

With such verbs, the perfect often (but not always) loses sight of the prior action and focusses entirely on the ongoing relevance. The completed action of the verb *results in a new state*, and that is the ongoing relevance.[12]

The *aorist* would mean that the change of state happened, but not necessarily that the resulting state remains. The perfect does mean that the resulting state continues. See Figure 16.6.

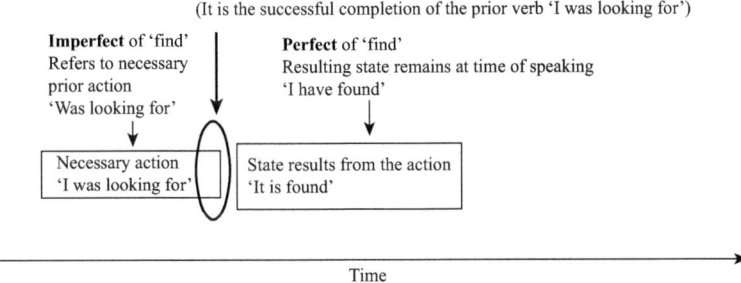

Figure 16.6 Result Verbs

> Καὶ εἰσελθὼν εἶπεν τῷ πατρί Ἰδοὺ εὕρηκα ὃς συνπορεύσεταί μοι Tob 5:9
> Going in, he said to his father: 'Look, <u>I have found</u> one who will go with me.'
> Both the completion of the action and the consequence are expressed: the search is over, and he has a companion.

> χάριτί ἐστε σεσῳσμένοι Eph 2:5
> By grace <u>you have been saved</u>
> The context, before and after, is a recounting of the one-off events that saved us, described with aorists. However, this perfect, and the nearly identical one a few verses later (v8), are a foretaste of Paul's exposition of what it means *to be in a saved state now*.

---

[12] Such verbs are sometimes called 'climaxes'.

δίψυχοί εἰσιν· οὔτε γὰρ ζῶσιν οὔτε τεθνήκασιν. Herm. Sim. 8.7.1
they are in two minds, for neither do they live, nor are they dead.
> There is no sense here of 'they have died'; the perfect is used in parallel with the state ζῶσιν. See also Matt 2:20.

ἡ γὰρ ὕπανδρος γυνὴ τῷ ζῶντι ἀνδρὶ δέδεται Rom 7:2
For the married woman is bound to her living husband
> There is no reference here to her *having been* bound; the point is that she continues to be bound while her husband lives. The purpose of the analogy is to show that the *binding ends* when the husband dies; the prior act of binding is irrelevant.

Even with such verbs, the past event can remain in view and be even more prominent than the ongoing state:

Ἐλάτεια κατείληπται. Demosthenes, *Cor.* 18.169
Elateia has fallen.
> The point is not so much the fallen condition of Elateia, but the news that the enemy has attacked and captured the city.

4.2.3 Perfect with States

FURTHER READING: FANNING 4.5.1.1

Consider verbs which express a state, rather than an action. The *present* tells us that I am currently in the state: βασιλεύω 'I am king'.

The *aorist* of states is ambiguous in two ways, as we know. First, it can refer to the entry to the state, and normally implies that you are still in the state ('ingressive'). However, rarely, it can mean that you entered the state for a while and then left it. Ἐβασίλευσεν in 1 Esd 1 means 'he became king' and 'he was king for a while', referring to different kings (see **EM 7** 5.1.2). Second, as we keep seeing, the aorist neither confirms nor denies that there is an ongoing relevance to the past action.

The *perfect* removes all ambiguity. It states categorically that you remain in the state (which the aorist doesn't say), and refers to a time when you entered it (which the present doesn't tell you).[13]

---

[13] Classical Greek used the perfect of states to intensify the meaning (see *CGCG* 33.37; Rijksbaron 10.1; Fanning 4.5.1.1):

πολλὰ δὲ **θαυμάζων** [present] Λεπτίνου κατὰ τὸν νόμον, ἐν μάλιστα τεθαύμακα [perfect] πάντων ... Demosthenes, *Lept.* 143
While **I am amazed** at many things from Leptines, concerning his law, I am utterly astonished at one more than all the others ...

While this use doesn't occur in the GNT, some NT grammars do use this same label 'intensive perfect', but to refer to something quite different.

Ἐν τῷ ἀκοῦσαι ὑμᾶς τὴν φωνὴν τῆς κερατίνης καὶ ἐρεῖτε Βεβασίλευκεν βασιλεὺς Ἀβεσσαλὼμ ἐν Χεβρών. 2 Kgdms 15:10

The moment you hear the blast of the horn you are to say: 'King Absalom has become king at Hebron.'

The event in question is a sort-of coronation, and the ongoing relevance is that he is now the king, but both are central to the proclamation. The prior event explains the new state.

See Figures 16.7, 16.8.

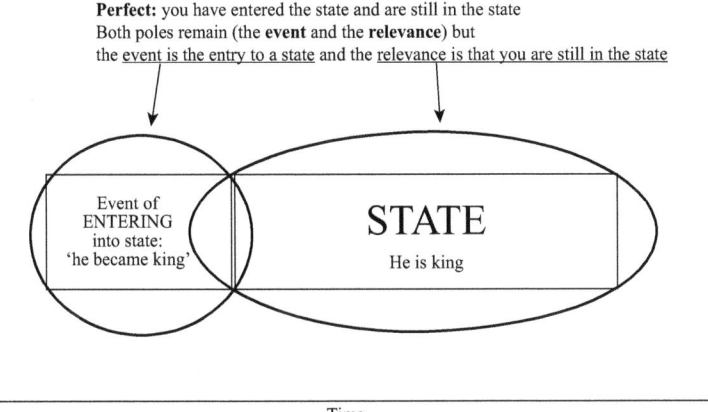

Figure 16.7 Perfect of States

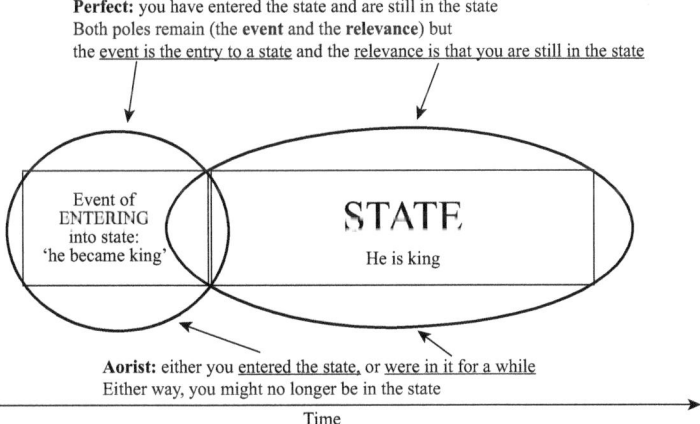

Figure 16.8 Aorist vs Perfect of States

Notice the difference between the aorist and perfect of *states* and of *verbs of result* (figure 16.6 in **EM 16** 4.2.2). With states, the meaning of the verb is the state

(I am king); we don't know how you enter the state, but the perfect implies that you have (I have become king) and the aorist can refer to that event (I became king). With verbs of result, the meaning of the verb *is the entry to the state* (I killed, I healed), and the state itself is only implied.

Further examples:

> οἶδα γὰρ ᾧ <u>πεπίστευκα</u>, καὶ πέπεισμαι ὅτι … 2 Tim 1:12
> for I know in whom <u>I have put my trust</u>, and am convinced that …
> > πεπίστευκα doesn't merely mean that I believe now, but points me back to a definitive event of making my mind up. On πέπεισμαι, see **EM 16** 4.4.2.

> ἔστιν ὁ κατηγορῶν ὑμῶν Μωσῆς,[14] εἰς ὃν ὑμεῖς <u>ἠλπίκατε</u> John 5:45
> There is one who accuses you: Moses, in whom <u>you have put your hope</u> *and the irony is that you continue to hope in him even though he is the one accusing you.*

> ἡ δὲ ὄντως χήρα καὶ μεμονωμένη <u>ἤλπικεν</u> ἐπὶ τὸν Θεόν … ἡ δὲ σπαταλῶσα, ζῶσα τέθνηκε 1 Tim 5:5–6
> the one who is a widow and left to herself <u>has put her hope</u> in God *and continues to hope in him, because she has no one else to help her … As for the one who indulges herself, she is dead even while she lives.*
> > On τέθνηκε, see **EM 16** 4.2.2.

4.3 Greek vs English

We need to keep our focus on the meaning conveyed in Greek texts, and not on the problems caused by translation.[15]

4.3.1 Perfect vs Present in English (Beware: 'Intensive' vs 'Extensive')

The Greek perfect combines a past event with a present relevance. An author may well want to put more stress on the past event or on the present relevance: as you read the examples in **EM 16** 4.2.1, you can probably see the emphasis being more towards one or the other in each case. If you feel that the emphasis is strongly one way, you might want to convey that in English translation: 'you *are* saved' rather than 'you *have been* saved'. However, resist the temptation to call this perfect by some label, as though you were identifying a point of *Greek*. What some grammars divide into 'intensive' vs 'extensive' is simply the **default** perfect in *Greek*, but with emphases that generate differences in *English*.[16]

---

[14] A variant spelling.
[15] We have seen the same principle in **EM 7** 5.2.2.
[16] For example, Wallace 574–7.

4.3.2 Greek Perfect vs Greek Aorist Illustrated

ἡ πίστις σου σέσωκέ [perfect] σε. καὶ ἐσώθη [aorist] ἡ γυνὴ ἀπὸ τῆς ὥρας ἐκείνης. Matt 9:22
'Your faith has healed you.' And she was healed from that hour.

Jesus' words to the woman address her desire to be well; so he assures her that her faith hasn't merely brought about an act of healing, but that it has left her in a healed state (the ongoing relevance of the act). Matthew's report of the action to his readers is less interested in the ongoing state of the woman than in the miraculous act of healing.

The Greek author's choice between aorist and perfect is not because of a difference in the event, or even a difference in the ongoing effects of the event; it is the *author's choice* to emphasise an ongoing relevance or not.[17]

As we will see next, English binds the author more than Greek does: you can't use a perfect in certain circumstances, and you must use one in others. Greek has a free choice, which makes the perfect less common but also more significant.

4.3.3 Perfect vs Past Simple in English

FURTHER READING: VS 200D

In **EM 7** 5.2.2 we discussed the difference between the Greek and English perfects. English is much less free to use a perfect than Greek is. It has to be used when the time of the action includes 'now' and cannot be used otherwise. That means that English speakers have to rearrange their sentences to make or avoid the point that the perfect makes: ongoing relevance.

When translating, rather than understanding, Greek, this causes problems. We discussed the so-called 'constative' aorist, where English forces a perfect that is not intended in Greek (**EM 7** 5.2.2). Let me remind you again that translation is not your aim, but reading Greek with understanding. There is no notion of 'constative' in the Greek text, but it is forced on you by English grammar.

Now we see a similar problem: a perfect in Greek that translators feel is too pointed in English:

ὅτε δὲ γέγονα ἀνήρ, κατήργηκα τὰ τοῦ νηπίου 1 Cor 13:11
but when I became a grown-man, I set aside what is childish ['the things of a child']
The English 'when I have become ... I have set aside' would mean something else.

Particularly in epistles, there is a tendency for translators to choose to set aside the force of the perfect even when English will allow it. This seems to be particularly

---

[17] As a result, some would argue that this is the most fruitful tense for the exegete to understand (MH I:140–1). Accordingly, this chapter gives much more space to understanding the perfect than to chapters on other verb forms.

true when the author is narrating historical events. At that point, it is particularly important to pay attention: the author is emphatically flagging up the ongoing relevance of a historical action:

> [Following a number of aorists retelling the events of salvation, vv11–14] καὶ αὐτὸ ἦρκεν ἐκ τοῦ μέσου, προσηλώσας αὐτὸ τῷ σταυρῷ Col 2:14
> ... and this he has set aside from our midst, nailing it to the cross. Many translations have 'he set aside', losing the sense that this setting aside had an ongoing relevance for Paul's readers.

English forces a choice between opposites. An aorist verb cannot mean what a perfect verb means, and vice versa. However, the Greek aorist *does not deny* what the Greek perfect tells you.

An author using the perfect tells you that there is an ongoing relevance, and invites you to find it. When the author uses the aorist, he does *not deny* that there is some ongoing relevance. This makes the Greek perfect relatively rare, and that much more interesting when you find it.

4.4 Minor Matters

4.4.1 Aoristic

> FURTHER READING: B-D-R 342; WALLACE 578–9; vS 200F

This is the fourth of the stages in **EM 16** 4.1.[18] It is disputed whether this had begun by the time of the GNT, and it is certainly rare in the GNT. See Figure 16.9.

For example:[19]

> καὶ εἴληφεν ὁ ἄγγελος τὸ λιβανωτόν Rev 8:5
> The angel picked up the censer.

> ὃς εὑρὼν ἕνα πολύτιμον μαργαρίτην, ἀπελθὼν πέπρακε πάντα ὅσα εἶχε. Matt 13:46
> ... who, on finding one most precious pearl, went and sold everything, as much as he had.

Remember, though, that the relevance of the perfect is often something that needs to be inferred. The fact that we can't spot it doesn't necessarily mean that there is none to find. For example, some authors would consider the following aoristic, whereas I think it makes sense as a normal perfect:

---

[18] For further details of this final stage: Horrocks 4.7.7, 5.3, 5.11.1, 6.5.2, 10.2.1. For a thorough examination of its possible existence in and around the GNT, see MH I:141–6.
[19] Crellin, 'Semantics', *GVR*, §7.

τοῦτο δὲ ὅλον γέγονεν, ἵνα πληρωθῇ τὸ ῥηθὲν διὰ τοῦ προφήτου, λέγοντος ... Matt 21:4

This whole thing <u>has taken place</u>, so that what was spoken by the prophet might be fulfilled: '...'

Matthew is pointing out that a prophecy (quoted after this statement) which the reader is waiting to see fulfilled *already stands fulfilled*.

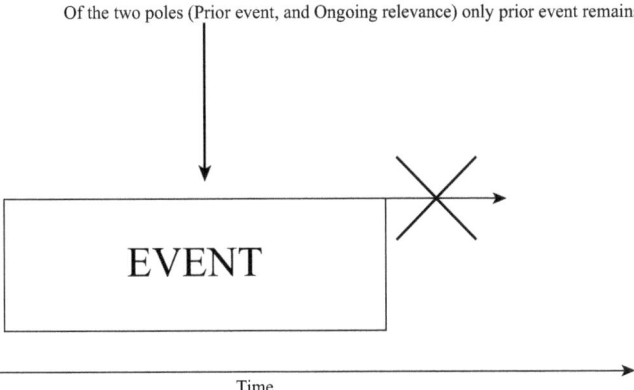

Figure 16.9 Aoristic Perfect

4.4.2 Certain Frozen Verbs: Present Stative Perfect

FURTHER READING: *CGCG* 38.36; vS 200B; WALLACE 579–81

This is the original stage of meaning in **EM 16** 4.1, and remains only with a few verbs, all of them states. It communicates only a present state; the fact that some action must have put you in that state is not relevant. These few verbs still occur often enough, including: οἶδα,[20] πέποιθα and ἕστηκα (and its compounds).[21] You learn this meaning as a matter of vocab: it is not an exegetical decision. See Figure 16.10.

ἰδού, ὁ κριτὴς πρὸ τῶν θυρῶν <u>ἕστηκεν</u> Jas 5:9
Look: the judge <u>is standing</u> at <u>the door</u>.
    You might feel that 'I stand' implies 'I have stood up', but notice that there is no hint of that at all here.

Compare:

Aorist: <u>ἕστησα</u> τὰς <u>θύρας</u> 2 Esd 17:1
<u>I stood</u> the doors <u>up</u>

---

[20] This perfect has been frozen, and you never meet it in the present (**EH 18** 1.2–3).
[21] Further examples in Michael Aubrey, 'The Greek Perfect', *LNTG*, 68–70.

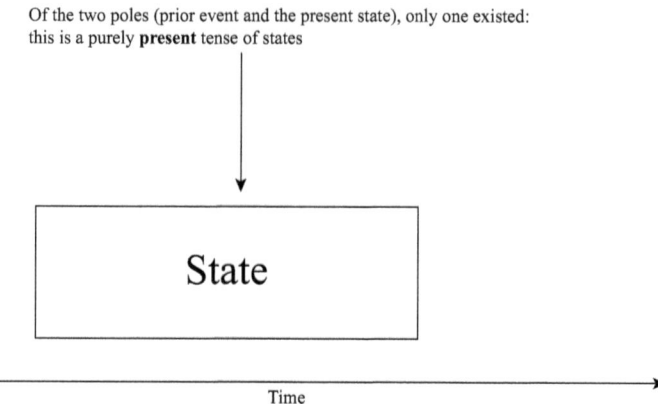

Figure 16.10 Perfect as Present Tense of States

Further examples:

> μύριαι μυριάδες <u>ἑστήκασιν</u> ἐνώπιον αὐτοῦ 1 En. 14:22
> Myriads of myriads <u>stand</u> before him.
>
> Ἀλλὰ καὶ ἡ περιτομὴ ἐφ' ᾗ <u>πεποίθασιν</u> κατήργηται Barn. 9.4
> But even the circumcision in which <u>they trust</u> has been destroyed
>
> Ἑλλὰς δή, τί <u>πέποιθας</u> ὑπ' ἀνδράσιν ἡγεμόνεσσιν … ; Sib. Or. 3.545
> Greece, why <u>do you trust</u> in men who govern … ?
>
> <u>οἶδα</u> γὰρ ὅτι ἀέναός ἐστιν ὁ ἐκλύειν με μέλλων Job 19:25
> For <u>I know</u> that there is an eternal one, who is about to free me.
>
> ἀλλ' <u>οἴδασιν</u> πάντες οἱ υἱοὶ Ἰσραὴλ ὅτι οὐκ ἔστι μου θυγάτηρ.
>   Prot. Jas. 17.1
> But all the sons of Israel <u>know</u> that she is not my daughter.
>
> Perfect: <u>ἕστηκα</u> ἐπὶ τὴν πηγὴν τοῦ ὕδατος Gen 24:43
> <u>I am standing</u> [not <u>I have stood something up</u>] by the source of water

4.4.3 Obvious Rhetorical Uses (Very Rare)

FURTHER READING: vS 200H–I; B-D-R 344; *CGCG* 33.38

The present force of the 'ongoing relevance' of the perfect might explain why it takes on some of the minority uses of the present tense (**EM 2** 5); these are very rare and also very obvious in their meaning.

> κατενόησε γὰρ ἑαυτὸν, καὶ <u>ἀπελήλυθε</u>, καὶ εὐθέως ἐπελάθετο ὁποῖος
>   ἦν Jas 1:24

For he looks [aorist] at himself, then <u>departs [perfect]</u>, and promptly forgets [aorist] what he resembles.

The context makes it obvious that the verbs are **gnomic**.

ὅστις γὰρ ὅλον τὸν νόμον τηρήσει, πταίσει δὲ ἐν ἑνί, <u>γέγονε</u> πάντων ἔνοχος. Jas 2:10
for anyone who keeps [future] the whole law, and yet trips up [future] over one thing, <u>becomes [perfect]</u> guilty of all.

The two future tenses τηρήσει and πταίσει point to a future condition: **EM 19** 5.1.3, so the perfect has a **futuristic** sense.

4.5 Uses and Contexts of the Pluperfect Indicative

FURTHER READING: vS 201; WALLACE 583–6

4.5.1 Default Pluperfect

The pluperfect does exactly what you would expect: it refers to a prior event with ongoing relevance in the past. The point in time when the relevance continues is in the past of the author, so that the prior event is earlier still. See Figure 16.3.

ἀνὴρ Αἰθίοψ ... ὃς <u>ἐληλύθει</u> προσκυνήσων εἰς Ἰερουσαλήμ, Acts 8:27
An Ethiopian ... who <u>had come</u> to worship in Jerusalem,

ἦν δὲ ... Βαραββᾶς μετὰ τῶν συστασιαστῶν δεδεμένος, οἵτινες ἐν τῇ στάσει φόνον <u>πεποιήκεισαν</u> Mark 15:7
There was ... Barabbas among the imprisoned insurrectionists, who <u>had committed</u> murder during the insurrection.

4.5.2 Pluperfect with Verbs of Result

καὶ ὤρθρισαν οἱ ἄνδρες τῆς πόλεως τὸ πρωΐ, καὶ ἰδοὺ <u>καθῄρητο</u> τὸ θυσιαστήριον τοῦ Βάαλ, καὶ τὸ ἄλσος τὸ ἐπ' αὐτῷ <u>ὠλέθρευτο</u> Judg 6:28
The men of the city got up early in the morning, and look: Baal's altar <u>had been torn down</u>, and the grove around it <u>had been destroyed</u>!

4.5.3 Past Stative Pluperfect

For the handful of verbs whose perfect is a pure present tense, with no implication of past action (**EM 16** 4.4.2), the pluperfect is their imperfect.

πᾶς ὁ ὄχλος ἐπὶ τὸν αἰγιαλὸν <u>εἱστήκει</u> Matt 13:2
the whole crowd <u>was standing</u> on the beach

οὐκ <u>ᾔδεισαν</u> τί αὐτῷ ἀποκριθῶσι Mark 14:40
<u>they</u> didn't <u>know</u> what to answer him

κύκλῳ δὲ τῆς πύλης εἱστήκεισαν παρθένοι δώδεκα Herm. Sim. 9.2.3
around the door, twelve virgins were standing.

ᾔδει δὲ καὶ Ἰακὼβ ὅτι ὁ θεὸς συνεργεῖ τῇ ἁπλότητί μου. T. Iss. 3.7
And Jacob also knew that God was supporting my lack of guile.

5 PERFECT SYSTEM: OTHER MOODS

In addition to the uses below, the perfect participle, infinitive and subjunctive stand for indicative tenses in indirect discourse (**EM 10** 6).

5.1 Perfect Participle

FURTHER READING: FANNING 6.2.4; WALLACE 626

This does exactly what you would expect. The good news is that the Greek is easy to understand and delivers a lot of meaning. English translation struggles to capture the difference between perfect and aorist. However, you're not in the business of translating but of reading with understanding. *Understanding* the Greek text is easy and productive.

5.1.1 Attributive

Ongoing relevance of a past action:

> Ἐξάγαγε τοὺς ἄνδρας τοὺς εἰσπεπορευμένους εἰς τὴν οἰκίαν σου τὴν νύκτα Josh 2:3
> Bring out the men who have come into your house during the night.
> > Rahab can hardly bring them out if they entered during the night unless they continue to be there: past event with ongoing relevance.
>
> Δεῦτε, οἱ εὐλογημένοι[22] τοῦ πατρός μου, κληρονομήσατε τὴν ἡτοιμασμένην ὑμῖν βασιλείαν ἀπὸ καταβολῆς κόσμου Matt 25:34
> Come, blessed by my father, inherit the kingdom prepared for you from the creation of the universe.
> > Both participles convey the past event: there is a moment when you became blessed, there is a moment when the kingdom became prepared. They also very strongly convey the ongoing effect: you continue to be blessed, the kingdom remains prepared for you.
>
> Ἔλεγεν οὖν ὁ Ἰησοῦς πρὸς τοὺς πεπιστευκότας αὐτῷ Ἰουδαίους, Ἐὰν ὑμεῖς μείνητε ἐν τῷ λόγῳ τῷ ἐμῷ, John 8:31
> Jesus was saying to those Jews who had put their trust in him: 'If you remain in my word …'

---

[22] The perfect stem of this verb doesn't reduplicate.

The perfect participle identifies their past act of trust as relevant at the time of the action. They had become believers and were therefore worth addressing as those who might potentially remain in his word. The participle doesn't necessarily mean that they were still trusting Jesus at that point.

καὶ ὃς ἐὰν ἀπολελυμένην γαμήσῃ μοιχᾶται Matt 5:32
And whoever marries a <u>divorcée</u> commits adultery.

In the immediate context, he has been teaching that divorce *doesn't* generally absolve a couple from their marital status. The focus of the participle is on the woman's *ongoing* state as 'not marriable'. However, there is also a focus on the prior action (the act of divorce) as *failing* to make her marriable.

κηρύσσομεν Χριστὸν ἐσταυρωμένον, Ἰουδαίοις μὲν σκάνδαλον, Ἕλλησι δὲ μωρίαν 1 Cor 1:23
we proclaim Christ <u>crucified</u>, a scandal for Jews and folly for Greeks.

The past crucifixion remains enduringly relevant, in that it tells us what kind of Christ is proclaimed: the idea of a Christ who would have been crucified is such an unpopular idea.

ἰδοὺ ὁ μισθὸς τῶν ἐργατῶν… ὁ ἀπεστερημένος ἀφ' ὑμῶν κράζει Jas 5:4
Look: the pay due to the workers … which <u>you have withheld</u> from them, are crying out.

The focus is on both elements: the wages were withheld *at the point when they were due*, and they *remain* unpaid.

Focus more on ongoing relevance:

μιμνῄσκεσθε τῶν δεσμίων, ὡς συνδεδεμένοι Heb 13:3
remember the prisoners, as though <u>you were imprisoned with them</u>
Emphasis probably on the ongoing state of imprisonment, rather than the prior act of 'having been imprisoned'.

ἀγαλλιᾶσθε χαρᾷ ἀνεκλαλήτῳ καὶ δεδοξασμένῃ 1 Pet 1:8
rejoice with a joy that is inexpressible and <u>filled with glory</u>
Emphasis probably on the ongoing state of being full of glory.

μετὰ τῶν ζώντων καὶ μετὰ τῶν τεθνηκότων Ruth 2:20
with the living and with <u>the dead</u>

πᾶς ὁ ἁπτόμενος αὐτῶν τεθνηκότων ἀκάθαρτος ἔσται ἕως ἑσπέρας Lev 11:31
all who touch one of them <u>when they are dead</u> [i.e. who touches one of their carcasses] will be unclean until evening.

As we have seen for aorist and perfect indicatives, so also with participles. The aorist does not deny an ongoing relevance and (as in the example below) can be used in a context that tells you of the ongoing relevance. English translation may force your hand towards a perfect tense. Keep your eye on the Greek author's intention:

> οἱ οὐκ ἠλεημένοι, **νῦν δὲ ἐλεηθέντες** 1 Pet 2:10
> having not <u>received mercy</u> [perfect], but **<u>now</u> having received mercy [aorist]**
> The perfect participle describes the <u>ongoing condition</u> of not having received mercy, whereas the **aorist participle** describes the past event of receiving mercy, but as a property of the hearers in the **present**.

5.1.2 Attributive (Present Stative Verbs)

With verbs where the perfect has purely present meaning (**EH 16** 4.4.2), it just has a present meaning:

> εἰσί τινες τῶν ὧδε ἑστηκότων Mark 9:1
> there are some from among <u>those standing</u> here

> δύο λέοντες <u>ἑστηκότες</u> παρὰ τὰς χεῖρας 3 Kgdms 10:19
> two lions <u>standing</u> by the hands

> ὑπερασπιστής ἐστιν πᾶσιν τοῖς <u>πεποιθόσιν</u> ἐπ' αὐτῷ 2 Kgdms 22:31
> he is the champion of all who <u>trust</u> in him

> τυγχάνει γὰρ Ἑβραϊκοῖς γράμμασι καὶ φωνῇ λεγόμενα … καθὼς ὑπὸ τῶν <u>εἰδότων</u> προσαναφέρεται. Let. Aris. 1:30
> For they happen to speak [i.e. be written] in Hebrew letters and sound … as it was reported to me by <u>those who know</u>.

5.1.3 Adverbial

Adverbial perfect participles relate to the main verb like aorist participles (the event is in the past relative to the main verb) *plus* the sense of ongoing relevance *at the time of the main verb*:

> ὁ οὖν Ἰησοῦς <u>κεκοπιακὼς</u> ἐκ τῆς ὁδοιπορίας ἐκαθέζετο οὕτως ἐπὶ τῇ πηγῇ John 4:6
> Therefore Jesus, <u>because he had become tired</u> by his journey, was sitting at the well.
> The journey tired him out *and* he continued to be tired at the time of the main verb (sitting at the well). As with any other participle, implied connections between it and the main verb are also possible: here, *causal* (**EM 14** 4.2.2).

ἵνα ἄρτιος ᾖ ὁ τοῦ Θεοῦ ἄνθρωπος, πρὸς πᾶν ἔργον ἀγαθὸν
ἐξηρτισμένος 2 Tim 3:17
so that the man of God may be ready, <u>since he has become equipped</u> for every good deed.
He has been equipped fully *and* remains equipped at the time of the main verb (now). Implicit adverbial connection: causal.

πᾶς ὁ <u>δεδηγμένος</u> ἰδὼν αὐτὸν ζήσεται Num 21:8
anyone, after they look at it, will live <u>despite having been bitten</u>
The ongoing relevance of the snake bite is that the venom is still killing you. Hence the concessive connection: the main verb (ζήσεται) is true *despite* the expected ongoing relevance of a snake bite (δεδηγμένος).

5.1.4 Adverbial (Present Stative Verbs)

Adverbial participles of verbs with a purely present meaning in the perfect (**EH 16** 4.4.2) relate to main verbs like other *present* participles:

συμπαθείτω μοι <u>εἰδὼς</u> τὰ συνέχοντά με Ign. *Rom.* 6.3
let him sympathise with me <u>because he knows</u> what compels me

ἐκ γῆς γὰρ ἀνεβιώσκοντο πάντες, οὐδὲν <u>μεμνημένοι</u> τῶν πρόσθεν. Plato, *Pol.* 272a
for they all used to be brought back to life from the ground, <u>remembering</u> nothing about former things.

5.1.5 The Three Participle Aspects Side by Side

ὅτι πᾶν τὸ <u>γεγεννημένον</u> [perfect] ἐκ τοῦ Θεοῦ νικᾷ τὸν κόσμον· καὶ αὕτη ἐστὶν ἡ νίκη <u>ἡ νικήσασα</u> [aorist] τὸν κόσμον, ἡ πίστις ἡμῶν. τίς ἐστιν <u>ὁ νικῶν</u> [present] τὸν κόσμον, εἰ μὴ <u>ὁ πιστεύων</u> [present] ὅτι Ἰησοῦς ἐστιν ὁ υἱὸς τοῦ Θεοῦ; 1 John 5:4–5
Because everyone <u>who has been born</u> from God overcomes the world: and this is the victory <u>which has overcome</u> the world: our faith. Who is it that <u>overcomes</u> the world, other than <u>the one who believes</u> that Jesus is the Son of God?
The present participles describe someone as overcoming/believing in ongoing aspect, presumably habitual.
The aorist participle describes a victory that has overcome by the time of the letter being written (**EM 7** 5.1.3). It *does not deny* that there is an ongoing relevance (indeed, there almost certainly is one), but it does not highlight it. The focus is on the past action.
The *perfect* participle, though, highlights the ongoing relevance: that is, having been born of God means that one has a new nature which endures from that birth.

5.2 Perfect Imperative

The perfect imperative is *extremely* rare, and its meaning is obvious enough when you find it.

> καὶ εἶπε τῇ θαλάσσῃ, Σιώπα, πεφίμωσο. Mark 4:39
> He said to the sea: 'Shut up! Be silenced!'
> > The sea is being told to enter into a state of silence and to stay there, which fits the meaning of the perfect nicely.

With verbs where the perfect has purely present meaning:

> ἴστε[23] γὰρ ὅτι καὶ μετέπειτα Heb 12:17
> ... know that later ...

> ἴσθι[24] τότ' Αἰγύπτου ὀλοὸν γένος ἐγγὺς ὀλέθρου Sib. Or. 3.348
> Then know that the mortal race of Egypt is close to its destruction

5.3 Perfect Subjunctive

The verb table accompanying Chapter 21 will help you here: 'The Greek Verb in Full – λύω' in the **Online Material**.

As expected, the perfect subjunctive active is formed on the perfect active stem, and takes the endings of the present indicative active, with lengthened thematic vowels.

The perfect subjunctive middle/passive is always periphrastic (*ENTG* 20.3), taking the perfect middle/passive *participle* plus the subjunctive of εἰμί (*ENTG* 17.2.2).

The perfect subjunctive

- is used in the syntactical forms of the subjunctive: purpose, deliberation, etc. (*ENTG* 17 and 20.1.2)
- has the meaning of the perfect system: the ongoing relevance of a prior action.

> καὶ ὑπὲρ αὐτῶν ἐγὼ ἁγιάζω ἐμαυτόν, ἵνα καὶ αὐτοὶ ὦσιν ἡγιασμένοι ἐν ἀληθείᾳ John 17:19
> It is on their behalf that I sanctify myself, with the intention that they also should become, and remain, sanctified by the truth
> > An aorist would leave open the possibility that they would be sanctified for a while, while the perfect points to some ongoing relevance; their remaining in a state of sanctification is the most obvious.

---

[23] An older form of οἶδα in the 2p indicative/imperative (cf. οἴδατε in *ENTG* 18.1).
[24] 2s imperative of οἶδα.

Compare the aorist subjunctive:

> οἱ ἄνδρες, ἀγαπᾶτε τὰς γυναῖκας ἑαυτῶν, καθὼς καὶ ὁ Χριστὸς ἠγάπησε τὴν ἐκκλησίαν, καὶ ἑαυτὸν παρέδωκεν ὑπὲρ αὐτῆς· ἵνα αὐτὴν ἁγιάσῃ [aorist subjunctive], Eph 5:25–6
> Husbands, love your own wives, just as Christ also loved the church and handed himself over on her behalf, with the intention that <u>he should sanctify her</u>,
> While the context goes on to talk about the fact that the sanctification must endure up until judgment day, the focus of the aorist is not on the ongoing relevance of sanctifying, but on the event of sanctifying: a costly one, which husbands are to imitate by sacrificially loving their wives.
> As ever, the aorist does not *deny* that there is an ongoing relevance to the event, but it chooses not to highlight it. See also Heb 13:12.

5.4 Perfect Infinitive

The perfect infinitive also holds no surprises: as a noun, it captures the idea of a verb; specifically, the ongoing relevance of that verb's prior action:

> ... οὐδεὶς ἠδύνατο αὐτὸν δῆσαι, ⁴**διὰ τὸ αὐτὸν** πολλάκις πέδαις καὶ ἁλύσεσι δεδέσθαι, καὶ διεσπᾶσθαι ὑπ' αὐτοῦ τὰς ἁλύσεις, καὶ τὰς πέδας συντετρῖφθαι. Mark 5:3–4
> ... no one could tie him up, **because of his** <u>having</u> often <u>been tied up</u> with manacles and chains, and [**his**] <u>having broken off</u> the chains from him, and [**his**] <u>having shattered</u> the manacles.
> The ongoing relevance of δεδέσθαι is that he remained tied up at the point when the next thing happened, which is that he overpowered his chains, etc.; that overpowering is given as perfects too (διεσπᾶσθαι, συντετρῖφθαι), with the ongoing relevance that he then remained untied.

Here is Plato paraphrasing the ongoing result of an action (a perfect infinitive) as a noun which describes the product of that action:

> πότερον οὖν ταὐτόν δοκεῖ σοι εἶναι <u>μεμαθηκέναι</u> καὶ <u>πεπιστευκέναι</u>, καὶ **μάθησις** καὶ **πίστις**, ἢ ἄλλο τι; Plato, *Gorg.* 454c–d
> Therefore, which of these do you think: that '<u>having learnt</u>' and '<u>having believed</u>' (which is to say, '**knowledge**' and '**belief**') are the same, or different?
> Plato shows that '**belief**' is the product of <u>having come to believe</u> something, and that '**learning**' (the knowledge, not the process) is the product of <u>having learnt</u> something.

6   PERFECT: QUICK SUMMARY

The perfect system generally combines two poles: a prior action, with an ongoing relevance. Either of the two poles can be more or less prominent, or even absent altogether, for a variety of reasons. In the indicative, the ongoing relevance can be pinned down in time as 'now' (perfect indicative) or 'earlier' (pluperfect indicative).

The main exegetical task is to discern whether each of the two poles is present; if both, then which of them is prominent.

CHAPTER 17

The Subjunctive
—
Aspect in the Subjunctive

> **How to Use This Chapter**
>
> In this chapter, we meet the final mood that *ENTG* really covers: the subjunctive.
> In **Extra Help** you will see how easy it is to understand this new mood using the pattern we have followed so far for the verb.
> Simply work through *ENTG*, consulting the **Extra Help** below as you complete each section.
> In **Extra Material**, we will think about the aspect of the subjunctive mood.

1 SUBJUNCTIVE

1.1 After *ENTG* 17.2: Parsing Made Trivial

As a **mood**, the subjunctive is a new row, across all the columns (systems and voices) in our verb table. Your job now is to know which endings it has in each column.

It could hardly be much easier! The **only endings** you ever see on the subjunctive are the endings of the **present indicative**, whether **active** or **middle**. That's twelve endings in total.

> Make sure you're completely happy with the verb so far before tackling the subjunctive. Use "The Greek Verb So Far" for Chapter 17, in the **Online Material**. Did you get it perfectly right (apart from accents)? If so, read on. If not, repeat until perfect.

The endings are lengthened in the subjunctive. That makes them easy to spot, but beware of the two endings that are already long in the indicative: ω, η.

The **active** subjunctive takes the **active** endings; the **middle** takes the **middle** endings. The **aorist passive** takes *active* endings (just like the aorist passive indicative).

If the stem ends in θ it's **aorist passive**; σ **aorist**; **nothing, present**. See Table 17.1.

17 The Subjunctive

Table 17.1 Subjunctive Endings

Stem:	Present		Aorist		
	Active	Middle/Passive	Active	Middle	Passive
Endings:	Active	Middle	Active	Middle	*Active*

1.1.1 Parsing in More Detail

1 The subjunctive is always built on *present indicative* endings.
2 The subjunctive *lengthens the thematic vowel* in the endings.
   The 1s active ending has no visible thematic vowel, since it has already contracted: ω.
   The 2s middle ending has already lengthened the thematic vowel through contraction, so it cannot lengthen further: ε-σ-αι → εαι → ῃ and η-σ-αι → ηαι → ῃ
   The 3p active requires a bit of understanding of slippery sigma: ο-ντ-σ-ιν → ουσιν (*ENTG* 12.2.1); in the subjunctive: ω-ντ-σ-ιν → ωσιν.
3 The subjunctive uses active endings in the active; middle endings in the middle; but **active** endings in the **passive** (**cf. aorist passive**). It is built on the stems we have learnt: λυ-, λυσ-, λυθ-.

Further hints:

4 There is never an augment. Don't confuse the aorist subjunctive and future indicative.
5 Contract verbs are easy: the contract vowels *lengthen* in the aorist subjunctive (again, like the future indicative); they *disappear* in the present subjunctive because the lengthened thematic vowel contracts them to oblivion.

1.2 Before *ENTG* 17.3: Only in Set Constructions

Back in **EH 7** 1.1, I gave you a brief idea of what each mood does, and we now add the subjunctive:

> **Indicative** deals with the *real* world.
> (It doesn't have to deal with the world accurately or truthfully. It includes questions.)
> **Imperative** *changes* the world.
> '*Learn* your paradigms!'
> **Infinitive** is a *noun* which expresses the idea of a verb.
> 'What's your favourite thing? Do you love apples?' 'No: I love **to** read.'

Participle is an *adjective* which expresses the idea of a verb.
Was the man slow? No, he was a *running* man.

Subjunctive deals with *potential* worlds.
'If I *were to study* Greek, then ...'

Even though that might help you remember which mood is which, please engrave on your desk what *ENTG* says in 17.1:

> **The subjunctive is only used in set constructions.**

The only way to handle the subjunctive is to **memorise** the syntax of its uses; learn them like vocab or paradigms.

2 THE GREEK READINGS

2.1 Reading A: *Joseph & Aseneth* 24

The story so far ...

Joseph and Aseneth have visited Joseph's father, Jacob. His brothers Simeon and Levi have kept them safe from the danger of many jealous suitors, and Levi has particularly won Aseneth over with his prophesying.

Pharaoh's firstborn isn't giving up on Aseneth but is consumed with I-love-her-I-hate-her envy. Having heard of Simeon and Levi's brutality (Gen 34), he tries to bribe them into assassinating Joseph. They offer him violence instead, and we left him terrified of them. But was he also chastened?

24:1 Καὶ ἐλυπεῖτο ὁ υἱὸς Φαραὼ δι' Ἀσενὲθ καὶ ἔπασχεν. ²ᵃ ἐλαλήθη δὲ πρὸς

αὐτὸν ὅτι· Οἱ υἱοὶ ἄλλων γυναικῶν τοῦ Ἰακὼβ μισοῦσιν τὸν Ἰωσήφ. ²ᵇ ὁ δὲ

διελογίζετο ἐν ἑαυτῷ λέγων· Πράξουσιν οὗτοι ἣν ἂν διακονίαν αἰτήσω;

λαλῶ οὖν αὐτοῖς; ³ᵃ ἀπέστειλεν δὲ ὁ υἱὸς Φαραὼ ἀγγέλους ἵνα καλέσωσιν

αὐτούς. ³ᵇ ἦλθον δὲ Γὰδ καὶ Δὰν οἱ πρεσβύτεροι ἀδελφοὶ πρὸς αὐτὸν νυκτός.

⁴ καὶ εἶπον τῷ υἱῷ Φαραώ· Λάλει, ὃ γὰρ ἂν θέλημα βούλῃ πράξομεν. ⁵ ὁ δὲ

κελεύει τοῖς διακόνοις αὐτοῦ· Μὴ ἀκούσητε πρὸς τῇ θύρᾳ, ὅπως λαλήσω τοῖς ἀνδράσι τούτοις. ⁶τότε λέγει· Ζωὴν καὶ θάνατον ὁμολογῶ ὑμῖν· ἐν οὖν τῇ σοφίᾳ μὴ λάβητε τὸν θάνατον. ⁷γινώσκω γὰρ ὅτι ἄνδρες ἰσχύοντές ἐστε καὶ ἀδικεῖτε τοὺς ἐχθροὺς ὑμῶν. ⁸ἤκουσα δὲ τοῦ Ἰωσὴφ λέγοντος τῷ Φαραώ, καὶ ἑκατηγόρει ὕμων λέγων ὅτι Δὰν καὶ Γὰδ οὐκ εἰσὶν ἀδελφοὶ αὐτοῦ. ⁹καὶ εἶπεν· Ἀποκτανθεὶς ὁ πατήρ μου, ἀνέλω αὐτοὺς ἵνα μὴ κληρονομήσωσιν, διότι οὗτοι με πεπωλήκασι τοῖς Ἰσμαηλίταις; ¹¹ὁ δὲ Φαραὼ ἀπεκρίθη· Καλῶς λελάληκας. ἀποκτείνωμεν αὐτούς· οὐ μὴ ᾖ σωτηρία πάσαις ταῖς γενεαῖς αὐτῶν. ¹²οἱ δὲ ἄνδρες ἀκούσαντες, ἐφοβήθησαν καὶ ἀπεκρίθησαν· Κύριε, τὶ ποιήσωμεν; ¹³ὁ δὲ λεγεί· Ἐγὼ μὲν ἀποκτενῶ τὸν πατέρα μου τῇ νυκτὶ ταύτῃ, διότι ὁ Φαραὼ ὡς πατήρ ἐστι τῷ Ἰωσήφ, ἀποκτείνατε δὲ ὑμεῖς τὸν Ἰωσὴφ ἵνα σχῶ τὴν Ἀσενέθ.

¹⁴ᵃἆρα εἶπον Δὰν καὶ Γάδ· Ἡμεῖς ποιήσομεν ὅσα λελάληκας ἡμῖν.

¹⁴ᵇἀκηκόαμεν γὰρ τοῦ Ἰωσὴφ λέγοντος πρὸς τὴν Ἀσενέθ· ¹⁴ᶜΠορεύου εἰς τὸν ἀγρόν, διότι καιρός ἐστι τῶν καρπῶν. ¹⁶διό ἡμεῖς πορευσόμεθα νυκτὸς ἵνα μὴ ἀποκαλυφθῶμεν ὑπὸ τοῦ ἡλίου, καὶ κρυβησόμεθα ὑπὸ τῶν δένδρων. ¹⁷ἀλλὰ σὺ λαβὲ μετὰ σεαυτοῦ ἑκατὸν ἄνδρας καὶ πορεύου ἔμπροσθεν. ¹⁸καὶ φεύξεται Ἀσενὲθ ὡς ἄνεμος ἀλλὰ πεσεῖται εἰς τὰς χεῖράς σου, καὶ ποιήσεις αὐτὴν κατὰ ἣν ἂν ἐπιθυμίαν ἔχῃς. ¹⁹καὶ μετὰ ταῦτα ἀποκτενοῦμεν τὸν Ἰωσὴφ λυπούμενον δι' Ἀσενέθ. ²⁰καὶ ἐχάρη ὁ υἱὸς Φαραώ, ἀκούσας τῶν ῥημάτων τούτων. ²¹καὶ ἐλθόντες ἐκρύβησαν μετὰ τριῶν χιλιάδων στρατιωτῶν ὅπως μὴ βλέπωνται ὑπὸ Ἀσενέθ.

2.1.1 Vocabulary

ἀδικέω – I do wrong, injure
ἀκούω – Principal Parts: 2. ἀκούσω;
3. ἤκουσα; 4. ἀκήκοα
ἀναιρέω – Principal Parts: 2.
ἀναιρήσω; 3. ἀνεῖλον; 6.
ἀναιρεθήσομαι
ἀποκτείνω – Principal Parts: 2.
ἀποκτενῶ; 3. ἀπέκτεινα; 6.
ἀπεκτάνθην

κληρονομέω – I inherit
κρύβω – I hide; Principal Parts: 6.
κρυβήσομαι
πίπτω – Principal Parts: 2.
πεσοῦμαι
πρός – near (+ dat)
πωλέω – I sell

2.2 Reading B: John 3:14–23

¹⁴ καὶ καθὼς Μωσῆς ὕψωσε τὸν ὄφιν ἐν τῇ ἐρήμῳ, οὕτως ὑψωθῆναι δεῖ τὸν υἱὸν τοῦ ἀνθρώπου· ¹⁵ ἵνα πᾶς ὁ πιστεύων εἰς αὐτὸν μὴ ἀπόληται, ἀλλ᾽ ἔχῃ ζωὴν αἰώνιον.

¹⁶ Οὕτω γὰρ ἠγάπησεν ὁ Θεὸς τὸν κόσμον, ὥστε τὸν υἱὸν αὐτοῦ τὸν μονογενῆ ἔδωκεν, ἵνα πᾶς ὁ πιστεύων εἰς αὐτὸν μὴ ἀπόληται, ἀλλ᾽ ἔχῃ ζωὴν αἰώνιον.

¹⁷ οὐ γὰρ ἀπέστειλεν ὁ Θεὸς τὸν υἱὸν αὐτοῦ εἰς τὸν κόσμον ἵνα κρίνῃ τὸν κόσμον, ἀλλ᾽ ἵνα σωθῇ ὁ κόσμος δι᾽ αὐτοῦ. ¹⁸ ὁ πιστεύων εἰς αὐτὸν οὐ κρίνεται· ὁ δὲ μὴ πιστεύων ἤδη κέκριται, ὅτι μὴ πεπίστευκεν εἰς τὸ ὄνομα τοῦ μονογενοῦς υἱοῦ τοῦ Θεοῦ. ¹⁹ αὕτη δέ ἐστιν ἡ κρίσις, ὅτι τὸ φῶς ἐλήλυθεν εἰς τὸν κόσμον, καὶ ἠγάπησαν οἱ ἄνθρωποι μᾶλλον τὸ σκότος ἢ τὸ φῶς· ἦν γὰρ πονηρὰ αὐτῶν τὰ ἔργα. ²⁰ πᾶς γὰρ ὁ φαῦλα πράσσων μισεῖ τὸ φῶς, καὶ οὐκ ἔρχεται πρὸς τὸ φῶς, ἵνα μὴ ἐλεγχθῇ τὰ ἔργα αὐτοῦ. ²¹ ὁ δὲ ποιῶν τὴν ἀλήθειαν, ἔρχεται πρὸς τὸ φῶς, ἵνα φανερωθῇ αὐτοῦ τὰ ἔργα, ὅτι ἐν Θεῷ ἐστιν εἰργασμένα.

²² Μετὰ ταῦτα ἦλθεν ὁ Ἰησοῦς καὶ οἱ μαθηταὶ αὐτοῦ εἰς τὴν Ἰουδαίαν γῆν· καὶ ἐκεῖ διέτριβε μετ' αὐτῶν καὶ ἐβάπτιζεν. ²³ ἦν δὲ καὶ Ἰωάννης βαπτίζων ἐν Αἰνὼν ἐγγὺς τοῦ Σαλείμ, ὅτι ὕδατα πολλὰ ἦν ἐκεῖ· καὶ παρεγίνοντο καὶ ἐβαπτίζοντο.

2.2.1 Vocabulary

ἀγαπάω – I love [parse as though it were ἀγαπέω]
ἀπόλλυμι – I perish [parse as though it were ἀπόλομαι]
διατρίβω – I remain a while
εἰργασμένος – perfect participle of ἐργάζομαι
ἐλέγχω – I expose
ἔρχομαι – Principal Parts: 2. ἐλεύσομαι; 3. ἦλθον; 4. ἐλήλυθα

μᾶλλον – rather
μονογενής, ές – only-begotten
οὕτω = οὕτως
ὄφις, εως, ὁ – snake
ὑψόω – I lift up [parse as though it were ὑψωω]
φανερόω – I reveal [parse as though it were φανερωω]
φαῦλος, η, ον – foul

3 ACCENTS

As with other finite verbs, the accent in subjunctives is recessive.

In the aorist passive subjunctive, bear in mind that the stem θη contracts with the endings, which are all long (because the thematic vowel is lengthened in the subjunctive). The rules of contract with accents (**EM 2** 3.1) then account for the forms: λυθή + ὦμεν → λυθῶμεν.

4 ASPECT IN THE SUBJUNCTIVE

> **In summary**
> Subjunctives used of commands and desires are analysed like imperatives.
> States: the subjunctive uses the *present by default*; the aorist either is ingressive or tells us that the state has become an action.
> Actions: there is no distinction between actions with/without an endpoint. The subjunctive uses the *aorist by default*; the present indicates any of the usual aspectual nuances of the present system.

4.1 Basic Expectation: Aorist

FURTHER READING: FANNING 6.1.3.2

Like all the 'other moods', there is no sense of absolute time in the subjunctive; by its nature the subjunctive almost always refers to something that is either in the future absolutely (hortatory, deliberative, prohibitions, emphatic negative future) or relative to the main verb (most purpose clauses). The choice of system is therefore aspectual, as we have come to expect in the other moods.

When the subjunctive is used for commands or desires (hortatory, deliberative, prohibition), its aspect should be analysed in the same way as imperatives (**EM 11** 5).

We only find the perfect subjunctive with verbs that have a frozen present stative meaning (**EM 16** 4.4.2).

Purpose clauses are overwhelmingly aorist, both when they use infinitives (**EM 8** 5.5.2) and subjunctives. This is probably because such constructions refer to a future event in general terms, viewing it as a whole. This would also explain why the 'emphatic negative future' subjunctive (οὐ μή + subj) is almost always aorist, even when the verb has no endpoint.

The question then becomes: when do authors use a present subjunctive (apart from in situations to be analysed as imperatives)?

4.2 States

We naturally expect a present for states.

> ὅς δ' ἂν ἔχῃ [present, state] τὸν βίον τοῦ κόσμου, καὶ θεωρῇ [present, state] τὸν ἀδελφὸν αὐτοῦ χρείαν ἔχοντα, καὶ κλείσῃ [aorist, action] τὰ σπλάγχνα αὐτοῦ ἀπ' αὐτοῦ ... 1 John 3:17
> If anyone were to have the possessions of the world, and were to see his brother in need, and were to close his heart ['bowels'] to him ...

The aorist appears where the state becomes an action, either through some resistance or by having an object (as in the following example):

> Ἐὰν ὑμεῖς μείνητε [aorist] ἐν τῷ λόγῳ τῷ ἐμῷ, John 8:31
> If you persevere in my word,

> καὶ ὃς ἐὰν μὴ δέξηται ὑμᾶς μηδὲ ἀκούσῃ [aorist] τοὺς λόγους ὑμῶν ... Matt 10:14
> as for anyone who doesn't receive you or who doesn't listen to your words ...

Also as expected, the aorist can be ingressive:

> ὁ δὲ ὄχλος ἐπετίμησεν αὐτοῖς ἵνα σιωπήσωσιν [aorist] Matt 20:30-1
> the crowd remonstrated with them, so that they would shut up.
> They were to enter the state of σιωπάω 'I am silent'.

> οὐκ ἤθελεν ἵνα τις γνῷ [aorist] Mark 9:30
> he didn't want that anyone should find out
> They would enter the state of γινώσκω 'I know'.

ἵνα πάντες πιστεύσωσι [aorist] δι' αὐτοῦ. John 1:7
so that everyone <u>would come to faith</u> through him
    They would enter the state of πιστεύω 'I believe'.

ἐὰν δὲ κοιμηθῇ [aorist passive] ὁ ἀνήρ αὐτῆς 1 Cor 7:39
but if her husband <u>falls asleep</u>
    He would enter the state of κοιμάω 'I am asleep'.

4.3 Actions

The distinction between actions with/without an endpoint is irrelevant in the subjunctive: the aorist is the default.

Consider first actions without an endpoint. Compare these almost identical uses of διώκω:

Μακάριοί ἐστε, ὅταν ὀνειδίσωσιν ὑμᾶς καὶ διώξωσι [aorist] Matt 5:11
Blessed are you, whenever they revile you and <u>persecute</u> you

ὅταν δὲ διώκωσιν [present] ὑμᾶς ἐν τῇ πόλει ταύτῃ, φεύγετε Matt 10:23
when they <u>persecute</u> you in that town, run away

The aorist views the action in a default way, simply as the whole action. You are blessed throughout the time of persecution. The present focusses on the action as ongoing: there is something you are to do *while* they persecute you. Don't endure it to the end, but flee.

Situations *with* an endpoint seem to work the same way: the default is the aorist, and the present is used to make some point. Compare these uses of προσφέρω / προσήνεγκον:

ἀναγκαῖον ἔχειν τι καὶ τοῦτον ὃ <u>προσενέγκῃ</u> [aorist]. Heb 8:3
it is necessary also for this one to have something which <u>he might offer</u>

ἐὰν οὖν <u>προσφέρῃς</u> [present] τὸ δῶρόν σου ἐπὶ τὸ θυσιαστήριον, κἀκεῖ μνησθῇς ὅτι ὁ ἀδελφός σου ἔχει τι κατὰ σοῦ, **ἄφες ἐκεῖ τὸ δῶρόν** ... Matt 5:23–4
therefore, if <u>you are in the act of offering</u> your gift at the altar, and there you remember that your brother holds something against you, **leave your gift right there** ...
The present subjunctive fits here because you are pointedly in the process of doing it, and are being told to *interrupt* the action.

With or without endpoints, then, the aorist is the default, whereas the present tells us something more. For example, 'here is what you are to do *during* the action' (see Table 17.2).

4 Aspect in the Subjunctive

Table 17.2 Aspect in Subjunctive

Aorist, whole action in view; 'simple' aspect	Present, 'ongoing aspect', time *during* the action is in view
ὃς δ' ἂν ποιήσῃ [aorist] Matt 5:19 whoever does [this]	Ὅταν ποιῇς [present] ἄριστον ἢ δεῖπνον ... Luke 14:12 Whenever you are laying on a banquet or a feast ...
Ὃς ἂν μὴ νηστεύσῃ [aorist] τὴν νηστείαν Barn. 7.3 Whoever does not observe ['fast'] the fast	Ὅταν δὲ νηστεύητε [present] ... Matt 6:16 But whenever you are fasting ...

We find the aspectual nuances we expect with the present system, such as habitual:

ὅταν λαλῇ τὸ ψεῦδος, ἐκ τῶν ἰδίων λαλεῖ John 8:44
when he utters what is false, it is out of his true self that he speaks

CHAPTER 18

Using Verbs

> **How to Use This Chapter**
>
> Follow the instructions throughout the **Extra Help** below, which will tell you when to work through various sections of *ENTG*. The instructions below are for the fourth edition of *ENTG*. If you have the third edition, please check the **Online Material**, which has different instructions for you for this chapter.
>
> The final three chapters of *ENTG* cover slightly more disjointed topics than previous chapters, filling in various gaps which would have been overwhelming earlier. If you have followed along with me on how to understand and memorise the verb, you will again reap a reward in this chapter.

1 BEFORE *ENTG* 18.1: FOUR VERBS

We can understand these four verbs easily as we have been doing throughout this *Reader*: skip all the explanations in *ENTG* 18.1, and just keep the tables.

1.1 Root Presents: δύναμαι, κάθημαι, κεῖμαι

These three verbs are easy to grasp if you remember two things. They are (1) never active (2) 'root presents'.

First, since Chapter 9 we have been used to verbs that never have active endings, such as ῥύομαι, ἔρχομαι. Review **EH 15** 2.3.2 on their meaning. These three new verbs are the same, and mean 'I am able', 'I sit', 'I lie'.

Second, in Chapter 11 we met some 'root aorists' (**EH 11** 1.2). These three verbs are **root presents**:[1]

- They have no thematic vowel.
- The 'endings proper' bolt straight onto the stem. Even though the stem ends in a vowel, there is no contraction.
- You can see that there is not always the slippery sigma in the 2s forms. Be prepared to see them either way (δύνῃ or δύνασαι).

That's it!

Above the table in *ENTG* 18.1, replace 'These are deponent, and hence have middle endings' with 'These are never active.'

---

[1] The explanations in *ENTG* are a helpful short-cut, because these endings look like perfect middle endings; however, with the rules we have learnt, we can see what they really are. There is no perfect meaning involved.

1.2 Frozen Perfect: οἶδα

Here again we have a verb that's very easy to understand, bearing in mind two things. It is (1) always in the **perfect system** (2) its meaning has become frozen as though it were in the **present system**.

Look at the endings for οἶδα in the table marked '**present**' (*ENTG* 18.1). Can you see that it has the **perfect** active endings (*ENTG* 16.2)? The stem doesn't look like a perfect active stem, lacking the κ and the reduplication. However, it is a **perfect** indicative active. Relabel the table 'perfect' rather than 'present'.

Remember that the perfect system means that a prior action is being portrayed as relevant (**EH 16** 1.1). What we have here is a verb that used to mean 'I see', and therefore, in the perfect, it meant 'I have seen, in a way that is now relevant'. One possible relevance would be 'I know [because I have seen]'. Eventually, it became frozen as meaning 'I know' in the present (without any hint of 'having seen').

It only occurs in the **perfect active stem** (**4th Principal Part**) without κ and without apparent reduplication (more on that, optionally, in **EH 18** 1.3). This frozen perfect meaning applies throughout οἶδα.

- The perfect indicative with present indicative meaning, as above.
- The pluperfect indicative with imperfect indicative meaning: the *historical indicative tense* of the perfect system with the meaning of the *historical indicative tense* of the present system. Replace 'Imperfect' with 'Pluperfect' in the table.
- The infinitive has the perfect active infinitive ending (see 'The Greek Verb So Far' for Chapter 18, in the **Online Material**), with present active infinitive meaning.
- The participle has the perfect active participle endings (see the footnote in *ENTG*, and cf. *ENTG* 16.2), with present active participle meaning.

> Parse οἶδα as *perfect* system.
> Understand as *present* system.

If your teacher tells you to follow *ENTG* instead, and parse as present system, that's fine too.

1.3 Optional for Language Enthusiasts: A Bit More on οἶδα and ὁράω

FURTHER READING: SMYTH 794–6; CGCG 18.23

Are you old enough to remember *video* cassettes? Video, from the Latin 'I see', and pronounced **wideo**.

That root [*wid*] existed in Latin's brother, Greek. The w sound died out (it used to be written F 'digamma'). Ϝιδ- became ιδ-, meaning 'I see'.

Because of that ϝ, the reduplication in the perfect stem looks unusual: οἰδ-. If you add the augment (in the pluperfect) you get an unusual ᾐδ. This ἰδ- root eventually ends up with two very different jobs (see Table 18.1).

Its **aorist** system means 'I saw'. It becomes the **second aorist** of ὁράω: ἔϝιδον → εἶδον.

Its **perfect** system means 'I have seen' but becomes frozen as 'I know' and lives as its own verb, with present meaning, known as οἶδα, with perfect endings and (unusual) reduplication, but no κ.

Table 18.1 ὁράω and οἶδα

Principal Part:	1. present	2. aorist	4. perfect active
ὁράω: I see	ὁράω	εἶδον	ἑώρακα I have seen
[ἰδ]: I see	*Lost*	↑	οἶδα I know

1.4 Embedding the Endings

Embed these in the usual way by writing out the verbs δύναμαι, κάθημαι, κεῖμαι, and by writing out οἶδα, being careful to add the translation 'I know'.

Tackle **Practice** 18.1.

Move on to *ENTG* 18.2 and return here before **Practice** 18.3.

2 AFTER *ENTG* 18.3: 3RD PERSON IMPERATIVE

Notice that these 3rd person imperatives always have the same beginning as the familiar 2nd plural imperatives. The 3rd singular, which you are familiar with, is the odd one out.

Tackle **Practice** 18.3.

3 BEFORE *ENTG* 18.4: PRINCIPAL PARTS

I introduced Principal Parts in **EH 11** 1.5. Remember that in my online vocab, I list the Principal Parts in order (the same order as *ENTG* 18.4), but I additionally give you the *imperfect* as though it were a Principal Part (before the future). However, in the vocab accompanying the **Readings** in this *Reader*, I conform to what you would expect. I list the true Principal Parts in order, or refer to them by number; if I give you an irregular imperfect, I list it separately.

Work through *ENTG* 18.4–5.

4 AFTER *ENTG* 18.5: ASPECT

As *ENTG* notes, aspect is a matter of some dispute among NT scholars. It may reassure you to know that the options entertained by Classicists are rather more limited.

4.1 Aspect and the Verbal Systems

Arranging the verb into our familiar systems, the table in *ENTG* 18.5 becomes Table 18.2.

Table 18.2 *ENTG* 18.5

System:	Present Ongoing	Aorist Simple	Future No aspect	Perfect Combinatory
Indicative	Action presented as ongoing + time	Action presented simply + time	Future action	Ongoing relevance + time
Participles	Simultaneous (ongoing at the time of the main verb)	Prior (action complete, viewed simply, by the time of the main verb)	EH 21 1.2	EH 16 5.1
Infinitive Imperative Subjunctive Optative	EH 8 5 EH 11 5 EH 17 4 EH 21 1.1.2		EH 21 1.2	EH 16 5

Remember that I warned you not to read too much into the aspect of the other moods until you've enjoyed some further study, apart from the participle (**EH 7** 1.2.2). I have indicated the sections of this *Reader* where you can follow up on this.

4.2 Aspect in Summary

When we describe what authors do by their choice of aspect, we often use metaphors of *space* and especially *point of view*, such as 'the imperfect tense draws you into the action' or 'the aorist indicative tense views the action as a whole'. While these are helpful, we need to avoid confusing the metaphor with what aspect actually means. Aspect is not about space, or point of view. Aspect is purely about time: aspect is the author's choice of how to *present* the action in *time*.

The **simple** aspect of the **aorist** presents **the action in its entirety**.[2] It refers to the whole action, from beginning to end.[3]

The **ongoing** aspect of the **present** refers to **a time** which is not the whole action.[4] It refers to a point in time, or a period of time, which doesn't include both the start and the end of the action.[5]

The **perfect** combines the ongoing aspect of the present (an ongoing relevance) with the simple aspect of the aorist (the prior event that led to that relevance).

The **future** is agnostic as far as aspect goes: it doesn't distinguish 'I will eat' from 'I will be eating'.

We will build on this understanding of aspect in the **Extra Material** on the verb throughout this *Reader*. Until then, bear in mind that the author's choice of aspect in the other moods, and especially in commands and prohibitions, is very hard for us to grasp. The writer or speaker will choose between the aorist and the present system based on quite a complicated set of factors, including: whether the action is complete; whether the action is repeated; whether the action is to be done generally or only now; whether the action is interruptible; whether the action was an unsuccessful attempt; and others.[6] Getting to know which factor was uppermost in the author's mind is an art, not a science. Don't get too excited by the aspect of the other moods (especially commands and prohibitions) until you've studied this further and read a lot more Greek texts.

When you read commentaries or hear others speaking about Greek verbs, be ready for them to use different terminology for the same ideas, or the same terminology with different meaning, or simply be different altogether. I really do feel your pain, and I'm sorry for this discouraging news. What it means in practice is that, when you're evaluating how an author exegetes the aspect of a verb, you need first to decide how that author understands aspect in the first place. If their theory of aspect is different from your own, there is little point engaging with their exposition at that point.

---

[2] Technically called 'perfective'.
[3] Please note what it doesn't do: it doesn't 'step back from the action' or 'view it from a distance' – just like in English, when, if you say 'I saw the match', you're referring to the whole event of watching the match, from the time you turned on the TV to when you switched it off. Your point of view or distance from the match are nothing to do with it. You're telling me: 'It happened.' In narrative, you might be setting the scene for the *time* of the action of the next verb as being after this aorist.
[4] Technically called 'imperfective'.
[5] Please note what it doesn't do: it doesn't 'step into the action' or 'view it from close up' – just like in English, when, if you say 'I was watching the match', you're referring to a point in time while you were watching the match, rather than referring to the whole *time* of the action. Your point of view or distance from the match are nothing to do with it. You're telling me: 'It was happening.' In narrative, you might be setting the scene for the time of the action of the next verb as being during that event.
[6] *CGCG* 33.65.

5 VOCAB: 2-2 ADJECTIVES

The footnote on 'compound adjectives' alerts you to a rare class of adjectives called 2-2. Like 3-3, they take the same declension endings in the masculine and feminine, as well as in the neuter. You'll find them listed as ἀκάθαρτος, ον.

6 THE GREEK READINGS

6.1 Reading A: *Joseph & Aseneth* 26–7

The story so far …

Pharaoh's son had tried, unsuccessfully, to bribe Simeon and Levi into murdering Joseph and kidnapping Aseneth. He then changed tack and lied to Dan and Gad, telling them that Joseph will kill them and their families. They're frightened enough to fall in with Pharaoh's son, and are lying in ambush, planning to kill Joseph and chase Aseneth into the hands of Pharaoh's son.

We have skipped chapter 25, in which Pharaoh's son attempted to assassinate Pharaoh but was foiled. He has taken his place to catch Aseneth. Dan and Gad's younger brothers remonstrated with them about their plan, but Dan and Gad have taken their places and are waiting for their victims to arrive.

26:1 Καὶ εἶπε Ἀσενὲθ πρὸς Ἰωσήφ· Πορεύσομαι εἰς τὸν ἀγρὸν ἡμῶν, ἀλλὰ φοβοῦμαι. ² εἶπεν δὲ αὐτῇ Ἰωσήφ· Μὴ φοβηθῇς, ἀλλὰ πορεύου, ὅτι ὁ κύριος παρέσται. ⁵ᵃ ἦλθεν οὖν Ἀσενὲθ ὥστε ἐπελθεῖν τὸν τόπον μετὰ τῶν τριῶν χιλιάδων ἀνδρῶν κειμένων. ⁵ᵇ τότε ἀνέβησαν ἐκ τῆς ἐνέδρας αὐτῶν καὶ ἐμάχοντο τοῖς δυνατοῖς Ἀσενέθ. ⁵ᶜ καὶ τοὺς δυνατοὺς τῆς Ἀσενὲθ πάντας ἀπέκτειναν. ⁶ ἄρα ἔφυγεν Ἀσενέθ.

⁷ᵃ Ἤδει δὲ Λευὶς ταῦτα πάντα, προφήτης ὤν, καὶ εἶπε τοῖς ἀδελφοῖς αὐτοῦ. ⁷ᵇ καὶ ἔλαβεν ἕκαστος αὐτῶν τὴν μάχαιραν αὐτοῦ τῇ δεξιᾷ καὶ ἔδραμον.

⁸ᵃ Ἔφευγεν δὲ Ἀσενέθ, ἀλλὰ ἰδοὺ ὁ υἱὸς Φαραὼ ἐνηδρεύκει αὐτῇ καὶ ἑκατὸν ἄνδρες μετ' αὐτοῦ. ⁸ᵇ εἶδεν δὲ αὐτὸν Ἀσενὲθ καὶ ἐφοβήθη. **27:1** ἐκάθητο δὲ

Βενιαμὴν μετ' αὐτῆς ἐπὶ τοῦ ὀχήματος. [2a] καὶ ἦν Βενιαμὴν ὡς ἐτῶν δέκα καὶ ὀκτώ, [2b] καὶ ἐδύνατο μάχεσθαι ὡς λέων πνευματικὸς φοβούμενος τὸν θεόν.

[3a] ἄρα καταβὰς Βενιαμὴν ἐκ τοῦ ὀχήματος ἔλαβε λίθον καὶ κατέβαλε τὸν υἱὸν Φαραὼ πατάσσων τὴν κεφαλὴν αὐτοῦ· [3b] ἔπεσεν δὲ οὗτος ἐκ τοῦ ἵππου αὐτοῦ τετραυματισμένος τραύματι μεγάλῳ. [4] Βενιαμὴν δὲ εὗρε λίθους ἑκατὸν [5] καὶ βαλὼν τοὺς λίθους Βενιαμὴν ἀπέκτεινε τοὺς ἑκατὸν ἄνδρας τοὺς παρόντας μετὰ τοῦ υἱοῦ Φαραὼ ἕνα ἕκαστον αὐτῶν.

[6a] Τότε Ῥουβὴμ καὶ Συμεών, Λευὶς καὶ Ἰούδας, Ἰσαχὰρ καὶ Ζαβουλὼν ἐδίωξαν ὀπίσω τῶν ἀνδρῶν τῶν κειμένων [6b] καὶ ἐπέπεσαν αὐτοῖς καὶ ἀπέκτειναν τοὺς τρεῖς χιλιάδας ἄνδρας οἱ ἓξ ἄνδρες. [7a] ἔφυγον δὲ Γὰδ καὶ Δὰν λέγοντες· [7b] Ἀναιρεθησόμεθα ὑπὸ τῶν ἀδελφῶν ἡμῶν καὶ ἀποτέθνηκεν ὁ υἱὸς Φαραὼ ἐν τῇ δεξιᾷ Βενιαμὴν [7c] καὶ πάντες οἱ μετ' αὐτοῦ ἀποτεθνήκασιν. [7d] καὶ νῦν, ἀποκτείνωμεν τὴν Ἀσενὲθ καὶ τὸν Βενιαμὴν καὶ φύγωμεν. [8a] καὶ ἦλθον ἔχοντες τὰς μαχαίρας αὐτῶν τὰς ἀκαθάρτας αἵματος. [8b] εἶδεν δὲ αὐτοὺς Ἀσενὲθ καὶ εἶπε· [8c] Κύριος ὁ θεός μου ὁ καθαρίσας με ἐκ τοῦ θανάτου, ὁ εἰπών μοι· [8d] Εἰς τὸν αἰῶνα σωθήσεται ἡ ψυχή σου, ῥῦσαί με ἐκ τῶν ἀνδρῶν τούτων. [8e] ἤκουσε δὲ κύριος ὁ θεὸς τὴν φωνὴν αὐτῆς καὶ ἐλύθησαν αἱ μάχαιραι ἀπὸ τῶν χειρῶν αὐτῶν.

6.1.1 Vocabulary

ἀποθνῄσκω – **Principal Parts: 2. ἀποθανοῦμαι, 3. ἀπέθανον, 4. ἀποτέθνηκα**
ἐνέδρα, ας, ἡ – ambush
ἐνεδρεύω – I lie in ambush, I prepare an ambush
ἐπερχόμαι – I arrive; Principal Parts: as ἐρχόμαι

ἐπιπίπτω – I fall upon + dat;
Principal Parts: as πίπτω
ἵππος, ου, ὁ – horse
καταβάλλω – I strike down
λέων, οντος, ὁ – lion

μάχομαι – I fight, make war
ὄχημα, ατος, τό – vehicle
πατάσσω – I strike
τραῦμα, άτος, τό – wound
τραυματίζω – I wound

6.2 Reading B: Acts 23:12–22

[12] Γενομένης δὲ ἡμέρας, ποιήσαντές τινες τῶν Ἰουδαίων συστροφήν, ἀνεθεμάτισαν ἑαυτούς, λέγοντες μήτε φαγεῖν μήτε πιεῖν ἕως οὗ ἀποκτείνωσι τὸν Παῦλον. [13] ἦσαν δὲ πλείους τεσσαράκοντα οἱ ταύτην τὴν συνωμοσίαν πεποιηκότες· [14] οἵτινες προσελθόντες τοῖς ἀρχιερεῦσι καὶ τοῖς πρεσβυτέροις εἶπον, Ἀναθέματι ἀνεθεματίσαμεν ἑαυτούς, μηδενὸς γεύσασθαι ἕως οὗ ἀποκτείνωμεν τὸν Παῦλον. [15] νῦν οὖν ὑμεῖς ἐμφανίσατε τῷ χιλιάρχῳ σὺν τῷ συνεδρίῳ, ὅπως αὔριον αὐτὸν καταγάγῃ πρὸς ὑμᾶς, ὡς μέλλοντας διαγινώσκειν ἀκριβέστερον τὰ περὶ αὐτοῦ· ἡμεῖς δέ, πρὸ τοῦ ἐγγίσαι αὐτόν, ἕτοιμοί ἐσμεν τοῦ ἀνελεῖν αὐτόν. [16] ἀκούσας δὲ ὁ υἱὸς τῆς ἀδελφῆς Παύλου τὴν ἐνέδραν, παραγενόμενος καὶ εἰσελθὼν εἰς τὴν παρεμβολήν, ἀπήγγειλε τῷ Παύλῳ. [17] προσκαλεσάμενος δὲ ὁ Παῦλος ἕνα τῶν ἑκατοντάρχων ἔφη, Τὸν νεανίαν τοῦτον ἀπάγαγε πρὸς τὸν χιλίαρχον· ἔχει γάρ τι ἀπαγγεῖλαί αὐτῷ. [18] ὁ μὲν οὖν παραλαβὼν αὐτὸν ἤγαγε πρὸς τὸν χιλίαρχον, καί φησιν, Ὁ δέσμιος Παῦλος προσκαλεσάμενός με ἠρώτησε τοῦτον τὸν νεανίαν ἀγαγεῖν πρός σε, ἔχοντά τι λαλῆσαί σοι. [19] ἐπιλαβόμενος δὲ τῆς χειρὸς αὐτοῦ ὁ χιλίαρχος, καὶ ἀναχωρήσας κατ' ἰδίαν, ἐπυνθάνετο, Τί ἐστιν ὃ ἔχεις ἀπαγγεῖλαί μοι; [20] εἶπε δὲ ὅτι Οἱ Ἰουδαῖοι συνέθεντο τοῦ ἐρωτῆσαί σε, ὅπως

αὔριον εἰς τὸ συνέδριον καταγάγῃς τὸν Παῦλον, ὡς μέλλοντές τι ἀκριβέστερον πυνθάνεσθαι περὶ αὐτοῦ. ²¹ σὺ οὖν μὴ πεισθῇς αὐτοῖς· ἐνεδρεύουσι γὰρ αὐτὸν ἐξ αὐτῶν ἄνδρες πλείους τεσσαράκοντα, οἵτινες ἀνεθεμάτισαν ἑαυτοὺς μήτε φαγεῖν μήτε πιεῖν ἕως οὗ ἀνέλωσιν αὐτόν· καὶ νῦν ἕτοιμοί εἰσι προσδεχόμενοι τὴν ἀπὸ σοῦ ἐπαγγελίαν. ²² ὁ μὲν οὖν χιλίαρχος ἀπέλυσε τὸν νεανίαν, παραγγείλας μηδενὶ ἐκλαλῆσαι ὅτι ταῦτα ἐνεφάνισας πρός με.

6.2.1 Vocabulary

ἀκριβέστερον – more thoroughly
ἀναιρέω – **Principal Parts: 2. ἀναιρήσω, 3. ἀνεῖλον**
ἀνάθεμα, ατος, τό – a curse
ἀναθεματίζω – I bind with a curse
ἀναχωρέω – I withdraw; Principal Parts: 3. ἀνεχώρησα
ἀπάγω – I bring before (+ πρός); Principal Parts as: ἄγω
αὔριον – tomorrow
γεύομαι – I taste
δέσμιος, ου, ὁ – prisoner
διαγινώσκω – I decide
ἑκατοντάρχης, ου, ὁ – centurion
ἐκλαλέω – I tell (+ acc of person told); Principal Parts as: λαλέω
ἐμφανίζω – I inform (+ dat of person informed; in this passage, as so often with verbs of speaking, you can use πρός instead of the dative); Principal Parts: 2. ἐμφανίσω, 3. ἐνεφάνισα, 6. ἐνεφανίσθην
ἐνέδρα, ας, ἡ – ambush
ἐνεδρεύω – I lie in ambush (+ acc of victim)
ἐπιλαμβάνομαι – I grasp; Principal Parts: 2. ἐπιλήψομαι, 3. ἐπελαβόμην

ἐρωτάω – **I ask (parse as though ἐρωτέω)**
ἕτοιμος, η, ον – ready
ἔφη – he said
κατάγω – I lead down; Principal Parts: as ἄγω
παρεμβολή, ῆς, ἡ – barracks
πείθω – **[imperfect ἔπειθον; Principal Parts: 2. πείσω, 3. ἔπεισα, 4. πέποιθα, 5. πέπεισμαι, 6. ἐπείσθην]**
πλείους – **more than**
προσδέχομαι – I await; Principal Parts: as δέχομαι
πυνθάνομαι – I ask
νεανίας, ου, ὁ – young man
συνέδριον, ου, τό – Sanhedrin
συνέθεντο – 'they have agreed' [you will be able to parse this in Chapter 19]
συνωμοσία, ας, ἡ – a conspiracy
συστροφή, ῆς, ἡ – a plot
τεσσαράκοντα – forty
χιλίαρχος, ου, ὁ – tribune ['commander of 1,000']
φησίν – he says

CHAPTER 19

Extra Verbs
—
Future Indicative

> **How to Use This Chapter**
>
> Follow the instructions throughout the **Extra Help** below, which will tell you when to work through various sections of *ENTG*.
>
> If you have followed along with me on how to understand and memorise the verb, you will again reap a reward in this chapter. So far you have met the major family of Greek verbs (-ω verbs), including one variation (-έω verbs, which have a contract vowel).
>
> This chapter introduces you to the remaining two variations on the -ω verbs, which have different contract vowels. There's nothing to them: we just need to get used to them.
>
> This chapter also introduces you to the second major family of Greek verbs: the -μι verbs.
>
> In the **Extra Material** you'll meet the few contexts in which the future tense can be found.

The verbs in this chapter have a bad reputation. If you've followed my method of building up your verb, you'll see just how straightforward these verbs really are! The **Extra Help** notes are a little fuller than usual to hold your hand through these beautiful, friendly, caring and virtuous verbs that have been slandered so.

It will help to understand *ENTG* 19.1 if we take 19.2 first.

1 BEFORE *ENTG* 19.2: CONTRACT VERBS

1.1 Contract Vowels

We have known for a while that some verbs have a contract ε at the end of their stem: ποιέω. This ε behaves predictably. It contracts with the endings according to fixed rules. It lengthens whenever a suffix is added to the stem: σ in the future stem, σα in the aorist stem, κα in the perfect active stem, θη in the passive stem.

In *ENTG* 19.2 we meet two more contract vowels that appear at the end of the stem of some verbs: α and ο. They behave exactly as above, but with their own rules of contract, which are in the table on *ENTG* 19.2.

Work through *ENTG* 19.2, including **Practice** 19.2, and then return here.

315

1.2 Thematic Vowels

We have also seen that after the stem, we find a thematic vowel before the ending proper. This vowel is ε, but becomes ο before a μ or ν. It is replaced by α in the aorist stem and the perfect active stem, and by an η in the passive stem. It is missing in the perfect middle/passive stem (**EH 16** 1.2), in root aorists (**EH 11** 1.2) and root presents (**EH 18** 1.1).

1.3 Infinitive Made Easy

With these in mind we can make the infinitive of all verbs (not just contracts) really easy.

All middle infinitive endings are **σθαι**. Before that we add the thematic vowel and, if there is one, the contract vowel. This accounts for all middle/passive infinitives of λύω, ποιέω, τιμάω, πληρόω.

The present active infinitive is **εν** (not ειν). The thematic vowel before it contracts to give λύειν. If there is a contract vowel, that will contract first, to give:

ποι-ε+ε+ε-ν	ποι-ει+ε-ν	ποιεῖν
τιμ-α+ε+ε-ν	τιμ-ᾱ+ε-ν	τιμᾶν
πληρ-ο+ε+ε-ν	πληρ-ου+ε-ν	πληροῦν

Each of λύειν, ποιεῖν, τιμᾶν and πληροῦν is easy to recognise as εν with some contractions.

That leaves the aorist active, perfect active, and passive stems. In each case the infinitive is ναι, with the thematic vowel. You can see it easily in perfect active λελυκ**έναι** and aorist passive λυθ**ῆναι**. The aorist active suffers from slippery sigma, so that λυσαναι ends up as λυσαι.

So we only have three infinitive endings: **σθαι, εν, ναι**. This will save us time in *ENTG* 19.1.

2 EXTRA HELP: BEFORE *ENTG* 19.1: μι VERBS

For the last eighteen chapters I have been insisting on memorising paradigms and getting them exactly right before moving on.

I'm changing that tune. This close to the end of the course is no time for nailing down every detail of new paradigms. Instead, enjoy the huge overlap between the -ω verb paradigms, which you already know, and the -μι verbs, which you are about to meet.

If you do about 10 per cent of the work, you can parse 90 per cent of these verbs. Doing an extra 90 per cent of work for the sake of the remaining 10 per cent of verbs isn't worth it at this stage.

2.1 After *ENTG* 19.1.1: The Stems

The stems are even easier to spot than with -ω verbs. You only need to ask three yes/no questions, each with one simple follow-up.

1 Does the stem end in θη?
    IF YES, is there a σ afterwards?
- θησ-: future passive (as usual) -δωθησ-; -τεθησ-; -σταθησ-
- θη-: aorist passive (as usual) -δωθη-; τεθη; -σταθη-

    IF NO:
2   Does the stem reduplicate?
        IF YES: does it reduplicate with ε or ι?
- ε: perfect stem (as usual, κ suffix if active, none if middle/passive) -δεδ-; -τεθ-; -εστ-
- ι: present stem -διδ-; -τιθ-; -ιστ-

        IF NO:
3   Is there a σ at the end of the stem?
- σα: first aorist (as usual) -στησα-
- σ: future (as usual) -δωσ-; -θησ-; -στησ-

Notice that all of the above are identical to the questions for -ω verbs, with the sole exception of the present stem reduplicating. If the answer to all of the above is no, you're dealing with:

- an aorist, which can break the rules:
  - aorists tend to lack a σα suffix altogether in the other moods
  - aorists can use a κα suffix in the indicative
  - ἵστημι has both a first (-στησα-) and second (-στα-) aorist, with different meanings.

2.1.1 Reduplication

As you can see, the perfect stem is formed in the same way as the perfect of -ω verbs. The present stem is also easy to spot, since it is the dictionary form.

The rules of reduplication are the same as the ones we have met before, but note two things:[1]

- If the stem begins with a vowel or σ, it reduplicates with a rough breathing ἱστ- not σιστ-.
- General rule: if the same aspirated consonant appears twice in a row, the first will lose the aspiration: τιθ- not θιθ-. To practise this, work out why ἐτίθην is imperfect active and ἐτέθην is aorist indicative passive.

---

[1] These apply in the perfect of -ω verbs too.

2.1.2 Contract Vowel

These verbs don't always have a thematic vowel, but they do have a *contract vowel*: στα θε δο. This lengthens unpredictably either fully (στη θη δω) or halfway (στα θει δου).

Now you can either work through *ENTG* 19.1.2 onwards (without the notes below) or else follow the notes below, which will lead you through *ENTG* in a different order.

2.2 Optional: Before *ENTG* 19.1.4: The Endings

We will return to *ENTG* 19.1.3 after we have looked at the basic endings.

2.2.1 Mostly the Same Endings

> Here are the few things you need, to fulfil **the 10/90 rule** I promised:
>
> 1 Three new endings on the present active indicative: μι ς σι. 'Missy!' There is no thematic vowel.
> 2 The masc nom sing participle, both present active and aorist active, is just the *half-lengthened contract vowel* followed by ς.
> 3 The 2s imperatives are tricky.

Once you understand the stems with contract vowels, you see that the endings are almost entirely interchangeable across the different -μι verbs, and almost always identical to the -ω endings anyway.

Here are some more notes to help you go beyond **the 10/90 rule**. Feel free to skip them for now.

2.2.2 Perfect System: Identical

All perfect endings are identical to λύω.

Note the pluperfect of ἵστημι. The reduplication happens as expected (**EH 19** 2.1.1), and the augment contracts with the reduplicating vowel:

> reduplication: στη → ἑστη
> augment: ε + ἑστη
> contraction: ε + ἑστη → εἱστη

2.2.3 Future System: Identical

All identical to λύω.

2.2.4 Subjunctives: Identical

All endings identical to λύω.

2.2.5 Infinitives

Always ναι when active or passive, always σθαι when middle, and always regular.

2.2.6 Participles

Participle endings are identical to λύω (with the one exception listed in **the 10/90 rule** above).

2.2.7 Imperatives

The 2s imperatives need learning for each stem. The other three are identical to λύω in every stem.

2.2.8 Present System

The indicative is identical to λύω, with the one exception listed in **the 10/90 rule** above.

The active imperative 2s is blank, so the ε thematic vowel contracts with the preceding contract vowel: ε + ε → ει; α + ε → η; ο + ε → ου. The middle 2s is σο, as it is for λύω, except that the intervocalic sigma is slippery in λύεσο → λύου, but remains in -μι verbs: δίδοσο.

2.2.9 Aorist System

The only real complications are in the aorist active and middle. The aorist passive is identical to λύω.

The aorist indicative endings are the same as for -ω verbs, regardless of whether the stem adds σ or κ. As expected, the 2nd aorist (the intransitive forms of ἵστημι) take the endings from the present stem (the imperfect indicative).

Outside the indicative, they use a *second* aorist, and copy the present stem endings, except in the imperative 2s, which needs learning.

Transitive ἵστημι is only active and uses a regular, first aorist throughout the moods, identical to λύω; you only need to learn the 2s imperative.

Now work through *ENTG* 19.1.3.
 Skip 19.1.4, then work through *ENTG* 19.1.5.

2.3 After *ENTG* 19.1.5: Vocab

Not all -μι verbs reduplicate in the present stem. How can you tell? It's the easiest thing in the world, since the present stem is the form you memorise as vocab: compare τίθημι and δίδωμι with __δείκνυμι.

The imperfect of φημί (ἔφη) is used as though it were aorist, and is interchangeable with εἶπε.

Generally, -μι verbs were dying out, and you would often see them with normal -ω verb endings (in the same way that some second aorists sometimes take first aorist endings, like εἶπον, εἶπα). You don't need to learn when δείκνυμι takes one set of endings or another, but be ready to see either.

Now complete the **Half-Way Practice**.

3 THE GREEK READINGS

The story so far ...

Pharaoh's son has tricked Dan and Gad (Joseph's half-brothers) into thinking that Joseph doesn't consider them brothers because they are not sons of Rachel or Leah (his father's wives), but of Bilhah and Zilpah (his father's wives' servants). He claims to have overheard Joseph and Pharaoh plotting to murder them and all their families as soon as their father dies. They set an ambush for Aseneth and Joseph, but didn't reckon with the remaining brothers, who intervened and overpowered the enemy forces. Aseneth was trapped and about to be killed by Dan and Gad. In answer to her prayer, their swords drop from their hands instead.

3.1 Reading A: *Joseph & Aseneth* 28

For your encouragement, there was nothing in the original passage that you could not have read, given a bit of help with vocab. The editing below was necessary only to give you practice with the contract and -μι verbs, and with the vocab of the chapter.

28:1 Καὶ εἶδον οἱ υἱοὶ Βάλλας καὶ Ζέλφας τὸ σημεῖον τὸ γεγονὸς καὶ ἐφοβήθησαν καὶ εἶπον· Κύριος νενίκηκεν ἡμᾶς ὑπὲρ Ἀσενέθ. ² καὶ ἔπεσον ἐπὶ τὰ πρόσωπα ἐπὶ τὴν γῆν καὶ ἠρώτησαν τῇ Ἀσενέθ· Ἄφες ἡμᾶς τὰς ἀδικίας, διότι κυρία ἡμῶν εἶ καὶ βασίλισσα καὶ ἡμεῖς ἠδικήσαμεν εἰς σὲ ἀκάθαρτα καὶ κατὰ τοῦ ἀδελφοῦ ἡμῶν Ἰωσήφ. ³ Ἀλλὰ νῦν ἀπέδωκεν ἡμῖν ὁ θεός, διὰ τοῦτο ἐπερωτῶμέν σου, οἱ δοῦλοί σου, ἐλέησον ἡμᾶς καὶ ῥῦσαι ἡμᾶς ἐκ τῶν χειρῶν τῶν ἀδελφῶν ἡμῶν, ἵνα μὴ ἀπολώμεθα ἀλλὰ ζῶμεν. ⁴ ἔφη δὲ αὐτοῖς

Ἀσενέθ· Μὴ φοβεῖσθε, ἀλλὰ συνίετε ὅτι οἱ ἀδελφοὶ ὑμῶν εἰσιν ἄνδρες δίκαιοι

καὶ μὴ ἀποδιδόντες κακὸν ἀντὶ κακοῦ τινι ἀνθρώπῳ. ⁵ πορεύθητε δὲ καὶ μὴ

φανερώσατε ἑαυτοὺς ἕως οὗ ἐξιλάσομαι αὐτοὺς περὶ ὑμῶν καὶ παύσω τὴν

ὀργὴν αὐτῶν καὶ τελειωθήσεται ἡ ἀγάπη αὐτῶν, διότι ἐτολμήσατε κοπιᾶσαι

ἐν μεγάλοις πρὸ αὐτῶν. ⁶ ἄρα μὴ φοβεῖσθε, διότι κρινεῖ κύριος ἀναμέσον ἐμοῦ

καὶ ὑμῶν καὶ στήσει ὑμᾶς. ⁷ ἀνέστησαν δὲ καὶ ἔφυγον Δὰν καὶ Γάδ. ⁸ καὶ ἰδοὺ

ἦλθον οἱ υἱοὶ Λίας τρέχοντες κατ' αὐτῶν, καὶ Ἀσενὲθ ἑστηκυῖα καὶ ἠσπάσατο

αὐτοὺς κλαίουσα. ⁹ Καὶ αὐτοὶ προσεκύνησαν ἐνώπιον αὐτῆς ἐπὶ τὴν γῆν

καὶ ἔκλαυσαν μετὰ φωνῆς μεγάλης καὶ ἐζήτουν τοὺς ἀδελφοὺς αὐτῶν τοῦ

ἀπολέσαι αὐτούς. ¹⁰ᵃ ἔφη δὲ πρὸς αὐτοὺς Ἀσενέθ· ¹⁰ᵇ Ἄφετε τῶν ἀδελφῶν ὑμῶν

καὶ μὴ δῶτε κρίμα κατὰ αὐτῶν καὶ μὴ ἐπιθῆτε κακὸν αὐτοῖς, ¹⁰ᶜ διότι κύριος

παρεστηκὼς οὐ παρέδωκέν με ἀλλὰ ἀπετέφρωσε τὰς μάχαιρας αὐτῶν ¹⁰ᵈ καὶ

ἀπώλοντο ἐκ τῶν χειρῶν αὐτῶν ὥστε γενέσθαι ὡς κηρίον ἀπὸ προσώπου

πυρός. ¹¹ᵃ τοῦτο οὖν ἱκανὸν ἡμῖν ἐστιν ὅτι δεδικαίωμαι τε ἐγὼ καὶ δεδικαίωται

Ἰωσὴφ ὑπὸ κυρίου· ¹¹ᵇ μὴ διψῶμεν τὸ αἷμα τῶν ἀδελφῶν ὑμῶν. ¹¹ᶜ λοιπὸν

ἰαθήτωσαν οἱ ἄνδρες οὗτοι εἰς τὸ πληρωθῆναι πᾶσαν δικαιοσύνην. ¹² ἔφη δὲ

Συμεὼν πρὸς Ἀσενέθ· Ἵνα τί ἐπιτιμᾷς ἡμῖν περὶ τῶν ἐχθρῶν σου; ¹³ οὐχί, ἀλλὰ

σταυρώσωμεν αὐτούς· δεῖ ἡμᾶς δεῖξαί σοι; διότι ἐβουλήθησαν κακὰ κατὰ τοῦ

πατρὸς ἡμῶν Ἰσραὴλ καὶ κατὰ τῆς διαθήκης τῆς μετὰ Ἀβραάμ.

3.1.1 Vocabulary

ἀναμέσον – between
ἀντί – in the place of; instead of; replacing (+ gen)
ἀποτεφρόω – I reduce (something) to ashes
Βάλλα, ας, ἡ – Bilhah
βασίλισσα, ης, ἡ – queen

ἐξιλάσκομαι – I appease, I propitiate; Principal Parts: 2. ἐξιλάσομαι; 3. ἐξιλασάμην
Ζέλφα, ας, ἡ – Zilpah
κηρίον, ου, τό – wax
κυρία, ας, ἡ – mistress
παύω – I end, I finish
πολεμέω – I fight
τολμάω – I dare

3.2 Reading B: John 18:5–25

To make the text the right length, sentences that require too much vocab have been skipped over.

Jesus and his disciples have gathered in a garden. Judas Iscariot is leading an armed band that wants to arrest Jesus. Jesus sees them coming, since they're carrying lanterns and torches at night, and asks them whom they're looking for.

⁵ ἀπεκρίθησαν αὐτῷ, Ἰησοῦν τὸν Ναζωραῖον. λέγει αὐτοῖς ὁ Ἰησοῦς, Ἐγώ εἰμι.

εἱστήκει δὲ καὶ Ἰούδας ὁ παραδιδοὺς αὐτὸν μετ' αὐτῶν. …

⁸ ἀπεκρίθη ὁ Ἰησοῦς, Εἶπον ὑμῖν ὅτι ἐγώ εἰμι· εἰ οὖν ἐμὲ ζητεῖτε, ἄφετε τούτους ὑπάγειν· ⁹ ἵνα πληρωθῇ ὁ λόγος ὃν εἶπεν ὅτι Οὓς δέδωκάς μοι, οὐκ ἀπώλεσα ἐξ αὐτῶν οὐδένα. …

¹¹ εἶπεν οὖν ὁ Ἰησοῦς τῷ Πέτρῳ, Βάλε τὴν μάχαιράν σου εἰς τὴν θήκην· τὸ ποτήριον ὃ δέδωκέ μοι ὁ πατήρ, οὐ μὴ πίω αὐτό; …

¹⁶ ὁ δὲ Πέτρος εἱστήκει πρὸς τῇ θύρᾳ ἔξω. …

¹⁸ εἱστήκεισαν δὲ οἱ δοῦλοι καὶ οἱ ὑπηρέται ἀνθρακιὰν πεποιηκότες, ὅτι ψύχος ἦν, καὶ ἐθερμαίνοντο· ἦν δὲ μετ' αὐτῶν ὁ Πέτρος ἑστὼς καὶ θερμαινόμενος.

¹⁹ Ὁ οὖν ἀρχιερεὺς ἠρώτησε τὸν Ἰησοῦν περὶ τῶν μαθητῶν αὐτοῦ, καὶ περὶ τῆς διδαχῆς αὐτοῦ. ²⁰ ἀπεκρίθη αὐτῷ ὁ Ἰησοῦς, Ἐγὼ παρρησίᾳ ἐλάλησα τῷ κόσμῳ· ἐγὼ πάντοτε ἐδίδαξα ἐν τῇ συναγωγῇ καὶ ἐν τῷ ἱερῷ, ὅπου πάντοτε οἱ Ἰουδαῖοι συνέρχονται, καὶ ἐν κρυπτῷ ἐλάλησα οὐδέν. ²¹ τί με ἐπερωτᾷς; ἐπερώτησον τοὺς ἀκηκοότας, τί ἐλάλησα αὐτοῖς· ἴδε, οὗτοι οἴδασιν ἃ εἶπον ἐγώ. ²² ταῦτα δὲ αὐτοῦ εἰπόντος, εἷς τῶν ὑπηρετῶν παρεστηκὼς ἔδωκε ῥάπισμα τῷ Ἰησοῦ, εἰπών, Οὕτως ἀποκρίνῃ τῷ ἀρχιερεῖ; ...

²⁴ ἀπέστειλεν οὖν αὐτὸν ὁ Ἄννας δεδεμένον πρὸς Καϊάφαν τὸν ἀρχιερέα. ²⁵ Ἦν δὲ Σίμων Πέτρος ἑστὼς καὶ θερμαινόμενος· εἶπον οὖν αὐτῷ, Μὴ καὶ σὺ ἐκ τῶν μαθητῶν αὐτοῦ εἶ; ἠρνήσατο ἐκεῖνος, καὶ εἶπεν, Οὐκ εἰμί.

3.2.1 Vocabulary

ἀνθρακιά, ᾶς, ἡ – charcoal fire
θερμαίνω – I warm [middle: reflexive]
θήκη, ης, ἡ – sheath

κρυπτός, ή, όν – secret, hidden
ῥάπισμα, ατος, τό – a slap to the face
ψῦχος, ους, τό – cold

4 ACCENTS

4.1 Contract Verbs

FURTHER READING: VS 11F

The rules of contract mean that any 'o' sound always wins; an 'a' sound will win over an 'e' sound if the 'a' comes first (**EH 11** 1.2.1). This has two consequences.

First: -άω contract verbs will always end either in a long 'o' sound (when there is an 'o' sound in the ending) or else in a long 'a' sound (when there is an 'e' sound in the ending). While you generally can't tell whether α is long or short, **any α in the ending of an -άω contract is long**:

ἠγάπας not ἤγαπας.

Second: -όω contract verbs. Normally, a final οι is short. However, when that οι is the result of a contraction of ο + ει, then it is long. Thus:

πληρό + ἐι → πληροῖ (not πλῆροι).

However, when the final οι, αι isn't the result of contraction, it remains short:

πληρό + ἐται → πληοῦται (not πληρο + ἐται → πληούται).

4.2 -μι Verbs

FURTHER READING: PROBERT 88

Generally, μι verbs follow the rules you would expect for contract verbs, namely, the accents are regressive before the contraction is resolved:

1s pres mid/pass subj: διδό + ώμαι → διδῶμαι

However, some forms make the accent regressive *after* contraction. These include the subjunctive and optative of -νυμι verbs, of perfects with κ and of *first* aorists, e.g.: δεικνύω; ἑστήκω; στήσω; δεικνύοιμι; ἑστήκοιμι; στήσαιμεν.

4.3 φημί

FURTHER READING: PROBERT 279D

Like εἰμί, the indicative forms are enclitic, apart from the 2s. Note that the 2s is not recessive: φής.

5 EXTRA MATERIAL: FUTURE

5.1 Contexts for the Future Indicative

FURTHER READING: VS 202; MURAOKA 28G

The future in indirect utterance is treated with all other indicative tenses in **EM 10** 6.

5.1.1 Default (Predictive a.k.a. Prospective) Future

This is by far the most common. It simply tells us that the action is in the future, and has nothing to say about aspect.

καὶ τοῦτο ποιήσομεν Heb 6:3
we will do this.

δώσω αὐτῷ φαγεῖν ἐκ τοῦ ξύλου τῆς ζωῆς Rev 2:7
I will give him [permission] to eat from the tree of life

5.1.2 Volitive

The future has become blurred with other forms of expressing desires, deliberations and even commands (subjunctive, optative and imperative), both in Greek itself and under pressure from translated Hebrew. As the translations below show, this isn't all that different in English.

> πορεύσομαι πρὸς τὸν πατέρα μου, καὶ ἐρῶ [future of λέγω] αὐτῷ, Πάτερ, ἥμαρτον Luke 15:18
> I will go to my father, and I will say to him, 'Father, I have sinned …'
> This isn't a prediction, but a decision.

> Τί οὖν ἐροῦμεν [future of λέγω] Ἀβραὰμ τὸν πατέρα ἡμῶν εὑρηκέναι κατὰ σάρκα; Rom 4:1
> Then what shall we say: that Abraham our father found according to the flesh?
> This is the equivalent of a deliberative subjunctive: εἴπωμεν [aorist subjunctive of λέγω], Ἐξ ἀνθρώπων 'Shall we say "It is from man"?'

> Οὐκ οἴδατε τὴν παραβολὴν ταύτην; καὶ **πῶς** πάσας τὰς παραβολὰς γνώσεσθε [future of γίνωσκω]; Mark 4:13
> Don't you grasp this parable? So how will you grasp any of the parables?
> This isn't asking for information about the future, but rhetorically questioning their ability.

Note especially in quotations from the LXX, a future for an imperative (capturing Hebrew grammar):

> Ἀγαπήσεις Κύριον τὸν Θεόν σου … Matt 22:37 citing Deut 6:5
> You shall love the Lord, your God …
> This is not a prediction, but a command.

5.1.3 Replacing Subjunctive or Optative

Because of the blurring above, you find the future indicative where you would expect a subjunctive or optative.

> Λέγω σοι, Πέτρε, οὐ μὴ φωνήσει [future indicative] σήμερον ἀλέκτωρ Luke 22:34
> I tell you, Peter: the cock will by no means crow today

CHAPTER 20

Final Pieces
—
Consolidation Greek Reading

> **How to Use This Chapter**
>
> In **Extra Help** you will find some notes to help you with these final topics, but you should view them as entirely optional. Simply work through *ENTG*, optionally consulting the **Extra Help** below as you complete each section.
> As usual, you will find **Greek Readings A** and **B**.
> As we have reached the end of *ENTG*, we offer **Greek Reading C** for consolidation. This is an extended passage from an early Christian text: completely unedited, with the usual vocab helps and online notes.
> Well done for making it this far!

1 *ENTG* 20

1.1 *ENTG* 20.1: Conditions

1.1.1 After *ENTG* 20.1.2: Contrary-to-Fact Conditions

Notice (Table 20.1) that contrary-to-fact conditions use *historical (augmented)* indicative tenses; the choice of stem generally conveys time.

Table 20.1 Stem and Conditions

Stem:	Present stem	Aorist stem	Perfect stem
Time:	Present	Past	Prior to past
Historical tense of the stem:	Imperfect	Aorist	Pluperfect

1.1.2 After *ENTG* 20.1.3: Examples of Pluperfect in Contrary-to-Fact Conditions

> εἰ δὲ ἐγνώκειτε [pluperfect] τί ἐστιν, Ἔλεον θέλω καὶ οὐ θυσίαν, οὐκ ἂν κατεδικάσατε [aorist] τοὺς ἀναιτίους. Matt 12:7
> if you <u>had understood</u> what this is, 'It is mercy that I desire, rather than sacrifice', then you <u>wouldn't have condemned</u> the innocent. The action in the <u>past [aorist]</u> was the result of a <u>prior</u> lack of understanding [pluperfect].

Ἀπολελύσθαι ἐδύνατο [aorist] ὁ ἄνθρωπος οὗτος, εἰ μὴ ἐπεκέκλητο [pluperfect] Καίσαρα. Acts 26:32
This man would have been able to be dismissed, if he hadn't appealed to Caesar.
Note the missing ἄν in the apodosis.

εἰ γὰρ ἦσαν ἐξ ἡμῶν, μεμενήκεισαν ἄν μεθ' ἡμῶν 1 John 2:19
for if they had been [imperfect] from us, they would have remained [pluperfect] with us.
Remember that εἰμί doesn't have a choice of stems, so it tends to use the imperfect tense for past and present tense for present, as here.

1.2 After *ENTG* 20.2: Genitive Absolute

You may find that it helps to understand this construction if you think about writing a Greek sentence.

Jesus' mother says to him, 'They have no wine.'
λέγει ἡ μήτηρ τοῦ Ἰησοῦ πρὸς αὐτόν, Οἶνον οὐκ ἔχουσι. (John 2:3)

What had happened to bring her to speak?

When the wine ran out, Jesus' mother says to him, 'They have no wine.'

So we want to add this branch to the tree:

The wine having run out.

What case should *wine* be in?
Unlike all the participles you've met so far, it does not modify anything already in the trunk of the tree. It stands alone, so we don't know what case to give it. The convention in Greek is that you use the genitive:

καὶ ὑστερήσαντος οἴνου, λέγει ἡ μήτηρ τοῦ Ἰησοῦ πρὸς αὐτόν, Οἶνον οὐκ ἔχουσι. (John 2:3)
And when the wine ran out, Jesus' mother says to him, 'They have no wine.'

1.3 After *ENTG* 20.3: Periphrastic Tenses

As with conditionals, these are quite intuitive and are also how English forms nearly all its tenses, so you would be right at home even if we didn't tell you about them.

Time is indicated by the choice of tense of εἰμί, which also indicates person and number. The choice of system for the participle determines the system of the verb. As we know, a tense is the combination of system + time, and these have been split between the form of εἰμί and the system of the participle. The information in a single tense is divided up as shown in Table 20.2.

Table 20.2 Periphrastic Tenses

Parsing	εἰμί	Participle	
Time (past, pres, fut)	Tense of εἰμί		⎫ Combine to give a tense
System (pres or perf)		System of participle	⎬
Person and number (1, 2, 3; sing pl)	Person and number of εἰμί		⎭
Voice (act, mid/pass)		Voice of participle	
Verb (λύω, ποιέω, etc.)		Participle	

You may find it helpful to take some verbs in indicative tenses (not aorists) and turn them into periphrastic tenses.

1.4 After *ENTG* 20.4: Comparative and Superlative

Comparatives in -ων follow the paradigm of πλείων, -ον (*ENTG* 12.4).

2 THE GREEK READINGS

2.1 Reading A: *Joseph & Aseneth* 28–9

Dan and Gad have seen that God is against them by the way that he has miraculously defeated them. They plead for mercy from Aseneth, who advises them to make themselves scarce. Simeon and his brothers are chasing after Dan and Gad, when Aseneth stands in their way and tells them to forgive their brothers. Simeon is unimpressed and reminds her of how heinous their plot was. What will she say to that?

For your encouragement, there was nothing in the original passage that you could not have read, given a bit of help with vocab. I have edited the passage only to give you practice with the genitive absolute, periphrastic tenses and comparatives (conditionals are in **Reading B***). Note that the periphrastic tenses below are a bit forced and do not represent normal style.*

[14] ἀλλὰ εἶπεν αὐτῷ Ἀσενέθ· Μὴ ἀποδῷς, ἀδελφέ, κακὸν ἀντὶ κακοῦ οὐδὲ τῷ ἐλαχιστοτέρῳ. μᾶλλον δὲ μνήσθητι ὅτι κύριος ἔσται κρίνων. [15] μετὰ δὲ ταῦτα ἦλθε πρὸς αὐτὴν Λευὶς [16] καὶ εἶπεν· Ἀληθῶς σέσωκας τοὺς ἄνδρας ἐκ τῆς ὀργῆς

ἡμῶν τοῦ μὴ ἀποκτεῖναι αὐτούς. **29:1** ὁ δὲ υἱὸς Φαραὼ ἀνέστη ἐκ τῆς γῆς, καὶ τὸ αἷμα αὐτοῦ ἦν ῥέον ἐκ τῆς κεφαλῆς αὐτοῦ εἰς τὸ στόμα αὐτοῦ. καὶ πτύοντος τούτου, ² ἔδραμεν ἐπ' αὐτὸν Βενιαμήν. ³ᵃ καὶ τοῦ Βενιαμὴν μέλλοντος ἀπολέσαι τὸν υἱὸν Φαραώ, παρεγένετο δραμὼν Λευίς. ³ᵇ καὶ ἐκράτησε τῆς χειρὸς αὐτοῦ καὶ εἶπεν· ³ᶜ Μὴ ποιήσῃς, ἀδελφέ, τὸ ἔργον τοῦτο. ³ᵈ μὴ γένοιτο, διότι ἡμεῖς ἄνδρες δίκαιοί ἐσμεν, ³ᵉ καὶ οὐκ ἔξεστιν ἀνδρὶ δικαίῳ ἀποδοῦναι κακὸν ἀντὶ κακοῦ οὐδὲ πεπτωκότα τραυματίσαι οὐδὲ διῶξαι τὸν ἐχθρὸν ἕως θανάτου. ⁴ ἀλλὰ θεραπεύσωμεν αὐτὸν καὶ ἐὰν ζήσῃ ἔσται ἡμῶν φίλος. ⁵ ἄρα ἀνέστησε Λευὶς τὸν υἱὸν Φαραὼ καὶ ἔνιψε τὸ πρόσωπον αὐτοῦ καὶ ἔδησε τελαμῶνα εἰς τὸ τραῦμα αὐτοῦ καὶ ἐπέθηκεν αὐτὸν ἐπὶ τὸν ἵππον αὐτοῦ. καὶ ἐνέγκας αὐτὸν πρὸς τὸν πατέρα αὐτοῦ ⁶ ἀπήγγειλαν αὐτῷ ἅπαντα τὰ γενόμενα. ⁷ᵃ ἀναστὰς οὖν Φαραὼ ἀπὸ τοῦ θρόνου αὐτοῦ προσεκύνησε τῷ Λευὶ ἐπὶ τὴν γῆν. ⁷ᵇ καὶ θεασαμένου τοῦ Φαραὼ τὸ σῶμα, ἐδίδου θυσίας ἐπὶ θυσιαστήριον. καὶ ἦν διδοὺς τὰ κρείσσονα ζῷα τὰ τοῦ Αἰγύπτου ὕπερ τοῦ ἔχοντος κακῶς. ⁸ τῇ δὲ τρίτῃ ἡμέρᾳ ἀπέθανεν ὁ υἱὸς Φαραὼ ἐκ τοῦ τραύματος τοῦ λίθου Βενιαμήν. ⁹ᵃ καὶ λυπηθεὶς Φαραὼ διὰ τὸν υἱὸν αὐτοῦ τὸν πρωτότοκον ἠσθένησεν. ⁹ᵇ καὶ προσκαλεσάμενος τὸν Ἰωσὴφ ηὐλόγησεν αὐτὸν λέγων· ⁹ᶜ Ποιμένες ἦσαν οἱ ἀδελφοί σου. σὺ δὲ ὢν μείζων αὐτῶν πάντοτε ἦν ἀγαπῶν αὐτούς. μήποτε καυχᾶσαι. ⁹ᵈ διὸ τέθεικα ὑπὸ τοὺς πόδας σου τὴν γῆν Αἰγύπτου. μικρὸν γὰρ ἀποθανοῦμαι. ¹⁰ καὶ ἀπέθανεν Φαραὼ ἐτῶν ἑκατὸν ἐννέα καὶ κατέλιπε τὸ διάδημα αὐτοῦ τῷ Ἰωσήφ. ¹¹ τότε εὖ ἦρξε Ἰωσὴφ ἐν Αἰγύπτῳ ἔτη τεσσαράκοντα ὀκτώ. ¹²ᵃ μετὰ δὲ ταῦτα ἔδωκεν Ἰωσὴφ τὸ διάδημα τῷ δικαιότατῳ υἱῷ τοῦ Φαραώ. [12b] καὶ ἦν Ἰωσὴφ ὡς πατὴρ αὐτῷ ἐν

Αἰγύπτῳ.

2.1.1 Vocabulary

ἀντί – in the place of; instead of; replacing (+ gen)
βασιλεύω – I rule as king
διάδημα, τος, τό – diadem
ἵππος, ου, ὁ – horse
πτύω – I spit

ῥέω – I flow
τελαμών, ῶνος, ὁ – bandage
τεσσαράκοντα – forty
τραῦμα, ατος, τό – wound
τραυματίζω – I wound

2.2 Reading B: Matt 24:22–8, 32–6, 43–4

[22] καὶ εἰ μὴ ἐκολοβώθησαν αἱ ἡμέραι ἐκεῖναι, οὐκ ἂν ἐσώθη πᾶσα σάρξ· διὰ δὲ τοὺς ἐκλεκτοὺς κολοβωθήσονται αἱ ἡμέραι ἐκεῖναι. [23] τότε ἐάν τις ὑμῖν εἴπῃ, Ἰδού, ὧδε ὁ Χριστός, ἤ ὧδε, μὴ πιστεύσητε. [24] ἐγερθήσονται γὰρ ψευδόχριστοι καὶ ψευδοπροφῆται, καὶ δώσουσι σημεῖα μεγάλα καὶ τέρατα, ὥστε πλανῆσαι, εἰ δυνατόν, καὶ τοὺς ἐκλεκτούς. [25] ἰδού, προείρηκα ὑμῖν. [26] ἐὰν οὖν εἴπωσιν ὑμῖν, Ἰδού, ἐν τῇ ἐρήμῳ ἐστί, μὴ ἐξέλθητε· Ἰδού, ἐν τοῖς ταμείοις, μὴ πιστεύσητε. [27] ὥσπερ γὰρ ἡ ἀστραπὴ ἐξέρχεται ἀπὸ ἀνατολῶν καὶ φαίνεται ἕως δυσμῶν, οὕτως ἔσται καὶ ἡ παρουσία τοῦ υἱοῦ τοῦ ἀνθρώπου. [28] ὅπου γὰρ ἐὰν ᾖ τὸ πτῶμα, ἐκεῖ συναχθήσονται οἱ ἀετοί. …

[32] Ἀπὸ δὲ τῆς συκῆς μάθετε τὴν παραβολήν· ὅταν ἤδη ὁ κλάδος αὐτῆς γένηται ἁπαλός, καὶ τὰ φύλλα ἐκφύῃ, γινώσκετε ὅτι ἐγγὺς τὸ θέρος· [33] οὕτω καὶ ὑμεῖς, ὅταν ἴδητε πάντα ταῦτα, γινώσκετε ὅτι ἐγγύς ἐστιν ἐπὶ θύραις. [34] ἀμὴν λέγω ὑμῖν, οὐ μὴ παρέλθῃ ἡ γενεὰ αὕτη, ἕως ἂν πάντα ταῦτα γένηται. [35] ὁ οὐρανὸς καὶ ἡ γῆ παρελεύσονται, οἱ δὲ λόγοι μου οὐ μὴ παρέλθωσι.

³⁶ περὶ δὲ τῆς ἡμέρας ἐκείνης καὶ τῆς ὥρας οὐδεὶς οἶδεν, οὐδὲ οἱ ἄγγελοι τῶν οὐρανῶν, εἰ μὴ ὁ πατήρ μου μόνος. ... ⁴³ ἐκεῖνο δὲ γινώσκετε, ὅτι εἰ ᾔδει ὁ οἰκοδεσπότης ποίᾳ φυλακῇ ὁ κλέπτης ἔρχεται, ἐγρηγόρησεν ἄν, καὶ οὐκ ἂν εἴασε διορυγῆναι τὴν οἰκίαν αὐτοῦ. ⁴⁴ διὰ τοῦτο καὶ ὑμεῖς γίνεσθε ἕτοιμοι· ὅτι ᾗ ὥρᾳ οὐ δοκεῖτε, ὁ υἱὸς τοῦ ἀνθρώπου ἔρχεται.

2.2.1 Vocabulary

ἀετός, οῦ, ὁ – eagle
ἀνατολή, ῆς, ἡ – east (both sing and pl)
ἁπαλός, ή, όν – tender
ἀστραπή, ῆς, ἡ – lightning
γρηγορέω – I remain wakeful
διορύσσω – I break in (aor pass inf: διορυγῆναι)
δυσμή, ῆς, ἡ – setting
ἐάω – I allow
ἐκλεκτός, ή, όν – chosen
ἐκφύω – I put out
ἕτοιμος, η, ον – prepared
θέρος, ους, τό – summer
κλάδος, ου, ὁ – branch

κλέπτης, ου, ὁ – thief
κολοβόω – I shorten
οἰκοδεσπότης, ου, ὁ – the one in charge of the house
οὕτω = οὕτως
προλέγω – I tell in advance; Principal Parts: as λέγω
πτῶμα, ατος, τό – corpse
συκῆ, ῆς, ἡ – fig tree
ταμεῖον, ου, τό – an inner room
τέρας, ατος, τό – a wonder
φύλλον, ου, τό – leaf, foliage
ψευδοπροφήτης, ου, ὁ – a fake prophet
ψευδόχριστος, ου, ὁ – a fake Christ

3 CONSOLIDATION OF CHAPTERS 1-20

So far, we have read some edited Greek texts from outside the NT, and some unedited NT texts. We move now to a taster of unedited Greek from outside the NT. This passage from the Greek Fathers will serve as consolidation for Chapters 1–20.

3.1 Reading C: 1 Clement 5–6

V. Ἀλλ' ἵνα τῶν ἀρχαίων ὑποδειγμάτων παυσώμεθα, ἔλθωμεν ἐπὶ τοὺς ἔγγιστα γενομένους ἀθλητάς· λάβωμεν τῆς γενεᾶς ἡμῶν τὰ γενναῖα ὑποδείγματα. ² Διὰ ζῆλον καὶ φθόνον οἱ μέγιστοι καὶ δικαιότατοι στύλοι ἐδιώχθησαν καὶ ἕως θανάτου ἤθλησαν. ³ Λάβωμεν πρὸ ὀφθαλμῶν ἡμῶν τοὺς ἀγαθοὺς ἀποστόλους· ⁴ Πέτρον, ὃς διὰ ζῆλον ἄδικον οὐχ ἕνα οὐδὲ δύο ἀλλὰ πλείονας ὑπήνεγκεν πόνους, καὶ οὕτω μαρτυρήσας ἐπορεύθη εἰς τὸν ὀφειλόμενον τόπον τῆς δόξης. ⁵ Διὰ ζῆλον καὶ ἔριν Παῦλος ὑπομονῆς βραβεῖον ὑπέδειξεν, ⁶ ἑπτάκις δεσμὰ φορέσας, φυγαδευθείς, λιθασθείς, κῆρυξ γενόμενος ἔν τε τῇ ἀνατολῇ καὶ ἐν τῇ δύσει, τὸ γενναῖον τῆς πίστεως αὐτοῦ κλέος ἔλαβεν, ⁷ δικαιοσύνην διδάξας ὅλον τὸν κόσμον καὶ ἐπὶ τὸ τέρμα τῆς δύσεως ἐλθών· καὶ μαρτυρήσας ἐπὶ τῶν ἡγουμένων, οὕτως ἀπηλλάγη τοῦ κόσμου καὶ εἰς τὸν ἅγιον τόπον ἐπορεύθη, ὑπομονῆς γενόμενος μέγιστος ὑπογραμμός.

VI. Τούτοις τοῖς ἀνδράσιν ὁσίως πολιτευσαμένοις συνηθροίσθη πολὺ πλῆθος ἐκλεκτῶν, οἵτινες πολλαῖς αἰκίαις καὶ βασάνοις, διὰ ζῆλος παθόντες, ὑπόδειγμα κάλλιστον ἐγένοντο ἐν ἡμῖν. ² Διὰ ζῆλος διωχθεῖσαι γυναῖκες αἰκίσματα δεινὰ καὶ ἀνόσια παθοῦσαι, ἐπὶ τὸν τῆς πίστεως βέβαιον δρόμον κατήντησαν καὶ ἔλαβον γέρας γενναῖον αἱ ἀσθενεῖς τῷ σώματι. ³ ζῆλος ἀπηλλοτρίωσεν γαμετὰς ἀνδρῶν καὶ ἠλλοίωσεν τὸ ῥηθὲν ὑπὸ τοῦ πατρὸς ἡμῶν Ἀδάμ, Τοῦτο νῦν ὀστοῦν ἐκ τῶν ὀστέων μου καὶ σὰρξ ἐκ τῆς σαρκός μου. ⁴ ζῆλος καὶ ἔρις πόλεις μεγάλας κατέστρεψεν καὶ ἔθνη μεγάλα ἐξερίζωσεν.

3.1.1 Vocabulary

ἄδικος, ον – unrighteous
ἀθλέω – I contend
ἀθλητής, οῦ, ὁ – a champion
αἰκία, ίας, ἡ – abuse
αἴκισμα, ατος, τό = αἰκία

ἀλλοιόω – I change
ἀνατολή, ῆς, ἡ – the act of rising; the East (i.e. where the sun rises)
ἀνόσιος, ον – unholy; by extension: evil.

ἀπαλλάσσω – I release; Principal Parts: 2. ἀπαλλάξομαι, 3. ἀπήλλαξα / ἀπηλλάγην
ἀπαλλοτριόω – I alienate
ἀρχαῖος, αία, αῖον – ancient, of old
βάσανος, ου, ἡ – torment
βέβαιος, α, ον – dependable
βραβεῖον, ου, τό – prize
γαμετή, ῆς, ἡ – wife
γενναῖος, α, ον – worthy
γέρας, ως, τό – prize
δεσμός, οῦ, ὁ – bond, fetter, chain
δρόμος, ου, ὁ – course, fixed trajectory
δύσις, εως, ἡ – the act of setting; the West (i.e. where the sun sets)
ἐκλεκτός, ή, όν – chosen
ἐκριζόω – I uproot (metaphorically of thorough destruction)
ἑπτάκις – seven times
ἔρις, ιδος, ἡ – rivalry
ζῆλος, ου / ους, ὁ / τό – zeal / envy (positive or negative)
καταντάω – I arrive
καταστρέφω – I subvert, overturn, destroy
κῆρυξ, υκος, ὁ – a herald
κλέος, ους, τό – fame; report
λιθάζω – I stone someone
ὁσίως – piously
ὀστέ-ον, οῦ, τό – bone (a contract noun, like νο-ός → νοῦς in **EH 13** 1.2.5)
παύω – I stop something
πολιτεύομαι – I am a citizen; by extension: how I lead my life
πόνος, ου, ὁ – painstaking effort
στῦλος, ου, ὁ – pillar; in the Church Fathers it refers to the 'pillars of the church' (cf. 'pillar of the community')
συναθροίζω – I assemble
τέρμα, ατος, τό – the furthest extent possible
ὑπογραμμός, οῦ, ὁ – a pattern
ὑπόδειγμα, ατος, τό – an example to imitate
ὑποδείκνυμι – I instruct; I point out
ὑποφέρω – I endure
φθόνος, ου, ὁ – envy (always negative)
φορέω – I bear
φυγαδεύω – I banish

CHAPTER 21

Next Steps
—
Atticising Greek (Optative; Future in Other Moods; Perfect in Other Moods; Hyperbaton)

> **How to Use This Chapter**
>
> Well done for making it this far! So, what's next?
> First, you'll find some advice on how to keep your Greek growing (and how to stop it from rusting). It's an easy concept to grasp: read a little each day.
> In **Extra Material** you find an introduction to some of the features of Greek that aren't covered in *ENTG* but which you still find in the GNT and literature from that era.

What should you do next, now that you have completed *ENTG*?
One thing: read Greek texts. **Read every day, at least for a couple of minutes.**
Which texts? Lots of texts. Read texts that you have already read; read ones that you haven't. Read NT texts and non-NT texts. Read Greek texts.
Ideally, you'll eventually take a further course of Greek. You need to learn how Greek authors communicate with their readers by going beyond the *Elements* of the language. You need to read lots of Greek texts and have some help on how (for example) the genitive or the imperfect can be used by an author:

> οὐχὶ δηναρίου συνεφώνησάς μοι; Matt 20:13
> This doesn't mean: 'Didn't you agree with me *of* a denarius?'

> ὁ δὲ Ἰωάννης διεκώλυεν αὐτὸν λέγων Matt 3:14
> This doesn't mean 'John was stopping him, saying:'

If you haven't got access to a decent course like that, the **Extra Material** throughout this *Reader* introduces you to some of these topics. We cover how verbs work and how cases work quite thoroughly. The same **Greek Readings** will do the job again, but this time with more advanced notes and questions in the **Online Material**.
What resources should you have?
Obviously, you need a copy of the GNT, and a way of looking up the words of vocab that you don't know. You can buy a lexicon (what we call a Greek dictionary) and a copy of the GNT, or you can get a 'Reader's edition' of the GNT, which

will give you the vocab you need at the foot of every page. That saves a fabulous amount of time and makes it easy to make progress.

For texts outside the GNT, an excellent place to start is Bradley H. McLean, *Hellenistic and Biblical Greek: A Graduated Reader* (Cambridge: Cambridge University Press, 2014). It has the vocab you need at the foot of each text, and the passages are carefully chosen to give you a wide exposure to the literature of the time.

You might also invest in a decent reference grammar. A good one-stop shop is Heinrich von Siebenthal, *Ancient Greek Grammar for the Study of the New Testament* (Oxford: Peter Lang, 2019). First, it covers the little irregular bits which don't belong in *ENTG*, and will give you even more help understanding the patterns of nouns, verbs and everything else. When you're reading a form that you don't recognise, it will be your friend. Second, it covers lots of further topics that I could have included in the **Extra Material**, and which you will want to master eventually.

Let's return to the main thing: a bit of Greek each day. If you do nothing else, when you open your NT to read it daily, using whatever schedule or plan you have, always start in Greek. After a few minutes, carry on with English so that you don't limit how much NT you can read. However, you will quickly see how much more Greek text you can read in those few minutes. Even now, you'll have no problem reading a verse of John in a couple of minutes. Soon it will be a paragraph. Before you know it, a chapter of John will be doable in five to ten minutes. John is especially easy, so when you're reading a chapter of that you'll still only be reading a paragraph of 1 Corinthians or half a verse of Hebrews. This is how you make progress and keep using Greek.

If you use Greek for preaching or teaching, and if you keep reading daily as above, something exciting will happen after a few years. It will *save you time* to do all your preparation from Greek, rather than from translations.

Please don't let your Greek rust again. You have put in all this hard work, and now you just need *a few minutes each day* to keep it up and capitalise on your investment. I know that's hard to do, but the rewards are wonderful.

1 EXTRA MATERIAL: ATTICISING GREEK

There are features of Greek which were dropping out of the language by the age of the NT and are so infrequent that *ENTG* doesn't cover them. Here, I give you a very basic introduction to the main ones which you will meet as you read through the GNT. As *ENTG* 20.5 warns you, these are more likely in 'Atticising' passages, which hanker for Classical style. Within the NT, that includes Luke-Acts, Hebrews, 1 Peter, James and (though he is usually restrained) occasionally Paul.

The main features below don't come together in a single NT passage. You can find them in passages such as 4 Macc 4–5, but, by their very nature, such texts are too difficult to belong in this *Reader*.

1.1 Optative

1.1.1 Morphology

FURTHER READING: vS 64D, 76-9

See 'The Greek Verb in Full – λύω' in the **Online Material**. Notice these basics as you look at the table:

- The endings proper are:
    - all active forms: nearly the same as the pres indic act of -μι verbs (-μι -ς -σι -μεν -τε **-εν**)
    - all middle forms: the *historical* middle endings; in 2s the 'slippery sigma' disappears but without contraction
    - aorist passive: *historical active* endings
    - future passive: *historical middle* endings.
- The optative adds ι or ιη *after the thematic vowel*. The thematic vowel changes to ο *except*
    - the aorist active and middle changes to α, as expected, but
    - the aorist passive remains ε.
- You find the expected contractions in contract verbs, according to the rules we've learnt.
- -μι verbs are the easiest of them all, simply adding ι or ιη to the contract vowel.

The optative of εἰμί is easy: εἴη plus the aorist indicative endings ν ς – μεν τε σαν.

1.1.2 Syntax

vS 211

We have met the optative in indirect utterance (**EM 10** 6.5). There are three other, very closely related, uses of the optative. All are very rare in the NT and the Greek of the period. Each can be found with or without **ἄν**, which makes no difference to the meaning.

The optative can express a **desire** (sometimes as a polite request) which is considered to be plausible ('**obtainable wish**'). It can express a theoretical possibility, something that is being considered by the speaker ('**potential optative**'). It isn't always obvious which is which. Examples:

> ὁ δὲ Θεὸς τῆς ἐλπίδος πληρώσαι [aorist active optative 3s] ὑμᾶς πάσης χαρᾶς Rom 15:13
> <u>may</u> the God of hope <u>fill</u> you with all joy ...
> **Desire**

> πῶς γὰρ <u>ἂν δυναίμην</u> [present middle/passive optative 1s] ἐὰν μή τις ὁδηγήσει με Acts 8:31
> for how <u>would I be able</u> to unless someone guides me?
> **Potential**

The '**potential optative**' was used in some types of conditional sentences in older Greek, either in the protasis (with εἰ) or the apodosis (with or without ἄν). In NT grammars, these get labelled '4th class conditions'. There are no complete 4th class conditional sentences in the NT and scarcely any in that era.

> οὐδ' **εἰ** πάντες ἔλθοιεν [aorist active optative 3p] Πέρσαι, πλήθει [dative of reference] γε οὐχ ὑπερβαλοίμεθ' [aorist middle optative 1p] **ἄν** τοὺς πολεμίους. Xenophon, *Cyr.* 2.1.8
> Even **if** all the Persians <u>were to come</u>, even then <u>we wouldn't outdo</u> the enemy, as far as our numbers are concerned.

The aspect of the optative in these three uses should be analysed as imperatives (**EM 11** 5).

> χαίροιεν [present] οἱ Ἱεροσολυμεῖται 4 Macc 4:22
> The Jerusalemites <u>should rejoice</u>
>> χαίρω has no endpoint, so the present optative is as expected. Likewise for states: Luke 1:62.

> τίς δ' ἄρα γνοίη [aorist] ὅτι εὕροιμι [aorist] αὐτὸν καὶ ἔλθοιμι [aorist] εἰς τέλος; Job 23:3
> So then, how <u>might I come to know</u> so that <u>I might find</u> him and <u>arrive at the end</u>?
>> γινώσκω aorist optative of a state: ingressive.
>> εὑρίσκω aorist optative as expected.
>> ἔρχομαι by itself has no endpoint, but τέλος (!) supplies it, so it becomes aorist, as expected.
>> See also Job 11:5–6; Diogn. 7.3.

1.2 Future in Other Moods

This is the easiest thing in the world to parse: add σ to the present stem and endings. For the future passive, add middle endings to the future-passive stem. See 'The Greek Verb in Full – λύω' in the **Online Material**. The meaning is the same as in the future indicative: it points forward, without any sense of aspect.

We have met the future infinitive, participle and optative in indirect utterance (**EM 10** 6).

Future participles can be attributive or adverbial. When adverbial participles are future, it is common sense that they will refer to purpose or result (rather than to something that happened before or alongside the main verb).

> πορεύομαι εἰς Ἰερουσαλήμ, <u>τὰ ἐν αὐτῇ συναντήσοντά</u> [future active participle neut acc pl συναντάω] μοι μὴ εἰδώς Acts 20:22
> I'm going to Jerusalem, not knowing <u>the things which will meet</u> me there
>> **Attributive**

ἴδωμεν εἰ ἔρχεται Ἠλίας σώσων [future active participle masc nom sing σώζω] αὐτόν Matt 27:49
let's see whether Elijah is coming to save him.
Adverbial, purpose

1.3 Perfect: Remaining Moods

See 'The Greek Verb in Full – λύω' in the **Online Material**. As with the future, the form of the verb and its uses are predictable.

The perfect imperative is built on the two perfect stems and adds the corresponding endings from the present stem. Note that the 2s middle ending doesn't lose the slippery sigma (because there is no thematic vowel before it), so you see -σο in the perfect, whereas the present contracts to ου. Likewise, the perfect subjunctive and optative. However, the middle/passive forms are always periphrastic: a middle/passive perfect participle with the subjunctive or optative of εἰμί.

Apart from standing in for other tenses in indirect utterance (**EM 10** 6), these forms are almost always used with verbs that have a frozen present meaning in the perfect (**EM 16** 4.4.2).

Ταῦτα ἔγραψα ὑμῖν ... ἵνα εἰδῆτε ὅτι ζωὴν ἔχετε αἰώνιον 1 John 5:13
I'm writing these things to you ... so that you might know that you have eternal life.

1.4 Hyperbaton

Further Reading: *CGCG* 60.18; Efrosini Deligianni, 'Hyperbaton', *EAGLL*, §3

In 1 John 5:13 above, notice the phrase ζωὴν ἔχετε αἰώνιον. The noun and its modifier (ζωὴν αἰώνιον) have been split up by a word that doesn't belong there: ἔχετε. This is known as '**hyperbaton**'.

If the *modifier* has been moved forward, that probably implies strong emphasis on the modifier, contrasting either with something in the context or in your expectation.

πάντα ἀφεθήσεται τοῖς υἱοῖς τῶν ἀνθρώπων τὰ ἁμαρτήματα καὶ βλασφημίαι ὅσας ἂν βλασφημήσωσιν· [29] ὃς δ' ἂν βλασφημήσῃ εἰς τὸ Πνεῦμα τὸ Ἅγιον, οὐκ ἔχει ἄφεσιν εἰς τὸν αἰῶνα Mark 3:28–9
Every single transgression will be forgiven the sons of men – even as many blasphemies as they utter – [29] but whoever blasphemes against the Holy Spirit, he lacks forgiveness for all time! The pulling forward of πάντα from τὰ ἁμαρτήματα sets up the very pointed counter-example in v29 as the *one* thing that is excluded from '*every* transgression'.

> ὤφειλε κατὰ πάντα τοῖς ἀδελφοῖς ὁμοιωθῆναι, ἵνα <u>ἐλεήμων</u> γένηται καὶ <u>πιστὸς ἀρχιερεὺς</u> τὰ πρὸς τὸν Θεόν, εἰς τὸ ἱλάσκεσθαι τὰς ἁμαρτίας τοῦ λαοῦ. Heb 2:17
> It was necessary for him to be made similar, in every respect, to his brothers, so that he would become a <u>*merciful* and faithful high-priest</u> concerning God's business, in order to bring about mercy ['make propitiation'] for the people's sins.
>
> Note how one modifier (πιστός) remains in its expected place, which highlights even more that ἐλεήμων has been singled out.

What if the noun *being modified* is what has been moved forward?

You know that Greek word order is flexible in places, such as the elements of the 'trunk', and the choice between sandwich or repeated-article constructions. *Why* an author makes those choices involves many factors, including the surrounding sentences and paragraphs, and is too big and complex a topic for this book. This kind of hyperbaton belongs in that category. For now, don't be thrown by it when you meet it. I offer you (tentatively) one suggestion of what the author might be doing. The author seems to be helping you follow the topic (whether pointing forward to a new topic or pointing backwards to tell you that the topic remains).

> συνέδραμε πρὸς αὐτοὺς <u>πᾶς ὁ λαὸς</u> ἐπὶ τῇ στοᾷ τῇ καλουμένῃ Σολομῶντος, **ἔκθαμβοι**. ἰδὼν δὲ Πέτρος ἀπεκρίνατο πρὸς τὸν λαόν, Ἄνδρες Ἰσραηλῖται, τί **θαυμάζετε** ἐπὶ τούτῳ ...; Acts 3:11–12
> <u>All the people</u> ran up to them, to the portico called 'Solomon's' **amazed**. But Peter, seeing it, answered them [i.e. responded to their astonishment]: 'Men, Israelites, why are you **amazed** ...?'
>
> The hyperbaton which leaves ἔκθαμβοι at the end helps us to see the link with Peter's speech, which uses the etymologically related θαυμάζω. This is why he's *answering* (ἀπεκρίνατο) the crowd: responding to their astonishment.

In 1 John 5:13 (above) ζωὴν αἰώνιον has been split, with ζωή pulled forward. John has just mentioned ζωή four times in vv11–13, concluding the penultimate section of his letter. As he now opens his conclusion, he wants to flag up that ζωή is still the topic. He's summarising what he wants them to know, 'I'm writing these things to you ... so that you might know', and uses hyperbaton to highlight *life* as the content. In other words: 'what I've been saying about life – *that* was for you'.

> ἵνα εἰδῆτε ὅτι <u>ζωὴν</u> ἔχετε <u>αἰώνιον</u> 1 John 5:13
> 'that you may know that you have *that* eternal life'

Indexes

Topics

Entries are sorted alphabetically, with Greek words following English words.
Bold page numbers indicate the more significant entries for a topic.
Cross-references (*See* or *See Also*) to a subentry will include the main entry first, separated by a comma, e.g.:

Ablaut. See pronunciation, vowel lengthening

unless the cross-reference is from a subentry within the same main entry, e.g.:
accents

 contonation. *See* rules of pitch

Cross-references to multiple entries are separated by semicolons.

Ablaut. See pronunciation, vowel lengthening
accents, 3, 8
 accented paradigms. *See* online material
 acute, 12, **13**, 14
 augment, 59
 breathings, 13
 circumflex, 12, **13**, 14, 22
 compound verbs, 59
 contonation. *See* rules of pitch
 contract verbs, 22, 323–4
 contracts in -όω, 14
 contrastive pronouns, 158
 differences in meaning, 12
 enclitics, **82–5**, 161, 177, **182–7**, 324
 enclitics combining with proclitics, 84
 enclitics starting a sentence, 83
 exceptions, 59, 145, 200, 224
 finite verbs, 22
 grave, 12, **13**
 imperative vs indicative, 119–20
 infinitives. *See* non-finite verbs
 introduction, 11
 liquid verbs, 189, **200**
 morae, 14, *See Also* vowel length
 non-finite verbs, 22
 nouns, 46
 optative endings, 14
 paradigms. *See* online material
 participles. *See* non-finite verbs
 persistent, 46
 pitch. *See* rules of pitch
 preparatory use of ἔστι, 84
 proclitics, 23, 46, 59, 161
 proclitics combining with enclitics, 84
 question words, 218, *See Also* correlatives
 quoting Greek words out of context, 12, 14, **15**
 reduplication, 59
 regressive, 22
 relative pronoun, 172–3
 rule of limitation, **14–15**, 22
 rule of limitation with contract verbs, 119
 rules of pitch, 12, 13, 22
 subjunctive, 302
 syllables, **8**, 12
 vocabulary. *See* online material
 vowel length, 12
 why they are worth learning, 11
 εἰμί, 84
 μι verbs, 324
 οι, αι, 14
 -σαι, 145
accusative, 161–8
 adverbial, 163
 'cognate', 164, 165
 direct object, **161–3**, **162**, 165

double accusative, 162
  in apposition, 54
  internal object, **163–4**, 165, 166
  manner, **164–5**, 166
  measure, 166–7, *See Also* cases, time and space
  reference, 165–6
  reference vs respect, 166
  respect, 165–6
  respect vs reference, 166
  space. *See* cases, time and space
  subject of infinitive, 162
  time. *See* cases, time and space
ad sensum, 226
adjective
  as modifier, 72–3
  attributive, 72–3
  predicative, 73
adjective formation
  2-2, 311
  3-1-3, 222
  3-3, 215–16
  consonant declension, 215–16, 222
  slippery sigma, 215
agents, 66
agreement
  ad sensum, 226
  parsing not appearance, 43, 215
Aktionsart, 86
anger rule. *See* noun formation, ιρε rule
aorist contexts, 120–36
  complexive. *See* default (states)
  default, 121–3
  default (states), 124
  dramatic, 134
  entering a state. *See* ingressive
  epistolary, 133
  futuristic, 134
  global. *See* default, *See* default (states)
  gnomic, 134
  ingressive, 124
  ingressive only with states, 126
  narrative mainline, 126
  non-narrative contexts, 126–8
  present mental states, 134
  relative past, 126–8
  Semitic, 134
  summary, 135
  time in a state. *See* default (states)
aorist indicative. *See* aorist tense
aorist system. *See Also* aorist, exegetical cautions; aorist tense; verb formation
  aspect in the other moods, 149, 245–7
  coincident participle, 239
  imperative, 201, **206–8**, **206–7**, 208–9
  imperative commanding repeated actions, 207, **208–9**, 208, 210
  imperative in prayers, 207
  indirect discourse, 178
  infinitive, 150, 151, 152
  ingressive, 152, 303
  not necessarily a single event, 154
  participle, 237, 238
  participle compared with perfect participle, 290
  relative time (prior), **178**, 237
  subjunctive, 302–3, 303
aorist tense. *See Also* aorist contexts; aorist, exegetical cautions; aorist system; verb formation
  aspect, 87, **120–8**, **310**
  aspect compared with present, 121
  'constative', 130, 280
  'consummative', 130
  default past tense, 87, 120
  does not deny ongoing relevance, 286
  'effective', 130
  global, 130
  imperfect, compared, 88, 120, 121, 122
  ingressive, 201, 284
  narrative alternation with imperfect, 100–1
  narrative mainline, 100
  ongoing relevance, 130
  perfect tense, compared, 120, **129–32**, 268, 280, 281, 282, 284, **285**
  single meaning, 149
  situation types with completion point, 122
  situation types without completion point, 121
  states, **123–6**, 149, 282
  successful completion, 122, 126
  summary by genre, 129
  time, 120–8

aorist tense (*cont.*)
  with completion point, 149
  without completion point, 149
aorist, exegetical cautions
  'constative', 129–32, 285
  'consummative', 128–9
  dramatic, 135
  futuristic, 135
  imperative commanding repeated
      actions, 207, **208–9**, 208, 210
  not necessarily a single event, 120, **121**,
      132–3
  punctiliar. *See* not necessarily a single
      event
  unnecessary categories, 128–33
article
  endings, 41
  neuter endings -ο vs -ον, 172
  relative pronoun, compared, 172
aspect, 86, 309–11
  Aktionsart, **247**, 268
  anterior. *See* combinative
  author's choice, 86, 152, **309**
  combinative, 310, *See Also* 'aspect' under
      perfect system; perfect tense
  definition, 309–11
  imperfective. *See* ongoing
  lexical. *See* situation types
  metaphors describing, 309
  ongoing, 88, **310**, *See Also* 'aspect' under
      present system; present tense;
      imperfect tense
  perfect. *See* combinative
  perfective. *See* simple
  simple, 87, **310**, *See Also* 'aspect' under
      aorist system; aorist tense
  situation type, **247**, 268
  stative. *See* combinative
  system, 89
  time, 309
aspect in the indicative. *See Also* 'aspect'
      under aorist tense, etc.
  combined with time, 23, **88–9**, 90–1
  past tenses compared, 86–7, 121
  tenses, 23, **88–9**, **90–1**
aspect in the other moods. *See Also* 'aspect'
      under 'imperative' etc.

basic principles, 146–7
complementary infinitive, 153
Hebraisms, 153
indirect discourse, **178**, 181
indirect speech, 152
participle, 237
purpose clauses, 153, 303
relative time, **178**, 181, 237
situation type, 146–7
systems vs tenses, 113, 116
translated Hebrew, 153
aspect, exegetical cautions
  humility, 211
  not about point of view, 309
  not about space, 309
  not nature of event, 121
  not situation type, **247**, 268
  other moods, 309, 310
  over-exegesis, **152–4**, 211
atelic. *See* situation types, actions without
      completion point
athematic verbs. *See* verb formation, μι
      verbs
Attic. *See* Classical Greek
Atticisms, 335
  conditions, 337
  dramatic aorist, 134
  future in other moods, 337–8
  future participle, 238, 337
  hyperbaton, 338–9
  indirect questions, 181
  middle, 259
  optative, 181, **336–7**
  participle in indirect discourse, 248
attributive. *See* modifiers, attributive
augment. *See* verb formation, *See* verb
      parsing
authorial intent, **227**, 334, *See Also* reading
      with understanding, *See Also*
      discourse analysis
adverbial participles, 233–45, 240–2
aspect, 86, 152, 209–11
explicit, 70, 269
explicit adverbial connections with
      participles, 235
explicitly comparative, 60
explicitly conative, 30, 105

explicitly concessive, 244
explicitly desiderative, 106
explicitly ingressive, 126
explicitly iterative, 103
explicitly of duration in a state, 125
explicitly of measure, 167
explicitly voluntative, 106
hyperbaton, 339
imperative, 208, **209–11**
ongoing relevance, 131, 278, 285
present tense, 27, 32
relative clauses, 173
word order, 225

cases. *See Also* accusative, etc.
apposition, 54
general uses, 54
prepositions, 54
time and space, 167–8
verbs, 54
categories. *See* reading with understanding, cautions regarding labels
cautions. *See* exegetical cautions
Classical Greek, 111, 134, *See Also* Atticisms
aspect of future, 153
changes over time, 262, 276–8
correlative form distinctions, 183
future participle, 238, 337
genitive absolute. *See* participle, adverbial, genitive absolute
gnomic aorist, 134
indirect questions, 181
optative, 181
participle in indirect discourse, 248
passive endings, 262
perfect of states, 282
perfect tense labels, 278
specialised middle meanings, 259
climaxes. *See* situation types, actions with completion point, resultant state verbs
commands. *See* imperative; indirect discourse; optative; future; volitive
companion website. *See* online material
comparative, 328

compensatory lengthening. *See* pronunciation, vowel lengthening
complementary infinitive. *See* infinitive, complementary
completable actions. *See* situation types, actions with completion point
completion point. *See* situation types, actions with completion point
conditions, 326–7, 337, *See Also* participles, adverbial nuances
conjunctions, 159, **168–71**
consonant declension. *See* noun formation, third declension
constructio ad sensum. *See* ad sensum
contract vowel. *See* noun formation, *See* verb formation
correlatives, 182–7

dative, 37, *See Also* dative contexts
abstract nouns, 69
basic meanings, 57
exegetical cautions, 60
genitive, compared, 66
indirect object, 60–3
instrumental, 63–8
interest. *See* dative contexts, advantage and disadvantage
location, 68, *See Also* cases, time and space
locative, 68–70, *See Also* cases, time and space
metaphors, 69
perfect passive verbs, 63
with adjectives, 60
with adverbs, 60
with participles, 60
with verbs, 60–1
γίνομαι. *See* dative contexts, possession
εἰμί. *See* dative contexts, possession
ὑπάρχω. *See* dative contexts, possession
dative contexts, 59–71
advantage, 61
agent, 62
association, 66
cause, 67
cognate, **64–6**, 236
disadvantage, 61

dative contexts (*cont.*)
  ethical, **62**, 259
  in apposition, 54
  indirect object, 61
  instrument, **63–4**, 67
  location in space or time, 68–9, See Also cases, time and space
  locative vs reference, 68, **69–70**
  measure, 60
  possession, 62
  reference, 67–8
  reference vs locative, 68, **69–70**
  respect, 67–8
  space, 68–9, See Also cases, time and space
  sphere, 69
  time, 68–9, See Also cases, time and space
demonstrative pronouns, 157
  predication, 158
demonstrative words, 182–7
deponent. *See* voice
desires. *See* imperative; imperfect tense contexts, volitive; indirect discourse; optative; subjunctive; future tense, volitive
dictionaries. *See* reference works, lexica
digamma, 307
diphthong, 7, 12
  iota subscript, 40
direct reflexive. *See* voice, middle
discourse analysis
  adverbial participle, 240–2
  conjunctions, 159, **168–71**
  demonstratives, 157
  hyperbaton, 339
  narrative, 100–1, 169
  narrative vs non-narrative, 129–32
  non-narrative, 126–8

endings. *See* noun formation, *See* verb formation
endpoint. *See* situation types, actions with completion point
English vs Greek
  adverbial nuances, 230, 235
  adverbial participles vs finite verbs, 233
  aorist vs English perfect, 129–32, 285

aorist vs pluperfect, 126
aspect, 93, 113
cases vs word order, 155
cognative accusative, 165
conative, 30
conjunctions, 168–71
'consummative' aorist, 129
dative, 60, 61
dative 'with', 63
demonstratives, 157
descriptive genitive, 49
desiderative, 106
direct object vs indirect object, 60, 162
direct reflexive, 258
durative present, 26
English perfect tense, 26, 264
epistolary aorist, 133
ethical dative, 62
future tense, 93, 94
genitive of comparison, 53
genitive of time and space, 50
go and..., 206
grooming, 258
historical present, 33
imperative and participles, 243
imperfect, 86
imperfect tense, 93, 94
indirect discourse, 173, 178, 179
indirect object vs direct object, 60, 162
indirect reflexive, 258
letter writing, 133
marked vs unmarked choices, 208, 261, 286, 292, 293, 295
middle meaning, 259
participles, 117
past simple, 86
perfect participle, 290
perfect vs aorist, 285
perfect vs past simple, 285
perfect vs present, 284
pluperfect vs aorist, 126
present tense, 16, **24**, 32, 93, 94
relative past, 126
short-lived states, 26, 101
situation types, 149
tenses, 86–9, 87–8
verbal genitives, 52

Indexes   345

voice, 257, **260**, 261
word order vs cases, 155
English, US, 259, 264
exegesis. *See* reading with understanding
exegetical cautions. *See* reading with understanding, *See* 'exegetical cautions' under aorist tense; aspect; dative; imperative; imperfect tense; participles; perfect tense; present tense; situation types
exhaling. *See* pronunciation, aspirated

future indicative. *See* future tense
future system. *See Also* future tense; verb formation
   aspect, 153, **310**
   aspect in the other moods, 245–7
   indirect discourse, 178
   other moods, 337–8
   participle, **237**, **238**, 337
   relative time (subsequent), **178**, 237
future tense. *See Also* future system
   aspect, 87
   contexts, 324–6
   default, 324
   predictive, 324
   prospective, 324
   replacing optative, 325
   replacing subjunctive, 325
   volitive, 325

genitive, 37, **46–55**
   ablative. *See* 'from'
   action. *See* subjective
   appertunances. *See* pertaining to ...
   apposition. *See* in apposition, *See* of apposition
   association, 48
   cognate head noun. *See* subjective
   comparison, 53
   contents, 50
   dative, compared, 66
   described, 49
   descriptive, 49
   destination, 48
   emphasised quality. *See* described

epexegetical. *See* explanatory
   explanatory, 50
   'from', 53
   in apposition, 54
   material, 50
   objective, 51
   'of'. *See* pertaining to ...
   of apposition, 50
   origin, 48
   partitive, 48, 50, *See Also* cases, time and space
   pertaining to ..., 47–53
   possession, 48
   pretii. See price
   price, 51
   proper. *See* pertaining to ...
   quality. *See* descriptive
   relationship, 48
   separation, 53
   source, 48
   space, 50, *See Also* cases, time and space
   subjective, 51
   time, 50, *See Also* cases, time and space
   value. *See* price
   verbal. *See* subjective
genitive absolute. *See* participles, adverbial, genitive absolute
gnomic. *See* proverbial expressions
grammars. *See* reference works
grammatical aspect. *See* aspect
Greek vs English. *See* English vs Greek

head noun, **37**, 47
Hebraisms
   aspect of infinitive, 153
   cognate dative. *See* dative contexts, cognate
   instrument, 63
   participle of manner, 236
   Semitic aorist, 134
   volitive future, 325
   ἐν + dat, 63
   ב of instrument, 63
historical present. *See* present tense contexts
Holy Spirit. *See* dative contexts, agent
hyperbaton, 338–9

illocutionary acts. *See* present tense contexts, performative; voice, middle, speech acts
imperative, *See Also* prohibitions
  advance warning, 205
  aspect, 113, **200-12**, 209-11, *See Also* aspect, in the other moods
  aspect vs context, 210, 211
  author's choice of aspect, 209-11
  begin, 202, **204-6**
  continuing, 202, **203**
  core sense of aspect, 200
  emphatic, 202, **203-4**
  equivalent expressions, 180, 201
  exegetical cautions, 114, 211
  formation, 113
  generic situations, 208-9
  habit, 202-3, 207
  immediative, 204-6
  ironic, 204
  lengthy, 205, 207
  motion, 206
  participles, 241, **242**
  prayers, 207
  process, 205, 207
  resistance, 204
  situation type, 201-2
  urgent, 202, **203-4**
imperfect indicative. *See* imperfect tense
imperfect tense. *See Also* imperfect tense contexts; imperfect tense, exegetical cautions; present system; verb formation
  aorist, compared, 88, 120, 121, 122
  aspect, 88, **99**, **103-7**, **310**
  marked past tense, 120
  narrative alternation with aorist, 100-1
  narrative background, 100
  past time, 99, 101-3
  resultant state. *See* imperfect tense contexts, immediative
  similar to present tense, 24, 36, 99, 100, 101, 109
  situation types with completion point, 122
  situation types without completion point, 121
  states, 101

imperfect tense contexts, 99-112
  conative, 104-5
  conative vs voluntative, 105
  customary, 102-3
  descriptive, 101-2
  desiderative, 106
  habitual, 102-3
  immediative, 111
  inceptive, **106**, 109-11, *See Also* immediative
  iterative, 102-3
  summary, 107
  voluntative, 105
  voluntative vs conative, 105
imperfect tense, exegetical cautions, 100, 107-12
  inceptive, 109-11
  'linear', 109
  not necessarily repeated, 109
imperfective aspect. *See* aspect, ongoing
indefinite pronoun. *See* pronouns, indefinite
indicative tenses. *See* tenses
indirect commands. *See* indirect discourse, commands
indirect discourse, 177-82
  aspect, 152
  basic approach, 173-5
  commands, 180-1
  complementary participle, 180, **247-51**
  general principles, 177
  infinitive, **178-80**, 180
  other mood, 177
  participle, 180, **247-51**
  perfect stem, 338
  persons, **177**, 181
  questions, 181
  relative time, 177
  statements, 178-80
  subjunctive, 180
  summary chart, 182
  supplementary participle, 180, **247-51**
  systems and relative time, **178**, 181
  tense shifting, 177
  time, 177
  time shifting, 174
  wishes, 180-1

ὅτι, 178
ὡς, 178
indirect object, 37
indirect questions. *See* indirect discourse
indirect reflexive. *See* voice, middle
indirect speech. *See* indirect discourse
indirect statement. *See* indirect discourse
indirect utterance. *See* indirect discourse
indirect wishes. *See* indirect discourse, wishes
infinitive
   aspect, **146–55**, 201
   aspect and situation type, 150–1, 151–2, 152
   complementary, 153
   complementary vs indirect discourse, 179
   indirect commands or wishes, 180, 201
   indirect discourse, 152, **178–80**
   indirect discourse vs complementary, 179
   purpose, 153
   subject, 162
   subject in indirect discourse, 179
instruments, 66
interpretation. *See* reading with understanding
interruptible actions. *See* situation types, actions with completion point
iota subscript, 40
irregular verbs. *See* verb formation, irregular

labels. *See* reading with understanding, cautions regarding labels
learning. *See* memorisation
lexica. *See* reference works
lexical aspect, 86, *See Also* situation types
lexically determined meanings
   aorist of resultant state verbs, 128
   consummative, 129
   direct reflexive, 258
   frozen perfects, 239, 287, 289, 303, 307, 338
   past stative perfects, 289
   perfective present, 33
   present stative perfects, 239, 287, 307, 338
   verbs which are always middle, 260
liquid verbs. *See* verb formation, liquid verbs
little words, 159, **168–71**, 175, **182–7**

Magnificat, 134
manner
   accusative, 164–5
   adverbs, 163
   dative, **63–4**, 163
   participles, 163, **236**
   prepositions, 163
   ways of expressing, 163
   τρόπος, 163
meaning overruling grammar. *See ad sensum*
means. *See* dative contexts, instrument
media tantum. *See* voice
memorisation, 17–18
   adjectives, 215–16
   article, 38
   consonant declension nouns, 212
   feminine nouns, 38
   masculine nouns, 38
   neuter nouns, 38
   nouns, 213
   paradigms, 17–18, 220
   participles, 228–29
   perfect stem, 268
   prepositions, 56
   verbs, 90
   vocabulary, **17–18**, 156, 159, 162, **168**, **170**, 175, 182–7, 320
   vocabulary essential to parsing, **142**, 187, 191–2, 213, 215–16, **230**, 255
αὐτός, 38, 42
modifiers, **37**, 47
   adjective, 72–3
   article, **72–3**, 73, **74–5**
   as nouns, 74–5
   attributive, 72–3
   attributive vs predicative, 74
   genitive, 37, 72
   hyperbaton, 338–9
   nominal, 74–5
   participle, 116, 230
   predicative, 73
   predicative vs attributive, 74
   prepositions, 55, 72
   pronouns, 74
   repeated article construction, 72–3
   sandwich construction, 72
   substantival, 74–5

moods, 298
motion, verbs of, 206
movable *v*, 16, 90, 96

narrative contexts, 33, 100–1, 126, 129–32
never-active verbs. *See* voice
next steps, 334–5
   daily reading, 334
   need for further study, 16, 38, 93, 114, 197, 256, 268, 309, 310, **334**
nominal. *See* modifiers, nominal
nominative, 225–8
   absolute, 225–6
   address, 226
   appellation, 226
   in apposition, 54
   naming, 226
   pendent, 225–6
   vocative, 226
non-narrative contexts, 100, 126–8, 129–32
noun formation. *See Also* noun formation, first, second and third declension
   Ablaut. *See* vowel lengthening
   contract rules, 137, 188, 220
   neuter ending rules, 38
   thematic vowel, **39**, 40, 41, 212
   vowel lengthening, 39, 41, *See Also* pronunciation, vowel lengthening
   ιρε rule, 41
noun formation, first declension
   feminine endings, **39–41**, 39
   feminine endings simplified, 41
   masculine nouns, 142
   Ἰησοῦς, 42
noun formation, second declension
   masculine endings, 39
   neuter endings -ο vs -ον, 43
noun formation, third declension, 212–15, 219–23
   contract stems, 220–2
   contract vowels, 219
   endings, 212
   nominative singular, **213–14**, 221
   siren rule. *See* pronunciation, word endings
   slippery sigma, 213
   summary, 222

-εύς, -έως, ὁ, 220
-ις, -εως, ἡ / ὁ, 221
Νηρεύς rule. *See* pronunciation, word endings
νοῦς, 222
-ος, ους, τό, 220
-ύς, -ύος, 221

older Greek. *See* Classical Greek
online material, 3
   accented paradigms, **3**, 8, 22, **38**, 46, 158, 172, 173, 216
   accented vocabulary, **3**, 8, **17**, 191, 268, 308
   answers to study questions, 2
   answers to study questions based on Extra Material, 2
   errata, 1
   instructions for third edition of *ENTG*, **3**, 85, 251, 263, 306
   notes accompanying Greek Readings, **2**, 36, 192, 326
   notes based on Extra Material, **2**, 334
   noun tables, 4, 42, 142, 215
   parsing puzzle, 230
   study questions accompanying Greek Readings, **2**, 36
   study questions based on Extra Material, **2**, 334
   translation of Greek Readings, **2**, 197
   verb tables, **4**, 112, 139, 187, 191, 251, 266, 267, 270, 294, 297, 307, 336, 337, 338
optative
   aspect, **201**, 337
   replaced by future tense, 325
optional *v*. *See* movable *v*
other moods, 113, *See Also* imperative, etc.
   systems vs tenses, 116

paradigms. *See* memorisation, paradigms
participles, 232–51, *See Also* participles, adverbial; participles, adverbial nuances
   are adjectives, 114, 229, 232
   article, 115
   as nouns. *See* nominal
   aspect, 116, **245–7**

aspects compared, 293
attributive, 229
circumstantial. *See* participles, adverbial
complementary, 180, **247–51**
exegetical cautions, 234, 236–7, 237
formation, 114
implicit connections. *See* participles, adverbial nuances
indirect discourse, 180, **247–51**
meaning, 114–16
meanings, 229–30
nominal, 117, 229
parsing, 228–9
predicative, 230
relative time, 237–40
substantival. *See* nominal
supplementary, 180, **247–51**
systems and relative time, 237
systems vs tenses, 116
verbal meaning, 115, 229
with objects, 116
participles, adverbial, 115, 230, **233–45**
attendant circumstance. *See* stylistic
author's choice, 233–5, 240–2
coincident, 239
exegesis, 243
genitive absolute, **244–5**, 327
no article, 245
not connected to the subject, 243
stylistic, 233, **242–3**
vs main verb, 240
participles, adverbial nuances, 230, **235–7**
causal, 235
concessive, 235
conditional, 235
instrumental. *See* means
manner, 236, 239
means, 236, 239
pleonastic, 236
purpose, 235
redundant, 236
relative time, 237, **238–9**, **239**
result, 235
temporal, 235
passiva tantum. See voice
past contexts, 33
perception, verbs of, 248, 260, 261

perfect indicative. *See* perfect tense
perfect system, 263–70, **276–90**, **296**, *See Also* perfect tense, *See Also* pluperfect tense, *See Also* verb formation
aspect, 263–5, 310
aspect in the other moods, 245–7
frozen perfects, 303, *See Also* perfect tense, frozen perfects
imperative, 294
indirect discourse, 178
infinitive, 295–6
ongoing relevance, 263–5
other moods, 290–6
participle, 237, **238**, 267, **290–4**
participle compared with aorist participle, 290
prior event, 263–5
relative time (concurrent ongoing relevance), **178**, 237
subjunctive, **294–5**, 303
perfect tense, 266–7, *See Also* perfect system, *See Also* perfect tense contexts, *See Also* verb formation
aorist (ingressive), compared, 284
aorist, compared, 120, **129–32**, 268, 280, 281, 282, **285**
aspect, 267, 278, *See Also* perfect system, aspect
endpoint, 280
evolution. *See* stages of development
exegetical cautions, 278, 284, 286
'extensive', 284
frozen perfects, 239, **287–8**, 307, 338
historical events in epistles, 285
indicating responsibility, 279
'intensive', 282, 284
judicial contexts, 279
logical arguments, 279
marked present tense, 120, 268
meaning, 267
ongoing relevance, 130, 278, 281, 285
poles of meaning, 276–8, 284
present stative. *See* frozen perfects
present tense, compared, 282
prior event, 278, 281, 282

perfect tense (*cont.*)
  resultant state verbs. *See* perfect tense contexts, resultative
  simple aspect, 280
  stages of development, 276–8
  states, 282–4
  time, 266, 267
  verbs of result, 284
perfect tense contexts, 278–84
  aoristic, 286–7
  default, 278–81
  futuristic, 289
  gnomic, 289
  resultative, 281–2
  rhetorical, 288–9
periphrastic tenses. *See* tenses, periphrastic
pluperfect indicative. *See* pluperfect tense
pluperfect tense, 268, *See Also* perfect system, *See Also* verb formation
  aspect. *See* perfect tense, aspect
  default, 289
  frozen perfects, 289
  narrative contexts, 100
  past stative. *See* frozen perfects
  verbs of result, 289
post-NT Greek, 276
post-positive, 161
predicative. *See* modifiers, predicative
predictive contexts, 32
prepositional branch. *See* modifiers, prepositions
present indicative. *See* present tense
present system, *See Also* present tense; imperfect tense; verb formation
  aspect, 89
  aspect in the other moods, 149, 245–7
  contexts of indicative tenses, 107
  imperative, 201, **202–6**, 208–9
  imperative commanding beginning, 204–6
  imperative commanding continuing, 203
  imperative commanding habits, 202–3
  imperative commanding with urgency, 203–4
  indirect discourse, 178
  infinitive, 150, 151, 152
  not present time, 89, 266

participle, **237**, 238, 239
relative time (concurrent), **178**, 237
present tense, 23–36, *See Also* present system, *See Also* present tense contexts, *See Also* verb formation
  aspect, 23, **29–33**
  aspect compared with aorist, 121
  default present tense, 24
  exegetical cautions, 34
  ongoing aspect, 310
  perfect tense, compared, 282
  similar to imperfect tense, 24, 36, 99, 100, 101, 109
  states, 25, 282
  time, 23, **25–9**
  unfinished actions, 29
present tense contexts, 24–35
  aoristic. *See* performative
  characteristic, 26–8
  conative, 30, *See Also* voluntative
  conative vs voluntative, 31
  customary, 26–8
  descriptive, 25–6
  durative, 26
  futuristic, 31–3, *See Also* voluntative
  futuristic vs voluntative, 31
  gnomic, 28–9
  habitual, **26–8**
  historical, 33
  historical present, 100
  instantaneous. *See* performative
  iterative, 26–8
  perfective, 33
  performative, 29
  predictive contexts, 32
  prophetic contexts, 32
  proverbial expressions. *See* gnomic
  summary, 34–6, 107
  voluntative, 30–31, *See Also* conative, *See Also* futuristic
  voluntative vs conative, 31
  voluntative vs futuristic, 31
principal parts, 308, *See* verb formation, principal parts
prohibitions, 209, *See* imperative; indirect discourse; optative; subjunctive

pronouns. *See* modifiers, pronouns, *See Also* demonstrative pronouns; relative pronoun
  contrastive, 158
  indefinite, 183
  neuter endings -ο vs -ον, 172
  word order, 159
pronunciation, 7, 12
  aspirated, 56, 95, 253, 317
  combinations, 56
  consonant groups. *See* pronunciation, stops
  iota subscript, 40
  rough breathings, 56, 95, 317
  shorthand consonants, 56, 95, 253
  smooth breathings, 95
  stops, 96
  unaspirated, 56, 95, 253
  voiced, 95
  vowel lengthening, 189, 190, 213, 214
  word endings, 188, 214, 253
  β, 253
  γ, 253
  δ, 253
  F, 307
  ζ, 96, 253
  θ, 56, 95, 253, *See Also* verb formation, 'thlippery theta'
  κ, 56, 253
  λ, 189
  μ, 140, 189
  ν, 189, *See Also* movable ν
  ξ, 95
  π, 56, 253
  ρ, 189
  σ, 137, 140, 189, 253, *See Also* slippery sigma (under verb formation, noun formation, adjective formation)
  τ, 253
  τ, 56
  φ, 56, 95, 253
  χ, 56, 95, 253
  ψ, 95
prophetic contexts, 32
proverbial expressions. *See* 'gnomic' under aorist contexts; Classical Greek;
   perfect tense contexts; present tense context
purely privative opposition. *See* English vs Greek, marked vs unmarked choices
purpose clauses
  aspect, 153, 303
  indirect commands or wishes, 180

question words, 182–7
questions. *See* indirect discourse, questions

reading with understanding, 4–6, *See Also* exegetical cautions, *See Also* authorial intent, *See Also* discourse analysis
  ad sensum, 226
  cautions regarding labels, 24, 35, 46, 47, 48, 52, 70, 128–33, 161, 166, 236–7
  indirect statements, 174
  meaning overruling grammar. *See ad sensum*
  not translating, 107, **117**, 129, 130, 131, 132, **155–6**, **168–71**, 174, 233, 249, 259, 260, 284–6, 290, **335**
  parsing and meaning, 43, 89, 94, 113, 114
  perfect participle, 290
  present tense, 16
  vocabulary, 156, 159, **168**, **170**, 175, 256, 259, 261, 262
  voice. *See* voice
  wrong grammar. *See ad sensum*
reference. *See* accusative, reference; dative contexts, reference
reference works, 334–5
  lexica, 256, 261, 262, **335**
reflexive. *See* voice, middle
relative clause, 171–3
relative pronoun, 171
  accents, 172–3
  ambiguous, 173
  article, compared, 172
  endings, 172
repeated article construction. *See* modifiers:repeated article construction

resources. *See* online material, *See* reference works
respect. *See* accusative, respect; dative contexts, respect
rhetorical effect, 29, 225, 288–9, 325
root aorists. *See* verb formation, root aorists
root presents. *See* verb formation, root presents

sandwich construction. *See* modifiers:sandwich construction
second aorists. *See* verb formation, second aorists
sentence structure. *See* word order
shorthand consonants. See pronunciation, shorthand consonants
siren rule. *See* pronunciation, word endings
situation types, 147–9, *See Also* situation types, states, *See Also* situation types, actions with completion point, *See Also* situation types, actions without completion point
  aspect in the other moods, 146–7
  changing in context, 148, *See Also* situation types, states, becoming activites in context, *See Also* situation types, actions without completion point, completion point supplied
  language-specific, 149
  not the same as aspect, **247**, 268
  words with different senses, 148
situation types, actions with completion point, 30, 104, **147–9**
  accomplishments, 122
  aorist as default aspect, 149
  aorist tense, 122
  aspect choice, **149**, **150–1**, 201
  climaxes. *See* resultant state verbs
  imperfect tense, 104
  present tense, 30
  resistance, 30, 31, 104, 105
  resultant state verbs, 128, 281–2
  successful completion, 122, 126
situation types, actions without completion point, 104, **147–9**

aorist tense, 121
aspect choice, **149**, 151–2, 201
completion point supplied, **148**, 151, 201
present as default aspect, 149
situation types, states, 147–9
  aorist tense, 123–6
  aspect choice, **149**, 152, 201
  becoming activities in context, **148**, 303
  imperfect tense, 101
  perfect tense, 282–4
  present as default aspect, 149
  present tense, 25, 28
  vs resultant state verbs, 281
slippery sigma. *See* verb formation, noun formation, adjective formation
small words. *See* little words
sometimes-active verbs. *See* voice
speech acts. *See* present tense contexts, performative; voice, middle, speech acts
spelling, 56
square of stops. *See* pronunciation, stops
states. *See* situation types, states
stative. *See* situation types, states
stem. *See* verb systems; verb formation
subjunctive, 297–9
  aorist as default aspect, 302–3
  aspect, 201, 302–6
  indirect commands or wishes, 180
  perfect, 303
  replaced by future tense, 325
  set constructions, 298
substantival. See modifiers, substantival
syntactical categories. *See* reading with understanding, cautions regarding labels
syntactical labels. *See* reading with understanding, cautions regarding labels

telic. *See* situation types, actions with completion point
tenses, **86–9**, **89**, 137, *See* present tense, etc
  combining aspect and time, 23
  periphrastic, 327–8
  related to each other, 87
thematic vowels. *See* noun formation, *See* verb formation

translation. *See* reading with
    understanding
Trinity. *See* dative contexts, agent
trunk and branches
    modifiers. *See* modifiers
    predicative. *See* modifiers, predicative
    word order of trunk elements. *See* word
        order, sentence constituents

understanding. *See* reading with
    understanding

verb. *See* aspect; tenses (and 'aorist tense'
        etc.); verb systems (and 'aorist
        system' etc.); verb formation; verb
        parsing; voice
verb formation, *See Also* verb parsing, *See
        Also* future system
    aorist endings, 89
    aorist endings compared with imperfect,
        90
    aorist passive. *See* passive stem, *See*
        passive stem
    aorist passive endings, 252
    aorist stem, **88**, 90–1
    aorist tense, 90–1
    augment, 88, 93, 94, 96, 191, 298
    building your verb, 18, 93, 96, 139, 254
    compound verbs, 191
    contract vowel, 18, 19, 96, 298, 315–16
    contract vowel in μι verbs, 318
    contract vowel rules, 137, 188, 220
    endings, 19, 89, 93, 96
    future endings, 90–1
    future passive. *See* passive stem, *See*
        passive stem
    future passive endings, 252
    future stem, **88**, 90–1
    future tense, 90–1
    historical endings, 89, 137, **188**
    historical tenses, **88–8**, 88–9, 89, 90–1,
        269
    imperfect endings compared with aorist,
        90
    imperfect tense, 90–1
    infinitive, 316
    intervocalic sigma, 137, **189**, 266, 319,
        338

irregular. *See* liquid verbs; passive stem;
    perfect stem; principal parts; root
    aorists; root presents; second
    aorists
liquid verbs, 189–91
middle endings, 136–9
'middle men', 229, 267
middle participle, 229, 267
optative, 336
passive, 251–4
passive endings, 252
passive stem, 252
perfect endings, 266–7
perfect imperative, 338
perfect optative, 338
perfect participle, 267
perfect stem, 265–6, 267
perfect subjunctive, 294, 338
perfect tense, 266–7
pluperfect tense, 269
present endings, 89, 90–1
present stem, **88**, 90–1
present tense, 90–1
principal endings, 137, **266–7**
principal parts, 191–2, 252, 265
principal tenses, **88–9**, 88–9, 90–1
reduplication, 265, 269, 317
root, 93, 96
root aorists, 188–9
root presents, 306–7
second aorists, 187–8
siren rule. *See* pronunciation, word
    endings
slippery sigma, 137, 140, 189, 266, 298,
    319, 338
stem, 19, 93, 96, 252, 317–18
system, 252
thematic vowel, 89, 93, 96, 137, 252, 266,
    269, 298, 316, 318
'thlippery theta', 253
time, 88–9
voice changes, 191, *See Also* principal parts
vowel lengthening. *See* pronunciation,
    vowel lengthening
εἰμί, 140–2
μι verbs, 316–20
Νηρεύς rule. *See* pronunciation, word
    endings

verb parsing, **89**, 113, *See Also* verb
    formation
  aorist tense, 89, 90–1
  augment, 113, 187, 269
  future tense, 90–1
  imperfect tense, 90–1
  liquid verbs, 189–91
  participles, 228–9
  present tense, 89, 90–1
  root aorists, 188–9
  root presents, 306–7
  second aorists, 187–8
  subjunctive, 297–8
  voice, 140
  μι verbs, 317–18
verb stems. *See* verb systems; verb
    formation
verb systems, 90–1
  aspect, **88–9**, 89, **90–1**, **309**
  indirect discourse, **178**, 181
  moods, 113
  participle, 237
  relative time, **178**, 181, 237
  tenses, 88–9, 90–1
verb types. *See* situation types
verbal aspect. *See* aspect
vocabulary, 8
  accented. *See* online material
  John's Gospel, 17
  memorisation. *See* memorisation,
    vocabulary
  parsing. *See* memorisation, vocabulary
    essential to parsing
voice, *See Also* verb formation
  active does not deny subject-
    affectedness, 261
  deponent. *See* voice, never-active verbs
  media tantum. See voice, never-active
    verbs
  parsing and meaning, 255–6
  passiva tantum. See voice, never-active
    verbs
  sometimes-active verbs, 255–6, **258–9**
voice, middle, 139, **257–63**
  definition, 258
  direct reflexive, 256, **258**, 260, 261
  indirect reflexive, **258–9**, 260, 261

  passive included, 261
  subject-affected, **258**, 259, 260, 261
voice, never-active verbs, 255–6, **259–61**,
    306–7
  always-passive verbs, 261–3
  choice of endings, 255, 262
  meaning families, 260
  not 'deponent', 260
voice, passive, 255, 261
vowel lengthening. *See* noun formation,
    See pronunciation, vowel
    lengthening
website. *See* online material
what to do after this book. *See* next steps
why read extra-biblical texts, 4–6
wishes. *See* imperative; imperfect tense
    contexts, volitive; indirect
    discourse; optative; subjunctive;
    future tense, volitive

Wooster, Bertie, 10
word endings. *See* pronunciation, word
    endings
word order, 155, *See Also* discourse
    analysis, *See Also* modifiers
  adverbial participle, 240–2
  emphasis, 225
  hyperbaton, 338–9
  modifiers before/after main verb, 240
  pronouns, 159
  sentence constituents, 17, 38
wrong grammar. *See ad sensum*

α-declension. *See* noun formation, first
    declension

ιρε rule. *See* noun formation, ιρε rule

μι verbs. *See* verb formation, μι verbs

Νηρεύς rule. *See* pronunciation, word
    endings

ο-declension. *See* noun formation, second
    declension

οἶδα, 307

Ancient Texts

Classical Authors
Aesop
  Fab.
    The Goose That Laid the Golden Eggs, 80
    The Wolf and the Lamb, 81
Appian
  Bell. civ.
    5.4, 133
  Pun.
    77, 101
Aristophanes
  Vesp.
    907–9, 280
Aristotle
  Rhet.
    2h.7.1, 152
Demosthenes
  1 Olynth.
    13, 125
  Andr.
    22.16, 280
  Cor.
    18.169, 282
    18.207, 31
  Lept.
    143, 282
Euclid
  Elements CN 1, 28
Euripides
  Iph. taur.
    847, 34
Herodotus
  Hist.
    7.144.3, 51
    7.169, 52
  Interview with Pericles, 79
Pausanias
  Descr.
    6.9.9, 33
Pindar
  Ol.
    13.59, 246
Plato
  Apol.
    23c, 27
  Gorg.
    454c–d, 295
  Leg.
    627c, 48
  Menex.
    249d, 34
  Pol.
    272a, 293
  Tim.
    21b, 133
Plutarch
  Cic.
    47.5, 101
Sophocles
  Aj.
    1257–8, 245
  Oed. tyr.
    1451, 69
Thucydides
  P.W.
    2.4.1, 125
    2.13.3, 50
    3.75.1, 105
    6.11.2, 31
Xenophon
  Anab.
    1.5.2, 122
    4.2.12, 103
    6.1.26, 34
  Cyr.
    1.3.7, 148
    2.1.8, 337
    2.1.24, 111
    6.4.3, 123
  Mem.
    3.6.2, 62
    300!, 81

Greek Old Testament

Gen
- 2:15, 151
- 2:16–17, 64
- 5:22, 124
- 12:6, 103
- 15:13, 167
- 19:8, 84
- 19:14, 32
- 24:43, 288
- 31:38, 26
- 32:6, 31
- 34, 299
- 37:10, 169
- 39:10, 103

Exod
- 2:15, 105
- 8:6, 167
- 12:23, 154
- 22:7, 151
- 30:20, 258
- 34:12, 258
- 34:22, 62

Lev
- 11:31, 291

Num
- 7:89, 153
- 11:5, 102
- 21:8, 293
- 22:5, 280
- 22:38, 33

Deut
- 1:3, 121
- 2:8, 164, 166
- 6:5, 325
- 31:19, 148

Josh
- 2:3, 290

Judg
- 6:28, 289
- 19:16–17, 123

Ruth
- 2:20, 291

1 Kgdms (= 1 Sam)
- 1:8, 128
- 1:23, 133
- 20:32, 279
- 24:5, 128
- 24:7, 128
- 24:7–8, 128

2 Kgdms (= 2 Sam)
- 22:31, 292

3 Kgdms (= 1 Kings)
- 2:14–16, 203
- 10:19, 292
- 18:17, 246
- 20:2, 48

4 Kgdms (= 2 Kings)
- 2:5, 32
- 5:18, 151
- 6:25, 51

1 Chr
- 17:26, 158

2 Chr
- 6:42, 52
- 27:5, 102

1 Esd
- 1:33, 125
- 1:37, 125
- 7:9, 60
- 8:80, 31

2 Esd (= Ezra-Neh)
- 16:14, 104
- 17:1, 287

Jdt
- 12:16, 101

Tob
- 5:9, 281

1 Macc
- 3:3, 61, 63
- 6:13, 25
- 8:25, 64
- 9:43, 49
- 10:19, 132

2 Macc
- 9:25–6, 279

3 Macc
- 7:6, 249

Ps
- 103:4, 162

Prov
- 1:20, 28
- 3:12, 29
- 27:6, 52

Eccl
  3:5, 154
Job
  11:5–6, 337
  19:25, 288
  23:3, 337
Wis
  7:1, 83
Sir
  37:12, 249
  51:7, 105
Zech
  1:15, 25
Isa
  28:24, 151
Jer
  16:20, 158
  43:23, 103
Lam
  2:6, 49
Ezek
  21:11, 152
4 Macc
  4–5, 335
  4:7, 105
  4:22, 337

Old Testament Pseudepigrapha
  'The Rich Man and the Precious Stone',
    77
  1 En.
    1:4, 49
    6:2, 125
    14:22, 288
    21:9, 125
    23:2–4, 246
  Georgius Monachus Hamartolus
    Chronicon 4.11, 77
  Jos. Asen.
    1, 97
    1–2, 100
    1–3, 127
    1:1, 127
    1:2, 127
    1:9, 127
    1:11, 127
    1:13, 127
    1:14, 127
    2–3, 117
    2:1, 127
    2:11, 127
    2:16, 127
    3, 100
    3:1, 127
    4, 143
    5, 159
    6, 175
    7, 193
    8–9, 194
    10, 216
    11–12, 223
    13, 224
    14–17, 231
    18–19, 256
    20–1, 270
    22–3, 273
    22:10a, 68
    24, 299
    24:1, 163
    25, 311
    26–7, 311
    28:1–13, 320
    28:14–29, 328
  Jub
    2:2, 68
  Let. Aris.
    1:30, 292
    218, 60
  Sib. Or.
    3.45, 32
    3.348, 294
    3.545, 288
  T. Benj.
    3.6–7, 129
  T. Dan.
    4.4, 246
  T. Iss.
    3.7, 290
  T. Jos.
    7.3, 32
  T. Naph.
    1.11, 162
  T. Sim.
    2.13, 122, 127

New Testament
Matt
   1:19, 236
   1:20, 209
   2:3, 54
   2:13, 206
   2:14, 51
   2:18, 106
   2:20, 282
   3:1, 168
   3:14, 105, 334
   3:16, 248
   4:4, 33
   4:17, 110
   4:18, 115
   4:23, 167
   5:11, 304
   5:14, 52
   5:16, 159
   5:19, 305
   5:23–24, 304
   5:24, 203
   5:32, 291
   6:9–12, 207
   6:16–17, 208
   6:16, 305
   6:20, 202
   7:8, 28
   7:24, 159
   8:9, 83
   8:25, 201
   9:22, 285
   10:14, 303
   10:23, 304
   10:27, 201
   11:1, 151
   11:12, 26
   12:7, 326
   13:2, 289
   13:6, 168
   13:14, 65, 236
   13:24, 154
   13:29, 239
   13:46, 286
   14:19, 154
   15:4, 65
   15:22–5, 204
   15:31, 244
   16:1, 238
   16:7, 110
   16:8, 110
   16:21, 110
   16:23, 75
   17:15, 26
   17:17, 206
   18:28, 48
   19:17–19, 207
   19:17, 207
   19:19, 207
   20:13, 51, 334
   20:30–1, 303
   21:2–6, 154
   21:4, 287
   21:7, 148
   21:16, 25
   22:37, 325
   23:2, 27, 134
   23:3, 27
   23:4, 27, 63
   23:13, 246
   24:22–8, 330
   24:32–6, 330
   24:43–4, 330
   24:49, 126
   25:34, 290
   25:35, 124
   26:16, 110
   26:17–46, 110
   26:26–7, 202
   26:46, 110
   26:47, 110, 245
   26:55, 102
   26:58, 101
   26:60, 154
   26:63, 124
   26:64, 248
   26:65, 132
   27:4, 240
   27:16, 102
   27:31, 122, 123
   27:49, 338
   27:58, 157

28:19, 207
Mark
  1:20, 233, 234, 241
  1:27, 181
  1:30-1, 106, 111
  1:30, 48
  2:14, 206
  3:21, 152
  3:28-9, 338
  4:13, 325
  4:37, 150
  4:39, 201, 294
  4:41, 164
  5:11, 50
  5:21, 245
  5:29, 69
  5:3-4, 295
  5:33, 239
  6:1, 33
  6:16, 115
  6:52, 232
  7:3, 27
  8:2, 26
  9:1, 292
  9:22-4, 204
  9:30, 303
  9:41, 50
  10:33, 61
  12:41, 102
  13:1, 48
  13:35, 167
  14:1, 101
  14:40, 289
  15:7, 289
  15:20, 33
  15:29-30, 226
Luke
  1:29, 181
  1:51-4, 134
  1:59-60, 226
  1:59, 106
  1:62, 337
  2:8, 164
  2:36, 246
  3:4, 205
  3:9, 27
  3:12, 150
  3:21, 150
  4:8, 165
  4:41, 178
  5:3, 181
  5:20, 52
  6:37, 209
  7:29, 165
  8:42, 101
  8:46, 249
  8:52, 122, 209
  9:54, 162
  10:29, 235
  11:3, 207
  11:17, 28
  11:30, 61
  11:37, 180
  11:43, 54
  12:40, 32
  14:9, 162
  14:12, 305
  14:13, 208
  14:16-17, 205
  15:16, 102
  15:18, 325
  16:4, 134
  16:16, 110
  16:27, 180
  17:10, 279
  17:20, 181, 183
  18:20, 209
  19:13, 209
  19:41, 126
  20:9, 153
  22:19, 202
  22:34, 325
  22:63, 122
  22:66, 122
  23:6, 181
  23:15, 63
  23:18, 204
  23:21, 236
  23:34, 109
  24:24, 126
John
  1:1-2, 157

1:6–7, 158
1:7, 304
1:37, 60
1:43, 180
2:3, 327
2:21, 157
3, 174
3:1–2, 51
3:3–13, 271
3:14–23, 301
3:29, 65
4:5, 126
4:6, 292
4:16, 206
4:50, 32
5:18, 235
5:39, 179
5:45, 284
6:6, 235
6:9, 84
6:19, 166
6:31, 132
7:12, 169
8:7, 248
8:31, 290, 303
8:41, 26
8:44, 54, 305
9:15, 181, 183
9:25, 235
10:3, 27
11:3, 25
11:5, 107
11:14, 131
11:36, 107
12:3, 50
16:22, 32
16:24, 205
16:33, 131
17:19, 294
18:20, 133, 154
18:5–25, 322
19:15, 203
19:22, 280
20:1, 248
20:17, 32
20:31, 236

21:8, 50, 167
Acts
1:3, 75
3:11–12, 339
3:12, 25
3:26, 244
5:8, 51
5:41, 236
7:25, 102
7:33, 53
7:40, 225
7:44, 62
7:51, 67
7:60, 61, 64
8:27, 289
8:30, 26
8:31, 336
9:6, 207
9:11–15, 204
10:28, 178
11:17, 244
11:26, 151
12:2, 63
12:4, 240
12:8, 205
12:25, 240
13:10, 248
13:12, 125
13:41, 260
15:8, 240
15:11, 179
15:20, 53
16:18, 29, 167
17:9, 235
17:18, 178
17:29, 49
20:20, 151
20:22, 337
21:40, 64
22:5, 238
23:12–22, 313
23:14, 65
25:5, 84
26:32, 327
27:13, 179
28:17, 239

Rom
 1:9–10, 34
 3:22, 53
 4:1, 325
 5:17, 49
 6:19, 164
 7:2, 282
 7:16, 66
 8:33, 247
 9:2, 62
 9:3, 179
 12:14, 202
 13:4, 62
 13:14, 207
 14:1, 67
 15:13, 336
 15:16, 238
1 Cor
 1:4, 34
 1:23, 291
 3:5, 125
 4:9, 164, 166
 7:39, 304
 7:40, 179
 8:10, 249
 9:7, 63
 11:28, 203
 13:11, 285
 14:36, 129
 15:10, 54
 15:33, 29
 16:5, 31
2 Cor
 4:7, 49
 5.11, 31
 7:5, 245
 7:7, 159
 8:9, 125
 12:7, 67
 13:4, 28
 13:12, 207
Gal
 1:9, 29
 1:10, 30
 3:15, 163
 4, 170

 4:1, 170
 4:7, 170
 4:8, 170
 4:9, 170
 4:20, 106
 4:21, 204
 5:4, 30
 6:11, 134
 6:14, 62
Eph
 1:3–14, 235
 1:13, 240
 1:15, 73
 2:5, 67, 281
 2:8, 281
 4:1, 153
 4:8, 165
 4:11, 168
 4:14, 50
 4:15, 165
 5:25–6, 295
 6:14–15, 241, 242
 6:14–17, 50
 6:15, 48
Phil
 1:7, 163
 1:20–1, 149
 2:12, 133
Col
 2:11–14, 286
 2:14, 286
 2:6–7, 202
 3:1, 75
 3:2, 75
 4:9, 166
1 Thess
 1:8, 129, 278
 5:7, 51
 5:18, 158
2 Thess
 3:11, 249
 3:17, 27
1 Tim
 1:12, 34
 1:19, 70, 240
 4:4, 235

4:16, 68
5:5–6, 284
5:8, 53
5:18, 244
6:3, 84
6:20, 209
2 Tim
  1:9, 65
  1:12, 284
  1:13, 132
  2:2, 151
  2:24, 260
  3:8, 166
  3:17, 293
  4:7–8, 280
Phlm
  1–24, 197
  13, 106
Heb
  2:3, 239
  2:17, 164, 339
  3:2, 68
  3:9, 133
  3:18, 179
  5:7, 232
  5:11, 67
  6:3, 324
  6:4–6, 246
  8:3, 304
  9:7, 50
  10:20, 61
  10:29, 60
  11:13, 133
  12:17, 294
  12:18–25, 279
  13:3, 291
  13:12, 295
Jas
  1:5, 61, 232, 246
  1:11, 134
  1:24, 288
  2:8, 25
  2:10, 289
  2:20, 152
  5:4, 279, 291
  5:9, 287

1 Pet
  1:1, 51
  1:8, 238, 291
  1:17, 209
  2:10, 292
  4:12, 244
  5:10, 244
  3:1–2, 238
2 Pet
  1:12, 244
1 John
  2:1, 54
  2:19, 327
  3:17, 303
  5:13, 338, 339
  5:4–5, 293
2 John
  4, 249
3 John
  15, 205
Jude
  20–1, 242
Rev
  1:9, 53
  2:7, 324
  5:5, 129, 131
  5:13, 249
  8:5, 286
  11:6, 154
  12:17, 148
  14:4, 60
  14:8–10, 50
  16:9, 165
  17:6, 164
  17:12, 32

Texts around the New Testament
Acts Pil.
  Prologue, 162
  1.1, 69
  8.1, 244
  14.1, 246
Dio Chrysostom
  Ven.
    7.62, 162
Gos. Pet.

3.6, 111
3.9, 66
Inf. Gos. Thom.
    4.2, 69
Philo
    Confusion
        191, 106
    Sacrifices
        55, 164
    Unchangeable
        134, 27
Prot. Jas.
    1.4, 166
    13.1, 123
    17.1, 288

Greek Church Fathers
1 Clem.
    Salutation, 53
    3.4, 52
    5–6, 331
    5.7, 162
    24.4, 163
    35.9, 124
    59.3, 152
    61.3, 154
2 Clem.
    8.3, 150, 154
    16.3, 49
Barn.
    5.6, 70
    7.3, 305
    8.1, 151
    9.4, 288

    10.3, 29
Did.
    1.1, 48
    7.1, 208
Diogn.
    5.6, 27
    5.8, 69
    7.3, 337
Herm. Sim.
    2.7, 28
    5.1.3, 29
    8.7.1, 282
    9.1.2, 69
    9.2.3, 290
Herm. Vis.
    3.13.4, 33
Ign.
    Pol.
        2.2, 165
    Rom.
        6.3, 293
    Smyrn.
        4.2, 165
    Trall.
        2.3, 163
Mart. Pol.
    8.2, 105
    12.2, 64
    22.2, 66
    23.2, 66
Pol.
    Phil.
        3.3, 279
        9.2, 122

For EU product safety concerns, contact us at Calle de José Abascal, 56–1°,
28003 Madrid, Spain or eugpsr@cambridge.org.

www.ingramcontent.com/pod-product-compliance
Ingram Content Group UK Ltd.
Pitfield, Milton Keynes, MK11 3LW, UK
UKHW022111260226
468464UK00019B/419